INTELLECTUAL JOURNEYS OF RECENT, MOSTLY "DEFUNCT" ECONOMISTS

Touro College Press

INTELLECTUAL JOURNEYS OF RECENT, MOSTLY "DEFUNCT" ECONOMISTS

With a Foreword by
VICTOR R. FUCHS

MICHAEL SZENBERG
Touro College and University System

LALL RAMRATTAN
University of California, Berkeley Extension

Touro College Press

Library of Congress Cataloging-in-Publication Data:
A catalog record for this book is available from the Library of Congress.
ISBN 978-1-61811-466-2 (hardback)
ISBN 978-1-61811-467-9 (electronic)

Published by Touro College Press and Academic Studies Press.
Typeset, printed and distributed by Academic Studies Press.
Cover design by Ivan Grave

Touro College Press
Michael A. Shmidman and Simcha Fishbane, Editors
27 West 23rd Street
New York, NY 10010
USA
touropress.admin@touro.edu

Academic Studies Press
28 Montfern Avenue
Brighton, MA 02135
USA
press@academicstudiespress.com
www.academicstudiespress.com

B"H

Dedicated to the memory of my sister, Esther,
for teaching me how to read
and for bringing me to these shores;
to the memory of my parents, my father Henoch for his wisdom
and my mother, Sara, for giving birth to me—twice;
to my children Naomi and Avi
their spouses Marc and Tova;
to my grandchildren,
Elki and Chaim, Batya, Chanoch, Devorah and Nachum,
Ephraim, Ayala, Jacob,
and to my great-grandchildren,
Chanoch and Fegila
To my wife, Miriam;
And to the righteous German officer who took my immediate family to a hiding place just days before the last transport to Auschwitz, where most of my family perished.

—M.S.

To my wife, Noreena, my kids,
Devi, Shanti, Hari, and Rani, and my grandchildren,
Brian and Sabrina. I will love them forever.

—L.R.

Table of Contents

Foreword

The trajectory of the history of economic thought is not a happy one. What was once a robust field of research and publication is now of marginal interest to just a few economists. When I began graduate work in 1950 at Columbia University, history of economic thought was a well established field of concentration. The faculty included Joseph Dorfman, author of a five volume work, *The Economic Mind in American Civilization* (1946-1959), and Wesley Claire Mitchell, who taught and wrote about *Types of Economic Theory: From Mercantilism to Institutionalism* (1967). Most significantly, George Stigler, winner of the Nobel Prize in Economics in 1982, was on the faculty. Stigler's PhD thesis at the University of Chicago, *Production and Distribution Theories* (1941), was just the first of his many contributions to the history of economic thought, contributions that, for the subjects covered, have been deemed "unmatched by any other historian of economic thought" (T. Sowell, in *The new Palgrave, A dictionary of economics*, J. Eatwell, M. Milgate, & P. Newman [Eds.] [London: The Macmillan Press, 1987]: vol. 4, 498).

Despite having regularly offered a course on the history of thought, even Stigler finally acknowledged that "the history of economics is no longer a major academic subject; it is not taught at a professional level at most great universities" (*Memoirs of an unregulated economist* [New York: Basic Books, 1988]: 207). As David Colander has written, "The profession has far too little knowledge of its past and of how past theory and discussion relate to current theory, models, and problems" (Review of *The economic crisis in retrospect: Explanations by great economists*, G. P. West III & R. M. Whayles [Eds.], in *Journal of Economic Literature*, LII[3] [September, 2014]: 864).

Enter our hero, Michael Szenberg. Sometimes alone, sometimes with Lall Ramrattan as a collaborator, Szenberg has devoted a significant portion of his career to editing and authoring books that, in the words of one reviewer, will be most useful to "historians of thought interested in recent history" (A. M. Diamond, Review of *Reflections of eminent economists,* M. Szenberg & L. Ramrattan [Eds.]. [Cheltenham, UK: Edward Elgar, 2004]).

Szenberg served as editor-in-chief of *The American Economist* from 1972 to 2011. During that period he invited leading economists to contribute essays on their "philosophy of life." These essays and others invited by Szenberg that had not appeared in the journal were collected and edited by him and published as *Eminent Economists* (Cambridge University Press, 1982). In reviewing this work, I wrote that it "provides a rare opportunity to sit down with an Arrow, a Samuelson, or a Tinbergen and learn that there is more to economics (and economists) than the world of theorems and econometric models."

The success of *Eminent Economists*—it was translated into seven foreign languages—led Szenberg (with Ramrattan) to conceive, assemble, and edit numerous other collections of invited papers including *Passion and Craft, Economists at Work* (1999), *Reflections of Eminent Economists* (2004), *Samuelson Economics and the 21st Century* (2006), and *Eminent Economists II* (2013).

In addition to editing the works of other economists, Szenberg has authored books that also contribute to understanding economics and economists of the past century. Most notable is an excellent comprehensive biography of Franco Modigliani (2008) and an equally fine but more focused one on Paul A. Samuelson (2006).

Intellectual Journeys of Recent, Mostly "Defunct" Economists is the work of Szenberg and Ramrattan, not a collection of papers written by other economists. It brings together in one volume their thoughts, most of which have been previously published in diverse outlets. They discuss the work of fifteen economists, ranging alphabetically from Allais to Samuelson and historically from Keynes to Stanley Fischer. It is not a book to be consumed in one gulp or even a few sittings. Neither is it a reference work that takes the place of a dictionary or an encylopedia. Rather the reader should approach it as a rich, varied intellectual buffet about leading economists to be sampled as interest and need dictate. Readers who believe they already know as much about

Samuelson as they desire are unlikely to feel the same way about Adolph Lowe or Robert Heilbroner, two luminaries of the New School.

In this book, as in all his many volumes over more than two decades, Szenberg has provided a service for future economists. Just as journalism is said to be the first draft of history, so Szenberg and his collaborators can be said to have provided valuable material for future historians of economic thought.

Victor R. Fuchs

Preface and Acknowledgements

No book emerges *ex nihilo*. An ideal setting was presented by Touro College Press under the leadership of editors Dr. Michael Shmidman and Dr. Simcha Fishbane. This is our first book under their guidance. In fact, they are our Cicerone, being aware of our long-term interest in biographical aspects of scientists.

The book's contents reflect our conviction that constructing a biographical inventory of the most creative minds among economists is important in advancing the frontiers of economics and allied sciences. As the 1972 Nobel laureate Kenneth Arrow noted in his Foreword to our *Reflections of Eminent Economists*, "it provides material for the future historian of economic thought." The collection of essays, some written specifically for this volume, offers us personal and scientific data about wise and accomplished lives, and will serve as a source for deepening our understanding of the social history of economics. In a very important way, we expand our own lives by studying the lives of other scientists. Thus, we follow the wisdom in Voltaire's *Candide* (1759), whose protagonist urged, "*Infant cultivar notre jardin*"—we must cultivate our own garden.

We are most grateful to Drs. Michael Shmidman and Simcha Fishbane for giving birth to this volume, their support along the way, and for making this publication possible. Dr. Herb Basser provided his insightful and critical comments with speed and precision. Their enthusiastic guidance and editorial sensibility made this a better book.

We also owe great thanks to Leah Pollack Epshteyn for her exceptional organizational and editorial assistance on this project, as well as her warmth, attention to detail, and friendship. Meghan Vicks, Acquisitions Editor at Academic Studies Press, graciously responded to our queries and provided able assistance.

My intellectual debt continues with the members of the executive board of Omicron Delta Epsilon, the international honor society in economics, for being an important source of inspiration, encouragement, and support. Many thanks to Professors Mary Ellen Benedict, Joseph Santos, Kathryn A. Nantz, Alan Grant, Stacey Jones, Ali H. M. Zadeh, Ihsuan Li, Subarna Samanta, Farhang Niroomand, and Paul Grimes. For their enduring support and deep friendship, I wish to thank Professors Iuliana Ismailescu and Oscar Camargo. Thanks also to Shari Schwartz for her remarkable literary gifts. I must also mention Sadia Afridi, Ester Robbins Budek, Lisa Ferraro, Laura Garcia, Yelena Glantz, Jennifer Loftus, Larisa Parkhomovskaya, Andrea Pascarelli, Sandra Shpilberg, Marina Slavina, Janet Ulman, Aleena Wee, and Lisa Youel—my past talented and devoted graduate research assistants who have helped directly and indirectly in more ways than I can list to make this book the offspring of our partnership.

Thanks also to my most important champion, Dr. Victor R. Fuchs, past president of the American Economic Association and Henry J. Kaiser, Jr. Professor Emeritus at Stanford University. I know that my life would have been less without him. He has extended to us many kindnesses in the past, and unhesitatingly agreed to pen the Foreword to this volume.

Special thanks to Touro's Vice Presidents, Stanley Boylan and Robert Goldschmidt, and Deans Barry Bressler, Sabra Brock, Moshe Sokol, and Marian Stoltz-Loike, for their ongoing support and commitment to scholarly endeavors, and helping me navigate Touro's waters.

My deepest gratitude goes to Dr. Alan Kadish, President of Touro College and University System, for his extraordinary leadership, dedication to excellence, kindness, cheerfulness, and inspiration.

The process of bringing these essays together was all joy for Lall and me. We hope this panoramic book will prove to be a useful supplementary reading in various courses in money and banking, as well as courses in national income analysis where considerable emphasis is placed on issues of economic policy. The work of the economists we researched contains elements characteristic of great literature—pathos and wit that provoke an itch to seize the secrets of their creative power.

General Introduction

The essays in this volume span approximately twenty years of collaboration by the authors of this book. They are, however, classified not by the time during which they were written, but rather by the schools of economics in which each author shows most specialization. The purpose of this introduction is to provide some background on the authors' works and make them easier for readers to follow.

Some entries have been written especially for this collection. These include the essays about the contributions of Robert Aumann, Gary Becker, and Adolph Lowe. Robert Aumann pushed cooperative game theory to its logical limit. Gary Becker masterfully applied and extended microeconomics to social capital. Adolph Lowe extended the Marxian sectorial model to explain growth under capitalism and socialism. All exemplify creative thinking in economics, and it was imperative that they be included in this collection. But the works of the new entrants alone are not sufficient to illustrate creative activities in economics. While not an exhaustive list of sub-disciplines, the other entries cover the broader subject areas such as macroeconomics, microeconomics, monetary economics, Keynesian economics, and Decision theories.

Each piece in this collection is structured to bring out the main contributions of the economists discussed. For some, this includes multiple achievements, which leads to further subdivision of their work. We discuss their main thoughts with the backdrop of some prerequisite information to enable at least an essential understanding of their theories. In some cases, mostly for the Nobel Laureates, some knowledge of their contributions is already in the public domain. But many of the authors, because of the fields in which they specialized or the time in which they wrote, have to be discovered for their contributions.

Readers may observe that the lengths of the entries are uneven. The shorter pieces were the result of limitations of space or time. Some sources limited the number of words, and others required the input be made with a very short deadline. Thus, the comprehensiveness of each entry is not uniform throughout this volume.

As a prelude to the main works below, we provide some related materials as to the publication of each piece.

Part I: John M. Keynes (1883-1946), Franco Modigliani (1918-2003), and Stanley Fischer (1943-)

Part I of the collection begins with John Maynard Keynes, the dominant economic thinker of the twentieth century, whose ideas have profoundly affected the theory and practice of modern macroeconomics. The version we present here spans his important works. A version of it was published in Thomas Cate's book *Keynes's General Theory: Seventy-five Years Later* (Cheltenham Glos: Edward Elgar, 2012).

The next entry in Part I centers on the Nobel Laureate Franco Modigliani. We have had occasion to write several pieces about Modigliani, who was a professor at the MIT Sloan School of Management and MIT Department of Economics. The work presented here was first published in *The American Economist*, 48(1) (Spring 2004): 3-8.

The last entry in Part I focuses on Stanley Fischer. He brings new insights of Keynesian economics to the debate between New Keynesians and New Classical economics. His views maintain the Keynesian wage rigidity perspective over the price stickiness debate in the literature. This piece was published in *An Encyclopedia of Keynesian Economics*, 2nd edition, edited by Thomas Cate (Cheltenham Glos: Edward Elgar, 2013), 194-200.

Part II: Paul A. Samuelson (1915-2009)

Part II represents the work of the 1970 Nobel laureate Paul Anthony Samuelson, who won the prize for his scientific works in economics. Samuelson had a hand in directing the evolution of economics in the latter half of the twentieth century. For the fruits of his work, he is widely regarded as the leader of neoclassical economics. This piece was published in *The American Economist*, 55(2) (Fall 2010), 67-82.

Part III: Milton Friedman (1912-2006)

Milton Friedman is a household name, perhaps due to his popular public television show *Free to Choose*. He was the most influential leader of the monetarist school. But his most scientific work was done on the consumption function, where he advocated the permanent income hypothesis. In 1976, Friedman won the Nobel Prize for his achievements in the field of "consumption analysis, monetary history and theory, and for his demonstration of the complexity of stabilization policy." This entry was published in *The American Economist*, 52(1) (Spring 2008), 23-38.

Part IV: John Kenneth Galbraith (1908-2006)

John Kenneth Galbraith was an American ambassador during the Kennedy Administration, as well as a leading institutional economist. He was a prolific author and wrote four dozen books, including several novels, and published more than a thousand articles and essays on various subjects. Among his most famous works was a popular trilogy on economics, *American Capitalism* (1952), *The Affluent Society* (1958), and *The New Industrial State* (1967). Galbraith's books on economic topics were bestsellers from the 1950s through the 2000s. The piece included here is from *The American Economist*, 55(1) (Spring 2010), 31-45. It was incorporated in *John Kenneth Galbraith: The Economic Legacy, Volume IV*, edited by Stephen Dunn (London: Routledge, 2012).

Part V: Adolph Lowe (1893-1995)

Adolph Lowe represents the Marxian school. The piece included here was specifically written for this work. Because of his vast contribution to methodology, sociology, and economics, we survey only Lowe's work on business cycles, economic growth, and his much-lauded exposition of Adam Smith's economics system.

Part VI: Lawrence Klein (1920-2013)

After his dissertation on the Keynesian Revolution, Lawrence Klein set to work on the application of the Keynesian system using the tools of econometrics. Klein received the Nobel Prize for economics in 1980 for "the creation of economic models and their application to the analysis of economic fluctuations and economic policies." The piece included here is taken from *An Encyclopedia of Keynesian Economics* (London and New York: Edward Elgar, 2013), 372-378.

Part VII: Gerard Debreu (1921-2004), John Hicks (1904-1989), and Maurice Allais (1911-2010)

Gerard Debreu received the Nobel Prize in 1983 for his contributions to general equilibrium economics. He brought his influence of Bourbaki mathematics to economics, creating a long-lasting research program in that area. The piece included in this volume is from *The American Economist,* 49(1) (2005), 3-15.

John Hicks straddles the economics of Leon Walras and John Maynard Keynes. Hicks received the Nobel Prize in economics in 1972 for his contributions to general equilibrium theory and welfare economics. The piece included in this volume is from *The International Encyclopedia of Social Sciences,* 2nd Edition (London and New York: Macmillan Reference, 2007).

Maurice Allais received the Nobel Prize in economics in 1988 for his "pioneering contributions to the theory of markets and efficient utilization of resources." He is also known for the Allais paradox in utility, preference, and probability theory. His writings were translated later into English, which perhaps delayed his recognition in the English-speaking world. The entry here is from *The American Economist,* 56(1) (2011), 104-122.

Part VIII: Gary Becker (1930-2014)

Gary Becker established economics on a strong sociological foundation. Expanding standard microeconomics to include social capital, he made the family the atomic structure of economics. From this he made logical developments in the areas of discrimination and human capital. He received the Nobel Prize in 1992 "for having extended the domain of microeconomic analysis to a wide range of human behavior and interaction, including nonmarket behavior." This essay was written specifically for this volume.

Part IX: Robert Aumann (1930-)

Robert Aumann received the Nobel Prize for his contributions to game theory. In particular, his award was in the area of cooperative game theory, which embraces the dictum that if you want peace, you must prepare for war. Aumann is a professor at the Center for the Study of Rationality in the Hebrew University of Jerusalem in Israel. This essay was written specifically for this volume.

Part X: Robert Heilbroner (1919-2005)

Robert Heilbroner was influenced by Joseph Schumpeter and later by Adolph Lowe. Like so many economists, he stood on the ground of classical thought, including Marxism. He is best known for his work *The Worldly Philosophers: The Lives, Times and Ideas of the Great Economic Thinkers* (7th ed.) (New York: Simon & Schuster, 1999), a bestselling introduction to classical economic thought. The entry in this book is from *The American Economist*, 49(2) (2005), 16-32.

Part XI: Abram Bergson (1914-2003)

Abram Bergson's place in the history of economic thought is in the area of welfare economics. He did pioneering work that revolves around constructing a social welfare function, which is supposed to aggregate benefits of individuals to the whole society. Such work is welcomed by researchers who wish to measure economic benefits and optimal performance of an economy. The entry in this text is taken from *The American Economist*, 7(2) (2003), 3-5.

PART I

KEYNESIAN ECONOMICS

John Maynard Keynes, Franco Modigliani, Stanley Fischer

John Maynard Keynes

John Maynard Keynes (1883-1946) was the eldest son to Florence Ada and John Neville Keynes. His siblings were Gotfriey and Margret. Keynes went to an all-boys school, Eton College, and then to King's College Cambridge, where he graduated in mathematics. At Cambridge, he started studying economics under Alfred Marshall. Scoring very low on the Civil Service Exam, he was not hired by the British Treasury, so he settled for his first job in the Revenue, Statistics and Commerce Department of the India Office.

Introduction

Keynes's views evolved over time, maturing into the Keynesian framework of *The General Theory of Employment Interest and Money (GT)* (Keynes, 1936). To study the impact of his views on economic theories and policies, we need to peek through the various windows of his major works in order to cope with the novelties of the general theory. A panoramic view of the impact of Keynes' economic theories and policies started with his defense of the gold-exchange standard in his first book, *Indian Currency and Finance* (*ICF*) (Keynes, 1913) and culminated with his arguments for the Bretton Woods system in 1944. In this chapter, we first briefly summarize some essential works of Keynes in order to discuss the impact of his theories and polices.

Economics of Indian Currency and Finance

In the *ICF*, Keynes gave "a discussion of currency evolution in general" (Keynes, 1913: 11). His position in the *ICF* was that gold itself has become a managed currency, implying that the role of the monetary authority was to ensure an adequate amount of gold supply to match the currencies outstanding. This was not a problem when gold discovery was common in the first half of the nineteenth century, but as new discoveries became scarce, countries found it necessary to economize on gold, which is an idea that Keynes credited to "[David] Ricardo, who pointed out that a currency is in is most perfect state, when it consists of cheap material, but of an equal value with the gold it professes to represent" (Keynes, 1971: vol. XV, 70).

In the *ICF*, Keynes was discussing the evolution of the gold standard theory to a gold-exchange standard. In a typical gold-exchange standard, one country's currency is tied to gold, and the other countries' currencies are tied to that gold backed currency (Sawyer & Sprinkle, 2008). This yields a fixed exchange rate between the currencies, for if 1 ounce of gold = $20 in the US, and £5 in the UK, then the exchange rate will be fixed at $4 = £1.

To be sure, the idea of economizing on gold was fathered by Adam Smith, who compared gold and silver to a road that grows nothing, which farmers use to transport goods to the market. Replacing gold with notes is like converting the road to a field, making it productive (Smith, *Wealth of Nations*, Cannan ed., vol. 2 [1930], 28, 78, cited in von Mises, 1980: 332). J. B. Say summarized the issue this way: "The celebrated Ricardo, has . . . proposed an ingenious plan, making the Bank or corporate body, invested with the privilege of issuing the paper-money, liable to pay in bullion for its notes on demand. A note, actually convertible on demand into so much gold or silver bullion, cannot fall in value below the value of the bullion it purports to represent . . . so long as the issues of the paper do not exceed the wants of circulation, the holder will have no inducement to present it for conversion, because the bullion, when obtained, would not answer the purposes of circulation" (Say, 1880: 260).

Keynes also leaned on the works of Walter Bagehot in evolving the gold-exchange theory (Keynes, 1913: 22, 115, 125). He praised Bagehot for "the doctrine, namely, that in a time of panic the reserves of the Bank of England must, at a suitably high rate, be placed at the disposal of the public without stint and without delay" (Keynes, 1971 [1913]: 115). "Bagehot's rule was to raise Bank Rate to stem an external gold drain and to lend freely in response to an internal drain; in the event of both internal and external drains, the Bank was to raise its discount rate to high levels but to continue to provide liquidity" (Eichengreen, 1985: 14).

The seed of gold-exchange standard Keynes planted in the *ICF* evolved into a "Proposal for an International Clearing Union" at Bretton Wood in 1944 (Horsefield, 1969: vol. III, 3-19). The chronicles of the International Monetary Fund (IMF) revealed that "Keynes had no need to borrow ideas; he had long before adumbrated a plan somewhat similar to White's Stabilization Fund in his *Treatise on Money* (1920), where he had conceived a Supernational Bank which would act as a central bank for central banks. What was needed now was to link such an institution with the control of exchange rates and to clothe it with disciplinary powers" (Horsefield, 1969: vol. I, 16). Such disciplinary power was demonstrated by his influence in making the IMF adopt his policy to declare a country's currency as "scarce," if the country does not take action to correct its surplus balance of payment (Keynes, 1971-89: vol. 25, 401-2, 474).

Tract on Monetary Reform (*TMR*)

In his *Tract on Monetary Reform* (TMR) (Keynes, 1971 [1923]), Keynes demonstrated how unemployment and other problems in the economy were related to the "instability of the standard of value" (Keynes, 1971 [1923]: xiv). Keynes made monetary stability an "either or" proposition between internal price stability and external foreign exchange rate stability, expressing his preference for internal over external stability because he thought that the latter would follow once the former was secured. Unemployment, expectation, loss of savings, excessive windfalls, and risk are all affected by the instability of the standard of value, which made the value of a currency dependent on its quantity and purchasing power, the quantity of money dependent on the loans and budgetary policies of the government, and the purchasing power dependent on the public feeling of "the trust or distrust" about the value of the currency (ibid.: xviii).

Keynes looked for an answer to the instability problem from the Cambridge version of the quantity theory, using the equation $n = p(k + rk')$, where n is currency notes, p is the index number of the cost of living, k is people's cash holdings, k' is people's cash deposits, and r is bank reserves (ibid.: 63). The model predicts that if the bracket items are constant, then the price level (p) will vary with the quantity of cash (n). The term inflation then relates to increases in cash ($\Delta n > 0$), increase in credit ($\Delta r < 0$), or increases in real balances ($[\Delta(k, k') < 0]$). Deflation is defined by reversing the inequality signs.

"The business of stabilizing the price level . . . consists partly in exercising a stabilizing influence over k and k', and, in so far as this fails or is impracticable, in deliberately varying n and r so as to *counterbalance* the movements of k and k'" (Keynes, 1971 [1923]: 68 [italics original]).

Stability in the *TMR* implies several broad activities. The goal of policies is to keep price changes in a normal range. This goal is guided by economic activities such as "the state of employment, the volume of production, the effective demand for credit as felt by the banks, the rate of interest on investments of various types, the volume of new issues, the flow of cash into circulation, the statistics of foreign trade and the level of the exchanges" (Keynes, 1971 [1923]: 148-149).

The *TMR* was written after the Genoa, Italy meeting in 1922 of countries calling for the old pre-World War I gold standard based on gold to be an international standard for settling debts, a link with the old stable system, and a means of accommodating producers vested interest in gold (Keynes, 1971 [1923]: 139). Ralph Hawtrey added that vested interest should extend beyond the producers to include the "gold holders and gold creditors. The greatest gold holders are the Central Banks" (Hawtrey, 1924: 231-232). Keynes opposed this throwback to the gold-exchange standard, which he once defended in the *ICF* above, because he thought that gold supply was scarce, implying an overvalued currency for the UK. For Keynes, "the gold standard is already a barbarous relic" (Keynes, 1971 [1923]: 138). While the UK got on to the pre-World War I standard in 1925, it was forced off it in 1931 because of problems with balance of payments (BOP), and by 1937 all countries got off the gold-exchange standard (Reinert, 2005: 249).

Keynes argued against the pre-war standard because at that time, most countries were off the gold standard: "In 1914, gold had not been the English standard for a century or the sole standard of any other country for half a century" (Keynes, 1971 [1923]: 8). While gold had an intrinsic value that is free from the dangers of a managed currency (ibid.: 133), after WWI, gold itself had become a managed currency. For instance, as most countries were off the gold standard, gold became oversupplied. The US, which was still on the gold standard, did not want its standard of value to depreciate. The value of gold was therefore kept at an artificial value, determined by the Federal Reserve Board of the US. Meanwhile, the world was inflating, and some economists thought that if countries were to return to the pre-war gold standard, the gold supply would be inadequate. Gustav Cassel of Germany predicted gold would appreciate in value (ibid.: 135). In summary, "in the modern world of paper currency and bank credit there is no escape from a 'managed' currency, whether we wish it or not; convertibility into gold will not alter the fact that the value of gold itself depends on the policy of the central banks" (ibid.: 136). According to one of his biographers,

> The central claim of the Tract is that by varying the amount of credit to the business sector, the banking system could even out fluctuations in business activity. The claim to have identified a controllable single variable—the supply of credit—capable of determining the level of prices and amount of activity in the economy as a whole is the start of macroeconomics. (Skidelsky, 1992: 153)

A Treatise on Money (TM)

Keynesian theory and policy showed a major advancement in his two books on *A Treatise on Money* (*TM*) (1930). We find in the *TM* more fundamental equations for monetary theory and economic activities, representing "the most stupendous transfiguration" of the quantity theory but still lacking a marginal utility theory of value basis (Hicks, 1982: vol. 2, 47). According to one of his most able biographers, we "get the best picture of his total contribution to economics in the *Treatise*. . . . The fact remains that the future student who wishes to get the full measure of Keynes' importance and influence as an economist will not do so unless he reads the *Treatise*" (Harrod, 1951: 403-404). We find in the *TM* a positive role for savings and investment, which was modified in the *GT*.

In the *TM*, Keynes "proposed . . . to break away from the traditional method of setting out from the total quantity of money . . . and to start instead . . . with the flow of the community's earnings or money income" (Keynes 1930: vol. I, 121). He proposed two equations (ibid.: 121-123):

$$P = \frac{E}{O} + \frac{I' - S}{R} = \frac{W}{e} + \frac{I' - S}{R} \quad (1)$$

$$\Pi = \frac{W}{e} + \frac{I - S}{O} \quad (2)$$

Where E is money income or earnings; o is output of goods; I' is part of E that is earned by the production of investment goods; S is savings; R is flow of consumption goods and services; W is rate of earnings per human effort; e is coefficient of efficiency (output per unit of effort); I is the increment of new investment goods, and Π is the price level of output as a whole.

The essence of these equations is that the price index matches with the cost of production index plus the profit index (Patinkin, 1982: 7). They are novel in one respect, that "the relationship of purchasing power of money . . . and the price level of output as a whole to the quantity and the velocity of circulation is not that direct character which the old-fashioned quantity equations . . . might lead one to suppose" (Keynes, 1930: vol. 1, 129-132). Because theories of over-investments, under-consumption, and under-savings predated Keynes' works, less originality may be ascribed to the prediction of the equations; namely, that savings need not equal investment. Keynes claimed that his theory was radically different from those, in that it made the crucial influence the *disparity* between investment and saving (Harrod, 1951: Biography, 409 [Italics original]).

Investments and savings can diverge, not because people would hoard or idle their savings, but because the motives governing them were different enough to cause disharmony. Savings was defined to exclude excess profits that cause produce to increase output, and business losses, the differences between actual and expected receipts that cause producers to refrain from wanting to reduce output. If we apply excess profits and loss as defined back to investment, then an accounting equality between savings and investments will be obtained.

If investment exceeds savings, then upswing and inflation are likely outcomes. Investments create money income to consumers for consumption goods and to producers for producer's goods. If the money income from both sources were all spent on consumer goods alone, i.e. none put into savings, then prices would rise because "more money would be applied in their purchase than had been earned in their production" (Harrod, 1951: 406). Conversely, if savings exceed investments, then downswings and unemployment are most likely (ibid.: 404).

The bank rate was the major policy instrument for price stability. Keynes elucidated this instrument in the Macmillan Committee (1930) before the publication of the *Treatise*. "High interest rates led to a contraction of credit, the restriction of capital outlay . . . falling off in buying power and a fall in prices . . . wages were very sticky, and severe unemployment and disequilibrium might remain for a long time" (Harrod, 1961: 416). "If we reduced our rates, more capital would be tempted aboard than could be financed by our excess of exports over imports" (Harrod, 1951: 416). Keynes was also supplementing the Bank rate policy with Public Works, and tariffs on trade, and the liquidity preference concepts at this time. The main policy implication of the equations is that investment should be kept close to savings for price stability.

The General Theory (GT)

As a model builder of a general theory, Keynes laid out the givens, the independent variables, and the dependent variables to lay the new ground for his system. The *givens* include the existing labor, equipment, techniques of production, degree of competition, tastes and habits of consumers, organizational structures, social structure, and distribution of national income. Givens means that we would not look at the effect of changes in any of these assumptions on the economy. The *independent variables* include the propensity to consume, dC / dY, the marginal efficiency of capital, $I = f(r)$, and the rate of interest, r. The *dependent variables* are the volume of employment and national income (Keynes, 1936: 245).

Keynes explained in three steps of how he came by his model. After the *Treatise on Money* was written he had a sudden realization of ". . . the psychological law that, when income increases, the gap between income and consumption will increase. . . . Then appreciable later, came the notion of interest being the measure of liquidity preference. . . . And last of all . . . the proper definition of the marginal efficiency of capital linked up one thing with another" (Keynes, 1936: vol. VII, xv). Consumption, liquidity preference, and the marginal efficiency of capital are the triumvirate propositions of the *GT* that provide the grist for the mill of subsequent thought on the *GT*.

To understand Keynes' model therefore, we have to fill in the answer to the question "Employment depends on . . ., and Income depends on . . .," Keynes insists, ". . . my doctrine of full employment is what the whole of my book is about! Everything else is a side issue to that. If you do not understand my doctrine of full employment, it is perfectly hopeless for you to attempt to explain the book to anyone" (Keynes, 1973: vol. XIV, 24).

How does the model work to achieve full employment? Starting with consumers not spending all of their income, "there must be an amount of current investment sufficient to absorb the excess of total output over what the community chooses to consume when employment is at the given level" (Keynes, 1936: 27). If that investment is not forthcoming, employers will not get enough revenue to induce them to maintain that level of employment. The inducement to invest will depend on the state of the marginal efficiency of capital and the rate of interest (ibid.: 27-28).

Keynes intended this model to explain slump conditions during the Great Depression. As Milton Friedman explained, "The great contraction . . . was the result of a collapse of demand for investment which in turn reflected a collapse of productive opportunities to use capital. Thus the engine and the motor of the great contraction was a collapse of investment transformed into a collapse of income by the multiplier process" (Friedman, 1970: 13). Similarly, as Paul Samuelson explained, "In the early 1930s, when banks were failing, firms were going bankrupt, and mortgages were in delinquency on a macro scale, it was sensible to worry about liquidity trap, vicious cycles of wage cuts and debt deflation, inelastic marginal efficiency schedules" (Samuelson, 1986: vol. 5, 292). He also stated, "By 1938, short-term interest rates had been forced so low that the liquidity-preference function of Keynes seemed required by the facts of the day" (ibid.: 290).

As expounded, the Keynesian model can be backcast to President Hoover's administration in 1931, with the Reconstruction Finance Corporation, an agency that made loans to states, local governments, and businesses in distress (Horwich, 1991: 132). It entered in President F. D. Roosevelt's administration through the young macroeconomist minds that were grappling with the New Deal to combat the Depression of the 1930s, although Roosevelt's Secretary of the Treasury, Henry Morgenthau, opposed it. While President Roosevelt was not familiar with the Keynesian model, "a number of your economists in the New Deal responded enthusiastically to this new approach and tried to apply it to the American situation. Keynesian economics led to the policy called 'priming the pump,' which held that one has to pour some water into a pump in order to get it started" (Davies, 1964: 44).

In fact, the Keynesian model gave a good ex-post forecast for the interwar period as well, when consumption increased at a decreasing rate, investment slackened when consumption eased up, the interest rate was not high, and unemployment stayed above ten percent during 1923-1929 (Lowe, 1965: 234-237). GDP growth was high during that period, but the model was not designed to explain that growth because the *givens*, particularly equipments and techniques, were not allowed to change. As with slump, Keynes drew implications of his model for prosperous times, declaring that "it is more important to avoid a descent into another slum than to stimulate . . . a still greater activity than we have" (ibid.).

Keynes' articles (*The Times*, January 12, 13, 14, 1937) focused policies in distressed areas where a "rightly distributed demand" was preferred to "a greater aggregate demand," and on the necessity of planning so as "to preserve as much stability of aggregate investment as we can manage at the right and appropriate level."

In another article in *The Times* on March 11, 1937, Keynes further expanded his model for normal times, foreshadowing the more modern models of inflation. For Keynes, inflation is not "merely that prices and wages are rising. . . . It is when increased demand is no longer capable of materially rising output and employment and mainly spends itself in rising prices that it is properly called inflation." That is a remarkable statement, leading T. Hutchinson, renowned economic methodologists, to declare that "Keynes can be said to have suggested a similar concept to that now called—following Professor Milton Friedman—a 'natural rate' of unemployment" (Hutchinson, 1977: 14). As we shall see below, Franco Modigliani and James Tobin were precursors with their NAIRU (Non-Accelerating Inflation Rate of Unemployment) model.

Keynes' triumvirate propositions do not comport well with his prior works, often creating a dilemma among the thought of his followers, who either see concordance with his prior work or perceive a complete break with them. One horn of the dilemma is to look for contrasts of Keynesian thought by superimposing his apparatus on the orthodox school, a comparison and contrast approach. Another approach is expanding and articulating Keynes's work from the classical and neoclassical viewpoints, creating varied Keynesian schools of thought. The rest of this chapter examines such diverse research projects.

Comparative Analysis of Various Snapshots of Keynes' Works.

We have now a more rounded picture that has developed from Keynes' initial thoughts in the *Indian Currency and Finance* (1913), through his more matured thought in the *General Theory* (1936), interpretative texts, and topical incidents such as World War I and the Great Depression, which establish a broad Keynesian tradition.

This view we portray of Keynes has solidified albeit with much disagreement about the sources and shifts in Keynesian ideas. In trying to find some concordances, if any, between Keynes' prior writing and the *GT*, we will discuss questions of precursors to his ideas, and possible paradigmatic shift from the classical positions, with a view to understand and trace the impact of his theory and policy. To aid in this discussion, we will rewrite the main thread of the Keynesian model in three propositional forms to help gather the ideas.

Many economists have held opinions on what to do when the invisible hand does not stabilize the market. As Keynes puts it, "There is no reason to suppose that there is 'an invisible hand,' an automatic control in the economic system which ensures of itself that the amount of active investment shall be continuously of the right proportion" (Keynes, *The Times*, 1937). John Hicks (1976: 216) argued that Keynes may have reacted to the ideas of Hawtrey's book, *Currency and Credit* (1919), for Keynes and Hawtrey questioned whether the self-regulating mechanism could stabilize the market. In this regard, we can formulate Keynes' triumvirate proposition as follows.

Proposition I:

The invisible hand or market forces cannot cope with involuntary unemployment.

As R. F. Khan, a student of Keynes, remarked, "Keynes' concept of the 'involuntary unemployment' constituted a resounding challenge to the established school of thought" (Kahn, 1976: 19) It may include structural and cyclical unemployment, but excludes such traditional definitions as frictional unemployment, seasonal unemployment, and unemployment due to intermittent demand for specialized resources (ibid.: 22). One idea of involuntary unemployment is that "the population generally is seldom doing as much work as it would like to do on the basis of current wage" (Keynes, 1936: 7). Christopher Pissarides, a modern innovator of unemployment models, elaborated this definition: "A person is said to be involuntarily unemployed if he sees people just like himself holding jobs that he would like to have, but which he is not offered" (Pissarides, 1989: 2) A second definition is that "more labor than is at present employed is usually available at the existing money-wage, even though the price of wage-goods is rising and consequently, the real wage falling" (Keynes, 1936: 10).

The most technical definition of involuntary unemployment Keynes gave is that "men are involuntarily unemployed if, in the event of a small rise in the price of wage-goods relatively to the money-wage, both the aggregate supply of labor willing to work for the current money-wage and the aggregate demand for it at that wage would be greater than the existing volume of employment" (ibid.: 15). Keynes then stated that "an alternative, though equivalent, criterion is ... a situation in which aggregate employment is inelastic in response to an increase in the effective demand for its output" (ibid.: 26). One question that has been raised is why Keynes included the aggregate supply of labor curve in the definition, since that curve can be backward bending as well as upward sloping (Kahn, 1976: 21). Another question, raised by Hicks, is the relationship between liquidity and output, which Hicks would rather call "Keynesian Unemployment, defining it by the consequence which he drew from its existence . . . unemployment which can be reduced by an increase in Liquidity" (Hicks, 1983: vol. 3, 127). As Hicks pointed out, however, this would make liquidity a factor of production, which Keynes did not say.

Several implications came out of these definitions of involuntary unemployment. The classics only addressed frictional and voluntary unemployment, resulting, for instance, from time lags and refusal to work, respectively. Keynes reduced their doctrine to two postulates. First, "the wage is equal to the marginal product of labour" (Keynes, 1936: 5). The second in effect says that workers balance the utility of wage with the disutility of work (ibid.: 5) Alvin Hansen, a contributor to the Keynesian IS-LM apparatus, explained two implications of the second proposition, namely, that workers will refuse employment when the real wage is cut, and that a cut in money-wage is a good mechanism for reducing real wages.

To say that unemployment is involuntary implies that some form of help may be necessary. Keynes wanted to emphasize that involuntary unemployment induces the response of government and nonprofit organizations to come to the rescue, thereby relieving the individual of the necessity of job searching, retraining, self-employment, or lower aspirations. The New Deal in the 1930s was a major example of Fiscal stimulus to relieve unemployment, and the Employment Act of 1946 has shifted responsibility to the Federal government to ensure maximum employment, production, and purchasing power (Okun, 1970: 37).

The Keynesian concept of wage rigidity is sometimes used as a cause of unemployment. Jacob Viner, in an early review of the *GT*, would link Keynesian unemployment to inflation rather than wage rigidity. He wrote: "In Keynes's classification of unemployment by its causes, unemployment due to downward-rigidity of money-wages, which for the 'classical' economists was the chief type of cyclical unemployment . . . finds no place. . . . In a world organized in accordance with Keynes's specifications, there would be a constant race between the printing press and the business agents of the trade unions with the problem of unemployment largely solved if the printing press could maintain a constant lead . . ." (Viner, 1936: 149).

Embellishing Viner's view is the idea that wage rigidity is absent in the *GT* where Keynes contrasted his model with the classical model, attacking the foundation of Say's law. In his Z-curve model, Keynes made the aggregate supply price of output, Z, depend on the number of people employed, N, or $Z = \phi(N)$, and the aggregate demand as $D = f(N)$. Therefore, for all values of employment, $f(N) = \phi(N)$ is a realization of Say's law. Keynes intended $Z = \phi(N)$ as a 45-degree line, and the consumption demand $D_1 = \chi(N)$ to go through the origin, remaining everywhere below the Z - *curve* for positive values of output. But aggregate demand is $D = D_1 + D_2$, where D_1 is consumption that is induced by income, and $D_2 = \phi(N) - \chi(N)$ is autonomous consumption, such as business expenditure on investments, which is affected by exogenous factors such as technology and population, factors that are independent of output and employment. Investment is necessary for the realization of output and employment. When added to D_1, D_2, it enables us to realize a point where $Z = D = N$, marking a position of effective demand, and demonstrating that Say's law does not hold.

As a model builder for Keynesian economics, Modigliani was aware of this point when he used the liquidity preference to explain unemployment without wage rigidity by the following casual reasoning: tight money will cause the rate of interest to rise. People will raise cash by liquidating money instruments or through borrowing. Investments and savings will fall and be followed by the fall of income and employment. The demand for money will then fall to equal its supply. By keeping policy makers on guard to supply an adequate quantity of money or in fixing the appropriate interest rate, the "rate of interest" to "output" adjustment consequent to a tight monetary policy will make unemployment an equilibrating mechanism (Modigliani, 1944).

Keynes extended his concept of stability so that it did not apply only to slump. To attain stability, policy makers should "preserve as much stability of aggregate investment . . . at the right and appropriate level" (Keynes, *The Times*, Jan 12-14, 1937). Stability also means to provide enough Liquidity to the system, for "a shortage of cash has nearly always played a significant part in turning the boom into a slump" (ibid.). The covering factors for stability are found in further propositions.

Proposition II:

Consumption (and not savings as the classical economist thought) will through a multiplier process expand output and employment.

In the Keynesian model, "savings and investment are determinates of the system, not determinants. They are twin results of the system's determinants, namely the propensity to consume, the schedule of the marginal efficiency of capital and the rate of interest" (Keynes, 1936: 183-184). "Saving, in fact, is a mere residual. The decision to consume and the decision to invest between them determine incomes" (ibid.: 64). "The traditional analysis has been aware that saving depends on income but it has overlooked the fact that income depends on investment, in such fashion that, when investment changes, income must necessarily change in just that degree which is necessary to make the change in saving equal to the change in investment" (ibid.: 184).

One interpretation of all this is: "A rise in the disposition to save meant a decline of consumption, and the latter a reduction of investment (dependent on consumption) and a fall in employment and hence a reduction of income, and since savings depends on income, a decline of savings; and therefore, savings equal investment; but only through a process by which the original additional savings become abortive" (Harris, 1955: 110-111). Symbolically, we can write $S = f(Y)$; $Y = f(I)$ or that $S = f[Y(I)]$. Then $\Delta I \rightarrow \Delta Y \rightarrow \Delta S$ such that $\Delta S = \Delta I$. Keynes finds consistency with D. H. Robertson's definition, namely, $Y_t = C_{t-1} + I_{t-1}$. Then, $S_t = I_{t-1} + (C_{t-1} - C_t)$ (Keynes, 1936: 78).

"The investment market can become congested through the shortage of cash. It can never become congested through the shortage of saving" (Keynes, 1937: 669).

"Saving has no special efficacy as compared with consumption, in releasing cash and restoring liquidity" (Keynes, 1938: 321).

Proposition III:

The interest rate is not determined in the capital market as the classical economist supposed.

The rate of interest is determined in stages. The first stage is through the propensity to consume, which splits a person's income into how much he will consume now versus how much he will consume in the future. The second stage is through the liquidity preference schedule. From the first stage, a person must determine in what form to hold his future consumption. This will be determined by his liquidity preference (Keynes, 1936: 166). "It should be obvious that the rate of interest cannot be a return to savings or waiting as such. For if a man hoards his savings in cash, he earns no interest, though he saves just as much as before. On the contrary, the mere definition of the rate of interest tells us in so many words that the rate of interest is the reward for parting with liquidity for a specified period" (ibid.: 167).

Hicks, Hansen, and Lerner, interpreters of Keynes, were not content to make $M = L(r)$, where M is the quantity of money, and r is the rate of interest (ibid.: 168). As Hansen puts it, "there is a liquidity preference curve for each income level. Until we know the income level, we cannot know what the rate or interest is" (Hansen, 1953, 148). Lerner has shown how the marginal efficiency, consumption, and liquidity preference schedule combine with the money supply to determine the rate of interest (Lerner, 1951: 265, cited in ibid.: 148-151). Hicks would revive the

Keynesian version of the liquidity preference schedule to include income, giving Keynes "a big step back to Marshallian orthodoxy, and his theory becomes hard to distinguish from the revised and qualified Marshallian theories" (Hicks, 1982: vol. 2, 108).

As a precursor, Hawtrey also focused on the interest rate policy, but Keynes preferred the long-term rate and Hawtrey preferred the short-term rate. Keynes cautions that "a low enough long-term rate of interest cannot be achieved if we allow it to be believed that better terms will be obtainable from time to time by those who keep their resources liquid. The long-term rate of interest must be kept continuously as near as possible to what we believe to be the long-term optimum. It is not suitable to be used as a short-period weapon" (ibid.). Keynes gave the rate of interest a central role in his liquidity preference model. As Keynes found that the long term rate could not be controlled well, he later switched to fiscal policies. He took on broader "financial policies—unemployment and the choice of an exchange rate and a standard for sterling" (Moggridge, 1992: 414). As mentioned above, Keynes preferred domestic policies such as price stability over international matters (Skidelsky, 1992: 20). Keynes perceived the value of the British currency was higher than the US dollar and did not want to peg it to gold. He was "unshackling money from gold" (ibid.: 154).

We find concerns of interest rate at the heart of Keynes' liquidity preference concept. Central to this concept is that given a choice of holding many different assets for transaction, speculative, or precautionary purposes, a person may not see an advantage in holding other assets in preference to money. According to Keynes, "an individual's Liquidity-preference is given by a schedule of the amounts of his resources, valued in terms of money or of wage-units, which he will wish to retain in the form of money in different sets of circumstance" (Keynes, 1936: 166).

In developing this concept of liquidity preference, Keynes reflected on what he called "the state of bearishness" in his *Treatise on Money*, but differentiated such a concept from liquidity preference (ibid.: 173). Recognizing that it is a difficult idea, Keynes likened it to the "propensity to hoard": "The concept of Hoarding may be regarded as a first approximation to the concept of Liquidity-preference. Indeed if we were to substitute 'propensity to hoard' for 'hoarding,' it would come to substantially the same thing. But if we mean by 'hoarding' an actual increase in cash-holding, it is an incomplete idea—and seriously misleading if it causes us to think of 'hoarding' and 'not-hoarding' as simple alternatives" (ibid.: 174).

Liquidity preference also gets entangled with the concept of hoarding. Interest is not a reward for "not-spending" but a reward of "not-hoarding" (ibid.: 174, 182). "It is convenient to reserve the term 'hoard' to mean the stock of liquid final goods, and the term 'stocks' to mean other forms of liquid capital" (Keynes, 1930: vol. 1, 116).

First Impact of Keynes: GT Model and Propositions

After the *GT* was written, its impact on theory and policy followed either the road of its interpreters, on the one hand, or the road of a revolution in macroeconomics on the other hand. The early interpreters, dubbed "the hydraulic-Keynesians" by Coddington (1983: 100), include John Hicks (1937) and Franco Modigliani (1944), who both considered special cases such as investment inelasticity, liquidity trap, and wage rigidity as causes of unemployment by interpreting Keynes through neoclassical economics, in which government expenditure can transcend the special cases by providing various flows in mechanical systems of stable relationships (Dow, 1985: 58-61). Later interpreters include the reconstituted reductionists (Coddington, 1983:105) such as Robert Clower, who thought that the Keynesian model did not clearly identify the fatal flaw of the orthodox model in explaining effective demand and unemployment, and that these Keynesian failures lead to further failure by his interpreters of his arguments (Clower, 1988: 81). Part of the research program of the interpreters was to reconcile the Keynesian vision with the orthodox system—what Joan Robinson called "bastard Keynesianism" (Minsky, 2008: ch. 1). Post-Keynesians, such as Luigi Pasinetti, question whether a break with Keynes from the classics had occurred, pointing to reconciliations that were going on "between the group of young economist who had been working with Keynes . . . and those economists who, after publication, tried to reconcile the *General Theory* with traditional thinking" (Pasinetti, 1999: 3). He concluded that a Keynesian revolution "might as yet remain unaccomplished," waiting for something analogous to the Arrow-Debreu formulation of Leon Walras to happen to Keynes (ibid.: 13).

Clower and later Axel Leijonhufvud presented a choice theoretic model—a reductionist model in the sense that it has objective function, constraints, and interdependence, in an effort reconcile the state of equilibrium quarrel between the Keynesian and orthodox (Coddington, 1983: 108). The focus according to Leijonhufvud was on "a distinction between what Keynes originally meant and what has become known as 'Keynesian economics'" (Pasinetti, 1999: 4). Clower and Leijonhufvud are reconstituted reductionists in the sense that they are not concerned with states of equilibrium, but with the schematization of trading at disequilibrium prices in choice theory, and the speed with which such prices adjust, which turned out to be slower than in a Walrasian process.

For this purpose of reconstruction, Leijonhufvud thinks that what took place between the *TMR* and *TM* was more relevant than what took place between the *TM* and *GT*. (Leijonhufvud, 1968: 22). As far as equilibrium is concerned, Keynes thought that the theory of employment as determined from the theory of demand and supply was abandoned in the classical system after it was hotly debated for a quarter of a century (Keynes, 1936: xv), and its demise was Ricardian economics, on which Marshall had superimposed marginal and substitution principles (ibid.: xxix) This interpretation does leave plenty of room for Clower and Leijonhufvud to maneuver in with their choice theoretic logic.

Within a choice theoretic model, disequilibrium can arise from what Clower called a dual hypothesis in a money economy. For demand to be effective, money has to be held by the public, and the demand of producers to hire labor for money is different from the decision of workers to spend money for output (Dow, 1985: 92).

Keynesian Revolution—In What Sense?

In the revolutionary sense, the Keynesian vision represents a break from a Walrasian model of exchange to a production model, which Keynes had in mind around 1932 when he was drafting a new book, *The Monetary Theory of Production* (Pasinetti, 1999: 8-10). The renowned American economist Wesley Mitchell, who visited Keynes in 1932, remarked that by 1933, Keynes "took the ground that we live not in a 'Real-Exchange Economy,' as Marshall's and Arthur Pigou's treatises seem to assume. It is a 'Monetary Economy' and the difference of great importance because changes in the volume of money exercise a marked influence. He [Keynes]concluded by saying 'that to work out in some detail a monetary theory of production to supplement the real-exchange theories, which we already possess . . . is the task on which I am now working'" (Mitchell, 1969: vol. 2, 826). When Keynes incorporated that idea into the *GT*, he actually stated in chapter I: "I shall argue that the postulates of the classical theory are applicable to a special case only and not to the general case, the situation which it assumes being a limiting point of the possible positions of equilibrium" (Keynes, 1936: 3).

Don Patinkin remarked, "The *Tract*, the *Treatise*, and the *General Theory*: this is the inter-war trilogy that marks the development of John Maynard Keynes's monetary thought from the quantity-theory tradition that he had inherited from his teachers at Cambridge; to his subsequent systematic attempt to dynamise and elaborate upon this theory and its applications; and, finally, to the revolutionary work with which he changed the face of monetary theory and defined its developmental framework for years to come" (Patinkin, 1976: 249).

Keynes' thought descended from Rev. Thomas R. Malthus rather than Ricardo, and it came to his mind in stages beginning with the psychological law of consumption; then, the determination of interest rate from liquidity preference; and finally, the role of the marginal efficiency of capital schedule in the goods market (Keynes, 1936: xv). By declaring Malthus as the source of his ideas, Keynes opted for the study of the "nature and causes" rather than the "distribution" of wealth (ibid.: 4). He was looking for the fundamental theory that causes "actual employment." The fruit of his erudition was to put in place of the classical model a short-run macroeconomic model based on fixed capital, saving-investment identity, and disequilibrium. Some of its claims to novelty include liquidity preference, expectation, effective demand, and the multiplier effects. We examined his point of view for its consequential impacts below.

Standing on the Shoulders of Giants

In building his model, Keynes pulled some of his earlier thought together, while standing on the shoulder of giants. Malthus and Hawtrey were giants in regard to the principle of effective demand. "Malthus, indeed, had vehemently opposed Ricardo's doctrine that it was impossible for effective demand to be deficient; but vainly. For, since Malthus was unable to explain clearly . . . how and why effective demand could be deficient or excessive, he failed to furnish an alternative construction; and Ricardo conquered England as completely as the holy Inquisition conquered Spain" (Keynes, 1936: 32). Keynes, however, did not mention Hawtrey's clear definition of effective demand, which he wrote of as early as 1913: "producers . . . supply in response to a demand, but only to an effective demand" (Hawtrey, 1913: 4). Again, "The whole value of the manufacturer's effort in producing the goods depends upon there being an effective demand for them when they are completed" (ibid.: 78). Also, we should note that "only those who earn money contribute to the aggregate effective demand" (ibid.: 224).

Keynes also had precursors for his theory of liquidity preference. John Hicks noted that the idea "the demand for money depends on the rate of interest" was set by another Cambridge economist, F. Lavington, as early as 1921 (Hicks, 1982: vol. 2, 106). Keynes, however, developed it into a fundamental theory, where "an individual's Liquidity-preference is given by a schedule of the amounts of his resources, valued in terms of money or of wage-units, which he will wish to retain in the form of money in different sets of circumstance" (Keynes, 1936: 166). He wrote it in equation form as $M = L(r)$, where M is the quantity of money and r is the rate of interest (ibid.: 168). Keynes distinguished his idea of liquidity preference from this early thought of "the state of bearishness" in the *TM*, because the rate of interest was not a determinant in that state (ibid.: 173).

The ideas of the MPC (Marginal Propensity to Consume), MPS (Marginal Propensity to Save), and the multiplier also had prior claimants to the *GT*. In equilibrium, Keynes proposed that "employment will depend on aggregate supply, the propensity to consume, and investment" (Keynes, 1936: 29). In this model, the change in income, measured in wage units, exceeds the change in consumption, also in wage units. Changes in investment have a multiplier effect on changes in income, which he named the *investment multiplier*. "Mr. Kahn's multiplier is a little different from this, being what we may call the *employment multiplier*" (ibid.: 115). Keynes thought that "the conception of the multiplier was first introduced into economic theory by Richard F. Kahn in his article on 'The Relation of Home Investment to Unemployment' (*Economic Journal*, June 1931)" (ibid.: 113). Others have sourced the concept to several other authors (see Coleman, 19).

Keynesian Novelties of the *General Theory*

Sometimes economists speak of a Keynesian revolution as a paradigm shift in economics. For Lawrence Klein, "the revolution was solely the development of the theory of effective demand; i.e., a theory of the determination of the level of output as a whole" (Klein, 1966: 56). Leijonhufvud identified a paradigmatic shift from to Keynes from the classics, based on "a high incidence of 'conversion' . . . a massive migration into 'Keynesian economics' . . . Growth of Knowledge . . . in novel, worthwhile . . . curricula split general economic theory . . . into 'micro' and 'macro' segments" (Leijonhufvud, 1976: 83-84). For Mark Blaug, "Keynes is supposed to have surplanted . . . a network of interconnected sub-paradigms . . . best regarded as a Lakatosian SRP (Scientific Research Program)" (Blaug, 1976: 160-161).

Although Keynes did not use the term macroeconomics, the *GT* launched that subdiscipline, creating a paradigm shift in theory and policy that put government on the pedestal for stabilization and crisis management of the economy. In the terminology of the social scientists, the *GT* was "sufficiently unprecedented to attract an enduring group of adherents away from competing modes of scientific activity. Simultaneously, it was sufficiently open-ended to leave all sorts of problems for the redefined group of practitioners to resolve" (Kuhn, 1970: 10). Further, the *GT* was "recounted . . . by science textbooks. . . . These textbooks expound the body of accepted theory, illustrate many or all of its successful applications, and compare these applications with exemplary observations and experiments" (ibid.: 10). In other word, the students and practitioners of the Keynesian paradigm must be updated through books that interpret the *GT* (Pearce and Hoover, 1995: 184).

David Colander articulately described the impact of the *GT* as a new paradigm with the following syllogism: "researchers' needs and incentives determine which theory researchers use. . . . The first, which I call the article criteria, is a need to publish . . . a paradigm which is article laden is contagious; it will generate enormous interest and will spread quickly among the profession. . . . Whether a theory will have a lasting effect depends on second internal need. . . . To have a lasting effect a theory must be teachable" (Colander, 1988: 93-94).

As a scientific research program, Keynes departed from "methodological individualism" toward aggregates; concentrated on the short period analysis, and emphasized adjustment with output over prices (Blaug, 1976: 162). The new hard core of Keynesian thought revolves around underemployment, uncertainty, and expectation. Auxiliary hypotheses in the protective belt of Keynesian thought includes the consumption function, the multiplier, autonomous expenditures, speculative demand for money, and price stickiness (ibid.: 162). In similar vein, Hicks characterized the Keynesian revolution in terms of the "instability of capitalism . . . to be stabilized, by policy and by some instrument of policy" (Hicks, 1976: 217).

First Generation Keynesian Model of the Interpreters/ Reconcilers

John Hicks (1937) and Alvin Hansen (1953) have pioneered the first interpretation of Keynes with the classical and neoclassical school by building a Keynesian model using liquidity preference $M = L(r, Y)$, investment $I = I(r, Y)$, savings $S = S(r, Y)$, and saving-investment equilibrium $S = I$, where M is money, I is investment, S is savings, Y is income, and r is the rate of interest. Hicks admitted that his model of Keynes "was never intended as more than a representation of what appeared to be a central part of the Keynes theory" (Hicks, 1974: 6). In his "Mr. Keynes and the Classics" (Hicks, 1939), Hicks demonstrated how the marginal efficiency of capital (bond market), consumption (goods market), and liquidity preference (money market) can be looked at as two rather than three markets by the virtue of Walras' law, which says that one has a degree of freedom in studying n-markets.

Building on Hicks's framework, Modigliani (1944) offered a nine-equation Keynesian model, which sparked from the first Federal Reserve Board-Penn macro-econometric model in the US. Equations 1, 2, and 3 let the money market, investments, and savings be dependent on the rate of interest and income [M = L(r, Y), I = I(r, Y), and S = S(r, Y)]. Equation 4 denotes the equality between savings and investment [S = I]. Equation 5 is the money income [Y = P(X)]. Equation 6 is the production function [X = X(N)]. For Equation 7, we have a choice. We can deal with the relationship of N on W or the inverse, W on N. Say we write N = F(W/P), then the inverse would be W = F^{-1}(N)P. Equation 8 relates consumption to income and investment [C = Y–I]. Equation 9 relates wages to either its minimum or employment where the equation can take the form $W = \alpha w_0 + \beta F^{-1}(N)P$. If we let N_0 represent "full employment," then we can define the actual employment level as less than or greater than full employment ($N \leq N_0$ or $N > N_0$). In the former condition, $\alpha = 1$ and $\beta = 0$, and the formula becomes $W = w_0$. When $N > N_0$, $\alpha = 0$ and $\beta = 1$, and the formula becomes $W = F^{-1}(N)P$.

In sum, eight equations and one identity make up Modigliani's 1944 version of Keynesian economics. The variables are Income (X), Money (M), Consumption (C), Investment (I), Savings (S), Aggregate Demand (X^d), Employment (N), Labor Supply (N^s), Money Income (Y), Price of Output (P), the Price of Labor (W), and the Interest Rate (r). The fifth equation is pivotal for the determination of output and price, which are affected on the one hand by the control of money and on the other had by upward pressure on wage.

In a letter of March 31, 1937, Keynes related to Hicks that his model assumes that "increase in the quantity of money is capable of increasing employment. A strictly brought-up classical economist would not, I should say, admit that" (Keynes, 1973: vol. XIV, 79).

One strand of the money cum employment relations is that when the money wage rate is fixed, prices will also be fixed, and changes in the quantity of money will affect employment and output (Lowe, 1965: 229). Hicks opted for a short period in which he shown several way ways in which price and the rate of interest can be determined, namely "I. Prices determined by effective demand and supply for goods and services; interest by the demand for money; saving and investment a check equation. II. Prices determined by the quantity of money; interest by the saving and investment; effective demand the check equation" (Keynes, 1973: vol. XIV, 82). Keynes, however, was not satisfied: "I do not really understand how you mean interest to be determined by saving and investment under II" (ibid.: 83), for interest is determined in the money market. Hicks' view was that Keynes "determine[s] the rate of interest by the demand-for-money equation—and this means that [Keynes would] have to pack an unconscionable lot into the demand for money" (ibid.: 73). Keynes maintained that the classics think that the rate of interest is a "non-monetary" phenomenon (ibid.: 80). Modigliani accepted the Hicksian view, stating that "in reconsidering the Keynesian system we shall essentially follow the lines suggested by J. R. Hicks in his fundamental paper, 'Mr. Keynes and the "Classics."' Our main task is to clarify and develop his arguments, taking into account later theoretical developments" (Modigliani, 1980: vol. 1, 26).

The interpreters of the Hicksian view had the natural inclination to use classical concepts such as Say's Law, Walras' Law, and Homogeneity postulate. Nevertheless Keynes stood firm on the aggregate basis, leaving room for other post-Keynesians to expand and articulate his research program. A dominant line of thought was to let consumption lead to production and employment. As Hyman Minsky puts it, "To Keynes consumption, for the purpose of employment theory, was a part of aggregate effective demand. Aggregate effective demand, when introduced into the inverse of the aggregate-supply function, generated the demand for labor. Thus consumption to Keynes always involved current production" (Minksy, 2008: 25). In Keynes's words, "the actual level of output and employment depends not on the capacity to produce or on the pre-existing level of income, but on the current decisions to produce—which depends in turn on current decisions to invest and on present expectations of current and prospective consumption" (Keynes, 1936: vol. VII, xxxii).

Thus far we see that the revolutionary aspect of Keynes' theory holds that "the pure theory of what determines the actual employment of the available resources has seldom been examined in great detail" (Keynes, 1936: 4). Metaphorically, Keynes explained, "If . . . money is the drink which stimulates the system to activity . . . there may be several slips between the cup and the lip" (ibid.: 171). These slips are grounded in the idea that when the money supply increases, the interest rate will fall. This occurs because "more money would flow into investment channels and raise prices of securities and investment goods, which is the same thing as reducing interest rates" (Harris, 1955: 55). But Keynes maintained that the interest rate may not fall because the public may increase its liquidity preference faster that the increase in money supply. Alongside the liquidity preference problem, when the interest rate falls, the investment demand schedule may fall faster than an expected fall in the rate of interest, creating an inelasticity situation. Finally, with the fall in the interest rate, investment may not have the expected increase on employment if the MPC is falling (Keynes, 1936: 171).

Neoclassical Synthesis

The impacts of the views of Hicks, Hansen, and Modigliani were codified into the neoclassical synthesis, which according the Hicks began to emerge from the works of Samuelson, Kenneth Arrow, Milton Friedman, and Don Patinkin. These authors "regarded [Hick's *Value and Capital*] as the beginning of their 'neo-classical synthesis'" (Hicks, 1983: vol. VIII, 361). Following Pigou's attack on Keynes' *GT*, a number of economists developed the wealth effect argument to counter Keynes, creating a niche for the neoclassical synthesis to hold that"if such wealth effects were properly integrated in the analysis, full price flexibility . . . was bound to remove all excess demands and supplies" (Grandmont, 1983: 1). Basically, the Pigou effect can restore full employment in a Keynesian setting because as wages and prices fall, real wealth will appreciate, prompting wealth holders to save less, lowering the saving schedule to correspond with lower investment in the classical capital market at full employment—an effect that would restore confidence in the orthodox equilibrium system, but would trigger the special cases of the haudralic system on Keynes' behalf.

One representation of the neoclassical synthesis is the Keynesian-cross diagram, equilibrium outlay of consumption, $C(Y)$, plus fixed investment, $\bar{I}$, plotted on a vertical axis, equals equilibrium output, Y, plotted on the horizontal axis. "The intersection of $C(Y) + \bar{I}$ with the 45° line gives us our simplest 'Keynesian-cross,' which logically is exactly like a 'Marshallian-cross' of supply and demand" (Samuelson, 1966: vol. 2, 199). Alternatively, one can solve for savings, and write $S(Y) = Y - C(Y) = \bar{I}$, which now plots positive and negative amounts of savings and investment on the vertical axis against income to obtain the same level of equilibrium income as the Keynesian-cross (ibid.: 1200).

Basically, the neoclassical synthesis used microanalysis and macroanalysis on "a managed economy which through skillful use of fiscal and monetary policy channeled the Keynesian forces of effective demand into behaving like a neoclassical model" (ibid.: 1544). Its prediction transcends what Samuelson called Keynes' "depression version," where cheaper credit is an inoperable policy in the face of the special cases. Among the predictions of the neoclassical synthesis are: 1.) Expansionary monetary policy and austere fiscal policy mixes would deepen capital and cause the economy to grow (ibid.). Here the tight fiscal measure prevents demand-pull inflation, and the easy monetary policy assumes that the accelerator (K/Y) is not fixed, so as to allow the *deepening* of capital in the short run to take place. 2.) "Government policy could hope to use the levers of fiscal and monetary policy to cause the IS and LM curves of the Keynesian system to shift so as to achieve an equilibrium intersection nearer to full employment and with a mix between capital formation and real consumption that could be shifted toward investment by greater emphasis upon expansionary credit policy and on austere fiscal policy" (Samuelson, 1986: vol. 5, 293).

As Arrow put it, the neoclassical synthesis "held that achievement of full employment requires Keynesian intervention but that neoclassical theory is valid when full employment is reached. Let $W(g)$ be the Walrasian system, and $K(g)$ be the 'true' system, where g is a parameter representing government action (fiscal or monetary). The Samuelson-Keynes view of the world is that full employment is a valid proposition in $K(g)$ only for special values of g, whereas full employment holds in $W(g)$ for all g" (Arrow, 1967: 735). If g^* is such that full employment holds in $K(g^*)$, can it be true that theorems valid in $W(g^*)$ are also valid in $K(g^*)$? Obviously, the two systems do not respond similarly to changes in g, since full employment remains valid in one but not in the other. However, one might argue that the appropriate criterion is that the response of the economic behavior predicted by $K(g^*)$ to shifts in parameters of the system other than government actions (for example, technological change, shifts in demand for exports) be quantitatively, or at least qualitatively, the same as for $W(g^*)$. There is no a priori reason to believe this, and any brief consideration of possible K- models makes the proposition seem unlikely, except possibly at a more sophisticated level of analysis than has yet been achieved.

The neoclassical synthesis loosened up on some of Keynes' assumptions, particularly relating to existing labor, equipments, and the techniques of production. "In his 1937 *Eugenics Review* article 'The Economic [C]onsequences of a Declining Population,' Keynes was already aware of the effects associated with different exponential rates of natural growth," presenting an avenue through which to expand and articulate the Keynesian paradigm (Samuelson, 1966: vol. 2, 1543). In his "Economic Possibilities for our Grandchildren," Keynes looked favorably on capital accumulation, writing that "the modern age opened, I think, with the accumulation of capital which began in the sixteenth century" (Keynes, 1963 [1930]: 361). In his *TMR*, Keynes looked at the accumulation of capital historically, through the development of three classes of society—the investing, business, and earning class (Keynes, 1971 [1923]: 3-4), where he went at length to lay out the history and importance of capital accumulation for these classes as follows: the *investment society* was fully developed when investors "parted with his real property permanently, in return either of a perpetual annuity fixed in terms of money or for a terminable annuity and the repayment of the principal in money at the end of the term" (ibid.: 5). Thus he underscored that investors "owned neither buildings, nor land, nor businesses, nor precious metals, but titles to an annual income in legal-tendered money" (ibid.: 12). *The business person* borrows money to take advantage of expected profits. When the value of money falls, they repay loans with cheaper money. Further gains accrue to the business class because one usually "buys before one sells," and in that process, one stands to gain from "better prices than one expected." A third source of gain for the business class arises from the difference between the money interest rate on which one borrows funds, and the real interest rate established by the market. As for *the earning class,* how changes in the value of money during inflation affect these wage earners is more uncertain. As wages tend to lag behind prices, the value of real wages tends to fall during periods of rising prices (ibid.: 26). It is not alarming, therefore, that during the 1950s, when models of capital accumulation and technical change developed, one would want to reexamine Keynes' assumption of them in the *GT*, and this was an important task of the neoclassical synthesis (Samuelson, 1966, Vol. 2. 1543-1544).

Keynes's main purpose in the *GT* "is to deal with difficult questions of theory, and only in the second place with the applications of this theory to practice" (Keynes, 1936: vol. VII, xxi). Concerns with applications have created a division in the literature. A star among Keynes's students, Joan Robinson, set the stage of this research with the view that "On the plane of theory, the main point of the *General Theory* was to break out of the cocoon of equilibrium and consider the nature of life lived in time—the difference between yesterday and tomorrow. Here and now, the past is irrevocable and the future is unknown" (Robinson, 1980: vol. IV, 95). In the 1930s, the Keynesian model took the form of a few relationships. "They were constructed on the basis of a consumption function, and investment function, a liquidity preference function, and some other simple concepts. But an apparatus of such elementary concepts reveals itself entirely insufficient for the complex and differentiated problems one is facing if one attempts to formulate an adequate economic policy applying to post-war society. This implies harmonization of many antagonistic interests, consideration of many sectors of production, many social categories, etc." (Frisch, 1966 [1960]: 2). A third view, summarized by Franklin Fisher, was "whether (and how) an economy could get stuck at an underemployment equilibrium . . . an economy that gets close enough to such a point will not escape from it without an exogenous change in circumstance... the question of underemployment equilibrium has a general setting ... it involves a stability analysis to justify it" (Fisher, 1989: 9).

An important part of the neoclassical synthesis was to address, not answer, the problems characterized by Robinson and Ragnar Frisch, and Fisher, for which Samuelson proposed the "correspondence principle": "in the absence of precise quantitative data he [the economist] must infer analytically the qualitative direction of movement of a complex system" (Samuelson, 1947: 258). He evolved the "correspondence principle," whereby the comparative statical behavior of a system is seen to be closely related to its dynamical stability properties" (ibid.: 351). For instance, consider a system such as $dp / dt = k(D - S)$, where p is price, k is a constant, D is quantity demand, and S is quantity supplied. By adding the hypothesis that if D shifts to the right, prices will rise, we can make inferences of dynamic stability (Samuelson, 1966: vol. 2, 1771) In short, the *correspondence principle* enunciates "the relationship between the stability conditions of dynamics and the evaluation of displacements in comparative statics" (Samuelson, 1947: 350)

Economists are very one-sided about the performance of the neoclassical synthesis. Arrow sided with the neoclassical basis: "The theory of the perfect market is in an interesting way complementary to Keynesian theory. We have never been able to integrate Keynesian view-points into standard neoclassical theory, in terms of individual motivation, yet this theory, with its various modifications, has been a most serviceable tool of prediction and control. In fact, it is useful in domains where competitive theory fails and vice versa. Neither theory is good, however, at predicting dynamic processes"(Arrow, 1984: vol. 4, 158).

The post-Keynesian, Paul Davidson, has a partiality for authenticity, opposing Samuelson for triangulating between "gross substitution," where any interest bearing capital can substitute for money; "money neutrality," where money is neutral on its effect of output; and "ergodic hypothesis," where "in an ergodic system where the future can be reliable predicted . . . where the gross substitution axiom underlies all demand curves, then as long as prices are flexible, money must be neutral and the system automatically adjusts to full employment equilibrium" (Davidson, 2007: vol. 4, 214-215).

The neoclassical synthesis also assumed a fixed money wage model, and therefore does not encompass the overall picture of the *GT*, where Keynes argued that "the money-wage and other factor costs are constant per unit of labor employed . . . solely to facilitate the exposition. The essential character of the argument is precisely the same whether or not money-wages, etc., are liable to change" (Keynes, 1936: vol. VII, 27). As reviewed by Peter Howitt (1990: 9) Patinkin (1948) set the stage of a comprehensive picture of the *GT* by building a Keynesian model sympathetic to the classical view where the real-balance effect guarantees full employment. Following his treatment of the labor market, Clower (1965) began a reappraisal, and Leijonhufvud (1968) began his reconstruction, followed by Robert Barro and Gene Grossman's (1971) integration of these theories. The new classical and New Keynesian School subsequently developed to address further problems with these models.

The neoclassical synthesis dominated macroeconomics until the mid 1970, when crises developed (Blanchard and Fischer, 1989: 26-27). Keynesian economics became the mainstream doctrine from 1936 to the mid-1960s, but was challenged by New Classical economics from the mid-1970s to mid-1980s, and the New Keynesians in the mid-1980s. As Davidson puts it, "Consequently in the 1970s academic literature, the Monetarists easily defeated the Samuelson's neoclassical synthesis Keynesian. . . . New Keynesian theory was developed to replace Samuelson's Keynesians. Just as Friedman's Monetarism had conquered Samuelson's brand of Keynesianism, New Classical theory easily made a mockery of the New Keynesians' approach" (Davidson, 2007: Vol. 4, 208-209).

Friedman Monetary Counter Revolution

According to the monetarist Milton Freidman, "the basic source of the [Keynesian] revolution and the reaction against the quantity theory of money was a historical event, namely the great contraction or depression. In the United Kingdom the contraction started in 1925 when Britain went back on gold at the pre-war parity and ended in 1931 when Britain went off gold. In the United States, the contraction started in 1929 and ended when the US went off gold in early 1933. In both countries, economic conditions were depressed for years after the contraction itself had ended and an expansion had begun" (Friedman, 1970: 11).

Keynes' point of view about the Fisherian Quantity theory of money is that velocity of circulation of money would adapt so as to avoid equi-proportional changes in the money supply and prices, thereby shifting the focus from the quantity of money to autonomous spending, mainly business and government expenditures, which are independent of income (ibid.: 12-13). Even the *TMR* (1923), where Keynes followed the Cambridge quantity theory, explains that "inflationary experiences could condition expectations of future inflation which would exert a feedback effect upon the demand for cash holdings and the demand for bank deposits. This induced increase in velocity . . . would serve to fuel the inflationary process still further and generate still further expectations of future inflationary trends" (Shaw, 1983: 31). As variable velocity will dampen the effect of money, Keynes turned to autonomous and induced consumption, where autonomous spending has a multiplier impact on output, which will have a lagged effect on prices, a phenomenon determined in the latter half of the 1950s; first, by a decline in the WPI for crude materials, then for intermediate materials, then for finished products, and finally for consumer commodities (Moore, 1971: 6).

One view of the Keynesian counterrevolution sense is that, "the model which Keynes called his 'general theory' is but a special case of the Classical theory, obtained by imposing certain restrictive assumptions on the latter . . . models which do not assume perfect information are 'special cases' of the perfect information model" (Leijonhufvud, 1968: 394). As we know, Keynes wrote: "I shall argue that the postulates of the classical theory are applicable to a special case only and not to the general case, the situation which it assumes being a limiting point of the possible positions of equilibrium" (Keynes, 1936: 3). According to Samuelson, the "new classical economics" of Robert Lucas, Tom Sargent, Barro, and others is truly a counterrevolution and the same cannot be said of "monetarism" (Samuelson, 1986: vol. 5, 213). He meant "counterrevolution" in the sense of "market clearing."

In place of the quantity theory that he developed in his earlier works, Keynes put in place new "underlying presuppositions" that "constrain and determine belief" in Keynesian economics (Maki, 2001: 8). For instance, Keynes' contribution to the liquidity preference Schedule, with the Hicks, Hansen, and Abba Lerner revision mentioned above, was also a springboard for subsequent development for both the monetarist and Keynesian schools. On the monetarist side, "[Phillip] Cagan's equation . . . is a simplified form of the standard Keynes (1936)-Hicks (1937) LM curve . . . real money demand on date t depends positively on aggregate real output Y_t, and negatively on the nominal interest rate i_{t+1} between dates t and $t + 1$" (Obstfeld and Rogoff, 1996: 516). If the real rate of interest is constant, the nominal rate will move with expected inflation, allowing Cagan to make the demand for money dependent on expected inflation.

The monetarists perceive a gap between actual and unexpected prices, and not rigid wages or involuntary employment as the causes of lower output and employment. The gap is a result of workers misperceiving money wages for real wages, a misperception that can happen when a cut in effective demand lowers prices and nominal wages. In that situation, workers will supply less labor, which will increase real wages, and reduce employment and output, a phenomenon that is demonstrated by making the supply of labor curve dependent on expected prices. Friedman sees these adjustments as temporary, not warranting a stabilizing Keynesian policy that runs the risk of becoming more destabilizing as targeting an unknown inflation rate can create volatility, and that the adjustment will come to an end when expectations are realized (Modigliani, 1985: vol. 6, 14).

Expectation in the Direction of Foresight and Prediction of the Keynesian Model

Although Keynes presented the groundwork for a theory of expectation in economics that foreshadowed the adaptive and rational expectation theories that developed in the latter half of the twentieth century, the development of his theory is in a state of degeneration currently. The theory took form in his *A Treatise on Probability* (*TP*) (1921), where he attempted both a subject and objective theory of induction using probability theory not in the form direct knowledge, but in the form of an argument (Keynes, 1921: 3). Keynes turned against the old argument that "the probable is that which usually happens" (ibid.: 86), and stood beside David Hume, who hypothesized that "while past experience gives rise to a psychological anticipation of some events rather than of others, no ground has been given for the validity of this superior anticipation" (ibid.: 88). Logicians have called this "the problem of the validity of inference from past to future generalizations" (Stebbing, 1961: 414). In writing his *TP* dissertation, Keynes was influenced about objective probability relationship by his teachers, G. E. Moore, Alfred Whitehead, and Bertrand Russell on arguments of the form: "If p, probable q," but later, at the urging of Frank Ramsey and others, he turned to a more subjective theory, which characterizes the exposition he gave of expectation in the *GT*.

Keynes did not give a clear definition of probability in the statistical sense, but offered a psychological definition that suggests "*comparisons* of the respective weights which attach to different arguments . . . that probability is, in the full and literal sense of the word, measurable" (Keynes, 1921: 21). What is measured in the *TP* is the "degree of rational belief" of a proposition, based on some evidence that is given, and Keynes' emphasis was on the logical, formal, or objective aspect of probability, not the frequency ratio (Fisher, 1923: 46). Keynes said that he worked his way into the idea that probability was a relation through the influence of Russell's *Principia Mathematica*, which was concerned with laying mathematics on the foundation of logic (Keynes, 1921: 125).

Keynes originally stated that we must have knowledge of the premises, *h*, of an argument to a certain degree, α, which will give us some rational belief in the conclusion, *a*, of the argument, so that "there is a *probability-relation* of degree α between *a* and *h*" (ibid.: 4) We can therefore write the probability, *P*, of *a* as $P = a / h$ (ibid.: 43, 121). In brief, Keynes proposed a "generalized frequency theory" that places "propositions rather than events" as the subject matter of probability theory (ibid.: 110). Even in his early proposal in the *TP*, Keynes noted that probability plays a secondary role in expectation analysis: "of probability we can say no more than that it is a lower degree of rational belief than certainty" (ibid.: 16).

According to Ramsey, a fundamental criticism of Keynes's view of expectation in the *TP* is that "there really do not seem to be any such things as the probability relation" that Keynes described between *a* and *h* (Ramsey, 1931 [1960]: 161). Ramsey instead proposed a betting quotient alternative to

Keynes' theory that measures the degree of belief a person has in a proposition by the amount of money that person would be willing to bet on the proposition being true (Keynes, 1971 [1923]: xx). Responding to Ramsey's criticism, Keynes accepted a distinction between formal logic, human logic, and descriptive psychology, holding that "the calculus of probabilities belongs to formal logic. But the basis of our degrees of belief—or the *a priori* probabilities, as they used to be called—is part of our human outfit" (Keynes, 1933 [1972]: vol. 10, 335, 118 [Meridian edition]).

With the subjective view of probability, the works of Keynes began to look like beads strung on a necklace. In his *Tract* (1923), Keynes explained that expectation of an increase in price will create demand for cash and bank deposits, increasing the velocity of circulation of money, and increasing inflation further. In his *Treatise* (1930), the expected prices of stock and bonds affect the rate of interest, which in turn can create inflation or deflation (Shaw, 1984: 31). For instance, an investor will hold more stocks and less savings deposits if stock prices are expected to rise, and *vice versa*. According to Bradley Bateman, Keynes had the view of expectation that would characterize the *GT* by the fall of 1933; namely, that expectation affected the financial market through liquidity preference, affected investments through prospective quasi-rents, and affected employment through entrepreneurs' expectation of income, where the latter was short-term, and the former two were long-term expectation concepts (Bateman, 1996: 124).

In the *GT*, Keynes likens speculation to bubbles on a steady stream of enterprise. In that state, they can do no harm, unless the enterprise becomes the bubbles on a whirlpool of speculation (Keynes, 1936: 159). In this situation, "about the stock market as a casino, he describes the behavior of short-term speculators chasing immediate capital gains . . . trying to guess what other individuals guess other individuals will guess about capital gains" (Begg, 1982: 19). In his *Quarterly Journal of Economics* (1937) article, Keynes refocused his meaning of expectation to the point that he regarded the future as uncertain in the sense that "there is no scientific basis on which to form any calculable probability whatever. We simple do not know," and therefore, we should fall back on the things we know, on convention, which takes the form of three rules—using the present as a better guide for the future than the past, using the existing state of option on prices and output as "correct summing up of future prospects," and confirming with the behavior of the majority or the average, i.e., conventional judgment (Keynes, 1937: 214).

The model of the *GT* was built on the view that "The factors, which we take as given, influence our independent variables, but do not completely determine them" (Keynes, 1936: vol. VII, 245-246). Existing equipment, a given, is necessary for the determination of the marginal efficiency of capital (MEC), an independent variable, but is not sufficient for the determination of MEC because an additional variable; namely, the state of long-term expectation, is required as well but is not known. Similarly, the interest rate depends on the liquidity preference and the quantity of money. The givens will require the specification of three other variables for the existence of a solution for national income and employment: 1) the propensity to consume, attitude to liquidity, and expectation of future yield; 2) the wage-unit specified by collective bargaining; and 3) the quantity of money (Keynes, 1936: 246-247). We can operate in the Keynesian economy where the economy is "unchanging" or "changing," and the agent's view can be "fixed and reliable in all respects," where "all things are foreseen from the beginning," where "expectations are liable to disappointment," and where "expectations concerning the future affect what we do to-day" (ibid.: 293-294).

The picture depicted of Keynesian expectation is an underlying instability of economic activities due to speculation and spontaneous optimism. He stated that "our decision to do something positive . . . can only be taken as a result of animal spirits—of a spontaneous urge to action rather than inaction, and not as the outcome of . . . probabilities" (ibid.: 161). By a post-Keynesian account, convention rules investment demand through (1) profit expectation, (2) animal spirit, (3) risk, (4) supply of finance, and (5) the urge to accumulate. (Khan, 1984) We should note that "There are not two separate factors affecting the rate of investment, namely, the schedule of the marginal efficiency of capital and the state of confidence. The state of confidence is relevant because it is one of the major factors determining the former, which is the same as the invest demand-schedule" (Keynes, 1936: 149).

Keynes' conventional view of long-term expectation cause him to be "skeptical of the success of a merely monetary policy directed towards influencing the rate of interest" (ibid.: 164). For him, "our desire to hold money as a store of wealth is a barometer of the degree of our distrust of our own calculations and conventions concerning the future.... The possession of actual money lulls our disquietude; and the premium we require to make us part with money is a measure of the degree of our disquietude" (Keynes, 1973: vol. XIV, 116). People's desire for cash can lead to a liquidity trap situation where "after the rate of interest has fallen to a certain level, liquidity preference may become virtually absolute" (Keynes, 1936: 207).

Impact of Keynes' Views on Expectation

Many interpretations found a home in the house of expectation that Keynes built. Some categorical views of expectation spreads over short and long-term, exogenous and endogenous, ex ante and ex post, perfect and imperfect markets, and forms the foundation of different schools of beliefs on expectation. Cutting through the rhetoric, a modern writer wrote, "Any explanation of economic action requires some explanation of how economics actors think about the future" (McCloskey, 1985: 88). The impact of Keynes' expectation includes John Hicks using a day-to-day model for up to a week to develop his elasticity of expectation hypothesis, the Arrow-Debreu model of competitive equilibrium that found current and expected prices will jointly clear supply and demand equations in present and future markets, and Jean-Michel Grandmonth formulated an intertemporal model, that extended the Arrow-Debreu model for sequences of time periods. G. L. S. Shackle developed non-probabilistic statements about the next period output, x, such as that it is impossible, possible, or surprising if it would reach a specified high or low level, very surprised it occurs, etc. The adaptive expectation found a home in the Federal Reserve Board's MPS (Mathematical Programming System) model, one of the first large-scale econometric models that were built in the 1960s, where expectation was captured in the form of lag structure both to parameters and error terms.

Cagan introduced the adaptive expectation model $\log_e(M / P) = -\alpha E\gamma$, where the demand for money function depends on the expected rate of change in prices, E, and two constants, α and λ, where actual rate of change of prices was "approximated by the difference between the logarithms of successive values of the index of prices" (Cagan, 1956: 35). This model was incorporated into the Phillips curve analysis, which dominated research in the third quarter of the last century. As Robert Solow presented the problem, of the post WW II recessions of 1948-1949, 1953-1954, and 1957-1958, only in the latter recession did price increase, signaling a need for expected price analysis, which the Phillips's curve was suited because it embodied an adaptive expected mechanism that could lend interpretation from the cost-push versus demand-pull points of view (Solow, 2002: 71-73).

For the early post-Keynesians, such as Modigliani, the adaptive model was a good predictor of what Keynes call short-term expectation, which was "concerned with the price which a manufacturer can expect to get for his 'finished' output at the time when he commits himself to starting the process which will produce it" (Keynes, 1936: vol. 7, 46). Modigliani added the Non-Inflationary Rate of Unemployment (NIRU) concept to the model to underscore a "*critical* rate of unemployment such that, as long as unemployment does not fall below it, inflation can be expected to decline" (Modigliani and Papademos, 1980: 188-189). If the expected price, p^* is equal to the price in the last period, p_{t-1}, the difference between actual price and expected price, $p - p_{t-1}$, will be some function of the unemployment rate, and NIRU will be a solution to that function (Modigliani and Papademos, 1989: 175-176).

The test of the pudding is in eating it. The Keynesian model was baked with many restrictions in order to make identifications of its equations possible. In statistical terms, a Keynesian restriction for the consumption function occurs when we exclude other independent variables in the system besides income. Other statistical restrictions of a Keynesian system include the coefficients of the error term, and the classification of variables such as the money supply as exogenous, and variables such as prices and output as endogenous. Lucas and Sargent have criticized the Keynesian models for omitting important microeconomics restrictions, such as the way individuals set their expectations, and for not perusing a general equilibrium approach, noting that "microeconomic theory has very damaging implications for the restrictions conventionally used to identify Keynesian macroeconometric models.... Furthermore ... there is a point beyond which Keynesian models must suspend the hypothesis either of cleared markets or of optimizing agents" (Lucas and Sargent, 1981: vol. 1, 295, 299, 301). In that regard, Lucas and Sargent have extended Walrasian and Marshallian concepts of price, taking to the case where price provides information in the sense of the Rational Expectation Hypothesis (REH) sense that causes drifts in structural parameters of their models.

Through his microeconomic and general equilibrium specification, Lucas has made the REH hypothesis operational. On the microeconomic side, an individual at time t will form an expectation about price, p_{it}, based on all the information available, Ω_{it}, before making the forecast. This is operational in the sense that all the forecaster has to do is replace expression of the form $E(p_{it} \mid \Omega_{it})$ with values resulting from applying the mathematical expectation operator, E, on them, conditioned by the information we have. This procedure improves the adaptive expectation mechanism by making it less likely to underestimate the actual price increases when the inflation rate is accelerating, and ensuring that it does not ignore relevant information in the formation of the expectation (Pesaran, 1987: 18-19). As Lucas Papademos and Modigliani described it, the Phillips curve relationships were unstable because "they resulted from actions of economic agents induced by unanticipated price fluctuations under conditions of imperfect information. Expectation errors could persist, resulting in transitory output fluctuation, but in the long run actual and expected price changes could not deviate systematically. Consequently, in the steady state there is a unique 'natural' full-employment output level which is invariant to permanent inflation" (Papademos and Modigliani, 1990: 415).

Faith in the RE hypothesis is still being determined. Some economists see it as a generalization of Keynes' view of expectation in the beauty contest context, which can be written in modern terminology as $y_{it} = \lambda_i E(y_{it} \mid \Omega_{it}) + \omega_{it}$, where y is long term expectation, t is time (approximately three months), ω_{it} is the atmosphere of mass psychology, and Ω_{it} is the state of the news. Investors, i, calculate the average expectation, E, such as in a beauty contest where competitors must pick out the prettiest face among photographs that are published in a newspaper (Pesaran, 1987: 277). The Keynesian expected outcome is realized when λ_i is set equal to the inverse of the number of answers, say $1 / N$ and ω_{it} is zero. As these latter parameters can be different in general, Keynesian expectation is a special case of the REH.

Originally, the leading monetarist Friedman rejected the REH hypothesis. REH "denied the real evils of systematic mismanagement of money" (Samuelson, 1986. vol. 5, 292). A quick view of this occurs if we take the conditional expectation of both sides of the Lucas aggregate supply curve: $Y = Y_n + a(P - P_e) + error$, which will yield the result that policy makers can only affect the variance of output, Y, around its natural level, Y_n, since the expected value of prices, P, about their expect value, P_e, will be zero (Beggs, 1980: 294). Minimizing the variance was found germane to this approach based on REH and the Lucas supply curve, and Sargent and Wallace found that a monetary policy rule, one that is beyond the Friedman x-percent rule that does not have a feedback mechanism, and perhaps more in the spirit of Taylor rule, will do the job (Sargent and Wallace, 1981: 200).

Phelps advocated dropping the equilibrium framework, for a more non-Walrasian framework, which yields results more in line with Samuelson's views that oppose the REH. Large-scale econometric models for the REH are still not within reach. To improve predictions, Finn Kydland and Edward Prescott have used time-consistent computational experiments in econometric models, subsequent to the REH revolution. These models allow policy makers such as the Federal Reserve, to have no concern about wrong models or wrong goals, or even histories and reputation, because they need only choose sequentially. The modern literature also developed a non-Walrasian equilibrium concept that depends on current prices, and the expectation of future prices based on past and current prices. Thus, the economic agents are able to carry out all their preferred actions in current markets.

General Equilibrium (GE) and Expectation

Keynes was formally concerned with temporary equilibrium, and because of his emphasis on expectation and speculation, he was more concerned with failure of the price mechanism than with finding equilibrium prices (Arrow and Hahn, 1971: 347). A temporary equilibrium is a Hicksian short-run mechanism that chops time up into discrete periods in which one can find current prices, and interest rates that equate aggregate demand and supply (Grandmont, 1983: 3). In making short-run decisions, traders treat rational expectation in an exogenous way by discounting to the present value of variables.

In the Arrow-Debreu model, the economy is completely defined by a commodity space, the number household, consumption sets, ordering of consumption bundles, and consumer endowments (Hahn, 1985: 32). This model followed Hicks in "regarding commodities at different dates as different commodities," and it "proved the existence of present and future prices which jointly equilibrated supply and demand on all markets, present and future"

(Arrow, 1983: vol. 2, 227). As Gerard Debreu puts it, "A contract for the transfer of a commodity now specifies, in addition to its physical properties, its location and its date. . . . This new definition of a commodity allows one to obtain a theory of uncertainty free from any probability concept" (Debreu, 1959: 98).

In the Arrow-Debreu model, expectations are usually incorporated into the parameter of a utility function. Aviad Heifetz and Herakles Polemarchakis (1998, 172) have illustrated this for two goods, x, y, three individuals, and a Cobb-Douglas utility function can be written as: $u = x^{\alpha^i(t)} y^{(1-\alpha)^i(t)}$, where i is individual and t is time. Here, the expectations are built into the exponential coefficient. For instance, we can set $\alpha^1(t) = at^1 + bt^2 + \gamma c^3 + d$, $a^2(t) = at^2 + bt^3 + ct^1 + d$, and $a^3(t) = at^3 + bt^1 + ct^2 + d$. The individuals can observe their state space, t^i, and prices, p. We can proceed in the Keynesian parlance to the notion that "expectations in the sense of probability distribution over states of nature are included in the notion of preferences . . . we must adjoin at least expectations concerning future terms at which trade can take places. These will be conditional expectation. . . . One non-Keynesian proposal is to take the expected price to be conditioned by the state of nature and so independent of observed prices . . . a more or less uncertain future casts a shadow over the present, and not only are we closer to Keynes but, more importantly to reality" (Hahn, 1985: 34).

Following Leonard Savage, the Arrow-Debreu "look before you leap" attitude can be modeled in a world of different states and actions. A decision maker may choose action f, over many actions, f, g, h, etc, if certain states of nature such as good or bad prevails, yielding outcomes such as $f(Good) = Outcome_1$, and $f(Bad) = Outcome_2$ (Savage, 1972: 15). Given a probable range of uncertainty [0.1, 0.2], payoffs of 80 and 21 if state I occurs, and payoffs 20 and 30 if state II occurs, for agents A1, and A2 respectively, then the expected payoff for A1 is 29, and for A2 is 28.65, using the average probability of 0.15. The agent will choose 29 to maximize its expected payoff. Using a minimax strategy, we would use a probability of 0.1 on A1 expected value, and 0.2 on agent A2 expected value to get 26 and 28.2 payoffs respectively. But we have to use a mixture of probability as well. Calculating the mixture of returns for states I and II, and solving for the probability that would maximize the minimum value would yield a probability of 0.13, which in turn puts the payoff at 28.6 (Champernowne, 1969: 99-103).

Roy Radner (1968) was the first to extend such thinking to the Arrow-Debreu model, which he later developed into a model with rational expectation. Radner defines excess demand functions, Z, that are affected not only by a $p \in \Pi$, but by the states of nature $s \in S$, e definRa (Radner, 1979: 659). Radner's model is Full Revealing Rational Expectation Equilibrium (FRREE) if a one-to-one mapping can be found between the price function, and an allocation f_s for each $s \in S$, such that $f_s(a)$ maximizes the agent, u, state dependent utility function $E[u_a(x) \mid s]$, subject to its budget constraint $px \leq pe(a)$. This GE model, however, is found for a economy without money and liquidity, which are important pillars of Keynesian thinking (Radner, 1968).

A prospect, therefore, exists to incorporate Walrasian GE into Keynesian thought. For the RE model, price, p, is dependent on state of nature, s (Hahn, 1983: 228). In this model, however, many equilibrium prices exist, so that "I must have a view of which of the equilibria other agents think the economy is in before I can formulate 'the true model'" (Hahn, 1983: 228). In this sense, "Keynes . . . was not at all averse to the idea of rational expectations equilibria—he called them bootstrap equilibria" (ibid.: 229).

Game Theory and Expectation

Expectation in a GE setting can be expressed as a game. Debrue has expressed GE in terms of a game in the following way: "Let the first agent choose an action a_1 in the *a priori* given set A_1, and the second agent choose an action a_2 in the *a priori* given set A_2. Knowing a_2, the first agent has a set $\mu_1(a_2)$ of equivalent reactions. Similarly, knowing a_1, the second agent has a set $\mu_2(a_1)$ of equivalent reactions. $\mu_1(a_2)$ and $\mu_2(a_1)$ may be one-element sets, but in the important case of an economy with some producers operating under constant returns to scale, they will not be. The state $a = (a_1, a_2)$ is an equilibrium if and only if $a_1 \in \mu_1(a_2)$ and as $a_2 \in \mu_2(a_1)$, that is if and only if $a \in \mu(a) = \mu_1(a_2) \times \mu_2(a_1)$" (Debreu, 1983: 90–91). This Cournot and Nash type of game has solutions in terms of a fixed point solution of a correspondence (Debreu, 1982: 700). It treats expectation in the exogenous sense, and rationality has to do with each player choosing strategies to maximize expected payoff.

Robert Aumann and Jacques Dreze (2008) have shown how expectation solutions in some games are possible, using common knowledge rationality (CKR) and common prior assumption (CPA). CKR for players 1 and 2 mean "more than just that both 1 and knows it; we require also that 1 knows that 2 knows it, 2 knows that 1 knows it, 1 knows that 2 knows that 1 knows it, and so on" (Aumann, 2000: 593). For m-agents, we would have the statement "everyone knows that the fact is true" preceded by the expression "everyone knows that" m-1 times. People tend to have common knowledge if they are "present when the event happens and see each other there." Sources of common knowledge include public events, rules of a game, and contract (Geanakoplos, 1992: 54). Agents want to know when events, actions, optimizing behavior, and rationality are common knowledge. In Rational Expectation models of economics, economic agents forecast using model that are built on the assumption that the "public knows the models that are being used by the policy maker," and that all economic agents know the model on which they form their expectations (Ribeiro and Werlang, 1989: 74).

The definition of CPA is more complex. Recall that a prior probability means knowing beforehand the likely outcome of an event such as throwing a die and showing an ace. As there are 6 outcomes, the prior probability is $P(1) = 1/6$. The CPA roughly says that "differences in probability estimates of distinct individuals should be explained by differences in information and experience" (Aumann, 2000: vol. 1, 603). This is the Harsanyi doctrine, which in essence implies that all people are created equal with respect to probability and the absence of information. If we go back in time to a point where all the agents have the same information, then they will have the same prior probability distribution. In practice, if we want the CPA for stable operations in Iraq, we will have to estimate it from information from the news, intelligence reports, or accept the commander's estimate.

Given CKR and CPA, a rational belief system emerges, and RE is an expected outcome of some types of players in a rational system of the game. Two theorems summarize the information on this rational expectation game (Aumann and Dreze, 2008: 73-74):

> Theorem A: *The expectation of any two-person zero-sum game situation with common knowledge of rationality* (CKR) *and common priors* (CP) *is the value of the underlying game.*

Theorem B: *The rational expectations in a game G are precisely the conditional payoffs to correlated equilibria in the doubled game 2G.*

Consider a two player game of chicken with Rowena's strategies types {T, B}, Colin's strategies {L, R,}, and payoffs TL = (6, 6), TR = (2, 7), BL = (7, 2), and BR = (0, 0). The players will attach probability to their beliefs in the outcomes of {TL, TR, BL, BR}. Player Rowena's probability may be {.5, .5, .875, .125}, and Player Colin's probability may be {.5, .875, .5, .125}, respectively. The player rationality will be determined by their expected outcome. Rowena's expectation that a type B outcome will occur is $E_{\text{Rowena}}(B) = (7^{*}.875) + (0^{*}.125) = 6.125$. If we calculate Colin's expectation of playing type R, we get 6.125 as well.

The players' probability of playing a game can be calculated if their common priors are known. In the game of chicken, if the common prior, $\pi(t)$, are given as TL = 7/22, TR = 7/22, BL = 7/22, and BR = 1/22, then Rowena's probability $\pi_{Rowena}(L \mid B) = \pi(t) / \pi(t_i) = 7/22/(7/22 + 1/22) = 7/8 = .875$. In a similar manner, we can get $\pi_{Rowena}(R \mid B) = .125$, and $\pi_{Rowena}(R \mid L) = \pi_{Rowena}(L \mid T) = .5$.

This dramatic illustration of the game of chicken is that although CKR and CPA are known, Rowen's expectation of B and Colin's expectation of R are inconsistent because the expected payoffs of {6.125, 6.125} are outside of the feasible payoff space, which can be drawn by plotting all the payoffs for {TL, TR, BL, BR} in a Cartesian plane. The explanation is based on the dictum that even though people are witnesses to an event, they have different information.

Aumann has advocated that people cannot agree to disagree. His basic research "proves that a group of agents who once agreed about the probability of some proposition for which their current probabilities are common knowledge must still agree, even if those probabilities reflect disparate observations" (Hild, Jeffrey, and Risse, 1999: 92). Given common knowledge between two individuals with the same prior, it cannot be the case that "individual 1 assigns probability η_1 to some event and individual 2 assigns probability $\eta_2 \neq \eta_1$ to the same event" (Osborne and Rubinstein, 1994: 75). This is because their common beliefs are updated by true beliefs. "Player 1's prior $p^1(\omega)$ for each given state ω of the world is common knowledge. If it were not, then the description of ω would be incomplete; we would be able to split ω into several states, depending on the various possibilities for $p^1(\omega)$" (Aumann, 2000: vol. 1, 606).

In summary, Keynes spoke of stationary versus shifting equilibrium, meaning by "the latter the theory of a system in which changing views about the future are capable of influencing the present situation" (Keynes, 1936: 293). This gave way to the adaptive model that individuals adopt an error-correcting device because they do not know the environment they face, which puts them in a disequilibrium situation based on incorrect expectations. This led to adoption of the short-run Phillips curve, which allows an efficient turnpike path from disequilibrium to NAIRU equilibrium by allowing policy makers to steer the economy not down on a vertical line anchored on the natural rate of unemployment for an inflation rate above its critical level, but as "Keynesians oriented economists relied . . . upon the belief in the existence of a fairly stable relationships . . . they could trade off higher levels of employment at the cost of greater inflation and *vice versa*" (Shaw, 1984: 37). Edmund Phelps has underscored the Keynesian perspective of such a model where shifts in the underlying parameters that affect inflation and unemployment would cause swings in an economy, which is driven by "visions" and "fear" that requires a disequilibrium paradigm, such as was advocated by Keynes in Chapter 12 of his *General Theory* (Phelps, 2006: 12).

The Phillips curve analysis was expanded to address Abba Lerner's view in the 1940s, namely some constant time changes in expected price to account for the fact that workers tend to bargain for increases in wages during inflation. Later on, Modigliani NIRO-NIRU and Tobin NAIRU hypotheses were added, and were transferred into a price policy model through the incorporating of a mark-up on cost. In the long run then, when there is no supply shock, and when workers bargain for and receive increase in money wages equal to the inflation wage trends, the natural rate will be equal to the actual rate of unemployment.

The new classical school developed a version of the a supply curve, where output is equal to its natural level plus sum adjustment for deviation of actual from expected prices. Incorrect expectations, caused by misperception, result in deviations of the natural and actual level of output. This model highlights market imperfections and sticky prices. From $Y = Y_n + a(P - P_e)$, we can solve for price. We can change the prices by subtracting an expression for the previous price level $\pi = p - p_{t-1}$, and $\pi_e = p_e - p_{t-1}$. We can then obtain the short-run Phillips curve, and through Okun's law, we can relate deviations in output to deviations in unemployment from their natural level.

General Equilibrium models built all expectation into their parameters through a discounting to present value concept. Rational expectation modelers worked within that GE environment to explain the formation of expectation. Common knowledge assumptions were presumed to make the RE model work. Game theory furthers the development of these common assumption models in more mathematical forms. Research is currently going on in those directions.

General Impacts and Prospects of Keynesian Theories

Research in Keynesian economics for the last thirty years does not depict a single trend of their impact on current macroeconomic thought. They include theories such as rational expectations, random walk of GDP, real business cycle theory, and new Keynesian models. According to a leading textbook, "empirical support for these challenging ideas has not been as full and convincing as had been hoped by their proponents. What's more, the ideas in part contradict each other. . . . Even so, the impact of these concepts on both research and policy has been revolutionary" (Dornbusch et al., 2008: 550).

The New Classical School was formed in the 1980s in reaction to the disappointing performance of Keynesian economics in the 1970s. This school holds on to some cherished beliefs. According to Arrow, this school differs from the neoclassical synthesis school in that its practitioners want to reconcile Keynesian macroeconomics with the rational behavior of the individuals. (Arrow, 1991: xxii). They used a "complete" rather than an "incomplete" General Equilibrium model. According to Samuelson, "The new classical economics of rational expectations is a return with a vengeance to the pre-keynesian verities" (Samuelson, 1986: vol. 5, 291). "The 'new classical economics' of Robert Lucas, Thomas Sargent, Robert Barro, and other is truly a counterrevolution and the same cannot be said of 'monetarism.' If I can believe in Lucas market clearing, then I can no longer believe in the behavior equations and relations of the General Theory" (ibid.: 292). The new classical school thought that "it would be unsatisfactory to 'explain' [real-world business fluctuations] by easily correctable market failures . . . fluctuations had to reflect real or monetary disturbance, whose dynamic economic effects depended on cost of obtaining information, cost of adjustment, and so on" (Barro, 1989: 1).

The main postulate of the New Classical School is the maximizing behavior of individuals in markets that clear. This replaces the sticky wage assumption of the neoclassical synthesis school with the classical belief of harmony between the labor market and the economy, subject to incomplete information and shocks to the economy. This school can be restricted to the beliefs of the rational expectation school of thought, where the idea of expectation is linked to forecasts generated by true models of the economy. The principles of this school can be further restricted to the real business cycle school that deals with Walrasian General Equilibrium models that emphasize computation (Mankiw and Romer, 1991: 1).

According to George Akerlof, the school has at least six shortcomings—no involuntary unemployment, ineffectiveness of monetary policy, no acceleration of deflation theory, assumption of optimal saving behavior, and the last two: the model cannot explain volatile stock prices or the persistent self-destructive underclass (Akerlof, 2005: 473-474). According to Frank Hahn and Solow, the new classical macroeconomics "were claiming much more than could be deduced from fundamental neoclassical principles" (Hahn and Solow, 1995: vii).

In response to the New Classical School, the New Keynesian School was formed. "There are numerous different strands to New Keynesian Economics, taken in its broadest possible sense. One major element is the study of imperfect information and incomplete markets" (Greenwald and Stiglitz, 1987: 120). "They also espoused the Efficiency wage theories, Capital market imperfections, Credit rationing and a revised view of the role of monetary policy" (ibid.: 123).

The New Keynesian School took issue with the New Classical School by pointing out that wages may not adjust to allow full employment. For instance, firms do not just adjust their wage rates altogether on a certain day in the year but adjust their wage rates at different times in the year. Government intervention can aid the market by increasing employment and increasing effective demand.

Edmund Phelps has been a leader in assessing neoclassical and macroeconomics for a modern economy. He spotlighted the role of expectations on price and wage settings in the areas of employment, unemployment, and business cycles, cost inflation and difficulties of disinflation. In wage setting, he introduced "incentive wages"—each firm tries to pay a better rate to reduce the quit rate among employees. But as they try to get an advantage over each other, they end up in the industry standard pay scale, labor becomes expensive for all of them and employment falls and unemployment is created.

Keynes' Impact on International Economics

Besides mentioning that Keynes preferred internal to external stability, the impact of Keynes on international and now global economics is also significant. During the unemployment problems of the 1920s and 1930s, "Keynes argued that free trade should be abandoned in favor of protection in light of Britain's particular circumstance. This procedure called for tariffs to be imposed on imports. Keynes's views had a profound impact on economic theory and policy and were perceived as weakening the case for free trade for decades" (Irwin, 1996: 189).

"Keynes theory added, in the international context as in the analysis of closed economies, adjustments due to variations of output and effect demand" (Tobin, 1986: 38). Demand in a deficit country will decline, lowering income, output, and imports (ibid.: 43). Keynes was ahead of his time in policy rules. Regarding his *TMR*, we have alluded to his preference for price or domestic stability over exchange rate or external stability. "He recognized also that each country operating alone must sacrifice either internal or external stability unless some country adopts a credible rule for achieving price stability" (Meltzer, 1986: 66). The gold standard was a pricy way to maintain exchange rate stability, which made Keynes back away from it.

Keynes' concerns with unemployment in the 1920s and 1930s made him wary of free trade, which he earlier supported (Irwin, 1996: 189). Tariffs could "expand total employment when all labor was not fully utilized" (ibid.: 190). When the British government went off the gold standard in 1931, Keynes abandoned his protections effort and opted for monetary policy for internal balance (ibid.: 197-198).

Keynes' Impact on Economic Growth and Development

Keynes' emphasis on aggregate demand has influenced many growth and development models. "The emphasis on demand, reinforced by Keynesian theory, greatly influenced the early writings on development economics. The dynamic version of the Keynesian model (Harrod-Domar), dual economy model (Lewis); demand complementarity, balanced growth, and 'big-push'; these are among the central concepts of the 1950s" (Syrquin, 1988: 211). Demand side growth and development theories now co-exist with capital-deepening, endogenous growth models that incorporate technology and increasing returns in order to explain global growth phenomena.

Keynes remained relevant in his prognostication of the way debts should be handled. As the post-Keynesian Joan Robinson wrote: "In the industrial countries there is unemployment and underutilization of plant, and, in particular, extreme overcapacity for the production of steel. So there is unemployment and low profits in the industrial world for lack of demand. There is the third world which is supposed to be developing: development needs investment and investment needs steel. Here is an enormous real demand and an enormous real oversupply" (Robinson, 1984: 204). The oversupply is due to the mounting debt of third world countries during the 1970s. They have to use their export to service that debt instead of starting new demand. Keynes wrote a lot about war time debt, suggesting that if those "great debts are forgiven, a stimulus will be given to the solidarity and true friendliness of the nations lately associated" (Keynes, 1919,102). This is consistent also with Singer's interpretation of Keynes that "it is the proper job of finance to see that nothing is ever done on financial grounds . . . a development program ought to reflect the real conditions and needs of the country" (Singer, 1964: 102).

Keynes provided the platform for post-Keynesians to dive into growth theory. The linking of the rate of investment to GDP via the multiplier was the foundation for this take-off. The underlying parameters for growth in this model are investment and productivity, i.e., how much you invest and how much you get out of it (Bhagwati, 1998: 402). Holding productivity constant, i.e., treating it as a datum of the system, shifts the focus of development towards investment. Kahn pronounced the Keynesian case for development in the "basic proposition that it is possible to organize a higher rate of investment without thereby physically necessitating a lower aggregate of consumption" (Kahn, 1969: 82). As a modern author puts it, "In its simplest terms, economic growth is the result of abstention from current consumption" (Ray, 1998: 51). But Khan had in mind that "The consumption of those who benefit will increase by more than the reduction of the consumption of those who suffer" (Kahn, 1969: 82). The argument assumes an elasticity of supply such that when investment increases, it will raise demand, output, and consumption.

Keynes' thought in the General Theory also has bearing for development. Keynes enunciated two barriers to growth in the General Theory. One barrier deals with "the inherent tendency of the system towards unemployment, insufficient investment, and the resulting low-level equilibrium of low consumption, low savings, low investment, high unemployment, plenty of idle resources, and slow progress" (Singer, 1964: 5). The other barrier holds that at full employment, the marginal efficiency of capital will fall to zero (ibid.). This latter assumption, however, does not take into consideration that "technical progress and the increasing efficiency of production constantly create new investment opportunities at the same or a faster pace than that at which existing investment opportunities are being used up by capital accumulation (Singer, 1964, 66).

One branch of the post-Keynesian growth model followed Harror-Domar, relating the growth in output to the saving accelerator ratio. The resulting growth of output, $Y=c_e^{(s/v)t}$, where Y is output, s is the rate of savings, v is the capital-output ratio, t is time, and c is a constant, is unstable as t approaches infinity. Modern development theorists such as Jeffrey Sachs would emphasize that among other core sets of economic institution, "macroeconomic stability" is necessary, for instance, for growth in the modern globalized growth era (Sachs, 2005: 215).

Another branch of the post-Keynesian growth model followed Kaldor, and culminated in the Dual Pasinetti growth model. Nicholas Kaldor and Pasinetti argued that the profit rate depends on savings of the capitalists, while Modigliani and Samuelson argued for a dual theory where the the profit rate depends on workers' propensity to save (Ramrattan and Szenberg, 2007: 40). Keynesians see the Kaldor-Pasinetti version as overly concerned with production and distribution in the Ricardian and Marxian tradition, and opt for a version that emphasizes "the theory of output as a whole," which includes the laws of consumption, savings, the influence of loan on prices and wages, and the rate of interest (Keynes, 1936: xxvi xxvii).

A third branch of the post-Keynesian model integrated a more neoclassical tool, which was started by Solow and culminated in modern endogenous growth model by his student, Paul Romer. Solow's model emphasized capital-deepening and endogenous technology as the source of growth, which when augmented by increasing returns by Romer, has spotlighed a deeper vision of modern globalized growth. Sachs, however, sees the latter enhancement as explaining only growth "in countries with only about one-sixth of the world's population" (Sachs, 2005: 216).

Keynesian theory played a role in explaining growth in the Newly Industrialized Countries (NIC)—Singapore, Hong Kong, and South Korea, and the Newly Exporting Countries (NEC)—Malaysia, Thailand, the Philippines, and Indonesia (Reinert, 2005: 43). From 1947 to 1994, 21% of the World Bank loans went to East Asian countries. For the period of 1950-1994, Indonesia received 30%, China 28%, the Philippines 13%, Korea 12%, Thailand 7%, and Malaysia 5% of IBRD (International Bank for Reconstruction and Development) and IDA (International Development Association) loans to East Asia (Thomas and Stephens, Reader 3, 159).

Government involvement, a Keynesian prescription, was a key factor that channeled investments into growth. According to Joe Stiglitz, "the countries of East Asia grew because of globalization, but they managed it, shaped it, in ways that worked to their own advantage. It was only when they succumbed to outside pressures, only when they went faster and further with liberalization, that globalization no longer served them well" (Stiglitz, 2005: 230-231).

The Future Impact of the GT on Theory and Policies

The neoclassical synthesis did not cope well with the stagflation crises of the 1970s. This gave birth to the New Classical School that tried to usurp the role of the neoclassical synthesis by purging its wage stickiness assumption. The New Keynesian School tried to reinstate some Keynesian principles into the New Classical paradigm. Works in a new neoclassical synthesis (NNS) is currently going on in the direction of expanding the New Keynesian perspective in the areas of how government policies affect price stickiness and business cycles (Linnemann and Schabert, 2003).

One strand of post-Keynesian economics emphasized the effective demand approach of the *GT*. Paul Davidson, for instance, concluded that "as we entered the twenty-first century, only the Post Keynesians remain to carry-on in Keynes's analytical footsteps and develop Keynes's theory and policy prescription for the 21st century real world of economic globalization" (Davidson, 2007: vol. 4, 209). On the other hand, we witnessed research in the probability area being done in regard to GE and game theory, where the probability distribution of information that individual hold are an integral part of modeling information. The stability of expectation in such models does involve ergodic theory, which Davidson pointed out was not Keynesian. Howitt's (1990) development of the new classical model around the coordinating problem also implies this use of information.

Hicks wrote that the survival of "classical economics into the post-Keynesian epoch is not the same thing as the survivals of outmoded scientific theories . . . It survives because we have found that we have to attend, sometimes at least, to some of the things which Keynes left out" (Hicks, 1981: vol. 1, 234). Further, "There can be no doubt at all that Keynes wrote as he did because of the times in which he was living" (ibid.: 233). We add that the paradigm of the *GT* is not outmoded, and that while the Keynesian research program appears to degenerate in coping with topical anomalies, a group of practitioners are always working to turn it in the progressive direction, impacting theories and policies on the way.

References

Akerlof, G. A. (2005). *Explorations in pragmatic economics: Selected papers of George A. Akerlof.* Oxford: Oxford University Press.

Arrow, K. J. (1967). Samuelson collected. *The Journal of Political Economy,* 75(5), 730-737.

———. (1984). *Collected papers of Kenneth J. Arrow, Volume 4: The economics of information.* Cambridge, MA: Belknap Press of Harvard University Press.

———. (1983). *Collected papers of Kenneth J. Arrow, vol. 2: General equilibrium.* Cambridge, MA: Belknap Press of Harvard University Press.

———. (1991). *Issues in contemporary economics, vol. 1: Markets and welfare.* New York: New York University Press.

Arrow, K. J., & Hahn, F. H. (1971). *General competitive analysis.* San Francisco: Holden-Day, Inc.

Aumann, R. J. (2000). *Collected Papers,* Volume I. Cambridge, MA: MIT Press.

Aumann, R. J., & Dreze, J. H. (2008). Rational expectations in games. *American Economic Review,* 98(1), 72–86.

Barro, R. J. (Ed.). (1989). *Modern business cycle theory.* Cambridge, MA: Harvard University Press.

Bateman, B. W. (1996) *Keynes's uncertain revolution.* Ann Arbor: University of Michigan Press, 1996.

Begg, D. K. H. (1982). *The rational expectation in macroeconomics: Theories and evidence.* Baltimore, MD: Johns Hopkins University Press.

———. (1980, Jan.). Rational expectations and the non-neutrality of systematic monetary policy. *The Review of Economic Studies,* 47(2), 293-303.

Bhagwati, J. (1998). *A stream of windows: Unsettling reflections on trade, immigration, and democracy.* Cambridge, MA: MIT Press.

Blanchard, O. J., & Fischer, S. (1989). *Lectures on macroeconomics.* Cambridge, MA: MIT Press. (Fourth Printing, 1990).

Blaug, M. (1991). Afterwords. In N. de Marchi & M. Blaug, *Appraising economic theories: Studies in the methodology of research program.* Cheltenham: Edward Elgar Publishing Company.

———. (1976). Kuhn versus Lakatos or paradigms versus research programmes in the history of economics. In S. Latsis (Ed.), *Method and appraisal in economics* (149-180). Cambridge: Cambridge University Press.

Cagan, P. (1956). The monetary dynamics of hyperinflation." In M. Friedman (Ed.), *Studies in the quantity theory of money* (25-117). Chicago: University of Chicago Press.

Chambernowne, D. G. (1969). *Uncertainty and estimation in economics* (vol. 3). San Francisco: Holden Day.

Clower, R. W. (1988). "Keynes and the Classics Revisited." In O. F. Hamouda & J. N. Smithin (Eds.), *Keynes and public policy after fifty years, vol. 1: Economics and policy* (81-92). New York: New York University Press.

Colander, D. (1988). The evolution of Keynesian economics: From Keynes to new classical to new Keynesian. In O. F. Hamouda & J. N. Smithin (Eds.), *Keynes and public policy after fifty years, Volume I: Economics and policy* (92-100). New York: New York University Press.

Da Costa Werlang, S. R. (1989 [1987]). Common knowledge. In J. Eatwell, M. Milgate, & P. Newman (Eds.), *The new Palgrave: Game theory* (74-85). New York: W. W. Norton.

Davies, W. E. (1964). *The new deal: Interpretations.* New York: The Macmillan Company.

Debreu, G. (1982). Existence of competitive equilibrium. In K. J. Arrow & M. D. Itriligator (Eds.), *Handbook of mathematical economics* (vol. 2, 677–743). Amsterdam: Elsevier Science Publisher.

———. (1983, Dec. 8). Economic theory in the mathematical mode: Nobel memorial lecture. *Economic Science*, 87–102.

———. (1959). *Theory of value: An axiomatic analysis of economic equilibrium*. New Haven, CT: Yale University Press.

Dimand, R. W. (1988). *The origins of the Keynesian revolution*. Redwood City: Stanford University Press.

Dornbusch, R., Fischer, S., & Startz, R. (2008). *Macroeconomics* (10th ed.). New York: McGraw-Hill and Irwin.

Dow, S. C. (1985). *Macroeconomic thought: A methodological approach*. Oxford: Basil Blackwell Ltd.

Eichengreen, B. (Ed.). (1985). *The gold standard in theory and history*. New York: Methuen, Inc.

Fisher, Franklin M. *Disequilibrium Foundations of Equilibrium Economics*. Cambridge: Cambridge University Press, 1989 [1983].

Fisher, R. A. (1923). Mr. Keynes' *Treatise on probability*. *Eugenics Review*, 14, 46-50.

Flaschel, P. (1997). *Reiner Franke, and Willi Semmler, dynamic macroeconomics: Instability, fluctuations, and growth in monetary economies*. Cambridge, MA: MIT Press. (Second Printing, 1998).

Friedman, M. (1970). *The counter-revolution in monetary theory: First Wincott memorial lecture Delivered at the Senate House, University of London, 16 September, 1970* (7-28). London: The Institute of Economic Affairs.

Frisch, R. (1966 [1960]). *Maxima and minima: Theory and economic applications*. Chicago: Rand McNally & Company.

Geanakoplos, John. Common Knowledge. *The Journal of Economic Perspectives*, 6:4 (1992): 53-82.

Greenwald, B., & Stiglitz, J. E. (1987, Mar.). Keynesian, new Keynesian and new classical economics. *Oxford Economic Papers*, New Series, 39(1), 119-133.

Grandmont, J.-M. (1983). *Money and value: A reconsideration of classical and neoclassical monetary theories*. London: Cambridge University Press.

Heifetz, A., & Polemarchakis, H. M. (1998). Partial revelation with rational expectations. *Journal of Economic Theory*, 80, 171-181.

Hahn, F. (1992). Distinguished fellow: Honoring Roy Radner. *The Journal of Economic Perspectives*, 6(1), 181-194.

———. (1985). *Money, growth and stability*. Oxford: Basil Blackwell Ltd.

———. (1983). Comment. In R. Frydman & E. S. Phelps (Ed.), *Individual forecasting and aggregate outcome: Rational expectations examined* (223-230). Cambridge: Cambridge University Press, 1983.

Hahn, F., & Solow, R. (1995). *A critical essay on modern macroeconomic theory*. Cambridge, MA: MIT Press.

Hansen, A. H. (1953). *A guide to Keynes*. New York: McGraw-Hill.

Harris, S. E. (1955). *John Maynard Keynes: Economist and policy maker*. New York: Charles Scribner's Sons.

Hawtrey, R. G. (1924). Review of *A tract on monetary reform* by J. M. Keynes. *The Economic Journal*, 34(134), 227-235.

———. (1931). *The Gold Standard in Theory and Practice* (2nd ed.). London: Longmans, Green and Co.

Hild, M., Jeffrey, R., & Risse, M. (1999). Aumann's "now agreement" theorem generalized." In C. Bicchieri, R. Jeffrey, & B. Skyrms (Eds.), *The logic of strategy* (92-100). Oxford: Oxford University Press.

Hicks, J. (1974). *The crisis in Keynesian economics*. New York: Basic Books.

———. (1982). *Collected essays on economic theory: Money, interest and wages* (vol. II). Cambridge, MA: Harvard University Press.

———. (1983). *Collected essays on economic theory: Classics and moderns* (vol. III). Cambridge, MA: Harvard University Press,.

———. (1976). "Revolutions" in economics. In S. Latsis (Ed.), *Method and appraisal in economics* (207-218). London: Cambridge University Press.

———. (1937, Apr.). Mr Keynes and the classics: A suggested interpretation. *Econometrica*, 5(2), 147-159.

Horsefield, J. K. (1969). *The international monetary fund 1945-1965, volume I: Chronicles*. Washington, D.C.. International Monetary Fund.

———. (1969). *The international monetary fund 1945-1965, volume III: Documents*. Washington, D.C.: International Monetary Fund.

Horwich, G. (1991). Macroeconomics and macroeconomists as instruments of policy. In D. L. Weimer (Ed.), *Policy analysis and economics: Developments, tensions, prospects* (127-157). Boston: Kluwer Academic Publishers.

Howitt, P. (1990). *The Keynesian recovery and other essays*. Ann Arbor: University of Michigan Press.

Hutchison, T. W. (1977). *Keynes versus the "Keynesians" ...?: An essay in the thinking of J. M. Keynes and the accuracy of its interpretation by his followers*. London: Institute of Economic Affairs.

Irwin, D. A. (1996). *Against the tide: An intellectual history of free trade*. Princeton: Princeton University Press.

Kahn, R. F. (1984). *The making of Keynes' general theory*. Cambridge: Cambridge University Press.

———. (1976). Unemployment as Seen by the Keynesians. In G. D. N. Worswick (Ed.), *The concept and measurement of involuntary unemployment* (19-34). Boulder, CO: Westview Press.

———. (1969). The pace of development. In A. N. Agarwala & S. P. Singh (Eds.), *Accelerating investment in developing economies* (64-115). Oxford: Oxford University Press.

Keynes, J. M. (1963 [1930]). *Essays in persuasion*. New York: W. W. Norton and Company.

———. (1973). *The collected writings of John Maynard Keynes: The general theory and after, part II: Defense and development* (vol. XIV). London: Macmillan.

———. (1979). *The collected writings of John Maynard Keynes* (vol. XV). London: Macmillan

———. (1970 [1936]). *The collected writings of John Maynard Keynes: The general theory of employment interest and money* (vol. VII). London and New York: Macmillan and St. Martin's Press.

———. (1937, Feb.) The general theory of employment. *The Quarterly Journal of Economics*, 51(2), 209-223; reprinted in *The collected writings of John Maynard Keynes: The general Theory and after, part II: Defense and development* (vol. XIV, 109-123). London: Macmillan, 1973.

———. (1972 [1933]). *The collected writings of John Maynard Keynes: Essays in biography* (vol. X). London and New York: Macmillan and St. Martin's Press.

———. (1971 [1930]). *The collected writings of John Maynard Keynes: A treatise on money, Vol. I; The pure theory of money* (vol. V). London: Macmillan.

———. (1971 [1930]). *The collected writings of John Maynard Keynes: A treatise on money, vol. II; The applied theory of money* (vol. VI). London: Macmillan.

———. (1971 [1923]). *The collected writings of John Maynard Keynes: A tract on monetary reform* (vol. IV). London: Macmillan.

———. (1973 [1921]). *The collected writings of John Maynard Keynes: A treatise on probability* (vol. VIII). London: Macmillan.

Klein, L. R. (1966). *The Keynesian revolution* (2nd ed.). New York: The Macmillan Company.

Kuhn, T. S. (1970 [1962]). *The structure of scientific revolutions* (2nd ed.). Chicago: University of Chicago Press.

Leijonhufvud, A. (1976). Schools, "revolutions" and research programmes. In S. Latsis (Ed.), *Method and appraisal in economics* (65-108). London: Cambridge University Press.

Lerner, A. P. (1951). *Economics of employment.* New York: McGraw-Hill.

———. (1961). *Everybody's business: A re-examination of current assumptions in economics and public policy.* New York: Harper and Row.

Linnemann, L., & Schabert, A. (2003, Dec., part 1). Fiscal policy in the new neoclassical synthesis. *Journal of Money, Credit, and Banking,* 35(6), 35-36.

Lowe, A. (1965). *On economic knowledge.* New York: Harper & Row.

Lucas, R. E., Jr., & Sargent, T. J. (1981). After Keynesian macroeconomics. In R. E. Lucas, Jr. & T. J. Sargent (Eds.), *Rational expectations and econometric practice* (vol. I, 295-319). Minneapolis: University of Minnesota Press.

Maki, U. (2001). Economic ontology: What? Why? How? In U. Maki (Ed.), *The economic world view: Studies in the ontology of economics* (1-8). Cambridge: Cambridge University Press, 2001.

Malthus, Rev. T. R. (1962). 7 July 1821 letter. In P. Sraffa (Ed.), *The works and correspondence of David Ricardo* (vol. IX, 9-11). Cambridge: Cambridge University Press.

McCloskey, D. N. (1985). *The rhetoric of economics.* Madison: University of Wisconsin Press.

Meltzer, A. H. (1986). On monetary stability and monetary reform. In Y. Suzuki and M. Okabe (Eds.), *Toward a world of economic stability* (51-73). Tokyo: University of Tokyo Press.

Minsky, H. P. (2008). *John Maynard Keynes.* New York: McGraw Hill.

Mitchell, W. C. (1969). *Types of economic theory: From mercantilism to nstitutionalism* (vol. II). J. Dorfman, Ed. New York: Augustus M. Kelley Publishers.

Modigliani, F. (1944, Jan.). Liquidity reference and the theory of interest and money. *Econometrics,* 12, 45-88; reprinted in A. Abel (Ed.), *The collected papers of Franco Modigliani* (vol. 1, 23-68). (Cambridge, MA: MIT Press, 1986, [1980]).

———. (1986 [1980]). *The collected papers of Franco Modigliani* (vol. 1). A. Abel (Ed.). Cambridge, MA: MIT Press.

Modigliani, F., & Papademos, L. (1989). Monetary policy for the coming quarters: The conflicting views. In S. Johnson (Ed.), *The collected papers of Franco Modigliani* (vol. 4, 155-201). Cambridge, MA: MIT Press.

Moggridge, D. E. (1992). *Maynard Keynes: An economist's biography.* London: Routledge.

Moore, T. G. (1971, Dec.). U.S. income policy, its rationale and development. *American Enterprise Institute for Public Policy Research.* Special analysis 18.

Nachane, D. M., & Hatekart, N. R. (1995, Dec.). The bullionist controversy: An empirical reappraisal. *The Manchester School,* LXIII(4), 412-425.

Obstfeld, M., & Rogoff, K. (1996). *Foundations of international macroeconomics.* Cambridge, MA: MIT Press.

Osborne, M. J., & Rubinstein, A. (1994). *A course in game theory.* Cambridge, MA: MIT Press.

Pasinetti, L. L. (1999)., J. M. Keynes's "revolution": The major event of twentieth-century economics? In L. L. Pasinetti & B. Schefold (Eds.), *The impact of Keynes on economics in the 20th century* (3-15). London and New York: Edward Elgar.

Pissarides, C. A. (1989, Feb.). Unemployment and macroeconomics. *Economica,* New Series, 56(221), 1-14.

Patinkin, D. (1982). *Anticipations of the general theory? And other essays on Keynes.* Chicago: University of Chicago Press.

———. (1975, Jun.). The collected writings of John Maynard Keynes: From the tract to the general. *The Economic Journal*, 85(338), 249-271.

Pearce, K. A., & Hoover, K. D. (1995). Paul Samuelson and the textbook Keynesian model." In A. F. Cottrell & M. S. Lawlor (Eds.), *New perspectives on Keynes* (184). Durham, NC: Duke University Press.

Pesaran, M. H. (1987). *The limits to rational expectation.* Oxford: Basil Blackwell.

Phelps, E. (2006). Prospective shifts, speculative swings: Macro for the 21st century in the tradition of Paul Samuelson. In M. Szenberg, L. Ramrattan, and A. A. Gottesman (Eds.), *Samuelsonian economics and the 21st century* (66-87). New York: Oxford University Press.

Radner, R. (1979, May). Rational expectations equilibrium: Generic existence and the information revealed by prices. *Econometrica, 47*(3), 655-656.

———. (1968, Jan.). Competitive equilibrium under uncertainty. *Econometrica*, 36(1), 31-58.

Ramrattan, L., & Szenberg, M. (2007, Fall). Paul Samuelson and the dual Pasinetti theory. *The American Economist*, 51(2), 40-48.

Ray, D. (1998). *Development economics.* Princeton: Princeton University Press.

Ramsey, F. P. (1969 [1931]). *The foundations of mathematics.* Paterson, NJ: Littlefield, Adams and Co.

Reinert, K. A. (2005). *Windows on the World Economy.* Mason, OH: Thompson/South-Western.

Ricardo, D. (1962). *The works and correspondence of David Ricardo* (vols. I-IX). Piero Sraffa (Ed.). Cambridge: Cambridge University Press, 1962.

Robinson, J. (1984). Discussion. In R. F. Kahn (Ed.), *The making of Keynes' general theory* (203-205). Cambridge: Cambridge University Press.

———. (1980 [1973]). *Collected economic papers* (vols. I-V). Cambridge, MA: MIT Press.

Sachs, J. D. (2005). Globalization and patterns of economic growth. In M. M. Weinstein (Ed.), *Globalizaton: What's new?* (214-217). New York: Columbia University Press.

Samuelson, P. A. (1986). *The collected scientific papers of Paul A. Samuelson* (vol. 5). K. Crowley (Ed). Cambridge, MA: MIT Press.

Sargent, T. J., & Wallace, N. (1981). Rational expectations and the theory of economic policy. In R. E. Lucas, Jr. & T. J. Sargent (Eds.), *Rational expectations and econometric practice* (vol. I, 199-213). Minneapolis: University of Minnesota Press.

Savage, L. J. (1972). *The foundation of statistics.* New York: Dover Publications, Inc.

Sawyer, W. C., & Sprinkle, R. L. (2008). *International economics* (3rd ed.). Englewood Cliffs: Prentice Hall.

Say, J. B. (1971 [1880]). *A treatise on political economy or the production, distribution and consumption of wealth.* New York: Augustus M. Kelley Publishers.

Shaw, G. K. (1984). *Rational expectations: An elementary exposition.* New York: St. Martin's Press.

Singer, H. W. (1964). *International development: Growth and change.* New York: McGraw-Hill.

Skidelsky, R. (1992). *John Maynard Keynes: The economist as saviour, 1920-1937* (vol. 2). New York: The Penguin Press.

Solow, R. M. (2002). Analytical aspects of anti-inflation policy after 40 years. In K. Puttaswamiaiah (Ed.), *Paul Samuelson and the foundations of modern economics* (71-78). New Brunswick, NJ: Transaction Publishers.

Stiglitz, J. E. (2005). The overselling of globalization. In M. M. Weinstein (Ed.), *Globalizaton: What's new?* (228-261). New York: Columbia University Press.

Syrquin, M. (1988). Patterns of structural change. In H. Chenery & T. N. Srinivasan (Eds.), *Handbooks of development economics* (201-273). Amsterdam: Elsevier.

Tobin, J (1986). Are there reliable adjustment mechanisms? In Y. Suzuki & M. Okabe (Eds.), *Toward a world of economic stability* (37-50). Tokyo: University of Tokyo Press.

Vercelli, A. (1991). *Methodological foundation of macroeconomics: Keynes and Lucas.* Cambridge: Cambridge University Press.

Viner, J. (1936, Nov.). Review of Mr. Keynes on the cause of unemployment. *The Quarterly Journal of Economics*, 51(1), 147-167.

Von Mises, L. (1980 [1934]). *The theory of money and credit.* Indianapolis: Liberty Classics.

Franco Modigliani (1918–2003)

On September 25, 2003, the profession of economics and finance lost one of its prominent players. Born in Italy in 1918, Professor Franco Modigliani demonstrated his exceptional abilities at an early age when he enrolled in the University of Rome at the age of seventeen, two years ahead of the norm, and earned his first doctorate degree, Doctor Juris, in 1939, by studying on his own. Later that year, in response to the alarming developments in Europe, Modigliani landed in the United States just days before the beginning of World War II, where he attended the New School for Social Research in New York City, which provided a haven for European scholars who escaped Nazi Germany. At the New School, he studied with economists like Adolph Lowe and Jacob Marschak, and earned his PhD in economics in 1944. He then began a teaching career, holding positions at numerous institutions such as the New School for Social Research (1944–1949), Carnegie Institute of Technology (1952–1960), Northwestern University (1960–1962), and MIT (1962 until his death in 2003). He was also a research analyst at the Cowles Commission at the University of Chicago (1949–1952), and served as an advisor to numerous governmental bodies. Modigliani also served as president of the American Economic Association in 1976, and was awarded the Nobel Prize in 1985 for his achievements and contributions to the fields of economics and finance.

Modigliani is most known for the Keynesian liquidity preference (LP) theory. In fact, he started and ended his career with this now well-known theory. He wrote his dissertation on the liquidity preference at the New School in

1944, and his last published article on the subject of Keynes appeared in The American Economist (2003). His earlier presentation of LP was axiomatic in nature, where some of the assumptions were that LP is a sufficient condition to explain unemployment equilibrium, i.e., without the assumption of rigid wages, when the demand for money is infinitely elastic relative to a positive level of interest rates (Modigliani, 1944: 74). The dependence of the rate of interest (R) on money (M) is explained by rigid wages (W), where LP is not a sufficient or a necessary condition to explain underemployment equilibrium (ibid.: 76), and the conclusion of the LP theory is that if wages are flexible, then interest rates, savings, and investment propensities will determine prices (ibid.). Usually, the dominant theme of Modigliani's LP research program has been built around the special cases of wage rigidity and interest inelasticity. Tobin noted that Modigliani should also have mentioned the interest inelasticity of investment demand as "another and very important exception to the wage rigidity explanation of unemployment" (1987: 25). But, as we can see from Modigliani's last paper (2003), he concludes, in accordance with Keynes, that "the postulates of the classical theory are applicable to a special case only and not the general case, the situation which it assumes being a limiting point of the possible positions of equilibrium."

As Modigliani stated, "the present version differs from my previous papers, published throughout my career, starting from my first on 'Liquidity Preference.' The difference springs in part from the fact that the new presentation is meant to be understandable by a non-technical audience but in part it reflects my recent realization, that it is possible to use a model different from the prevailing one, which stresses the communality between Keynes and the classical theory. In fact, I will argue that the classical model is but a special case of Keynes's General Theory. It applies only to an economy in which wages (and prices) are highly flexible downward in response to 'excess supply,' and financial markets are unimportant. It should be obvious that this special case is of very little relevance to the present-day developed economies, and so are the analytical and policy conclusions that follow from it" (Modigliani, 2003: 3).

Modigliani (1988) has also had an opportunity to revisit what he elaborated on the famous Modigliani and Miller (MM) hypothesis. The first value-invariance proposition (Proposition I) states that the "market value of any firm is independent of its capital structure and is given by capitalizing its expected return at the rate ρ_k appropriate to its class" (Modigliani, 1980: 10). Meanwhile, the original proof is based on the arbitrage: "an investor can buy and sell stocks and bonds in such a way as to exchange one income stream for another . . . the value of the overpriced shares will fall and that of the under priced shares will rise, thereby tending to eliminate the discrepancy between the market value of the firm" (ibid.: 11). This proposition stood on the back of Proposition II, "concerning the rate of return on common stock in companies whose capital structure includes some debt" (ibid.: 13), and Proposition III, which "tells us only that the type of instrument used to finance an investment is irrelevant to the question of whether or not the investment is worthwhile" (ibid.: 34). According to Miller's assessment 30 years later, Proposition I with its arbitrage proof, is well accepted in the economics world today, but less so in corporate finance (2002: 421-422).

The adoption of the MM hypothesis has been overwhelming. Modigliani himself discovered that young cab drivers in the Washington, D.C. area were well informed of the MM hypothesis. However it is also important to mention that most cab drivers in that area at the time (with a foreign accent) were MBA students (Modigliani, 1988: 150). In MBA textbooks, and in the programs, students are taught how to calculate the discounted value of a unit of debt to the present time, add that to the value of equity in the marginal unit of capital, which is a residual equal to the marginal unit of capital less the amount paid to the bond holders, and consider the value of many financial assets besides debt and equity, and test the value-invariance principle with and without taxes on profits, and tax deductions on debt interest (Romer, 1996: 387). It is interesting to note that the robustness of the MM hypothesis stood up to the popular put-call parity analysis, or the Black-Scholes capital structure model: "The familiar Put-Call Parity Theorem . . . is really nothing more than the MM Proposition I in only a mildly concealing disguise!" (Miller, 2002: 434). However, the MM model had to confront a series of empirical distortions, which according to Tobin "include corporate income taxation, which is not neutral as between debt interest and dividends; the implications of leverage for probability of bankruptcy and loss of control; and economies of scale in borrowing which enable stockholders to borrow more cheaply through the corporation than individually" (Tobin, 1985: 241).

While looking at some regression results for 1960-1974, Tobin found a negative sigma coefficient, a dislike for dividend protection, and indifference toward or rejection of fixed debt service obligations, implying overall that "the stock market likes leverage, and prefers pay-out rather than retained earnings" (ibid.: 257).

Another study, by Stiglitz, examined more general conditions under which the MM hypothesis may hold, including Arrow-Debreu general equilibrium conditions, where securities are held based on varying states of the economy. Stiglitz found that "in the context of a general equilibrium state preference model that the M-M theorem holds under much more general conditions than those assumed in their original study . . . except that they must agree that there is zero probability of bankruptcy" (Stiglitz, 1979: 784).

In his response to the critics, Miller (2002: 425) pointed out that they were considering a general equilibrium approach from the inception, having drafted up an appendix to the original paper, but that the approach later took the form of three separate papers. An additional criticism was addressed toward various parameter assumptions of the model. For instance, varying dividend policies were accommodated either by a random error term that bridges the theoretical model to reality, or by a firm's "payout policies," which would tend to attract a certain "'clientele' consisting of those preferring its particular payout ratio" (Modigliani, 1980: 60). Another adjustment was made to the "method of taxing corporations on the valuation of firms," which was based on whether a firm should seek to maximize debt financing in their capital structure because of the tax advantage. In the philosophical sense of the argument, the authors did not find debt and equity financing to be either-or propositions, for they asserted that retained earnings can be a cheaper alternative (ibid.: 72). While Miller (2002: 444) thinks of the Tax Reform Act of 1986 as rare "supershocks," whose validation is yet to be seen, Modigliani (1998: 154) thinks it does point to a validation of the original position on taxes. Another area of Modigliani's fundamental contribution to economics is his life-cycle hypothesis of the consumption function. First, it was Keynes who initially proposed the absolute income hypothesis, implied in his psychological law of savings, where later some anomalies were found between long-run and short-run (cross-section) behavior of the consumption function. Briefly, the long-run marginal propensity to consume

(MPC) was converging to one, and the cross-section consumption function, say for socially diversified groups, had a smaller MPC and was drifting upward over time. Second, James Duesenberry's relative income hypothesis was in the mode of reconciling such observations, where personal consumption was based on the individual's relative position in the income distribution. Generally, during a downswing, households tend to dissave to keep up their consumption levels, thereby setting consumption on current income relative to previous peak period incomes. As recovery replaces lost income, consumption eventually manifests a "ratchet-effect," explaining the upward drift over time.

Modigliani dated his first formulation of the Life Cycle hypothesis to his 1954 article (Modigliani and Brumberg, 1954), prior to Friedman's work (1957). While Friedman claims to have done his most scientific work on the permanent income hypothesis, Modigliani placed Friedman's permanent income hypothesis under the umbrella of "important further developments" (Modigliani, 2002: 15). In fact, it is possible to find important similarities between the two contributors. Income now has two components, transitory and permanent, where transitory income is current income less permanent income. It is a known fact that consumers usually react slowly to transitory income changes because of habits and customs (Modigliani 1949). Later, when Modigliani solidified his thinking on this matter with his life-cycle hypothesis (Ando and Modigliani, 1963), he reached the final stage of the model's development, where a person's consumption is a function of his/her age group, resources, and returns on capital. At the student stage, for instance, the consumer is short of income and would borrow, or spend future income to consume at their current life-cycle spending level. In the meantime, a middle aged person with a higher participation rate and peak life-time earnings, is more likely to save and build up asset holdings. A retiree would tend to live by drawing down savings, returns from assets, other incomes such as SS, SSI, 401K, or even the contributions of children. Overall, it is evident that somehow consumers redistribute lifetime resources over their life cycle to maximize lifetime consumption. A marginal increase in (transitory) income affects consumption only if it increases a lifetime average income. As the mpc increases, it has a significant implication for a lower propensity to save, which is: 1 – MPC (Modigliani, 2003: 15).

Modigliani's and Friedman's contributions to the consumption function continue as a live research program in current literature. A 2003 Nobel Laureate in economics had this to say on the testing of Hall's theory of consumption in terms of the life cycle and permanent income hypothesis: "The theory was like manna from heaven to macro-econometricians. It was easily stated and understood, and appears to be easy to test" (Granger, 1999: 42-43). Central to this model is the fact that consumption follows a random walk model where the expected consumption of the next period should be equal to current consumption. In practical parlance, consumers will tend to adjust their individual consumption so that it will not differ from an expected level. This fact reinforces the underlying principle that consumers tend to smooth out spending over time, and that this practice relates to some uncertainty about income. If consumers have a quadratic utility function, then they will want to consume at the level where their future income will equal its mean value (Romer, 1996: 318). The life cycle model has also promoted research in terms of the type of instruments families use to finance retirement. This research has made it evident that most assets are in the "locked-up" form such as retirement programs, mortgages, life-insurance, and social security. "As long as families can make full use of locked-up accounts, their actual behavior will be almost the same as predicted by the life-cycle model" (Hall and Taylor, 1997: 284).

Modigliani was also involved in making fundamental contributions to post-Keynesian economics. He co-authored two articles with Samuelson, who generated much research in the area of long-term rates of return (Samuelson and Modigliani, 1966a, 1966b). They have jointly contributed what is known as the "anti-Pasinetti" theorem to the literature. Basically, the Pasinetti (1976: 276) theorem states: "The equilibrium rate of profit is determined by the natural rate of growth divided by the capitalists' propensity to save." This result occurred in the stability section of Pasinetti's original paper (ibid.: 275), where he derived it from the differential equation: $d/dt(P/Y) = f(I/Y - S/Y)$. It, therefore, remains an analysis of stability of a Keynesian model of income distribution. However, Samuelson and Modigliani's dual theorem brings worker's saving rate back into the picture. The literature on this debate is vast, and still ongoing. Samuelson (1991: 182), literally re-wrote the *New Palgrave Dictionary*'s view of the dual theorem thus: "the only balanced-growth equilibrium that could then possibly be obtained would be the anti-Pasinetti equilibrium with $(Y/K)^{**} = n/s_w$," where Y is full employment income, K is capital, n is the economy's growth rate, ** is the long-run equilibrium level, and s_w is workers propensity to save. In order to separate Modigliani's unique concerns on the "anti-Pasinetti" theorem, Kaldor, whose dual argument is based on Keynesian theory of the distribution of income, noted that "capitalists also spend some part of their capital gains . . . and, as Professor Modigliani has reminded us, the limited length of human life must add to such temptations" (1966: 316). Pasinetti (1936: 306), too, picked up on a concluding point in the original Samuelson and Modigliani article relating to permanent income influence on the long run rate of return.

It seems to us that what relates the argument to the Life Cycle hypothesis refers uniquely to Modigliani's work, and this has not received a significant attention in the literature. Modigliani will be remembered as a great inspirer to economists working on the scientific methods to validate, explain, or predict economic phenomena. He was an exceptional economist who always considered both economic theory and the real empirical world. He was also one of only a few remaining Keynesians, which makes his loss even more costly to the field. We are grateful for the research he has initiated in the many branches of economics, and we regret that we will not be able to see the articles he promised us on savings in China, a revisit of the MM hypothesis, and reflections on economics. Samuelson had this to say about his colleague, collaborator, and tennis partner: "He was a great teacher, intense and colorful. MIT was lucky to have him for forty years; he was a jewel in our crown, active to the end."

A vignette of the interaction between the editorial staff of *The American Economist* and Modigliani in the final year of his life is illustrative of his intensity, vibrancy, and great enthusiasm.

When he submitted his paper "The Keynesian Gospel According to Modigliani" to us for publication, he called five times leaving messages within the span of less than an hour. At later stages of production, his drive for perfection in correcting and revising the galleys and details of the graphs was truly remarkable. His mentoring of, and ultimately influence on, new elite generations of economists was so successful that at one point his protégés held top positions in ten of the major European central banks. He will be remembered as a man of extraordinary genius.

References

Ando, A., & Modigliani, F. (1963, Mar.). The "life cycle" hypothesis of saving: Aggregate implications and tests. *American Economic Review*, 53(1), 55-84.

Duesenberry, J. S. (1949). *Income, saving, and the theory of consumer behavior.* Cambridge, MA: Harvard University Press.

Friedman, M. (1957). *A theory of the consumption function.* Princeton: Princeton University Press.

Granger, C. W. J. (1999). *Empirical modeling in economics: Specification and evaluation.* London: Cambridge University Press.

Hall, R. E., & Taylor, J. B. (1997). *Macroeconomics* (5th ed.). New York: W. W. Norton & Company.

Kaldor, N. (1966, Oct.). Marginal productivity and the macro-economic theories of distribution: Comment on Samuelson and Modigliani. *The Review of Economic Studies*, 33(4), 309-319.

Keynes, J. M. (1979 [1936]). *The general theory of employment, interest and money.* London: Macmillan and Co. Ltd.

Miller, M. H. (2002). *Selected works of Merton H. Miller: A celebration of markets* (vol. II). Chicago: University of Chicago Press.

Modigliani, F. (2003, Spring). The Keynesian gospel according to Modigliani. *The American Economist*, 67(1), 3-24.

———. (1988, Autumn). MM—past, present, future. *The Journal of Economic Perspectives*, 2(4), 145-158.

———. (1980). *The collected papers of Franco Modigliani: The theory of finance and other essays* (vol. 3). A. Abel (Ed.). Cambridge, MA: MIT Press.

———. (1949). Fluctuations in the saving-income ratio: A problem in economic forecasting. In *Studies in Income and Wealth* (vol. 11, 369-444). New York: NBER.

———. (1944, Jan.). Liquidity preference and the theory of interest and money. *Econometrica*, 12(1), 45-88.

Modigliani, F., & Brumberg, R. (1954). Utility analysis and the consumption function: An interpretation of cross-section data. In K. K. Kurihara (Ed.), *Post-Keynesian economics* (388-436). New Brunswick, NJ: Rutgers University Press.

Pasinetti, Luigi L. "New Results in an Old Framework: Comment on Samuelson and Modigliani." *The Review of Economic Studies*, 33(4) (Oct. 1966): 303-306.

———. (1962). The rate of profit and income distribution in relation to the rate of economic growth. *Review of Economic Studies*, 29, 267-279.

Romer, D. (1996). *Advanced macroeconomics.* New York: McGraw-Hill.

Samuelson, P. A. (1991, Apr.). Extirpating error contamination concerning the post-Keynesian anti-Pasinetti equilibrium. *Oxford Economic Papers*, New Series, 43(2), 177-186.

Samuelson, P. A., & Modigliani, F. (1966a, Oct.). The Pasinetti paradox in neoclassical and more general models. *The Review of Economic Studies*, 33(4), 269-301.

———. (1966b). Marginal productivity and the macro-economic theories of distribution: Reply to Pasinetti and Robinson. *The Review of Economic Studies*, 33(4), 321-330.

Stiglitz, J. E. (1969, Dec.). A re-examination of the Modigliani-Miller theorem. *The American Economic Review*, 59(5), 784-793.

Tobin, J. (1985). *Essays in economics: Theory and policy* (3rd ed.). Cambridge, MA: MIT Press.

———. (1987). *Essays in economics: Macroeconomics.* Cambridge, MA: MIT Press.

Stanley Fischer (1943-)

Stanley Fischer was born in Lusaka, Zambia (formerly Rhodesia) on October 15, 1943. He was schooled in Rhodesia (now Zambia) and the prestigious London School of Economics, where he got his BSc in 1965, and MSc in economics in 1966. Fischer then attended MIT, where he earned his PhD in 1969, writing his doctoral dissertation on *Essays on Asset and Contingent Commodities*. He was an instructor at MIT in the spring semester of 1969, a post-doctoral fellow at the University of Chicago during 1969-1970, and assistant professor during 1970-1973. He rejoined MIT as an associate professor in 1973, and was a professor there during 1977-1999.

Professor Fischer is currently Governor of the Bank of Israel since May 2005. He was appointed for a second five-year term in May 2010, with glowing recommendations from today's President Shimon Peres and Prime Minister Benjamin Netanyahu. Other major positions he held include Vice Chairman of Citigroup, Inc. 2002–2005, Deputy Managing Director of the IMF from 1994 to 2002, and Chief Economist at the World Bank 1988–1990. Fischer has co-authored popular textbooks at all levels of economics, including an introductory text, *Economics*, with Rudiger Dornbusch and Richard Schmalensee, an intermediate text, *Intermediate Macroeconomics*, with Rudiger Dornbusch and Richard Startz, and an advance text, *Lecture in Macroeconomics*, with Olivier Jean Blanchard. His published articles are numerous, covering the areas of economic growth development, international trade, macroeconomics, inflation and stabilization, and economics of transitions. Like so many other MIT economists, he defends Keynesian economics and free trade.

Fischer's early brush with monetary policy occurred while he was assistant professor at the University of Chicago. Using the FRB-MIT-Penn econometric model for the US, he simulated the effects of the monetary policy rules (Cooper and Fischer, 1972). The result was that proportional control can be destabilizing to the economy. The simulation unearthed potential difficulty with model uncertainty, which echoed through the subsequent discovery of rational expectation models to the effect that the "adoption of a rule might modify the behavioral relations of the economy" (ibid.: 394). Commenting much later on monetary policy and uncertainty, Fischer distinguished model and net versus gross shocks uncertainties. By model uncertainty, he meant misspecification due to wrong theories, structural changes over time, and imperfect information. By shocks to the economy, he meant the ability to identify them, and to ascertain their degree of permanence (Fischer, 2003: 384).

Wage-Price Rigidities

Fischer is on the side of economists who hold that monetary policy can have real effects on output. The mechanism that transmits this effect starts in the labor market, where long-term wage contracts are negotiated. Contract wages must bring demand and supply in equilibrium in order to clear the labor market. This means that price must correspond with money wage to keep the real wage constant. For Fischer, labor contracts are set with time lags, $t - i$, so that the equality of the money wages W_t and prices P_t are constant, i.e., ${}_{t-i}W_t = {}_{t-i}P_t$, where $i = 1$ for one period lag, and $i = 2$ for two period lags, and t is the current time period (Fischer, 1977: 198).

A consequence of such long-term contracts is that "activists' monetary policy can affect the short-run behavior of real output, rational expectation not withstanding" (ibid.: 191). This is an important finding because New Keynesian economists who start with sticky wages have advocated activists' monetary policy to stabilize the economy. On the other hand, New Classical economists who start with sticky prices before sticky wages have shown that changing the money supply does not affect the natural rate of output when rational expectation is taken into account. Fischer demonstrated his activists' claim by working with a modified New Classical model developed by Sargent and Wallace (1975), demonstrating the idea that if both the government and the private sector have the same information, they would react to it rationally (Benassy, 2001: 46).

To bring out the role of long-term contracts in the New Keynesian Paradigm, we can look at the policy game played by the workers, the employers, and the government through its central bank policies (see Canzoneri, 1985). Long-term contracts are negotiated between the workers and employers. The contract wages are set based on the rational expectation of prices that will prevail over the life of the contracts, *Ep* If the actual price, *p*, is not what was expected, then the workers would be asked to supply more or less labor accordingly. The policy objective is to make contract wage reflect the difference between actual and expected prices, $\lambda[p - Ep]$ (Blanchard and Fischer, 1989: 523). The extent to which wages are indexed to price change will be important here. The proportional constant adjust partially or fully, $\lambda \leq 1$, to cost of living adjustment (COLA) built into long-term labor contracts indexed by the CPI or GDP deflator. (Dornbusch, Fischer, et al., 2008: 173) The indexation effect is normally taught of as reducing a two period contract to a one period contract, creating a spot rather than a future market for nominal wages.

The third player of the game, government, can change monetary supply in a way that stands on behalf of workers whose contracts wages are not indexed to prices. The order of playing the tri-party game is that workers and employers determine the contract wages, and then the government undertakes monetary policy. The three players are embroiled therefore, in a game whose outcome determines employment, output, and prices. In period $t-2$, the private sector, workers and employers, are locked into wages contracts that were negotiated in an earlier period, $t-1$. The government, however, is not so constrained, which gives it an information advantage over the private sector. The government can make a monetary policy that would react to shock that would, for instance, redress any price pressure that is put on wages fixed by long-term contracts. That Keynesian result will be ineffective, however, if the government is restrained only to the results in time period $t-1$ (Benassy, 2002: 217).

In essence, the Fischer model incorporated long-term wage contracts into a rational expectation model built by Sargent and Wallace (1975). A particular specification that Fischer made includes an aggregate demand equation that takes nominal money supply and its velocity of circulation as stochastic variables subject to random shocks. For instance, the velocity variable can be specified as a random walk model. A second equation models labor demand as a declining function of average wage. A third equation lays out the procedure for wage setting. A fourth equation describes an information set that staggers labor contracts such that neither current money supply nor its velocity is know at the time wages are chosen (Blanchard and Fischer, 1989: 415). A more comprehensive way of viewing this is through a welfare function explained by inflation, actual versus natural output, real exchange rate changes, and shocks (Persson and Tabellini, 2004: 2004). The welfare function is subject to shocks that may be symmetric or asymmetric. Usually private parties have only partial information of the shocks, whereas policy makers have superior information of the shocks in setting monetary policy and can use that superior information to stabilize the economy (ibid.: 2005).

Other researchers, Gray (1976), Phelps and Taylor (1977), Taylor (1980), and Calvo (1983), have emphasized different aspects of wage contracts. Gray emphasized wage indexation. Phelps and Taylor (1977: 165) think that "all prices and wages are reviewed and reset every period"; therefore, there are no long-term contracts like those in the model by Fischer. On the other hand, Fischer (1977: 203) considered their findings as dealing with price stickiness first and wage stickiness afterwards. An important part of the story is that the new classical economists have a partiality for price stickiness, which they trace back to David Hume (Taylor, 1999: 1011), while the New Keynesians start with wage rigidity postulated by Keynes. A large volume of the literature favors Calvo's contribution, which uses a single parameter taking the value of zero in a flexible system and a value of one in a fixed system, and other degrees of rigidities in the interval (0, 1) (Calvo, 1983). On the empirical side, during the most inflationary periods of 1973-1983 in the world economy, both Taylor and Fischer reached the conclusion that there is much evidence for as against sticky-wage or sticky-prices. (Taylor, 1987: 26). The middle ground is that as multi-period wage contracts are renewed over time, gradual adjustment takes place in the nominal wage rate, which can allow policy rules and government stabilization function to operate over the contractual period (Romer, 1996: 256; Shaw, 1984: 61).

Macro Policies

"Since Lucas's policy evaluation critique . . . there has been no accepted way of evaluating detailed policy proposals" (Fischer, 1990: 1168). Fischer found that "there is a continuum of monetary policies" between the traditional choice between rules and discretions (ibid.: 1181). This is in part due to the uncertainty over monetary policy and in part due to difficulty over managing rules. Fischer also defends a continuum of policy in the international arena (Dornbusch, Samuelson, and Fischer, 1977, 1980). It introduced money and payments systems in a barter trade model with an infinite number of commodities. International policies respond to changes in taste, productivity, and in a uniform way, technology.

Side-by-side with wage rigidity problems, Fischer has taken a strong position on the Keynesian liquidity trap situation. He is a staunch defender of the Lender of Last Resort (LOLR) function of the IMF and central banks. According to a leading post-Keynesian, "Stanley Fischer, first Managing Director of the International Monetary Fund, suggests turning in the IMF into a permanent international LOLR" (Davidson, 2007: 159). Fischer catalogs his position of this view for his tenure at the IMF in his 2004 book. In the face of the current great recession, he articulated another important variant of the LOLR role, namely a "market maker of last resort." In that role, the Federal Reserve has "managed to revitalize important financial markets that had failed during the crisis by means of its asset purchases in those specific markets" (Fischer, 2010: 5).

Fisher traces his view of LOLR to Bagehot's work, *Lombard Street,* written in 1892 (Fischer, 2004: 7) For the current great recession crisis, however, liquidity and solvency problems emerge simultaneously for both the Central Bank and the Government. We find that cooperation by the Treasury Department and the Federal Reserve on LOLR policy can prevent a financial meltdown. However, in other countries, "in Israel, the law provides that the central bank can intervene on its own to deal with a liquidity problem but needs the authorization of the Treasury and the government to take over an insolvent financial institution" (Fischer, 2011).

On the international scene, besides the LOLR function, central bank considers exchange rate and real exchange rate targets. Fischer is a free trader, exposing flexible exchange rate and capital mobility. He would, however, temper this view with an additional specification to the tradition one–instrument, one-goal policy in a two equation system such as monetary and fiscal policy targeting inflation and growth. A third equation will have a government intervention instrument with the goal to defend an exchange rate (ibid.). He defends the position that as a rule, the central bank should "never say never" (ibid.), and the one-instrument one-target a myth (Fischer, 2010).

Fischer had two notable opportunities to make his theories operational for the Israel economy, one as a consultant to Secretary of State George Shultz during 1983-1985, and now as the governor of the Bank of Israel. As a consultant, his goal was to help curb triple-digit inflation, falling reserves, and weak economic growth. His prescriptions were to cut the budget deficit, devalue, tighten monetary policy, and end wage indexation that could end inflationary momentum. It was a pain for gain approach, which the government half-heartedly embraced. As the Governor of the Bank of Israel, Fischer's policies are much more successful and trend-setting. It is more artistic in that he does not see any silver bullets to confront the great recession, and he advocates the aphorism that the central bank should "never say never." He did not see international coordination of policy as a necessary, since different countries were at different stages in their recovery from the crisis. Israel being ahead in recovery relative to the rest of the world, Fischer was ready to temper inflation with a rising interest rate. The inflow of capital that followed enhanced growth, but it also appreciated the shekel. The central bank, therefore, intervened, accumulating foreign reserves to defend its exchange rate. This policy had more than one target. Gaining control of Israel's budget stemmed the tide of political unrest in Egypt and Libya, and foreign reserves have doubled since the central bank started buying foreign currency in March 2008, maintaining an exchange rate that fosters its export industries. In spite of the pressure Fischer faces from increasing interest rates that are making housing unaffordable, he deserves an A for policy performance.

References

Benassy, J.-P. (2002). *The macroeconomics of imperfect competition and nonclearing markets: A dynamic general equilibrium approach*. Cambridge, MA: MIT Press.

———. (2001). On the optimality of activist policies with a less informed government. *Journal of Monetary Economics*, 47(1), 45-59.

Blanchard, O. J., & Fischer, S. (1989). *Lectures on macroeconomics*. Cambridge, MA: MIT Press.

Calvo, G. (1983). Staggered prices in a utility-maximizing framework. *Journal of Monetary Economics*, 12, 383-398.

Canzoneri, M. (1985). Monetary policy games and the role of private information. *The American Economic Review*, 75, 1056-1070.

Cooper, J. P., & Fischer, S. (1972). Simulations of monetary rules in the FRB-MIT-Penn model. *Journal of Money, Credit and Banking*, 4(2), 384-396.

Davidson, P. (2007). *Interpreting Keynes for the 21st century*. London: Macmillan).

Dornbusch, R., Fischer, S., & Startz, R. (2008). *Macroeconomics* (10th ed.). New York: McGraw-Hill/Irwin.

———. (1977). Comparative advantage, trade, and payments in a Ricardian model with a continuum of goods. *American Economic Review* 67(5), 823–839.

———. (1980). Heckscher-Ohlin trade theory with a continuum of goods. *Quarterly Journal of Economics*, 95(2), 203–224.

Fischer, S. (2011). Central bank lessons from the global crisis. 3rd P. R. Brahmananda Memorial Lecture. *Esocialsciences*. Retrieved from http://rbi.org.in/Upload/Publications/PDFs/SFL110211.pdf.

———. (2010). Myths of monetary policy. *Israel Economic Review*, 8(2), 1–5.

———. (2004). *IMP essays from a time of crisis: The international financial system, stabilization, and development*. Cambridge, MA: MIT Press.

———. (2003). *General overview*. In *Monetary policy and uncertainty: Adapting to a changing economy* (383-389). Kansas: The Federal Reserve Bank of Kansas City.

———. (1990). Rules versus discretion in monetary policy. In B. M. Friedman and F. H. Hahn (Eds.), *Handbook of monetary economics* (vol. 2, 1155-1184). Amsterdam: Elsevier Science Publishers B.V.

———. (1977). Long-term contracts, rational expectations, and the optimal money supply rule. *Journal of Political Economy*, 85(1), 191-205.

Fischer, S., Dornbusch, R., & Schmalensee, R. *Economics* (2nd ed.). New York: McGraw Hill.

Hall, R. E., & Taylor, J. B. (1997). *Macroeconomics* (5th ed.). New York: W. W. Norton and Company.

Keynes, J. M. (1936). *The general theory of employment interest and money*. London: Macmillan.

Layard, R., Nickell, S., & Jackman, R. (1994). *The unemployment crisis*. Oxford: Oxford University Press.

Persson, T., & Tabellini, G. (2005 [1995]). Double-edged incentives, intuitions and policy coordination. In G. M. Grossman & K. Rogoff (Ed.), *Handbook of international economics* (vol. 3, 1973-2030). Amsterdam: Elsevier.

Sargent, T. J., & Wallace, N. (1975). "Rational" expectations, the optimal monetary instrument, and the optimal money supply rule. *Journal of Political Economy*, 83(2), 241-254.

Taylor, J. (1999). Staggered price and wage setting in macroeconomics. In J. B. Taylor & M. Woodford (Eds.), *Handbook of macroeconomics* (vol. 1, 1009-1049). Amsterdam: Elsevier Science B.V.

———. (1987). A summary of the empirical and analytical results and the implications for international monetary policy. In Y. Suzuki & M. Okabe (Eds.), *Toward a world of economic stability: Optimal monetary framework and policy* (17-34). Tokyo: University of Tokyo Press.

———. (1980). Aggregate dynamics and staggered contracts. *Journal of Political Economy*, 88, 1-23.

PART II

NEOCLASSICAL ECONOMICS

Paul A. Samuelson

Paul A. Samuelson

Introduction

Paul Anthony Samuelson was born on May 15, 1915 in Gary, Indiana to Frank Samuelson and Ella Lipton. The family moved to Chicago, where Paul attended Hyde Park High School. He entered the University of Chicago at age sixteen, and took up economics after having heard a lecture on the Reverend T. R. Malthus. After graduating with a BA in 1935, he attended Harvard, where he earned an MA in 1936, and a PhD in 1941. He married a fellow student, Marion Crawford, in 1938, and after her death in 1978, he married Risha Clay Samuelson.

Samuelson's PhD thesis became the celebrated *Foundation of Economics Analysis*, published in 1947. A year later, he published his principles of economics, *Economics*, in 1948. Those two works bracketed his contributions from the simple to the complex aspects of economics that were imitated and have educated over a generation of economists.

Samuelson started his teaching career as an instructor at Harvard in 1940, but after a month moved to MIT as an assistant professor. He was an associate professor (1944), professor (1947), and institute professor (1966) at MIT. Samuelson received honorary doctoral degrees from the University of Chicago (1961), Oberlin College (1961), Indiana University (1966), and East Anglia University (1966). He was a pre doctoral fellow at Harvard University during 1935-1937, and a Ford Foundation Research Fellow during 1958-1959. His numerous awards include the David A. Wells Prize in 1941 from Harvard University, the John Bates Clark Medal from the American Economic

Association in 1947, and the Nobel Prize in Economics from the Bank of Sweden in 1970 for his scientific contributions to economics.

Because he did not like to compromise his thinking in economics, he turned down President Kennedy's requests to be the head of his economic council. However, he has been credited for educating the president on Keynesian economics, and he also was the one to encourage the tax cut that was implemented in the Johnson administration.

We have attempted multiple times over the years to appraise the works of Samuelson. Each of those contributions was specific to a certain task at hand, and even for those specific tasks, something surely had fallen through the cracks. Robert Solow has appreciated this monumental task of appraising Samuelson, noting that when he had edited a book on him, he soon realized that "the theory of overlapping-generations model had fallen through the cracks" (Solow, 2008: 35). In our "Ten Ways to Know Paul A. Samuelson," we overwhelmingly argued that he was a multi-faceted individual, a round rather than a flat character. Moving from his character to his works, we can say that his contribution is foundational in the sense that he milked all the ideas from the literature and fed them to us in palatable doses. We will examine how he did this in some detail for two areas, trade theory and capital theory, in this memoriam, and touch on other important works by way of summary and references.

Goals of Economics

Samuelson's goal was to understand the "behavior of mixed-economies of the American and Western European type" (Samuelson, 1986: vol. 3, 728). His means to this goal is scientific honesty. He holds that "science consist[s] of descriptions of empirical regularities" (ibid.: 772). Therefore, "a good economist has good judgment about economic reality" (ibid.: 775). One should not wonder why he often refers to Thomas Kuhn, for he holds that "economic analysis advances discontinuously. After a great forward step, time must be taken to consolidate the gains achieved" (Samuelson, 1966: vol. 2, 1140). Within this research program, Samuelson investigates reality with economic models, being well aware that "the science of economics does not provide simple answers to complex social problems" (ibid.: vol. 2, 1325). Economics for him is different in degree but not in kind from the physical sciences: "All sciences have the common task of describing and summarizing empirical reality. Economics is no exception" (ibid.: vol. 2, 1756). But unlike the falsificationists, he does not look at facts to kill a theory. Rather, he states, "In economics it takes a theory to kill a theory; facts can only dent the theorist's hide" (ibid.: vol. 2, 1568). In his many editions of his introductory textbook, Samuelson's representative definition of economics is:

> Economics is the study of how people and society end up choosing, with or without the use of money, to employ scarce productive resources that could have alternative uses, to produce various commodities and distribute them for consumption, now or in the future, among various persons and groups in society. It analyzes the costs and benefits of improving patterns of resource allocation. (Samuelson, 1980: 2)

First, this is a much developed definition from Adam Smith's concept:

> Political economy, considered as a branch of the science of a statesman or legislator, proposes two distinct objects: first, to provide a plentiful revenue or subsistence for the people, or more properly to enable them to provide such a revenue or subsistence for themselves; and secondly, to supply the state or commonwealth with a revenue sufficient for the public services. it proposes to enrich both the people and the sovereign. (Smith 2003: 397)

It incorporates the main ingredients of Lionel Robbins' celebrated definition to the effect that: "Economics is the science which studies human behavior as a relationship between ends and scarce means which have alternative uses" (Robbins, 1937: 7). We also see element of production, distribution, and consumption, which was the hallmark of J. B. Say: "the aim of political economy is to show the way in which wealth is produced, distributed and consumed" (German translation of Smith's WN, Paris, Guillamumin, 1881: vol. II, 1-2, note 2). The elements in his definition that characterize his contribution is that of dealing with future time and cost benefit analysis. Samuelson is known for bringing rigor and mathematics to economics. F. Hayek wrote that Samuelson espouses "physics as the science for economics to imitate" (Hayek, 1992: 5). The intention here is to criticize and not to praise Samuelson. But Samuelson has followed a long-standing tradition. According to Augustin Cournot, "There were authors, like Smith and Say, who, in writing on Political Economy, have preserved all the beauties of a purely literary style; but there are others, like Ricardo, who, when treating the most abstract questions, or when seeking great accuracy, have not been able to avoid algebra, and have only disguised it under arithmetical calculation of tiresome length" (Cournot, 1963 [1838]: 3). Even Alfred Marshall, the great classical economist, who preferred the "practical man's route" in explaining complex analysis such as trade theory, finds that "much that is most interesting from my point of view cannot, I think, be conveniently be reached by this route. . . . I always find that the best men are relieved when I go over the ground again, starting with aggregates and subordinating details" (Marshall, 1996: vol. 3, 85).

Method

Samuelson has evolved the "Operational" method of economics. He said: "My work in reveal[ed] preference, in *Foundation of Economic Analysis,* and in the several volumes of *Collected Scientific Papers,* consistently bears out this general methodological procedure" (Samuelson, 1986: vol. 5, 135 [italics original]). Basically, the procedure is "to learn what descriptions [new literature and mathematical paradigms] imply for observable data" (ibid.). With data on the one hand, and logic and theory on the other, operationalism seeks a correspondence of the two sides. "Samuelson's 'correspondence principle between comparative statics and dynamics' . . . shows how the problem of deriving operationally meaningful theorems in comparative statics is closely tied up with the problem of stability of equilibrium" (Morishima, 1964: 24). "By means of what I have called the Correspondence Principle between comparative statics and dynamics, definite operationally meaning theorems can be derived from so simple a hypothesis. One interested only in fruitful statics must study dynamics" (Samuelson, 1947: 5).

Between 1938 and 1946, John Hicks dealt with the stability question in only static terms. At best, he allowed price adjustments to take place within a short period such as one week, not accounting for price changes during the week. The short period analysis, he called "a series of temporary equlibria" (Hicks, 1979: 336). Samuelson turned his own methodology towards the development of operationally meaningful theory between comparative static and dynamic analysis in economics. One such operationally meaningful concept is the idea of stability of equilibrium. Prior to his *Foundation of Economics Analysis,* the idea of stability in economics was mainly static. In comparative static analysis, price changes were handled by shortening the period of adjustment to, say, a week. From a disequilibrium position, the adjustment to equilibrium from the static point of view would occur through a series of temporary equilbria. Samuelson's contribution made the period of adjustment momentary. He introduced the symbols: $dp/dt = H(q_D - q_S)$, where the term on the left is the rate of change of prices, dp with respect to changes of time, dt. H is a proportional constant, q is quantity, S is supply, and D is demand (Samuelson, 1966: vol. 1, 544). Stability occurs when as time goes to infinity, the solution of the differential equation breaks down, which in economic terms mean that "the supply curve cuts the demand curve from below" (Samuelson, 1947: 18).

Areas of Interest

Samuelson described himself as a generalist. He wrote: "I once claimed to be the last generalist in economics, writing and teaching such diverse subjects as international trade and econometrics, economic theory and business cycle, demography and labor economics, finance and monopolistic competition, history of doctrines and locational economics" (Samuelson, 1986: vol. 5, 800).

Samuelson's research areas in economics include methodology, welfare economics, linear programming, Keynesian economics, economic dynamics, international trade theory, and consumer theory. Modern economists consider him the undisputed leader of the Neoclassical School, a school of thought that uses the concepts of maximization and minimization as the foundation of economic thought. Samuelson laid such a foundation in his first book, *The Foundation of Economics* (1947), which he developed from his PhD dissertation at Harvard in 1941. In 1948, Samuelson published the first edition of another bestseller, *Economics*, a freshman college textbook that taught nearly two generations of young economists. Five volumes with over 5,000 words entitled *Collected Scientific Papers of Paul Samuelson* complement those two works.

Macroeconomics

In macroeconomics, Samuelson forged the "neoclassical synthesis" view, which adds the neoclassical economic foundation to Keynesian economic thought. From the fourth (1958) to the eleventh (1980) edition of his *Economics*, he held that economists have been synthesizing traditional theory with newer Keynesian thought on income distribution. He accepted the Keynesian synthesis as a revolutionary way to look "at how the entire gross national product is determined and how wages and prices and the rate of unemployment are determined with it" (Samuelson, 1986: vol. 5, 280). Looking through the Keynesian lenses, Samuelson saw that economic policies should operate from the point of view of a "mixed-economy," mixed because government works side-by-side with the private sector in our economic affairs. Economic cycles are generated when the traditional concept of the accelerator (constant capital to output in the naïve version) interacts with the Keynesian multiplier, a concept first conceptualized by Samuelson.

In 1958, Samuelson introduced the overlapping generation model (OLG), which is seen as a rival to the famous Arrow-Debreu general equilibrium (GE) model for the economy, and is a popular model in modern macroeconomic analysis (Samuelson, 1966: vol. 1, 219-234). The model allows intergenerational trading such as where a middle-aged person lends his savings to a younger person, expecting in return from the younger person's savings in a later period. "Break each life up into thirds: men produce one unit of product in period 1 and one unit in period 2; in period 3 they retire" (ibid.: 220). $U = U(C_1, C_2, C_3)$. represents the utility function on consumption in each period. The rate of interest is the price of exchange between current and future foods. $R_t = 1/(1 + i_t)$ is the discount rate. Equilibrium is achieved in periods when the discounted value of consumption equals the discounted value of production, or $C_1 + C_2R_t + C_3R_tR_{t+1} = 1 + 1R_t + 0R_tR_{t+1} = 1 + 1R_t$ (ibid.: 221).

If savings is income less consumption, we can specify the model from the savings and the people who save's points of view. $S_p(R_t, R_{t+1})$ is the saving function for p periods: 1, 2, 3. The population, B, at time, t, can be written as B_t. The population at different periods can be represented by a first period, B_t, a second period B_{t-1}, and a third period B_{t-2}. The equilibrium condition can then be represented as $B_tS_1(R_t,R_{t+1}) + B_{t-1}S_2(R_{t-1},R_t) + B_{t-2}S_3(R_{t-2},R_{t-1}) = 0$ (ibid.: 222). If all the Bs are the same (i.e. a stationary population), then $R_t = 1$. If B grows exponentially, then the equality of the discount rate with the population growth rate is also a solution. A solution means that there would be harmony between current and future savings and consumption plans across generations, and the model addresses how they would grow alongside zero and the actual growth rate in population. Considering further developments,

Solow elevated this model in the history of economic thought as follows: "this innocent little device of Samuelson's has been developed into a serious and quite general modeling strategy that uncovers equilibrium possibilities not to be found in standard Walrasian formulations" (Solow, 2006: 40).

Cambridge Controversy

In 1962 (Samuelson, 1966: vol. 1, 325-337) Samuelson derived a Walrasian-like production function by creating an index for capital from the many equations that capture the technique of production of firms that populate the economy. Using that surrogate capital index, he derived a surrogate production function (Wan, 1971: 100). The essence of the Cambridge controversy is about how the surrogate production captures certain stylized facts about neoclassical economics. According to C. E. Ferguson, "The essential issue may be put this way. If production functions are smoothly continuous and everywhere continuously differentiable, the neoclassical results hold (possible in a somewhat attenuated form if one allows for heterogeneous capital goods)" (Ferguson, 1975: 245). Among other things, smooth-differentiable production function allows more general analysis.

The problem of measuring capital came up with David Ricardo to which the roots of marginal analysis are traced. "The whole marginal analysis was born of Ricardo's attempt to explain the share of rent in the national income, and to show why some rents on some land were higher than on other . . . 'land' could be measured . . . in acres . . . adding together different acres weighted by their relative prices . . . the same could be done for labor . . . using relative wages as the basis of weights. With capital the problem was an entirely different one, since there was no unit in which we could reduce capital to homogeneous units" (Lutz and Hague, 1961: 305). As K. Wicksell puts it,

> Whereas labor and land are measured each in terms of its own technical unit (e.g. working days or months, acre *per annum*) capital . . . is reckoned . . . as a sum of exchange value—whether in money or as an average of products. In other words, each particular capital-good is measured by a unit extraneous to itself. [This] is a theoretical anomaly which disturbs the correspondence which would otherwise exist between all the factors of production. The productive contribution of a piece of technical capital, such as a steam engine, is determined not by its cost but by the horse-power which it develops, and by the excess or scarcity of similar machines. If capital were to

> be measured in technical units, the defect would be remedied and the correspondence would be complete. But, in that case, productive capital would have to be distributed into as many categories as there are kinds of tools, machinery, and materials, etc., and a unified treatment of the role of capital in production would be impossible. Even then we should only know the yield of the various objects at a particular moment, but nothing at all about the value of the goods themselves, which it is necessary to know in order to calculate the rate of interest, which in equilibrium is the same on all capital. (Wicksell, 1911: vol. 1, 149) [see *JEP* autumn 2003]

The measurement of capital is therefore among the top two problems in capital theory, the other being the capita-output ratio (Lutz, 1961: 9).

Leon Walras' view on capital is also foundational, although his model is different from Ricardo's (see Nell, 1967: 15-26). Walras postulated "a capital goods market, where capital goods are bought and sold. . . . They are demanded because of the land-services, labor and capital-services they render, or better, because the rent, wages and interest which these services yield" (Walras, 1954: 267). The price of the capital goods depends on the price of its services or its income. Net income is the gross income, p less the price of the capital goods, P, adjusted for depreciation, μ and insurance premiums, v, i.e, $\pi = [p - (\mu + v)P]$ (ibid.: 268). From this we get the rate of net income, $i = \pi / P$, suggesting that $p - (\mu + v)P = iP$ from which we can get the price of all capital goods (ibid.: 269). Walras suggested that we should not deduct depreciation or insurance charges for land, nor personal faculties (human capital), because they are natural and known. Land and personal faculties are hired in kind in the capital market, but capital proper is usually hired in the form of money in the money market. The proper capital goods are artificial (not natural), and are subject to cost of production, depreciation, and insurance premiums (ibid.: 271). "Capital formation consists . . . in the transformation of services into new capital goods, just as production consists in the transformation of services into consumer' goods" (ibid.: 282). Putting it all together, "Once the equilibrium has been establish[ed] in principle (through groping), exchange can take place immediately. Production, however, requires a certain lapse of time . . . equilibrium in production . . . will be established effectively through the reciprocal exchange between services employed and products manufactured within a given period of time during which no change in the data is allows" (ibid.: 242). A similar situation holds for capital formation (ibid.: 282). In the end, "Capital formation in a market ruled by free competition is an operation by which the excess of income over consumption can be transformed into such types and quantities of new capital goods proper as are best suited to yield the greatest possible satisfaction of wants" (ibid.: 305).

With this Walrasian background, we can appreciate Joan Robinson's position that

> A piece of equipment or a stock of raw materials, regarded as a product, has a price, like any other product, made up of prime cost plus a gross margin. These costs (direct and indirect) are composed of wages, rents, depreciation and net profit. The amount of net profit entering into the price of the product is, obviously, influenced by the general rate of profit prevailing in the industries concerned. Thus the value of capital depends upon the rate of profit. There is no way of presenting a quantity of capital in any realistic manner apart from the rate of profit, so that to say that profits measure, or represent or correspond to the marginal product of capital is meaningless. (Robinson, 1971: 601)

Yet we find attempts to construct aggregate production function in the style of J. B. Clark and Frank Ramsey, where the definition of capital represents a challenge.

From the macroeconomic point of view, the aggregate production function is written as $Y = f(K, L)$, which is read as output is a function of capital and labor, respectively. In equilibrium, the marginal product of labor is the wage rate. We usually set the marginal product of capital equal to the rate of interest, which is at the center of the controversy. Robinson sets up the controversy this way: "In 1961 I encountered Professor Samuelson on his home ground; in the course of an argument I happened to ask him: When you define the marginal product of labor, what do you keep constant? He seemed disconcerted, as though none of his pupils had ever asked that question, but next day he gave a clear answer. Either the physical inputs other than labor are kept constant, or the rate of profit on capital is kept constant. I found this satisfactory, for it destroys the doctrine that wages are regulated by marginal productivity" (Robinson, 1970: 310).

The problem has to do with time, or the time period of production. "Wicksell never used the term K . . . but always inserted the term T on the grounds that it is by allowing labor to use roundabout, time-consuming processes of production that capital raises the productivity of labor and thus is itself production" (Lutz, 1961: 10). But in a letter to Alfred Marshall, Wicksell wrote: "the theory of capital and interest cannot be regarded as complete yet. As I have tried to show several times . . . so long as capital is defined as a *sum of commodities* (or of value) the doctrine of the marginal productivity of capital as determining the rate of interest is never quite true and often not true at all—it is true individually, but not in respect of the whole capital of society" (Wicksell, 1905: vol. 3, 102 [italics original]).

Samuelson wrote several articles on the topic of capital theory that serve as a precursor to his 1962 milestone article, "Parable and Realism in Capital Theory: The Surrogate Production Function." His 1937 article, "Some Aspects of The Pure Theory of Capital," probed the aspect of time and timeless analysis of the production function (Samuelson, 1966: vol. 1, 161-188). He posited relationships for "constant rate of interest" and "the rate of interest itself in an unrestricted function of time" (ibid.: 163). Treating the rate of interest, r, as a constant, one can capitalize an income stream at the beginning and the end of a period, returning values $V(0, r)$, and $V(t, r)$ for time $t = 0$, and $t = t$, respectively. The internal rate of return, $\overline{r}$, makes the initial value of the investment zero, $V(0, \overline{r}) = 0$ (ibid.: 165-167). We can show that "at any instant of time the value of every investment account is unequivocally determined" (ibid.: 169). The income stream so determined will vary in the real world due to uncertainty, imputation of income, market imperfection, etc. (ibid.: 170).

The treatment of a constant rate of interest represents the condition of stationary society without capital accumulation. Making the rate of interest a function of time, $r = r(t)$, requires the consideration of an average rate, ρ. The relation of ρ to r is the same as the relationship of the margin to the average. The constancy of the rate of interest is seen as a special case of the variation of the rate of interest with time. The same relationship between perpetual income and value will hold for the constant and variable view of the interest rate (ibid.: 177).

In 1939, Samuelson further stated the analysis to show "some of the forces which help to determine the market rate of interest at which all can borrow or lend under ideal conditions" (Samuelson, 1939: 189-200). He categorized the analysis into discrete periods, and showed that the interest rate in any period equilibrates total asset holding with the total assets of all enterprises.

The approach he took "does not require the definition as a physical quantity" (Samuelson, 1939: 199).

In 1943, Samuelson considered dynamic, static, and stationary state conditions for the rate of interest to be zero (Samuelson, 1966: vol. 1, 201-211). After considering cases where capital should have a zero net productivity according to Frank Ramsey, and where the maximum output is never attained for a finite value of capital according to Frank Knight, Samuelson took the position "not to reify the limit by asking what really happens at a zero rate of interest, but rather to concentrate upon the dynamic path toward this limiting condition" (ibid.: 211).

In 1956, Samuelson and Solow extended consideration of the Ramsey zero interest and one capital-good model to heterogeneous capital goods (Samuelson, 1966: vol. 1, 261-286). This article set the stage to "reconstruct the composition of its diverse capital goods so that there may remain great heuristic value in the simpler J. B. Clark-Ramsey models of abstract capital substance" (ibid.: 261-262). Broadly speaking, the treatment of capital—fixed or circulating—can be looked at either as input or efficient output or consumption it generates. Simplifying, the Ramsey model maximizes all future utility of consumption, $U(C)$, constrained by a saving function, $f(s)$. The Ramsey model does not consider "differences between different kinds of goods and different kinds of labor, and suppose them to be expressed in terms of fixed standards, so that we can speak simply of quantities of capital, consumption and labor without discussing their particular forms" (Ramsey, 1928: 544). Samuelson and Solow's approach was to drop that assumption.

In a Clark-Ramsey framework, capital enters into the constraint, $f(s)$, in the initial period. In his 1961 paper on "The Evaluation of 'Social Income': Capital Formation and Wealth" (Samuelson, 1966: vol. 1, 299-324), Samuelson elaborated on this capital constraint. There was one output, produced from inputs, $F(K, L)$, which can be invested or consumed. Capital K can be changed to K_2 with twice the value of the original capital, which will no longer be produced. The production function for gross output is now $F(K+K_2, L)$, which is netted for depreciation at a rate equal to m. He used this model to answer an old "1935 debate between Pigou and Hayek as to the meaning of maintaining capital intact" (ibid.: 302). From this model also, the factors are rewarded their marginal products (ibid.: 304). The article "dealt with the problem of efficiency by valuing all capital in terms of new capital" (Lutz and Hague, 1960: 314). His treatment of depreciation seems to be dealing with mortality or accident as in the Walrasian insurance premium case (ibid.: 314). His income article, though, did not address the problem of measuring capital. The model avoided the "heterogeneity of capital goods. He had been able, with his methods, to avoid the problem of whether one was dealing with four- or five-year-old cars, or with different qualities of land as in Ricardo's theory" (ibid.: 315).

In his milestone article of 1962, Samuelson wanted to show that the surrogate production function, represented by a $w - r$ frontier, can be derived from heterogeneous capital goods as well as from an aggregate homogenous capital goods (Ferguson, 1972: 169). If we start with a heterogeneous set of capital-goods, each associated with labor, then "one need never speak of the production function, but rather should speak of a great number of separate production functions, which correspond to each activity and which and have no smooth substitutability properties" (Samuelson, 1966: vol. 1, 326). These have a linear programming-like structure that Samuelson explored in a book with others (Dorfman, Samuelson, and Solow, 1958), and in an independent piece on the subject (Samuelson, 1966: vol. 1, 287-298).

In general production has two sectors, one producing consumption goods, and one producing capital goods: A). $P_k = {}_{ak}W + b_k(r + \delta)P_k$, where the p is price, W is wage, r is the interest rate, δ is depreciation, k is the capital sector, a and b are labor requirements per unit of output, and B). $P_c = {}_{ac}W + bc(r + \delta)P_c$. Given the rate of interest, we can find the wage rate, and vice versa. One method to solve for them is to eliminate prices in each equation and then set the results equal to each other. The linearity comes out if we assume with Samuelson that $a_k = a_c$; $b_k = b_c$, for then we get $W/P_c = [1 - b_k(r + \delta)]/a_k$, which is a line (Samuelson, 1966: vol. 1, 337).

In stationary or steady state condition, a tradeoff frontier between wage and profit emerges. For a certain rate and wage level, we get a point on the $w - r$ frontier. The slope will be constant for a fixed proportion of labor and capital, yielding a straight line. Many such relationships exist for the various capital goods, yielding many negatively sloped straight lines in the $w - r$ plane.

If we parametize the coordinates of these points to time, we will find that the more roundabout a production process is, the steeper its $w - r$ frontier will be. This is because one process will be used at a much higher interest or profit rate in preference to another. As the interest rate is lowered, society will consider using one process rather than the other. This way, an envelope of all the straight lines will be formed, representing a piece-wise linear factor-price frontier. Samuelson wants to demonstrate that even in the "discrete-activity fixed-coefficient model of heterogeneous physical capital goods, the factor price (wage and interest rate) can still be given various long-run marginalism (i.e., partial derivative) interpretations" (ibid.: 322). P. Garegnani has shown that if we make the parameters of A) and B) defined for an interval in which the value of the functions are positive, then the curves will have a "smooth" envelope enclosing them (Garegnani, 1970: 412). This continuous feature makes a good comparison for a smooth frontier derived from the Clark-Ramsey model.

Samuelson then used the Clark-Ramsey homogenous capital model to approximate the $w-r$ of the discrete heterogeneous capital model. Let output depend on labor and capital: $Q = F(L, J)$. If the function is homogenous, we can factor out an input, yielding: $Q = LF(1, J/L)$. In equilibrium, $w = \partial Q/\partial L$, and $r = \partial Q / \partial J$. Taking their derivatives, and forming the ratio yields: $dw / dr = -(J / L)$, the slope of the frontier. The heterogeneous discrete capital case for deriving $w-r$ can be made arbitrary close to approximate the homogenous smooth capital case of deriving $w-r$.

Table 1 below shows a side-by-side comparison of the main results for the discrete versus the smooth models as they are presented in the literature (Ferguson, 1969: 253-257). Rows 4 and 5 indicate that the factor price frontier and the relative factor shares are the same in each case, respectively. We have made the special assumption in the discrete case that the frontier is a straight line, which is like to Karl Marx's assumption that the organic composition of capital is uniform across industries (Harcourt, 1972: 145). Dropping that assumption makes the frontier non-linear, and the second derivative of the frontier will be positive or negative depending on whether the capital-goods sector is labor-intensive or capital-intensive relative to the consumption goods sector (Ferguson, 1972: 262).

In his 1966 article, "A Summing Up," Samuelson wrote, "The fact of possible reswitching teaches us to suspect the simplest neoclassical parables" (Samuelson, 1972: vol. 3, 236). Reswitching is a situation where one technique is feasible at two different levels of the rate of interest. It can occur if two

TABLE 1: Smooth vs. Discrete Factor Price Frontier

Smooth Ramsey-Clark Model	Smooth Implication	Discrete Fixed Proportion Model	Discrete Implication
1. Q = F(K,L)	q = f(k) Per Capita form	1*a*. $M = C = \min\left(\frac{K}{a_K}.\frac{L}{a_L}\right)$	Fixed proportion function
2. W = f (k) – kf′ (f)	$\frac{dw}{dk} = -kf''(k)$	2*a*. $w = \frac{1}{a_L} - \frac{a_K}{a_L} r$	$\frac{dw}{dr} = -\frac{a_K}{a_L}$
3. · = f′ (k)	$\frac{dr}{dk} = f''(k)$	3*a*. $r = \frac{1}{a_K} - \frac{a_L}{a_K} w$	$\frac{dr}{dw} = -\frac{a_L}{a_K}$
4. $\frac{dw}{dr} = -kf''(k) / f''(k) = -k$	Factor Price Ratio	4*a*. $-\frac{dw}{dr} = \frac{a_K}{a_L} \div \frac{a_L}{a_K} = \frac{K}{L}$	Factor Price Ratio
5. $-\frac{r}{w}\frac{dw}{dr} = \frac{r}{w}k = \frac{rK}{wL}$	Relative Shares	5*a*. $\frac{r}{w}\frac{dw}{dr} = \frac{rK}{wL}$	Relative Shares

M is machines (capital goods). Source: Ferguson, 1969: 253-257.

frontiers intersect. Both Samuelson (ibid.: vol. 4, 136) and L. Pasinetti (2006: 151) point to Pierro Sraffa's work as fundamental to the origin of the reswitching debate. According to Pasinetti, the basic conclusion of the debate ends with Samuelson's admission that reswitching is possible (ibid.: 152).

In capital theory, Samuelson and Modigliani have worked on an "anti-Pasinetti" theorem, which holds that rate of profit is independent of the consumer propensity to save (Samuelson, 1972: vol. 3, 187-229). According to the Pasinetti theorem, the equilibrium rate of profit is determined by the natural rate of growth divide by the capitalists' propensity to save, independently of anything else in the model (Pasinetti, 1962: 276). Samuelson and Modigliani have proposed a dual to the Pasinetti primal theorem. While the primal theorem emphasized the capitalists' propensity to save, the dual theorem emphasizes the workers' propensity to save. The primal theorem relates to the profit-capital ratio; the dual theorem, the output-capital ratio, also referred to as the inverse of the naïve accelerator, or the average product of capital. We have developed this theory elsewhere (Ramrattan and Szenberg, 2007). Suffice to say that Pasinetti's view is in line with Robinson's argument that the profit rate is pivotal in the Cambridge controversy debate.

Samuelson's GE Approach to Trade Theory

Samuelson has made major contributions to trade theory. During his lifetime, his name was permanently appended to the Heckscher-Ohlin (HO) extension of the Ricardian comparative advantage theory for "adding substantial rigor to the analysis and expanded the original Heckscher-Ohlin model" (Applyard, IESS, 2007: vol. 2, 444). Sometimes, the honorific title "Ohlin Samuelson, or Ohlin-Learner-Samuelson theory" is used (de Marchi, 1976: 110).

At the outset, Samuelson acknowledged that some parts of his theory were foreshadowed by Abba Lerner (Lerner, 1953: 67). Both writers were influenced by Jacob Viner. Neil De Marchi's conversation with Lerner revealed that Viner had delivered a lecture at "LSE in 1931, in which he made use of the notions of opportunity cost and of consumer preferences in the form of transformation and indifference curves, to illustrate trade equilibrium" (De Marchi, 1976: 115). Samuelson, on the other hand, was a student of Viner. "Viner was my teacher," he wrote (Samuelson, 1977: vol. 4, 908), and his method was Socratic, an overhaul of Viner's teacher, Frank Tussig. Viner's major contributions to trade are his *Studies* (1937) and his *Lectures* (1953). Samuelson recalled that in his first lecture, Viner introduced continuum equilibrium, using the analogy of a balanced aquarium. He learned that calculus was a prerequisite for indifference and production possibility curve analysis. He wanted to elevate trade theory from its strong reliance on intuition to a more to a more theoretical level, where "the theorems are true consequences of the premises, and do not rest on *presumption* or *probability*" (Samuelson, 1966: vol. 2, 791) [italics original].

Samuelson put the production possibility and indifference curves to work in a general equilibrium framework. He kept that framework in focus through his works on trade, but has integrated his unique apparati, such as the revealed preference theory he discovered. Frank Hahn, leading GE theorist, underscored this view: "Samuelson's 1953 paper is a landmark in the integration of the international trade and general equilibrium theory" (Hahn, 1983: 44). He stated: "Samuelson made much of international trade theory an integral part of general equilibrium theory. By so doing he not only advanced the former but also advanced the latter" (ibid.: 48). One consequence of this approach was the concern with "conditions governing the existence, uniqueness and stability of general competitive equilibrium" (De Marchi, 1976: 112-113).

Another concern with Samuelson's General Equilibrium approach was its reversal of the traditional approach to trade theory. According to Paul Krugman, Samuelson's approach reversed the traditional approach to trade theory that worked from autarky to trade (Krugman, 1995: 1245). Samuelson divulged this foresight of GE in what is now termed his angel's parable:

> Let us suppose that in the beginning all factors were perfectly mobile and nationalism had not yet reared its ugly head. . . . [T]here would be one world price of food and clothing, one real wage, one real rent, and the world's land and labor would be divided between food and clothing production in a determinate way. . . . Now suppose that an angel came down from heaven and notified some fraction of all the labour and land units producing clothing that they were to be called Americans, the rest to be called Europeans; and some different fraction of the food industry that henceforth they were to carry American passports. Obviously, just giving people and areas national labels does not alter anything: it does not change commodity or factor prices or production patterns. But now turn a recording geographer loose, and what will he report? Two countries with quite different factor proportions,

but with identical wages and rents and identical modes of commodity production. (Samuelson, 1966: vol. 2, 882)

This parable served as a springboard for the later development of integrated trade theory, which is achieved in a world economy without boundaries (Krugman, 1995: 1244).

Samuelson's scientific approach to trade theory started with a hypothesis on gains from trade he laid out in 1938, an attempt to use numbers to validate and find a possible counter example in his 1939 paper, a problem with the prediction of the model in his Stolper-Samuelson model in 1941, and proof of the propositions he made in the late and early 1940s.

Samuelson's 1938 Paper

Samuelson developed his trade theories in a series of articles. His presentations have regular and unusual elements. In his 1938 paper (Samuelson, 1966: vol. 2, Item 60), the regular parts of trade theory he discussed involve the use of indifference and transformation curves. But already, he was using unusual elements of reveal preferences and GE. He made the first move by laying out the usual assumptions, assuming given taste and technology, one person or one country model, two goods (x, y), and two amount of productive services (a, b). Given b, a, and y, we can find the maximum amount of x that is produced. Given b, a, and x, we can find the maximum amount of y that is produced. The general representation is: $\varphi\ (x, y, a, b) = 0$. Now we can we can get the PPC by setting values for a and b, solving for y = f(x). To get the indifference, assign values for x and y, solving for b = f(a). The equilibrium condition for each country under autarky occurs at the tangency of these curves for their respective country. In this paper, Samuelson was not able to demonstrate that free or freer trade in some cases is better than all other kinds of trade. For gains from trade to take place in this model, a person or country can perform with less productive services (a, b) in trade, forgoing one commodity for another (x, y) to attain a higher indifference curve, or one gain by moving to a higher position on its preference scale at the expense of the other. The argument for gains from trade is inclusive because we need a welfare utility function to measure gain or losses. Samuelson concluded that "it is demonstrable that free trade (pure competition) leads to an equilibrium in which each country is better off than in the absence of trade. . . .

Nevertheless, this does not prove that each country is better off than under any other kind of trade; indeed, if all other are free trading, it always pays a single country not to trade freely" (Samuelson, 1966: vol. 2, 775).

Samuelson's 1939 Paper

The objective in his 1939 paper was to refine the conclusion of the 1938 paper to show that "*free* trade or some trade is to be preferred to *no* trade at all" (Samelson, 1966: vol. 2, 781). The theorem investigated was stated as follows:

> Samuelson Theorem I. (1939):"*the introduction of outside (relative) prices differing from those which would be established in our economy in isolation will result in some trade, and as a result every individual will be better off than he would be at the prices which prevailed in the isolated state.*" (ibid.: 786 [italics original])

Samuelson tried to find counterexamples for this theorem. He asked if there are any numbers for which the theorem is true. Using number for prices, *p*, and quantities, *q*, three commodities, and two factors prices, *w*, and factor quantities, *a*, he studied four scenarios or cases. The cases were used to validate the hypothesis that

$$\sum p'\overline{x}' - \sum w'a' \geq \sum p'\overline{x} - \sum w'a \tag{1}$$

$$s.t. \qquad \sum px = \sum p\overline{x} \tag{2}$$

Where the prime indicate preassigned prices and quantities, and the bar indicate optimal values. The summation runs over *n*, commodities, and *s*, factors. The "subject to" condition of Equation 2 requires that exports must be equal to imports. Trade is introduced as the existence of "an outside market in which there prevail certain arbitrarily established (relative) prices at which this country can buy or sell various commodities in unlimited amounts without changing those quoted prices" (Samuelson, 1966: vol. 2, 784-785).

As a first step in traditional proofs, Samuelson tried to put numbers into Equations 1 and 2 to find out how Theorem I would predict. Case I deals with autarky. It uses matching data for prices, consumption, and production for the three commodities. Cases II-IV use the same output number, but varying demand. All cases show varying factor prices and quantities. The conclusion is that "If at the primed set of price the individual would have bought the original combination of good $[X^0]$, and provided the original amounts of productive services $[A^0]$, the total algebraic cost would have been less than that of what he actually bought and sold $[X', A']$... it must necessarily follow from our inequality that $[X', A']$ is better than $[X^0, A^0]$. Thus our theorem is proved" (ibid.: 788-789].

The results will change if all individuals are not alike in preference and endowment. "Although it cannot be shown that every individual *is* made better off by the introduction of trade, it can be show that through trade ever individual *could* be made better off [or in the limiting case, no worse off]" (ibid.: 790) [italics original]. In Case I, the numbers show that, and that "trade may help some people and hurt other[s] . . . trade lovers are theoretically able to compensate trade haters for the harm done them, thereby making everyone better off" (ibid.: 795).

Samuelson's 1941 Paper

With his 1938 and 1939 papers, Samuelson was committed to the free trade doctrine. He even announced that proofs were forthcoming. In those regards, his Royal Economic Society, November 1941 piece with Wolfgang F. Stolper was a moment of pause. It is said that Samuelson delayed the publication of this paper. After all, the "argument seems to have relevance to the American discussion of protection versus free trade . . . labor is the relatively scarce factor in the American economy, it would appear that trade would necessarily lower the relative position of the laboring class as compared to owners of other factors of production" (ibid.: 832)

The purpose of this 1941 paper is to show "a special relationship between commodity and factor prices, namely, that an increase in the price of a commodity will bring about a more than proportionate increase in the price of the corresponding 'intensive' factor" (Chipman, 1969: 399). Usually, commodity prices are usually determined in the world market, and factor prices determined locally; but the theory applies also to when factors are traded internationally and goods are not. In the main, the mapping relates prices determined in the world market to prices determined locally.

The Stolper-Samuelson Model

The assumptions of the model are perfect competition, two countries, I and II, two homogenous goods, wheat (A), and watches (B), relative prices, P_a / P_b, two fixed factors, labor (L) and capital (C), fully employed with perfect factor mobility and the same production function (Samuelson, 1966: vol. 2, 835). Four additional assumptions—two relating to the HO model and two for case studies—are presumed.

1. Capital is abundant and labor is scarce;
2. Capital is more important in the production of wheat (A) than in the production of watches (B);
3. Capital is relatively more important in wheat (A) as the wage good;
4. Capital is relatively more important in watches (B) as the wage good. (Ibid.: 838)

The equations provided are:

$$L_a + L_b = L \tag{1}$$

$$C_a + C_b = C \tag{2}$$

$$A = A(L_a, C_a) \tag{3}$$

$$B = B(L_b, C_b) \tag{4}$$

Where the subscripts of the factors indicate the amount required to produce goods, wheat (A) or watches (B).

Prediction of the Stolper-Samuelson Model

Two propositions are explicitly stated in the form that "the introduction of trade lowers the proportion of capital to labor in each line and the prohibition of trade, as by a tariff, necessarily raises the proportion of capital to labor in each industry" (ibid.: 841). These have the consequence that 1). trade will lower the real wage of the scarce factor of production, and 2). protection will increase the real wage of the scarce factor of production. Jagdish Bhagwati summarized the literature under a third assumption, namely that factor intensity of import also matters, due to the works of Lloyd Metzler and Kelvin Lancaster, as summarized by Bhagwati (1983: vol. 1, 151).

A recent review by Alan Deardorff highlighted propositions 1) and 2) as forming the essential Stolper-Samuelson model (Deardorff, 1994: 12). John Chipman is credited with a "Weak Version," that is concerned with only factors that gain from a price increase, and a "Strong Version," that is concerned not only with factors that gain, but also with those that lose consequent to a price increase. Another characterization comes under the "Friends and Enemies Version," where "every good is a friend to some factor and an enemy to some other factor" (ibid.: 16). Yet another characterization is a "Correlated Version," which correlates a vector of goods prices, a vector of factor prices, and a matrix of factor requirement (ibid.: 18).

To determine the predictions of the model, we need to solve a consistent set of equations for their unknowns. Given the production functions above, equilibrium conditions require that the factor prices equal their marginal productivities. Since we assumed that the production functions for the two goods were the same, instead of writing two equations for labor, i.e., a wage rate equation each for wheat and watches, we can write one wage rate equation for labor, namely $w = P_a \partial A / \partial L_a = P_b \partial A / \partial L_b$. We can apply a similar reason for capital. Instead of writing two separate equations for the return on capital in each industry, we can write one equation for the return on capital, namely $r = P_a \partial A / \partial L_a = P_b \partial A / \partial L_b$. Along with the four equations above, we now have eight equations for the production side of the economy. We need equations on the demand side to close the system and to have a solution. We can add at least two more equations, one representing the demand for wheat and the other representing the demand for watches. With ten equations at hand, one is redundant according to Walras's law, leaving nine independent equations to solve for nine variables—two for quantity of labor in each industry, two quantities for capital used in each industry, total amount of watches and wheat, the real wage rate, the real return on capital, and the relative price of the two goods (Burmeister and Dorbell, 1970: Ch. 4; Takayama, 1972: 47).

Samuelson next examined the system through the Edgeworth-Bowley box, with the height represents Equation 1, the breath represents Equation 2, and isoquants are derived from Equations 3 and 4. In Figure 1, the southwest corner of the box represents production of wheat *A* and the northeast corner represents the production of watches *B*. The contract curve joining those two corners can be derived from the Lagrange function constraining the production of wheat *A*, by given amounts of watches $\bar{B}$. In equation form, maximize the function: $L = A(L_a, C_a) + \gamma[B(\bar{L} - L_a, \bar{C} - C_a) - \bar{B}]$, where the γ is the Lagrange multiplier (see Ferguson, 1962: 100). The way the box is constructed, the production of wheat, *A*, is assumed to be more capital-intensive that the

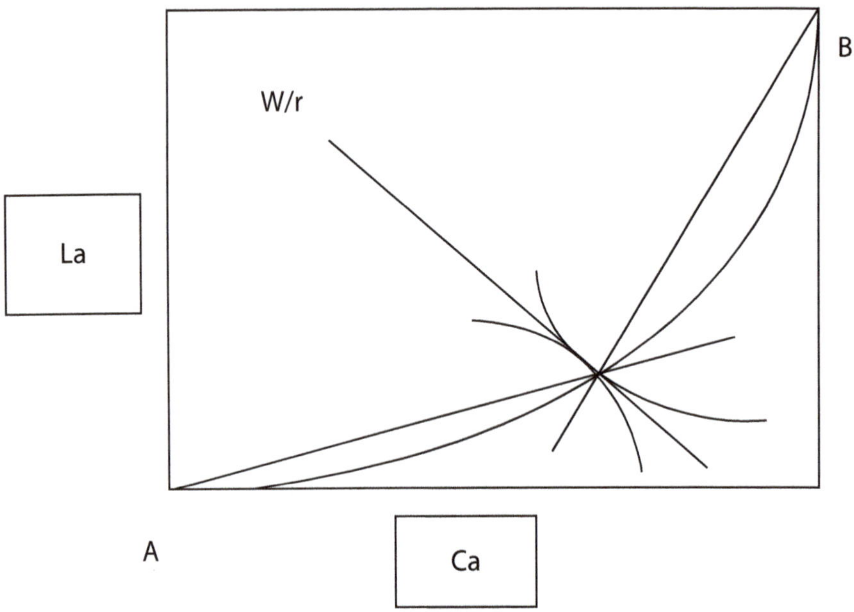

Figure 1 Edgeworth-Bowley Box.

production of watches, *B*, therefore, the curve bellies below the southwest to northeast diagonal. Points such as where the two straight lines from the origins intersect indicate no-trade, which we can call M.

The Case of Trade to No-trade

A higher point than M on the contract curve indicated, for example N, would represent trade. Movement from trade, N, to no-trade, M, is done through protections such as tariffs. It would make both industries, wheat (A) and watches (B), use more capital than labor, as the angle of the straight line with respect to the horizontal would be larger in Figure 1. More capital implies increased productivity for labor, the scarce factor. This means that the real wage to the worker will increase in terms of either the wage-good wheat, the wage-good watches, or a combination of both (Lancaster, 1957: 201).

But the theory argues that the real wage rate for the scarce factor should fall. By assumption b) of the model, the country is capital abundant. In conjunction with assumption 1), which lets wheat (A) be capital-intensive industry, there will be a tendency to expand the output of wheat (A) and contract the output of watches (B). This is achieved by transferring capital and labor from watch (B) production to wheat (A) production. The key point is that not enough capital will be transferred to employ all the labor released in the watch (B) industry because wheat production is more capital-intensive than watch production. For full employment of all the labor in the economy, therefore, the real wage of the scarce factor has to fall (Samuelson, 1966: vol. 2, 838).

A restriction of the argument is that as more capital-intensive output of wheat will be produced, some will be exported. Similarly, as less watches will be produced, some will be imported. Workers are paid by a wage-good by assumptions 1) and 2). If wheat (A) is the wage-good, then the workers receive wheat as payments, or if given watches (B), will exchange them for wheat as payment. When wheat is the wage-good, the net wheat imports = (labor force) x (marginal product of labor in wheat) – (production of wheat), or $I_a = L.MPL_a - A$. When watches are the wage-good, only capitalists will demand watches, so the Net Wheat import has to be re-written as $I'_b = L.MPC_b - B$. These two import constraints set break-even points for which the Stolper-Samuelson theorem holds. Using these two definitions of imports, Lancaster reached the conclusion that "*protection will raise the real wage of labour if, and only if, the country imports the labour intensive good*" (Lancaster, 1957: 209 [italics original]).

What is visible in the box corresponds with the algebra. Samuelson equates the overall $C / L = \bar{k}$ to a weighted average of the $C_a / L_a = k_a$ for the wheat industry, and $C_b / L_b = k_b$ for the watch industry. The weights are the labor share for the wheat and watch industry, i.e., $L_a / (L_a + L_a) == \lambda_a$, $L_b/(L_b + L_b) == \lambda_b$, respectively. We therefore have

$$\lambda_a k_a + \lambda_b k_b = \bar{k} \quad (5)$$

Akira Takayama has stated and proved the following lemma about Equation 5 (Takayama, 1972: 47-52):

> Lemma 1: *If* $k_a \gtreqless k_b$ *then* $\lambda_a \lesseqgtr \lambda_b$. The relationship predicts that if capital/labor in A is greater than in B, then the labor share in A is less than in B, and vice versa.
>
> Lemma 2: $d(p_a/p_b)/(p_a/p_b) = [\lambda_a - \lambda_b].[d(w / r) / (w / r)]$. This predicts that the percent change in the ratio of the factor prices will affect the

percentage change in the relative price of commodities through the differences of their labor share.

Lemma 3: The marginal product of capital increase in each industry as capital becomes more expensive than labor. In symbols, this lemma is expressed as follows:

$$d(r/p_a)/(r/p_a) = -\lambda_a \cdot [d(w/r)/(w/r)] \text{ and}$$
$$d(r/p_b)/(r/p_b) = -\lambda_b \cdot [d(w/r)/(w/r)]$$

Lemma 4: The factor price ratio, w/r, increases monotonically with the factor intensity, k_a and k_b.

Although Takayama developed a fifth lemma of his own that would help to solve the Stolper-Samuelson theorem, he resorted to the Edgeworth-Bowley box to illustrate the proof (ibid.: 94-96). We pick the story up from the argument that movement from trade to protection will use more capital in each industry, which translates to the argument that both k_a and k_b will rise for the two industries, with total capital and labor for the economy, $\bar{k}$, fixed. By lemma 4, the w/r will increase monotonically as k_a and k_b intensify. Now three critical phases of the proof are important in the two goods and two factors (2×2) case. First, protection on the imported goods will increase the price of imports in relation to exports at home. This is a juncture where several counteracting tendencies for prices to increase may occur, such as foreign retaliation to the protection. Second, the imported goods use the scarce factor intensively. Third, a rise in the price of the imported goods will increase the return to the scarce factor (ibid.: 562). For the 2×2, Samuelson argued that either the share of labor in the scarce factor industry, λ_a, or the share of labor in the abundant factor industry, λ_b, must be lowered. As not enough capital will be transferred to the capital-intensive wheat industry, the scarce factor share λ_b would be lowered (Samuelson, 1966: vol. 2, 838). This does not hold true in general, however, as the next section shows.

Samuelson's 1948, 1949, 1953, and 1967 Papers

The purpose of the 1948 paper is to probe the proof of Ohlin's partial equalization theorem that "(1) *free mobility of commodities in international trade can serve as a partial substitute for factor mobility* and (2) *will lead to a partial equalization of relative (and absolute) factor prices*" (ibid.: 847 [italics original]). Samuelson enunciated four propositions, of which the first two are proved, and the latter two are derived. The two main propositions are:

1. Given partial specialization and each country producing some of the two goods, factor price will be equalized, absolutely and relatively, by free trade.
2. If factor endowment are not too unequal, commodity mobility will always substitute perfectly for factor mobility. (ibid.: 853)

In his 1949 paper, Samuelson admitted that his 1948 paper, in which he argued that "free commodity trade will, under specified conditions, inevitable lead to complete factor-price equalization," was in need of further amplification (ibid.: 869). In the 1948 paper, he gave a relationship between wage/rent to the labor/land ratio that was tied to two countries, Europe and the US (Samuelson, 1969: 857). In 1949, he added a wage/rent to commodity price ratio (Samuelson, 1966: vol. 2, 876), and used a more integrated model, treating the world as a country.

Figure 2 below is an abridged diagram of Samuelson's 1949 paper, representing a generalization of the Stolper-Samuelson theorem. L is for labor, T is for land, C is for clothing, F is for food, w is the wage rate, r is rent, and P is commodity prices. Clothing is labor-intensive, and food is land-intensive.

This 1949-based Figure 2 incorporates Quadrant I of his 1948 paper side-by-side with the new diagram in Quadrant II showing the relationship of factor prices to commodity prices. We enter the diagram with the distance OM, which has a similar weighted average interpretation as Equation 5 above, where the commodities are clothing and food, and the factors are labor and land (ibid.: 858). The distance OM is a new expression for Equation 5 involving the following terms:

$$OM = \frac{\textit{total labor}}{\textit{total land}} = \frac{\textit{food land}}{\textit{total land}} \cdot \frac{\textit{food labor}}{\textit{food land}} + \frac{\textit{clothing land}}{\textit{total land}} \cdot \frac{\textit{clothing labor}}{\textit{clothing land}} \qquad (5')$$

Figure 2 indicates that OM can range between M' and M''. In between those points, both commodities, food and clothing, will be produced, marking the case of incomplete specialization. Outside of that range, only one commodity will be produced in each country, implying complete specialization.

The QQ line in Figure 2 represents a situation where the wage/rent ratio is the same for both industries. This underscores that the factor proportion will have to be the same in both industries. If the factor price ratios were not equal, we would have to draw two such lines, QQ and Q'Q' (not shown), which would represent different factor price ratios and different factor proportions. The different factor mix will result in different marginal productivities, which in equilibrium will yield different factor prices. With equal factor prices, however, we will have equal factor proportion in the first quadrant, corresponding to a unique commodity price ratio in the second quadrant. Samuelson summarized his 1949 paper with the finding that

> *Within any country: (a) an increase in the ratio of wages to rents will cause a define decrease in the proportion of labor to land in both industries; (b) to each determinate state of factor proportion in the two industries there will correspond one, and only one, commodity price ratio and a unique configuration of wages and rent; and (c) the change in factor proportions incident to an increase in wage/rents must be followed by a one-directional increase in clothing prices relative to food prices.* (Ibid.: 875 [italics original])

The rest of the 1949 paper lays out the mathematics behind Figure 2. Food and clothing are made homogenous functions of the inputs labor and land, $F = T_f f\,(L_f/T_f)$ and $C = T_c\, c\,(L_c/T_c)$ respectively. Partial derivatives for the marginal physical products for 1) labor in food, 2) land in food, 3) labor in clothing, and 4) land in clothing are taken. These marginal productivities are

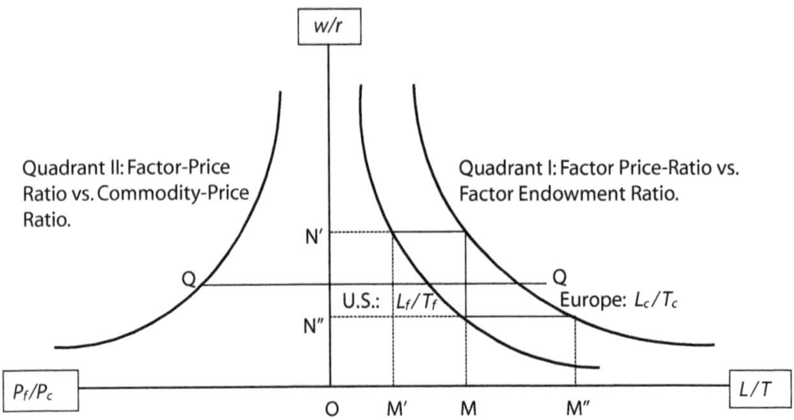

Figure 2 Factor-Price Ratio vs. Commodity-Price Ratio and Factor Endowment Ratio.

converted into values by multiplying by their respective prices. The values of labor in food and clothing industries are equated to form one equation. The values of land in both industries are then equated to form a second equation. We now have two equations with three variables. From Figure 2, the variables are L_c/T_c, L_f/T_f, and P_f/P_c. Given prices, we can then solve for the other two variables.

To solve the 2 × 2 system described above, Samuelson looked for a condition on the determinants to guarantee a solution. The condition is that the determinant of the Jacobian must not vanish. Technically, the Jacobian matrix is derived from a set of differentiable functions. Given a set of equations: $y_1 = 5x_2$ and $y_2 = x_1x_2$. The determinant of the Jacobian matrix can be written as:

$$Det[J(x)] = Det\begin{vmatrix} \partial y_1/\partial x_1 & \partial y_1/\partial x_2 \\ \partial y_2/\partial x_1 & \partial y_2/\partial x_2 \end{vmatrix} = \det\begin{vmatrix} 0 & 5 \\ x_2 & x_1 \end{vmatrix} = -5x_2 \qquad (6)$$

If the determinant of the Jacobian is zero, then the two equations are dependent, and no solution exists for the system. If the determinant is not equal to zero, then the equations are independent, meaning that we can solve for the unknown variables.

For Samuelson's 2 × 2 case, the determinant is derived from the commodity price ratio, the second derivative of the two homogenous production functions, and the differences in factor intensities. The following equation shows the Jacobian and its determinant for the Samuelson's 2 × 2 case:

$$\Delta = \begin{vmatrix} \frac{P_f}{P_c} f'' & -c'' \\ -\frac{P_f}{P_c}\frac{L_f}{T_f} f'' & +\frac{L_c}{T_c} c'' \end{vmatrix} = \frac{P_f}{P_c} f''c'' \left[\frac{L_c}{T_c} - \frac{L_f}{T_f} \right] \qquad (6')$$

In Equation 6', the f'' and c'' are the second derivatives of the food and clothing production functions, respectively, which will be negative because of production functions with diminishing returns. Prices and quantities are positive, and clothing is more labor-intensive, which makes the square bracket items positive. Because the Jacobian determinant did not vanish, Samuelson therefore concludes that the "equilibrium is unique" (ibid.: 880).

In his 1953 article, however, Samuelson recognized Alan Turing for informing him that the condition is not true "in the large" or globally (ibid.: 909). Global conditions are more complicated than local conditions. Local conditions deal with the value of a function in the neighborhood of a point. Global conditions deal with the behavior of a function over the domain, say an interval. For instance, between two points, $b > a$ on the x-axis, a function can rise or fall many times with varying amplitudes. Locally, many maxima and minima may exist in the interval. Globally, over the whole interval $b - a$, only one highest peak or one lowest trough is likely to exist (Frisch, 1965: 4).

In the 1953 article, Samuelson began to address more general cases beyond the 2×2 trade model. This means that he had to look for global conditions to find unique solutions of relationships between commodity and factor prices. He started to relate these prices with equations of the following form (Samuelson, 1966: vol. 2, 903):

$$P_i = A^i\,(w_1 \dots w_r)\ and\ [\partial p_i / \partial w_j] = [a_{ij}] \qquad (7)$$

Where p is commodity price with $i = 1 \dots n$, w is factor price with $j = 1 \dots r$, and the coefficient, $a_{i,j}$, represents the required amount of input, j, to produce a unit of the a good, i (ibid.: 889-890).

Samuelson considered three cases in interpreting Equation 7.

Case (i): *Equal Goods and Factors* ($n = r$): This case deals with the situation where the number of factors and goods are equal, the $n \times n$ case. The conclusion is that "if two countries have the same production functions, and if they do produce in common as many different goods as there are factors, and if the goods differ in their 'factor intensities,' and if there are no barriers to trade to produce commodity price differentials, then the absolute returns of every factor must be fully equalized" (ibid.: 893).

Case (ii): *More Goods than Factors* ($n > r$): In this case, the number of factors is less than the number of goods. We have more commodity equations than factors to be determined. This may be called an overdetermined system. Samuelson argued that if prices are arbitrarily fixed, then certain industries will shut down, reducing Case (ii) to Case (i). If the market determines prices, however, r factor prices will adjust to the market price, and the $\boldsymbol{n} - \boldsymbol{r}$ prices will require factor endowment to be determined.

We can look at Case (ii) from the point of view of least-square problems in regression analysis where the number of observations is greater than coefficients to be determined.

In such a case, we get the best solution. As in this statistically overdetermined system, we project the observation onto a line, similarly we can imagine projecting the factor price space into the commodity price space. We can think of the price space as the four walls of a room, and the factor space as just one wall. The projection is therefore a projection of the w-space to a subspace of the p-space. This projection restricts the commodity space from its n-dimension, to be compatible with the r-dimension of the factor space.

Case (iii): *More Factors than Goods* $(n < r)$: This is an underdetermined system characterized by less equations than unknowns to be solved. Samuelson proposed adding an equation for endowments to enable a solution.

Solution for Case (i) where the number of commodity and goods prices is $(n = r)$.

Essentially, Equation 7 is a mapping between commodity prices and factor prices, namely:

$$f : p \rightarrow w \quad \text{or} \quad p_i = f_i(w) \tag{8}$$

If $J_f(w) = \partial f_i(w) / \partial w_j$, then we can find $w = f_j^{-1} p$ for $j = 1 \ldots n$ (McKenzie, 1967: 272).

For $n = r = 2$, the global association between wages and prices were kept in alignment by their factor intensity. For instance, we could argue that a rise in the price of goods that were produced by a labor-intensive technique will lead to an increase in the price of labor to produce those goods. The non-vanishing of the Jacobian determinant discussed in Equation 7 satisfied that factor intensity condition. But in the large, as Turing pointed out to Samuelson, the determinant of the Jacobian may not vanish. The reason for non-vanishing Jacobian determinants in the large includes the occurrence of factor-intensity reversal, but as Ivor Pearce put it, "A 3 x 3 determinant can easily be zero for a great many reasons totally unconnected with factor intensities" (Pearce, 1979: 496).

In 1953, Samuelson refocused attention on the Jacobian of the a_{ij} of Equation 7 to satisfy the inverse requirements of Equation 8. Samuelson wrote: "Fortunately, the economics of the situation was clearer than my mathematical analysis; because all the elements of the Jacobian represented inputs or *a*'s, they were essentially one-signed; and this condition combined with the non-vanishing determinant, turns out to be sufficient to guarantee uniqueness in the large" (Samuelson, 1966: vol. 2, 903). He proceeded to give sufficient conditions for a unique solution for the global case. First, renumber the *p*'s and *w*'s in differentiable Equation 7, such that the successive principal minor of the partial derivatives are non-vanishing for all *w*'s (ibid.: 903). To refresh the terminology, given an element of a matrix, a minor is a matrix formed by deleting the row and column that is associated with the given element (Strand, 1988: 226). Let A be an $m \times n$ matrix, where $i = 1,...,m$ and $j = 1,..,n$. If $i = j$, A_{ij} is called a principal minor. These minors always involve the successive members on the principal diagonal, which is the diagonal running from the northeast to the southwest. Equation 9 below lists all the principal minors for the 2×2 case.

$$D_1 = \frac{P_f}{P_c} f'', \quad D_2 = \begin{vmatrix} \frac{P_f}{P_c} f'' & -c'' \\ -\frac{P_f}{P_c}\frac{L_f}{T_f} f'' & +\frac{L_c}{T_c} c'' \end{vmatrix} \tag{9}$$

According to Kenneth Arrow and Frank Hahn (1971: 242), Samuelson's 1953 "proposition paid insufficient attention to the domain of the mappings" between the *p*'s and *w*'s of Equation 7. David Gale and Hukukane Nikaido provided a counter example to illustrate this point. Given a mapping by the equations $f(x, y) = e^{2x} - y^2 + 3$, and $g(x, y) = 4e^{2x}y - y^3$, then $D_1 = 2e^{2x}$, and $D_2 = 2e^{2x}(4e^{2x} + 5y^2)$, which are both positive. But for the domain points (0,2) and (0, –2), the functions are mapped to the origin, which is zero (Gale and Nikaido, 1965: 82).

Gale and Nikaido provided the domain element by arguing that "if all principal submatrices of the Jacobian matrix have positive determinants the mapping is univalent in any rectangular region" (ibid.: 68). Formally speaking, the Gale-Nikaido theorem can be stated as follows:

> Given a map $F : R^n \rightarrow R^n$. Let the domain of the map be rectangular, i.e., $\Omega = \{x \in R^n : p_i \leq x \leq q_i, (i = 1,2,\ldots,n)\}$. Let the components of the map in that

> domain, $F(x) = f_i(x)$ be differentiable (C^1), i.e. its total differential exists at each point x of Ω. Then the mapping $F: \Omega \rightarrow R^n$ is univalent (one-to-one) if the Jacobian matrix, $J(x)$, has strictly positive principal minors, strictly negative principal minors, or is positive quasi-definite everywhere in a convex set Ω.

In the Gale-Nakaido theorem, the Jacobian matrix is called a $P-$ *matrix*. Positive quasi-definite means that for each vector $x \neq 0$, $x'Ax > 0$. Univalence of the mapping means that for each element in the domain there be only one element (image) in the range. As a practical matter, one can test this concept in the plane by using a vertical line on the graph to see if the line cuts the graph at only one point. But function defined globally may not refer to a point on a graph, or find its extrema over the real numbers, or when we look for undefined points for each element in the domain.

Samuelson's postscript to his 1965 paper proceeded to accommodate Gale and Nikaido's findings through "a naturally ordered set of principal minors . . . everywhere in the Euclidean n-space, bordered by two positive numbers" (Samuelson, 1966: vol. 2, 908). What is new here is that the sequence of principal minors has determinants that are bounded away from zero. This condition was earlier foreshadowed by Lionel McKenzie's dominant diagonal (DD) matrix. McKenzie argued that "an $n \times n$ matrix A is said to have a dominant diagonal if $|a_{ij}| > \Sigma_{i \neq j} |a_{ij}|$ for each j" (McKenzie, 1960: 47). In simple terms, the DD condition states that in each row of the a_{ij} matrix, the main diagonal element must be greater than the sum of the other row elements when the comparison is in absolute values terms. A dominant diagonal "means that each good can be identified with a factor that is uniquely important in the production of that good" (ibid.. 54). Gale and Nikaido provided a P-matrix that includes the DD matrix as a special case. "If a matrix with dominant diagonal has positive diagonal entries, then it is a P-matrix" (Gale and Nikaido, 1965: 84).

One problem with the Gale-Nikaido theorem is that it is "over-sufficient." According to Pearce, "for each condition of a rectilinear region satisfying the Gale-Nikaido condition and hence possessing an inverse, it is possible to construct an infinity of mapping not satisfying the conditions which nevertheless posses an inverse also" (Pearce, 1970: 525). Andreu Mas-collel has given two propositions in the direction of weakening the strong assumptions on the univalence condition of the Gale-Nikaido theorem. His two propositions are considered generalizations of the Gale-Nikaido theorem discussed above. The two propositions are listed as follows (Mas-collel, 1979a: 1105).

> Proposition I (Samuelson-Nikaido-Mas-collel): The restriction on principal minor of the input share function, $\frac{w}{f^i(w)} \cdot \frac{\partial f^i(w)}{\partial w^j}$, is irrelevant; all that matters is that the determinant of the function be uniformly bounded away from zero in order to attain global univalence within the strictly positive orthant, R^l_{++}.
>
> Proposition II (Gale-Nikaido-Mascollel): The condition of the cost function within the R^l_+ domain can be weakened, based on the general C^1 function on a compact polyhedral. (Mascollell, 1979b: 324).

Following his 1965 postscript, Samuelson answered a question raised by Bhagwati regarding the difference between the rental rate on capital, and the interest rate, which is a capitalization of the rental rate on capital. Working with the equation that GNP = NNP + Depreciation, he rewrote the price-cost equation for each industry (capital goods, food, and clothing) as $p_i = a_i w + b_i r p_0 + m_i b_i p_0$, where the a's, b's, and m's are labor, capital, and depreciation coefficients respectively, and p_0 is the price of capital goods. Samuelson then proceeded to apply the method of his modified Gale-Nikaido ideas in his postscript to discuss the solution (Samuelson, 1966: vol. 2, 912-915). The result indicated that the rate of interest is inversely related, and the real wage directly related to the wage-rental ratio (ibid.: 916).

In 1967, Samuelson summarized the factor-price equalization literature. He also perused the development of the use of factor endowment to bring about a solution. The model was now converted to a maximization problem using Lagrange multipliers (Samuelson, 1972: vol. 3, 351). The Hessian matrix formed for the partials of the Lagrangian equations do not satisfy the Gale-Nikaido conditions. "But the fact that its principal minors formed from crossing out any $r < n^2$ of the first n^2 rows and columns are of the sign needed for the maximum suffices, I believe, to assure univalence of the equation set" (ibid.: 351).

Modern orthodox texts on international trade seem to accept the Stolper-Samuelson and factor-price equalization theorem, at least in its 2 × 2 form. The general approach seem to be to write price-cost equations for two sectors and solve them simultaneously. For two sectors, A and B, we can let the prices, capital, and labor be $P_a = P_b = 100$, $C_a = 10$, $L_a = 60$, $C_b = 25$, and $L_b = 75$. We then get two equations of the forms 1). $100 = 25r + 75w$, and 2). $100 = 40r + 60w$. 100, whose solutions yield: $r = w = 1$. Now, suppose the second equation represents the sector with the abundant factor experiencing an increase in its price to 110. Resolving the equations now yields: $r = 1.5$; $w = 0.83$, showing that the percent increase in interest exceeds the percent fall in wages.

Regarding the factor-price equalization theorem, Hicks considered two sets of equations for the two countries, namely, $ar + bw = ar' + bw'$, and $cr + dw = cr' + dw'$.

The prime is used to distinguish the equation for the other country. Simultanuous solution yields: $r' - r = \frac{b}{a}(w - w') = \frac{d}{c}(w - w')$, where the ratios indicate capital-intensities.

Since capital-intensities can differ, they can differ only if $w - w'$ is the same, and therefore, $r = r'$ (Hicks, 1983: 226). Hicks concluded that "the analysis which emerges does not sound to be so unrealistic. It sounds to me like ringing true" (ibid.: 233).

According to Ronald Findlay, although the factor-price model is also credited to Lerner, it was Samuelson who first introduced it to the economic profession (Findlay, 1995: 7). Findlay quoted a rare citation of Samuelson, stating that also pointed out another of Samuelson's novel contributions in regards to the H-O model as well, which is worth quoting in full:

> Already in 1924 Ohlin has melded Heckscher and Walras. But neither then, nor in 1933 and 1967, did Ohlin descend from full generality to strong and manageable cases—such as two factors of production and two or more goods. What a pity. Not only did Ohlin leave to my generation these easy pickings, but in addition he would for the first time have really understood his own system had he played with graphable versions. (ibid.: 7)

Microeconomics

Samuelson's major contribution to microeconomics is in the area of consumer choice. Traditional theory predicts a consumer choice from assumptions abut their taste and preference. Samuelson begins with the assumption of choice, i.e., let the consumer select one item over another. This has become the theory of "revealed preference" (Varian, 2006: 99). Preferences are deduced for the choices the consumer makes in the market place, based on commodity prices and the consumer's income, moving the analysis for the realm of the observable taste and preference to the world of observable choices.

In his original paper, Samuelson gave three postulates: 1) a single-value function on prices and income, subject to a budget constraint; 2) homogeneity of order zero so as to make consumer behavior independent of the units of measurement of prices. Given vectors of two goods, ψ and ψ', with their respective price vectors, p and p'. Forming their inner product yields: $[\psi p]$, and $[\psi' p'], [\psi' p']$, we can make another observation: 3) "If this cost $[\psi' p]$ is less than or equal to the actual expenditure in the first period when the first batch of goods $[\psi p]$ was actually bought, then it means that the individual could have purchased the second batch of goods with the price and income of the first situation, but did not choose to do so. That is, the first batch $[\psi]$ was selected instead of $[\psi']$" (Samuelson, 1966: vol. 2, 7).

In making choices, a consumer needs to be consistent. "If an individual selects batch one over batch two, he does not at the same time select two over one" (ibid.: 7). In a latter note, Samuelson compacts the first two propositions with the third: "Postulates 1 and 2 are already implied in postulate 3, and hence may be omitted" (ibid.: 13).

With those assumptions, Samuelson pronounced that "even within the framework of the ordinary utility- and indifference- curve assumptions, it is believed to be possible to derive already known theorems quickly, and also to suggest new sets of conditions. Furthermore . . . the transitions from individual to market demand functions are considerably expedited" (ibid.: 23). But the revealed preference theory matured into an even more powerful rival research paradigm.

In 1950, Samuelson wrote: "I suddenly realized that we could dispense with almost all notions of utility; starting from a few logical axioms of demand consistency; I could derive the whole of the valid utility analysis as corollaries" (Samuelson, 1966: vol. 1, 90). He proceeded to make the following axioms.

- Weak axiom: If at the price and income of situation A you could have bought the goods actually bought at a different point B and if you actually chose not to, then A is defined to be "revealed to be better than" B. The basic postulate is that B is never to reveal itself to be also "better than" A. (ibid.)
- Strong axiom: If A reveals itself to be "better than" B, and if B reveals itself to be "better than" C, and if C reveals itself to be "better than" D, etc. . . . then I extend the definition of "revealed preference" and say that A can be defined to be "revealed to be better than" Z, the last in the chain. In such cases it is postulated that Z must never also be revealed to be better than A. (ibid.: 90–91)

In 1953, Samuelson elevated the revealed preference theory to the empirical domain: "consumption theory does definitely have some refutable empirical implications" (ibid.: 106), or we can "score the theory of revealed preference" (ibid.). Samuelson required a benchmark to allow refutation/scoring, for which he postulated this fundamental theorem: "Any good (simple or composite) that is known always to increase in demand when money income alone rises must definitely shrink in demand when its price alone rises" (ibid.: 107). He then proceeded "to show that within the framework of the narrowest version of revealed preference the important fundamental theorem, stated above, can be directly demonstrated (a) in commonsense words, (b) in geometrical argument, (c) by general analytic proof" (ibid.: 108).

A modern mathematical economist has appraised the revealed preference theory as follows: "Instead of deriving demand in a given wealth-price situation from the preferences, considered as the primitive concept, one can take the demand function (correspondence) directly as the primitive concept. If the demand function *f* reveals a certain 'consistency' of choices . . . one can show that there exists a preference relation . . . which will give rise to the demand function *f*" (Hildenbrand, 1974: 95).

Conclusion

Many attempts to look at Samuelson's contribution to economics have only been able to pick on his findings. Writers pick the fruits of his erudition but ignore the tree that generated them. Elsewhere, we have considered various ways to know Samuelson by viewing his character. We have also looked at him as a Wunderkind, and what of his view will survive in the twenty-first century. Here, we went behind his major topical contribution to feel the depth of his thoughts, particularly in the areas of capital and trade, and to use a Newtonian expression, leaving the sea of his discovery for others to investigate.

This memoriam took a peek at some trunks of the tree, not exploring its many branches. We looked at trade because Samuelson thinks that it is the one theory that is true but cannot be proved. We looked at capital theory because has engaged some of the best minds in economics for the last half a century on the two sides of the Atlantic. Research into trade and capital theory are still ongoing, and also in the areas we have touched only tangentially, as well as area we did not touch. No one will doubt that from the touch of Samuelson's hand, economics has become highly transparent and knowledge elevated, more so in some areas than in others.

References

Arrow, K. J., & Hahn, F. H. (1971). *General competitive analysis.* San Francisco: Holden-Day, Inc.

Bhagwati, J. (1983). *Essays in international economic theory: The theory of commercial policy* (vol. I). R. C. Freenstra (Ed.). Cambridge, MA: MIT Press.

Burmeister, E., & Dorbell, A. R. (1970). *Mathematical theories of economic growth* (chapter 4). New York: The Macmillan Company.

Chipman, J. S. (1969, Oct.). Factor price equalization and the Stolper-Samuelson theorem. *International Economic Review,* 10(3), 399-406.

Cournot, A. (1963 [1838]). *Researches into the mathematical principles of the theory of wealth.* Homewood, IL: Richard D. Irwin, Inc.

Deardorff, A. V., & N. Stern, R. N. (Eds.). (1994). *The Stolper-Samuelson theorem: A golden jubilee.* Ann Arbor: The University of Michigan Press.

De Marchi, N. (1976). Anomaly and the development of economics. In S. Latsis (Ed.), *Method and appraisal in economics* (109-127). Cambridge: Cambridge Unversity Press.

Dorfman, R., Samuelson, P. A., & Solow, R. M. (1958). *Linear programming and economic analysis.* New York: Dover Publication, Inc.

Ferguson, C. E. (1962, Oct.). Transformation curve in production theory: A pedagogical note. *Southern Economic Journal*, 29(2), 96-102.

———. (1975). *The neoclassical theory of production and distribution*. New York: Cambridge University Press.

Findlay, R. (1995). *Factor proportions, trade, and growth*. Cambridge, MA: MIT Press.

Frisch, R. (1966). *Maxima and minima: Theory and economic applications*. In collaboration with A. Nataf. Chicago: Rand McNally and Company.

Gale, D., & Nikaido, H. (1965). The Jacobian matrix and global univalence of mappings. In *Mathematische Annalen* (68-80); reprinted in P. Newman (Ed.), *Readings in Mathematical Economics* (81-93). Baltimore, MD: Johns Hopkins University Press.

Gandolfo, G. (1994). *International economics I: The pure theory of international trade* (2nd ed.). New York: Springer-Verlag.

Harcourt, G. C. (1972). *Some Cambridge controversies in the theory of capital*. Cambridge: Cambridge University Press.

Hayek, F. A. (1992). *Collected works* (vol. 4). Chicago: University of Chicago Press.

Hicks, J. (1983). *Collected essays on economic theory: Classics and moderns* (vol. III). Cambridge, MA: Harvard University Press.

Hildenbrand, W. (1974). *Core and equilibria of a large economy*. Princeton: Princeton University Press.

Krauss, M. B., & Johnson, H. G. (1974). *General equilibrium analysis*. London: George Allen and Unwin Ltd.

Krugman, P. (1995). Increasing returns, imperfect competition and the positive theory of international trade. In G. M. Grossman & K. Rogoff (Eds.), *Handbook of international economics, volume 3* (1243-1277). Amsterdam: Elsevier.

Lancaster, K. (1957, Jun.). Protection and real wages: A restatement. *The Economic Journal*, 67(266), 199-210.

Lerner, A. (1953). Factor prices and international trade. In *Essays in Economic Analysis*, 67-84. London: Macmillan and Co. Ltd.

Lutz, F. A. "The Essentials of Capital Theory." In *The Theory of Capital*, edited by Friedrich Lutz and D. C. Hague, 3-17. New York: Macmillan and Co. Ltd., St. Martin's Press, 1961.

Marshall, A. (2003 [1923]). *Money, credit, and commerce.* New York: Prometheus Books.

———. (1996). *The correspondence of Alfred Marshall, Volume Three: Towards the close, 1903-1924.* J. K. Whitaker (Ed.). Cambridge: Cambridge University Press.

Mas-collel, A. (1985). *The theory of general economic equilibrium: A differentiable approach.* New York: Cambridge University Press.

———. (1979a, Nov.). Homeomorphism of compact, convex sets and the Jacobian matrix. *Siam Journal of Mathematical Analysis,* 10(6), 1105-1109.

———. (1979b). Two propositions on the global univalence of systems of cost functions. In J. Green & J. Scheinkman (Eds.), *General equilibrium growth and trade* (323-331). New York: Academic Press.

McKenzie, L. W. (1960). Matrices with dominant diagonals and economic theory. In K. J. Arrow, S. Karlin, & P. Suppes (Ed.), *Mathematical methods in the social sciences* (47-62). Stanford: Stanford University Press, 1960.

———. (1967, Oct.). The inversion of cost functions: A counter-example. *International Economic Review,* 8(3), 271-278.

Nell, E. J. (1967). Theories of growth and theories of value. *Economic Development and Cultural Change,* 16, 15-26.

Pasinetti, L. L. (2006). Paul Samuelson and Piero Sraffa: Two prodigious minds at the opposite poles. In M. Szenberg, L. Ramrattan, & A. A. Gottesman (Ed.), *Samuelsonian Economics and the twenty-first century* (146-164). New York: Oxford University Press.

———. (1962, Oct.). Rate of profit and income distribution in relation to the rate of economic growth. *The Review of Economic Studies,* 29(4), 267-279.

Pearce, I. F. (1970). *International trade: A survey of principles and problems of the international economy.* New York: W. W. Norton and Company, Inc.

Ramrattan, L., & Szenberg, M. (2007, Fall). Paul Samuelson and the dual Pasinetti theory. *The American Economist,* 2, 40-48.

Ramsey, F. P. (1928, Dec.). A mathematical theory of saving. *The Economic Journal,* 38(152), 543-559.

Robbins, L. (1937). *An essay on the nature and Significance of economics science.* London: Macmillan.

Robinson, J. (1971, Sept.). The measure of capital: The end of the controversy. *The Economic Journal*, 81(323), 597-602.

———. (1970, May). Capital theory up to date. *The Canadian Journal of Economics*, 3(2), 309-317.

Samuelson, P. A. (1966). *The collected scientific papers of Paul A. Samuelson* (vols. 1-2). J. E. Stiglitz (Ed.). Cambridge, MA: MIT Press.

———. (1986). *The collected scientific papers of Paul A. Samuelson* (vol. 3). R. C. Merton (Ed.). Cambridge, MA: MIT Press.

———. (1986). *The collected scientific papers of Paul A. Samuelson* (vol. 4). H. Nagatani & K. Crowley (Eds.). Cambridge, MA: MIT Press.

———. (1986). *The collected scientific papers of Paul A. Samuelson* (vol. 5). Kate Crowley (Ed.). Cambridge, MA: MIT Press.

———. (1974 [1947]). *Foundations of economic analysis.* Harvard Economic Studies vol. 80. New York: Atheneum.

———. (1992). My life philosophy: Policy credos and working ways. In M. Szenberg (Ed.), *Eminent economists* (236-247). New York and London: Cambridge University Press.

———. (1980). *Economics.* New York: McGraw Hill Book Company.

Samuelson, P. A., & Nordhaus, W. D. (1995). *Economics* (15th ed.). New York: McGraw Hill.

Smith, A. (2003). *The Wealth of Nations.* New York: Bantam Classics.

Solow, R. (2006). Overlapping-generation. In M. Szenberg, L. Ramrattan, & A. A. Gottesman (Eds.), *Samuelsonian economics and the twenty-first century* (35-41). New York: Oxford University Press.

Strang, G. (1988). *Linear algebra and its applications* (3rd revised ed.). Pacific Grove, CA: Brooks/Cole Pub Co.

Szenberg, M., & Ramrattan, Lall. (2006). *Paul A. Samuelson, dictionary of american economists.* Devon: Thoemmes Press.

Szenberg, M., Ramrattan, L. & Gottesman, A. A. (2005). Paul A. Samuelson: Philosopher and theorist. *International Journal of Social Economics*, 32(4), 325-338.

———. (2006). Ten ways to know Paul Samuelson. In M. Szenberg, L. Ramrattan, & A. A. Gottesman (Ed.), *Samuelsonian economics and the twenty-first century* (xxii-xxx). New York: Oxford University Press.

Szenberg, M., Ramrattan, L., & Gottesman, A. A. (Eds.). (2006). *Samuelson economics and the twenty-first century*. New York: Oxford University Press.

Szenberg, M., Gottesman, A. A., & Ramrattan, L. (2005). *On being an economist*. New York: Jorge Pinto Books.

Takayama, A. (1972). *International trade: An approach to the theory.* New York: Holt, Rinehart and Winston, Inc.

Varian, H. R. (2006). Revealed preference. In M. Szenberg, L. Ramrattan, & A. A. Gottesman (Eds.), *Samuelsonian economics and the twenty-first century* (99-115). New York: Oxford University Press.

Viner, Jacob. *Studies in the Theory of International Trade.* New York: Harper & Brothers Publishers, 1937.

———. *International Trade and Economic Development: Lectures Delivered at the National University of Brazil.* Oxford: Oxford at the Clarendon Press, 1953 [1964].

Walras, L. (1969 [1926]). *Elements of pure economics.* (W. Jaffe, Trans.). New York, Augustus M. Kelley.

Wan, H. Y., Jr. (1971). *Economic growth.* New York: Harcourt Brace Jovanovich.

Wicksell, K. (1934 [1911]). *Lectures on political economy* (vol. I). London: George Routledge & Sons,.

———. (1996). Letter to Alfred Marshall, June 1, 1905. In J. K. Whitaker (Ed.), *The correspondence of Alfred Marshall, Volume Three: Towards the close, 1903-1924* (102). New York: Cambridge University Press.

PART III

MONETARISTS

Milton Friedman

Milton Friedman

Introduction

Milton Friedman was born in July 31, 1912, in Brooklyn, New York, to Jewish immigrants Jeno Saul Friedman and Sarah Ethel Landau, who immigrated to Brooklyn in 1890 and 1895, respectively. Friedman's parents came from Barehovo, Ukraine, which was formerly part of Hungary and Czechoslovakia. When Friedman was thirteen months old, his family moved to Rahway, New Jersey. His education included violin lessons, but he decided he did not have a talent for music. Friedman attended Washington Public School, where he skipped the sixth grade and transferred to Columbus School in the seventh grade, both public schools in Rahway. Ironically, he was nicknamed "Shallow" at that time. Although he attended Hebrew school in the afternoon after public school and was bar-mitzvahed, Friedman became an agnostic at the early age of twelve.

From 1924-1928, Friedman attended Rahway High School, where his favorite subjects were political science and geometry. Besides that, he participated in sports, won an oratory competition, and almost read out the local public library. He won a scholarship to attend Rutgers University in New Brunswick, New Jersey, then a private school. He had "a small purse," so he held two part-time jobs—at a men's department store at a wage of $4 a day, and waiting tables at a restaurant for the wage of a free lunch, as well as many other side jobs, including ROTC and a copy editor of the student newspaper while at Rutgers. Friedman said that the opportunity cost of the restaurant job was the only "C" grade he received.

Friedman intended to major in mathematics at Rutgers. He took the actuarial exams, but after failing some of them, he switched to economics. The economics department at Rutgers had two stalwart economists, Arthur F. Burns, who was writing his PhD at Columbia, and Homer Jones, who had been a student of Frank Knight, and completed graduate work at the University of Chicago. Friedman profusely praised them for their teaching, influence, and friendship. Friedman mentioned a seminar that Burns gave, which he attended with only one other student. The project was to go over Burns' dissertation: "That seminar imparted standards of scholarship—attention to detail, concern with scrupulous accuracy, checking of sources, and above all, openness to criticism—that have affected the whole of my subsequent scientific work" (Friedman and Friedman, 1998: 30). Friedman studied insurance and statistics with Jones. It was Jones who introduced Friedman to the "Chicago view" of individual freedom and the right reform policy. Friedman wrote that "had Homer not chosen to spend a couple of years teaching at Rutgers, I would almost certainly not have gone to Chicago." He also remarked that besides being at the bottom of the Great Depression, "becoming an economist seemed more relevant to the burning issues of the day than becoming an applied mathematician or an actuary" (ibid.: 33-34).

Friedman entered the University of Chicago in 1932. There he met Rose Director in Jacob Viner's class on "Price and Distribution Theory." Viner's policy was to seat students alphabetically, which put Friedman and Director next to each other. Eight years later, on June 25, 1938, they were married under full religious tradition in New York. At the University of Chicago, Friedman studied history of economic thought with Frank Knight, monetary theory with Lloyd Mints, and correlation and curve fitting with Henry Schultz. Friedman said: "I took courses enough to have the equivalent of a master's degree in mathematics—which stood me in very good stead in my later career" (ibid.: 39).

Friedman received his MA from the University of Chicago in 1933, and with the encouragement of Schultz, obtained a fellowship to study with Harold Hotelling at Columbia during 1933-1934, in his second year of graduate work. At Columbia, he studied mathematical statistics with Hotelling, Business Cycles and History of Thought with Westley C. Mitchell, and Pure Theory and Institutions with John Maurice Clark. Friedman recommend that "the ideal combination for a budding economist was a year of study [at] Chicago, which emphasized theory, followed by a year of study at Columbia which emphasized institutional influences and empirical work—but only in that order, not the reverse" (ibid.: 480). Friedman returned to Chicago in 1935, as a research assistant to Schultz. He wrote: "I ended up satisfying the requirements for a PhD other than the dissertation at both Chicago . . . and Columbia" (ibid.: 51). His PhD from Columbia in 1946 dealt with professional income distribution.

Having graduated, Friedman went to work in Washington, D.C. He wrote: "ironically, the New Deal was a lifesaver for us personally. The new government programs created a boom market for economists, especially in Washington. Absent the New Deal, it is far from clear that we could have gotten jobs as economists" (ibid.: 58). Friedman took a job with the National Resources Committee (NRC) for $2,600, annually, much more than his $1,600 assistant job with Schultz. The NRC job was in the statistical area, involving sample design, surveys, and the preparation of final reports on the cost of living index. After two years at the NRC, Friedman wrote, "I had become an expert on consumption studies, and had acquired experience with practical statistics that supplemented my knowledge of mathematical statistics, something that stood me in good stead throughout my scientific career" (ibid.: 66). At the NRC, Friedman developed a statistics test on "the analysis of ranks" to compete with "the analysis of variance," which is known as "Friedman's test" (Friedman, 1937, 1940).

In 1937, Friedman quit the NRC and moved to the National Bureau of Economic Research in New York, where he worked with the future Nobel Laureate Simon Kuznets on wealth and income distribution. His major task at the NBER was to work on income differentials among professionals, which by today's standards represents an early project on human capital. Friedman divided income into permanent, quasi-permanent, and transitory income, in order to study dynamic changes in income distribution over time, which led to his most important contribution in economics, the permanent income hypothesis (PIH).

Friedman's awards are too numerous to list. In 1951, Friedman won the John Bates Clark Medal honoring economists under age forty for outstanding achievement. In 1976, he won the Nobel Prize in economics for "his achievements in the field of consumption analysis, monetary history and theory, and for his demonstration of the complexity of stabilization policy." He was president of the American Economic Association in 1967 and economic adviser to presidents Richard Nixon and Ronald Reagan. In 1977, Friedman retired from the University of Chicago and became senior research fellow at the Hoover Institution at Stanford University, where he continued his research program in monetary economics and political and economic freedom.

Friedman's Place in the History of Economic Thought

Friedman earned a prominent place in the history of economic thought. Between 1960-1975, his research ideas had a commanding influence in macroeconomics. "Milton Friedman, who had returned to Chicago in 1946, was the primary architect of these policy views. Before that time he had written little on economic policy. . . . Friedman proceeded to establish three lines of work, which together constituted his fundamental contributions to the formation of the Chicago School. First, he revived the study of monetary economics. . . . He used the quantity theory of money, and refurbished and extended it. . . . Second, he presented strong defenses of laissez-faire policies . . . finally, he developed and employed modern price theory" (Stigler, 1988: 150-151). We use George Stigler's insight as a springboard for our assessment.

Monetary Theory

The quantity theory of money is the basis of Friedman's contribution to monetary economics. Basically, the theory relates money and its velocity of circulation to prices and transactions. Friedman restated the classical quantity theory in terms of a demand for money function. His restatement explained five types of assets for holding wealth: "(i) money (M), interpreted as claims or commodity units that are generally accepted in payments of debts at a fixed nominal value; (ii) bonds (B), interpreted as claims to time streams of payments that are fixed in nominal units, (iii) equities (E), interpreted as claims to state pro-rata shares of the returns of enterprises; (iv) physical non-human goods (G); and (v) human capital (H)" (Friedman, 1956: 3).

Analyzing the returns from the five assets yields a number of variables that affect the velocity of the circulation of money in the model Friedman (ibid.: 11) advanced with two pivotal equations:

$$\frac{M}{Y} = \frac{1}{v(r_b, r_e, \frac{1}{P}\frac{dP}{dt}, w, \frac{Y}{P}, u)} \qquad (1)$$

$$Y = v(r_b, r_e, \frac{1}{P}\frac{dP}{dt}, w, \frac{Y}{P}, u)M \tag{2}$$

where Y is income or returns to all forms of wealth, v is income velocity, P is price level, w is ratio of human to non-human capital, r_b is rate of interest on bonds, r_e is rate of interest on equity, u is taste and preference, and M is demand for money.

A question arises about the predictive ability of these equations. Equation 2 can be turned into a theory of output determination if the variables that affect velocity can be explained. Equation 1 can spotlight a theory of price by solving for price in terms of the other variables, particularly income determination. Friedman's restatement is now carried in textbooks in a simplified form as follows:

$$\frac{M^d}{p} = f(y_p, R - R_m, \pi^e - R_m) \tag{2a}$$

The income variable y_p is permanent income, which we explain more fully in the consumption function section. The other two terms explain that demand for money depends on the opportunity cost of holding money. The term $R - R_m$ measures deviation of financial return R, from the return on money, R_m, and the last term measures deviations of the returns of holding money from the expected inflation rate. A major difference between this specification form and the Keynesian demand function is that John Maynard Keynes prefers to separate the transaction and speculative demand, while Friedman is concerned more with total asset demand. This broader approach introduces more interest rates into the demand function, rather than just a single interest rate for a British console bond that never matures. Friedman's specification for the demand for money is amenable to empirical testing. He has evolved a technique for the estimation of the term structure of interest rates within the demand function. Friedman remarked, "the whole term structure, including yields for very long holding periods, affects the quantity of money demanded. There is no a priori reason to regard a 'short' rate or a 'long' rate as 'the' alternative cost of holding cash balances" (Friedman, 1977: 21). Following a suggestion by Robert Heller and Mohsin Khan (1979), Friedman and Anna J. Schwartz (1982) used the following two-step technique to incorporate the term structure into the demand for money function. First, they fitted a quadratic equation for the yield curve for each year from 1873 to 1975, in the form:

$$R_i(\tau) = a_{0i} + a_{1i}\tau + a_{2i}\tau^2 \tag{3}$$

where R_i is the yield per bond of year i, and τ represents years to maturity. In the second step, these parameters are used in place of the interest rate variables in the demand for money function, resulting in the estimated form (Friedman and Schwartz, 1982: 204):

$$\begin{aligned} \log m = {} & -1.93 + 1.21 \log y - 2.78 a_0 - 298 a_1 - 13{,}823 a_2 - 0.71 g_Y \\ & + 0.185\, S + 0.021\, W \end{aligned} \tag{4}$$

where the variables are in their log arithmetic form, g_Y is percentage change in nominal income, substituting for nominal yield on physical assets, S is a dummy variable for lower velocity in 1929-1954, W is a dummy variable for post war adjustment, y is real income per capita, and m is real balance per capita. The estimates were significant, and the r-square was 0.9916. Equation 4 has the power of economizing in having to fit equations that have to accommodate the entire term structure, such as the form:

$$M_t^d = f(y_t, R_{it} \dots R_{nt}) \tag{5}$$

where there are now many interest rates on financial assets, ranging from the shortest maturity, $t = 1$, to the longest, $t = n$. Equation 4 reduces the variables by restricting the parameters.

Both the Keynesian and the Friedman paradigms are still active for empirical research. Friedman's major argument against discretionary monetary policy is that it tends to be destabilizing because of lags. Modern extensions of macroeconomics within the CGE domain of research maintain this position (Blanchard and Fischer, 1990: 581).

The predictions of the quantity theory were backed by theoretical arguments. In 1969, Friedman advanced a model of his monetary theory is search of the optimum quantity of money. He likened it to a Japanese garden, characterized by simplicity and unity of a complex reality. He simplified monetary theory by making thirteen assumptions. The fixed assumptions included: 1) population, 2) taste, 3) physical resources, 4) technique, 5) a stationary state. He also assumed 6) competition, and 7) durable capital goods. The do-not assumptions included: 8) no exchange of capital goods, 9) no lending or borrowing, 10) only exchanges of money for services and vice versa allowed. The operational assumptions included: 11) flexible prices, 12) money is a fiat, and 13) money is a fixed number of pieces of paper, with a value of, say, $10,000 (Friedman, 1969: 2-3).

In this economy, people can hold money as a medium of circulation, or as a reserve. Assumption 5 posits a stationary but not static economy, where the latter would imply that people would conduct all transactions at one time, obviating the need for a circulatory function of money and even eliminating uncertainty. The amount of money citizens will want to hold depends on its velocity, which is assumed as ten percent. Therefore, given fiat money, citizens will want to hold $1,000 (10,000*0.1).

To see the model evolve, we introduce some money into the economy via a helicopter, which makes a one-time drop of a $1,000. Individuals will gather money equal in proportion to what they held before, which in this case will double their cash balance. But individuals are in stable equilibrium. Had they wished to double their cash balance, they would have done so by making some adjustment in the past. Individuals would now want to spend their excess cash balance, thanks to the helicopter incident. When others receive their spending, they too will be in the same situation of wanting to hold less cash balance. In this way the amount of money injected into the economy by the helicopter will translate into a proportional increase in prices, given the other fixed assumptions.

The bottom-line argument from Friedman's monetary theory is that monetary policies have strong influences on the economy. This potent influence has given birth to the aphorism that 'money matters,' whether in its weak form "money too matters" or in its strong form "only money matters." Because of the strong influence of money on economic activities, Friedman wanted to guard against the mismanagement of monetary policies. One thing to safeguard against is the lags with which changes in the money supply influence the economy. Because of these lags, Friedman thought the good intentions of the monetary policy makers to stabilize the economy might result in destabilization. He therefore became a staunch advocate for monetary policy rules, arguing against discretionary policies. Briefly, the debate of rules versus discretion started at the University of Chicago with the economist Henry Simons (1936). For Simons, the essential point for a test is to find stable and definite legislative rules of the game for economic freedom (Simons, 1936: 3). Given a tendency to hoard or dishoard money, or if many substitutes for currency and deposits exist, "near moneys," then the fixed scheme is easily defeated. Friedman (1969: 48) advocated the "5 percent and the 2 percent rules." In the 5 percent rule, "the aggregate quantity of money is automatically determined by the requirements of domestic stability" (Friedman, 1948: 252). The 5 percent rule addresses short-run phenomena such as rigidities and lags. The 2 percent rule is aimed at more long-run phenomena that require nominal interest rates to equal the opportunity cost of producing money for the interest rate to be approximately zero.

In Friedman and Schwartz's work *A Monetary History of the United States,* they subject the money matters hypothesis to several historical tests. Three tests stand out relating to price behavior for 1879-1914, to the World War I and World War II periods, and to the Federal Reserve's strict reserves policies in 1937-1938. To explain the inflation after 1896, we note that prices declined between 1879-1896 by approximately -0.93 percent annually, and increased between 1897-1914 by approximately 2.08 percent annually. Money to output increased between 1879-1896 by 2.29 percent annually, and between 1897-1914 by 4.23 percent annually, being driven up by new gold supply. Base money, defined as currency plus reserves, increased between 1879-1896 by 3.49 percent annually, and between 1897-1914 by 4.8 percent annually. One cannot rule out the possibility, therefore, of some association between money and prices after 1896. In the second case, between 1914-1920 money to output increased 8.45 percent annually, while the price level rose 10.84 percent annually. However, the differences were reversed between 1939-1948, when money to output increased 7.90 percent annually and price level increased 6.65 percent annually. Yet, we can say that the correlation between money and prices appears similar. In the third case, during the 1937-1938 recession, the Fed doubled required reserves, resulting in a decrease in the money stock by -0.37, a decrease in prices by –0.50, and a decrease in output by -8.23 percent during that one year; thus shedding light on the causation between money and economic activities.

An issue pointed out recently by Paul Krugman (2007) concerns the period 1929-1933. The money base increased from $6.05 billion in 1929 to $7.02 billion in 1933, while the money supply fell from $26.6 billion to $19.9 billion, reflecting bank failures. People seemed to have a high liquidity preference. At issue is whether the Fed that increased the money base should be blamed for the fall in the money supply. Friedman's point was that the Fed could have prevented bank failures.

Friedman's policy rules have taken on a different manifestation in the modern economy. In the hands of Finn E. Kydland and Edward C. Prescott (1977), policy rules are used to improve the social optimum. People's expectations change, for instance, with changes in new administrations in Washington. One frequent change in expectations of this sort regards taxing policies. Such changes, however, lead to other changes that may not lead to an optimum situation. With Robert Barro and David Gordon (1983), policy rules have a home in efforts to eliminate surprise inflation. In adjusting their expectation of inflation to eliminate surprise inflation, people's actions can lead to higher money supply and inflation. Policy rules can stop such expectations-driven inflation from occurring. Such adjustments can occur within a gaming situation where policy makers can break rules and cheat in order to get more employment by lowering inflation. In such games, policy makers put their reputation and credibility on the line.

Objections to Friedman's Monetary Positions

From the MIT perspective, the "Chicago view" was somewhat shallow. According to Paul Samuelson, "Dennis Robertson's Cambridge handbook on *Money,* and Alfred Marshall's unitary-elasticity demand for money were the alpha and omega of that allegedly subtle oral tradition. At the London School of Economics (LSE) and Harvard, the same macroeconomics prevailed" (Samuelson, 1986: 263). The framework did not measure up: "when at long last Milton Friedman came to write down in the 1970 *Journal of Political Economy* what his monetarism was analytically, it turned out to be one specification of the general Keynesian identities and behavior functions and not a very plausible one at that" (Samuelson, 1986: 262).

In a recent interview, Paul Samuelson, who studied the "Chicago view," put it under historical scrutiny. He underscored that Irving Fisher (1867-1947) was influenced by his financial losses during the Great Depression to lose faith in the belief that velocity was quasi-constant. Similarly, he underscored that Arthur Cecil Pigou (1877-1959) had retracted his criticisms of the Keynesian system. Samuelson then made a blanket attack on Friedman's monetary view as follows: "what those gods were modifying was much that Milton Friedman was renominating.... It is paradoxical that a keen intellect jumped on that old bandwagon just when technical changes in money and money substitutes . . . were realistically replacing the scalar M by a vector . . . the pity of it increases for one who adopts a simple theory of positivism.... Particularly venerable is a scholar who tries to test competing theories by submitting them to simplistic linear regressions with no sophisticated calculations of Granger causality, cointegration, collinearities and ill-conditioning, or a dozen other safeguard econometric mythologies" (Samuelson, 2007: 146).

Samuelson's objection does not negate the influence Friedman has had on monetary matters. Every student of economics has heard of his monetary policy rule, his natural rate hypothesis, that inflation is a monetary phenomenon, which is of paramount importance to modern policy makers. Friedman's monetarist appeal may be due to his influential logic. This is how he explained that inflation is a monetary phenomenon:

> Suppose the nominal quantity that people hold happens to correspond at current prices to a real quantity larger than that which they wish to hold. Individuals will then seek to dispose of what they regard as their excess money balances; they will try to pay out a larger sum of the purchase of securities, goods, and services, for the repayment of debts, as gifts than they are receiving from the corresponding sources. However, one man's expenditures are another's receipts. One man can reduce his nominal money balances only by persuading someone else to increase his. The community as a whole cannot in general spend more than it receives. . . . If prices and income are free to change, the attempt to spend more will raise the nominal volume of expenditures and receipts, which will lead to a bidding up of prices and perhaps also to increase in output. If prices are fixed . . . the attempt to spend more either will be matched by an increase in goods and services or will produce "shortages" and "queues." (Friedman, 1968: 434)

According to Franco Modigliani, Friedman's position was that wages were not rigid and unemployment involuntary as Keynes had supposed. The proper focus should be on deviation of the actual from the unexpected price changes. At the apparent level, an anticipated fall in demand is taken to be the cause of lower prices, output, and employment. What happens in fact is that workers fail to grasp the essence of the current fall in prices and nominal wages. For instance, workers misperceive a fall in money wages as a fall in real wages. They would then curtail the supply of labor, pushing up the real wage, reducing employment and output. All this would happen because a misperception has caused a cut in supply, and not because of the unanticipated fall in demand (Modigliani, 1986: 6). However, such a misperception cannot last but temporarily. The misperception will come to an end when expectations are realized. Friedman's novel insight is to reverse the Phillips curve argument that excess employment causes inflation. He made the argument that expected inflation causes excess employment, underscoring the aphorism that stabilization policies are themselves destabilizing. Such a dictum arises because full employment is an uncertain phenomenon. The parameters of the Phillips curve drift over time; therefore, targeting an unknown inflation rate might turn out to be incorrect, creating volatile movements. These considerations call for special policies, such as the constant growth in the money supply that would put the economy in an automatic mode, searching to find the unknown natural rate (ibid.: 14).

Following Friedman (1968) and Edmund S. Phelps (1967), Modigliani recognized that the Phillips curve relationships were unstable because "they resulted from actions of economic agents induced by unanticipated price fluctuations under conditions of imperfect information. Expectation errors could persist, resulting in transitory output fluctuation, but in the long run actual and expected price changes could not deviate systematically. Consequently, in the steady state there is a unique "natural full-employment output level which is invariant to permanent inflation" (Papademos and Modigliani, 1990: 415).

Other Novelties of Friedman's Research

Hyperinflation

Friedman held that "the quantity theorist accepts the empirical hypothesis that the demand for money is highly stable . . . the sharp rise in the velocity of circulation of money during hyperinflations is entirely consistent with a stable functional relation, as Phillip Cagan so clearly demonstrated" (Cagan, 1956: 16). Cagan's model for hyperinflation was pivotal for future development, as it incorporated the rate of change of expected prices. It is expressed as:

$$\log_e \frac{M}{P} = -\alpha E \gamma \qquad (3)$$

where the demand for money function is reduced to only the expected rate of change in prices, E, and two constants, a and λ. But E was loaded with forward-looking developments. It depended on the actual rate of change of prices that was "approximated by the difference between the logarithms of successive values of the index of prices" (ibid.: 35). It incorporated an adaptive mechanism and imitated permanent effects that Friedman was concerned with in his Consumption Function hypothesis.

Cagan's conclusion (ibid.: 91) was that "hyperinflation at least can be explained almost entirely in terms of the demand for money. This explanation places crucial importance on the supply of money . . . and involves the motives of government, with whom the authority to open and close the spigot of note issues ultimately lies."

Philosophy and Methodology

Friedman maintained a libertarian view of philosophy on the one hand, and a positive view of science on the other.

Laissez-faire

Three major premises cover Friedman in this area: Adam Smith's market system, The Declaration of Independence, and John Stuart Mill's idea that "over himself, over his own body and mind, the individual is sovereign" (Friedman and Friedman, 1979: 1-2). The philosophical underpinnings of these premises are found in their earlier book *Capitalism and Freedom.* In that work, we find that a "major theme is the role of competitive capitalism . . . as a system of economic freedom and a necessary condition for political freedom" (Friedman and Friedman, 1962: 4). It is fair to say that "through his books, his long-running column in *Newsweek,* his public television series *Free to Choose,* and countless speeches and television appearances, [Friedman] has consistently and eloquently made the case for individual freedom . . . he has expounded a wide-range of libertarian agenda, notable including abolition of the draft and decriminalization of the use of illegal drugs" (Boaz, 1997a: 292).

In his exposition of the *laissez-faire* concept, Friedman weaved his argument around social philosophic terms such as economic, political, and individual freedom. We have collected a sample of the usage of these terms, and then analyzed how Friedman used them to promote his point of view.

On Economic Freedom (EF)

> The free man will ask neither what his country can do for him nor what he can do for his country. He will ask rather "What can I and my compatriots do through government to help us discharge our individual responsibilities, to achieve our several goals and purposes, and above all, to protect or freedom?" (Friedman and Friedman, 1962: 2)

> . . . economic freedom is an end in itself . . . economic freedom is also an indispensable means towards the achievement of political freedom. (ibid.: 8)

> History suggests only that capitalism is a necessary condition for political freedom. Clearly it is not a sufficient condition. Fascist Italy, Fascist Spain, Germany at various times . . . Japan before World Wars I and II, tsarist Russia in the decades before World War I . . . are all societies that cannot conceivably be described as politically free. Yet, in each, private enterprise was the dominant form of economic organization. (ibid.: 10).

In the early nineteenth century, Jeremy Bentham and the Philosophical Radicals were inclined to regard political freedom as a means to economic freedom. They believed that the masses were being hampered by the restrictions that were imposed upon them, and that if political reforms gave the bulk of the people the vote, they would do what was good for them, which was "to vote for laissez faire . . . the triumph . . . was followed by a reaction toward increasing intervention by government . . . intellectual descendants of the Philosophical Radicals—Dicey, von Mises, Hayek, and Simons. . . . Their emphasis was on economic freedom as a means towards political freedom" (ibid.: 10).

On Political Freedom (PF)

> Political freedom means the absence of coercion of a man by his fellow men. (Friedman and Friedman, 1962: 15)

For F. A. Hayek, the state of liber7ty or freedom is "that condition of men in which coercion of some by others is reduced as much as is possible in society . . . The state in which a man is not subject to coercion by the arbitrary will of another or others is often also distinguished as 'individual' or 'personal' freedom" (Hayek, 1960: 11).

Relationship between IF and EF

Friedman's methodology is high on the scale of both individual freedom (IF) and economic freedom (EF), and his position is not to settle for an intermediate point between the two. In *Free to Choose,* he shuns market socialism, for instance, which will fall in the interval of the joint distribution of a function say, $F = f(IE,EF)$ Perhaps David Boaz had it right when he stated that Friedman is high on a 2-dimension scale of them, a libertarian view where one does not go out on a limb for just individual freedom as the liberals do, or for economic freedom as the conservatives do (Boaz, 1997b: 32).

Another shade of Friedman's view is that EF under competitive capitalism implies political freedom (PF). In propositional logic terminology, this can be stated as the existence of a competitive market economy (CME) such that EF implies PF:

$$\exists CME, EF \supset PF \tag{1}$$

First, we may study in what sense Friedman intends this implication to hold. Friedman holds that political freedom can be achieved quickly. In his visit to Czechoslovakia and Poland (*Free to Choose*, Tape 3), Friedman noted how, as a result of one demonstration, a government can be overturned; but one year later, economic freedom still had not been achieved. If we can in fact write that economic freedom follows political freedom, we must acknowledge that it will have to be with a long lag:

$$\exists CME, PF(t-i) \supset EF \tag{2}$$

In Equation 2, the lag$(t - i)$, in the case of those Former Soviet Union (FSU) economies, it has not materialized yet. If it turns out that economic freedom materializes in those FSUs, then we will be enlightened about how competitive markets work in that area. What is required for a successful transformation of those FSUs, according to Friedman, is for governments to move rapidly to put into place the institutions that would lead to economic freedom, for economic freedom is not based on race or culture, but on economic institutions based on free private markets.

Second, is it possible in the long run that political freedom with competitive market institutions will lead to economic freedom? Unless we can answer this question in the affirmative, we cannot use strict implicative arguments of Equation 1, because one of the three ways in which Equation 1 can be true is: *EF* is false and *PF* is true. How then can Friedman hold that economic freedom is necessary for political freedom? One sense of this statement to be true is in the *modal logic,* and not in the *propositional logic,* where the terms "possible" and "necessary" are related.

The "necessary" and the "possible" are foundational terms in Modal Logic, which is a branch of logic that goes back to Aristotle. For our purpose, "it is sounder to view modal logic as the indispensable core of logic, to view truth-functional logic as one of its fragments, and to view 'other' logics—epistemic, deontic, temporal, and the like—as accretions either upon modal logic . . . or upon its truth-functional components" (Bradley and Swartz, 1979: 219). Some of the modal possibilities in Friedman's argument can be listed as follows:

1. The economy can change into the same social state it was in before.
2. It can take another social form.
3. It can remain in an undeveloped state, where economic freedom through competitive markets can remain only a dream.
4. A former socialist country cannot be transformed into another form of society.

An example that Friedman discussed that had these possibilities is that of Yugoslavia, where Marshal Tito was able to break away from Stalin's Soviet Union. Yugoslavia remained a communist country but practiced decentralization. "The collapse of communism and its replacement by a market system, seems far less likely, though as incurable optimists, we do not rule it out completely. Similarly, once the aged Marshal Tito dies, Yugoslavia will experience political instability that may produce a reaction toward greater authoritarianism or, far less likely, a collapse of existing collectivist arrangements" (Friedman and Friedman, 1979: 56-57). It must be kept in mind that these transition stages do not bear the implications of Equation 1, but are only possibilities. For instance, Friedman explicitly condemned the approach of "democratic socialism," a system offered as a bridge between "totalitarian socialism," such as that of the former FSU, and capitalism as a system of economic freedom (Friedman and Friedman, 1962: 7-8). Then the implied question is the true value of this expression. Friedman stated that economic freedom is both an end and a means. As an end, it is "a component of freedom broadly understood" and an "indispensable means towards the achievement of political freedom" (Boaz, 1997a: 293). Keith Dixon faults Friedman for holding that "both political freedom and economic freedom may be construed in the same way" (Dixon, 1985: 25). They are rather desirable ends.

Positive Economic View

Friedman expanded and articulated a positive economic viewpoint. In doing so, he was reacting to the science of human action expounded by Ludwig von Mises. In *Human Action,* he wrote: "Action is will put into operation and transformed into an agency, is aiming at ends and goals, is ego's meaningful response to stimuli and to the conditions of its environment; it is a person's conscious adjustment to the state of the universe that determines his life" (von Mises, 1963: 11). One of von Mises' faithful students wrote: "The Fundamental praxeological axiom is that individual human beings *act*." To Rothbard (1970: 65), "Praxeology asserts the action axiom as true, and from this (together with a few empirical axioms—such as the existence of a variety of resources and individuals) are deduced, by the rules of logical inference, all the propositions of economics, each one of which is verbal and meaningful." So, for Rothbard (1951: 943), "This axiom of action is indisputable and important truth, and must form the basis for social theory." Although this is a broad definition, it has been narrowed in several ways in current popular applications to economics. A leading text, for instance, holds that the core of action is scarcity, from which economizing behavior and trade-offs follow, and it juxtaposed reactions, consequences, choices, and individualism to the "Economic Way of Thinking" (Heyne et al., 2003: 5).

Friedman was reacting to the soul of Austrian methodology called the "axiom of action." According to F. A. Hayek, the axiom's core feature is "logically the statements of theories [that] are independent of any particular experience" (Hayek, 1992: 148). This would make it a purely a priori science. As Rothbard puts it:

> We do not know, and may never know with certainty, the ultimate equation that will explain all electromagnetic and gravitational phenomena; but we do know that people act to achieve goals. And this knowledge is enough to

> elaborate the body of economic theory . . . the fact that people act to achieve goals implies that there is a scarcity of means to attain them. . . . Scarcity implies cost, which in a monetary system . . . are reflected in prices, and so forth. (1973: 315)

To label the action axiom a priori then puts it in opposition to the empirical models. Hayek assured us that the difference between von Mises' position and that of the falsificationist Karl Popper is "comparatively small," while a larger difference exists between them from the naïve empirical point of view (Hayek, 1992: 148).

Friedman then set out to create a general empirical economic method, specializing it to the positive view. Its central message is that we judge a theory by its ability to predict and explain phenomena. Friedman started by enunciating John Maynard Keynes' positive, normative, and instrumental viewpoints as the economic method. Positive economics is a system that can make correct predictions in economic matters. It requires a theory or hypothesis that has valid and meaningful predictions about economic phenomena not yet observed. The theory represents complex reality by way of an abstraction. A theory can be distinguished as a language where it will not have substantive content because it would be a tautology. However, a theory can also be described as a hypothesis where it will have substantive content for testing and validation.

Problems arise with Friedman's methodology when we note that theories have not only implications but also assumptions. Friedman defends the view that the realism of the assumptions is not a test of the hypothesis. For instance, if someone were to argue that imperfect competition has less realistic assumptions than perfect competition, Friedman would not consider that as a valid test to reject imperfect competition. The criteria for testing these models are their predictions and explanations of reality, and not the realism of their assumptions. To see the difference more logically, reasoning from realism of assumption to true theory is like a priori testing. In a priori reasoning, the state that P implies Q, $P \supset Q$, is true when both P and Q are true, both are false, and when P is false, Q is true. But Friedman's positive empirical view requires the true value of Q to be empirically true in order to make P true.

Friedman's positive economic doctrine has one element of uncertainty that has opened up an opportunity for other variants of positivism. Approximately twenty years ago, one of the authors wrote to Friedman on this matter that the number of times a theory must fail before we give it up is still an open question in his methodology. The question was why he criticized the US Department of Housing and Urban Development Section 8 program based on one empirical point about how the program allowed a tenant to live in an expensive apartment, paying more for rent than some of the private market rate tenants. This instance that he cited represented only one circumstance, which may be connected with a few others. The question then arises as to how many times must a program fail by his methodology before we abandon it. Friedman, with his every so charming wit, replied, "Enough is enough." We must realize that this is a serious criterion for the falsification of the positive doctrine. The methodology of science carries this innocent chat as two aspects of falsificationism, namely, naïve and sophisticated. In the naïve case, only one instance of a phenomena is enough to falsify a theory, while in the sophisticated case, one will have to accumulate enough anomalies and stay with a degenerating program long enough before rejecting it.

In this instance also, Friedman took the opportunity to point out that the question was in the vein of defending the "status quo." He was referring to his book, the "Tyranny of The Status Quo," 1984, in which he denounced government activities beyond what will be allowed under a free market mechanism. To defend those programs would mean to defend the status quo. To the extent that Friedman advocates programs such as the negative income tax, therefore, he does so from the point of view of stopping the movement away from free market goals, and not for the inherent characteristics of those programs.

Risk Analysis

Friedman presented a lucid explanation of the expected utility hypothesis (EUH) that telescoped further development (Friedman, 1976: 77-78). Given a stream of income, I_i, and their associated probabilities, P_i, the expected utility is the sum of their product. Utility enters when we form a function of income, $F(I)$, whose products with their respective probabilities generate a special function, $G = \sum_{i=1}^{\infty} P_i F(I_i)$. In the special instance where income is expected with certainty, $P_i = 1$, both the G and F functions have the same value or utility. Further development of this hypothesis turned on the uniqueness of specifying the utility function. Current literature suggests a concave function that can be written as: $U(butter,bread) = U(x_1,x_2) = -\exp[-x_1^5 + 2^{-x_2}]$ (Samuelson, 1986: 154). Risk enters if we consider the shapes of the utility function. The expected value of the prospect is a straight line probability weight of the prospects. The expected utility is the probability weighted average of the two utility functions. If we plot utility, $F(I)$, against income, I, then the average income yields three values of average utility, one for the expected utility, one for the utility function based on a concave shape, and one for the utility function based on a convex shape. A concave (from below) average utility function would measure aversion to risk and would be preferred to the expected average of the income. A convex (from below) average utility function would measure risk lovers, and yield the reverse preference. If we eliminate scale and origin from the utility function by the restrictions $I = 0$, $F(I) = 0$ and $I = 1$, $F(I) = 1$ $F(I)$ I = 0, then we can determine utility values for any values of income. However, without such restrictions, the utility function can take on recurrent concave (from below) shapes, making it unwise for someone to pay an infinite sum to play the St. Petersburg game.

We can use the EUH to clear up confusion about subjective and objective probability in experiments on expectation analysis. Given a choice between two prospects, we ask people to state their preference before a set of events, A and B in X, occurs. The offer might be to receive $1 if event A = [(H)ead, (Head)] or event B = [H, T; T, H; T, T] occurs when two coins are tossed. If the agent takes event B, then we regard the choice as putting higher probability to B. Utility values are absent since the agent gets $1 whether he chooses A or B. The probability of the outcome exceeds half, since both A and B are mutually exclusive and exhaustive events. Through repeated experiments, we need to find out the agent's indifference position, i.e., when he would put a 50-50 chance to A and B, or a probability of 0.25 to each of the four outcomes in the toss of the two coins. When we know the indifference position, we can tell when the agent's preference is greater or less than 50 percent. This way, the agents behave "as if" they associate personal probabilities with outcomes. If individuals as a group agree on their personal probabilities, the analysis is considered objective, resulting in risk analysis.

Although psychology is not involved in the personal probability analysis, agents do embrace some typical attitude and understanding in making their choices. "The dollar I win is not as worthwhile to me as the dollar I lose"

(Samuelson, 1986: 134). "A poor man generally obtains more utility than a rich man from an equal [money] gain" (Bernoulli, 1938: 24) (Samuelson, 1986: 147). "At fair odds. it is better to have a relatively large gain with small probability than to have a small gain with large probability" (ibid.: 154). Some other ways of expressing attitudes include: "leisure of gambling," the "love of danger," the "joy of expert gamesmanship" (ibid.: 136). The work of Savage illustrates a "look before you leap" attitude that reduces all decisions for the future to the present time. Assuming we have made a choice, f, over many actions, f, g, h, if the state of nature, which measures uncertainty, is either good or bad, then we will have logical outcomes that can be written as $f(Good) = Outcome_1$, and $f(Bad) = Outcome_2$ (Savage, 1972: 15). By imposing a simple order for choosing which actions among f, g, and h are available, we can have empirical models that either predict behavior, or normative models that make our decisions consistent. Further assumptions under the names of the "sure thing principle" or the "independence axiom" attempt to place order on the outcomes. In Savage's model, if one is neither delighted in risk, nor averse to risk, then he/she would maximize the mathematical expectation, which is the probability of the state times the outcome.

If one is risk averse, then he/she would maximize an EUF function, such as one developed by John von Neumann (Chambernowne, 1969: 98). The attitude that "the dollar I win is not as worthwhile to me as the dollar I lose" leads one to avoid even finite fair bets in their expectation. The utility function captures this attitude in its nonlinear form. While the mathematical expectation suggests that the game should be played infinitely, the nonlinear utility function suggests that agents would stop at a finite moment of play.

If the probability of the uncertain state of the world is unknown, then we look for a range of probabilities, a probability distribution. This means that the probability, P, lies within a certain range [0.1, 0.2]. We can use the average of the two endpoints, a minimax strategy, of a combination of the average and a minimax strategy to measure uncertainty. Following the discussion of Savage, if we have two states of uncertainty with payoffs 80 and 21 for state I, and payoffs 20 and 30 for state II, for agents A1 and A2 respectively, that the expected payoff for A1 is 29, and for A2 is 28.65, using the average probability of 0.15. The agent will choose 29 to maximize its expected payoff. Using a minimax strategy, we would use a probability of 0.1 on A1's expected value, and 0.2 on agent A2's expected value to get 26 and 28.2 payoffs, respectively. But we have to use a mixture of probabilities as well. Calculating the mixture of returns for states I and II, and solving for the probability that would maximize the minimum value, would yield a probability of 0.13, which in turn puts the payoff at 28.6 (Champernowne, 1969: 99-103).

Several steps have been made to: 1) link expectations of belief with classical probability theory; 2) link choices over uncertain prospects with classical probability; 3) link choices over uncertain acts that are consistent with probabilistically sophisticated belief over event likelihood (Machina and Schmeidler, 1992: 745-746).

We expect the economic agents to be rational in their expectations, in the sense of consistency of choice, conformity with self-interest and maximizing behavior, and following reason in general. The future can be in a good or bad state, making the expected outcome risky or uncertain. If conditions in the future look so bad as to render economic events unpredictable, then we may regard expectations as given, i.e., exogenous (Hicks, 1984: 7). Subjectively, economic agents may feel confident about an outcome, but such confidence varies among individuals. Objectively, individuals with the same information should reach the same expectation. We examine how economists incorporate expectation measures into their equilibrium or optimal models, a method called substantive rationality, or into their deliberating procedures, a method called procedural rationality (Simons, 1936: 130-132).

Consumption Function

Friedman advanced the permanent income hypothesis of the consumption in order to reconcile inconsistencies in the observations of short and long run marginal propensities to consume. The term permanent income is used because consumers spend from their lifetime resources. Friedman suggested an estimate of permanent income by a distributed lag method, where the lags reach backward into negative infinity. The degree of the lag occurred to a seventeenth-degree polynomial. The term "transitory income" is the difference between current and lifetime income. If you get paid for overtime, or a once in a while Christmas bonus, you may consider that income temporary. The tax cut in 1964 by President John F. Kennedy was permanent. The one year tax surcharge passed by President Lyndon B. Johnson in 1968, and the Economic Growth and

Tax Relief Reconciliation Act of 2001 (EGTRRA) passed by President George W. Bush are clearer examples of transitory phenomena. Because transitory income is consumed over many years, its effect on consumption may not be felt.

One way to distinguish temporary from permanent in reality is to plot the percentage change of per capita income and consumption over time. One notices that while the change in income has many sharp spikes, the change in consumption would not react to those spikes, and would be rather uniform over time. Therefore, we can assert that transitory income has a negligible effect on consumption.

Friedman (1957: 26) specified the consumption function as:

$$c_p = k(i, w, u)y_p$$

$$y = y_p + y_t$$

$$c = c_p + c_t$$

where p is permanent income, t is transitory income, i is interest rate, w is wealth, and u is taste and preference. One implication of these PIH equations is that consumption based on permanent income will be constant if the bracket items are constant over time. The consumer intends to consume from permanent income at a uniform rate. Saving depends on transitory income in the short run, but is independent of the permanent income. The literature suggests that we should estimate permanent income as a measure of past income plus a change in income from the past to the current period. This solves two problems: the last period income persists in the future, and the consumer will not likely treat the increase in income as being permanent. Having defined permanent income, we can now make consumption a function of it. Past income, change in income, and wealth drives determine consumption over time.

In PIH, growth leads to a decrease in saving because it sets up the expectation that future income will exceed current income, allowing people to spend more currently.

Friedman's Nonparametric Test

Because Friedman's test is not generally used by economists, we introduce it in this section using an example. In statistics, a parameter represents a population value such as the mean, variance, and standard deviation. A statistic is a calculation from a sample of a population. A nonparametric test considers less stringent conditions than a parametric test would. In particular, a nonparametric test does not involve knowledge of the distribution from which the sample is drawn.

Friedman's test is an alternative to a two-way analysis of the variance F-test. We do not use the F-test because we think that the data does not meet the assumptions for using. The data is ordinal, which means that it is ranked. Table 1 presents the ranked data of family income by types of expenditure in a two-way classification (Friedman, 1937: 677).

The inputs in Table 1 are ranked based on the standard deviations of the dollar values of cells, where the ranks by row are from 1 to 7, which is the

TABLE 1: Income and Rank of Standard Deviation for Friedman's Test

Category of Expenditure	Annual Family Income (Treatment or Stimulus)						
Expenditures	$750- $1,000	$1,000- $1,250	$1,250- 1,500	$1,500- $1,750	$1,750- $2,000	$2,000- 2,250	$2,250- $2,500
Housing	5	1	3	2	4	6	7
Household Operations	1	3	4	6	2	5	7
Food	1	2	7	3	5	4	6
Clothing	1	3	2	4	5	6	7
Furnishings	2	1	6	3	7	5	4
Transportation	1	2	3	6	5	4	7
Recreation	1	2	3	4	7	5	6
Personal Care	1	2	3	6	4	7	5
Medical Care	1	2	4	5	7	3	6
Education	1	2	4	5	3	6	7
Community Welfare	1	5	2	3	7	6	4
Vocation	1	5	2	4	3	6	7
Gifts	1	2	3	4	5	6	7
Others	5	4	7	2	6	1	3
Total:	23	36	53	57	70	70	83

number of columns, P. Each of these columns represents an income level that will stimulate a type of expenditure for row elements, n The test consists of:

Null hypothesis: H_0: That the p distributions of the family income are identical.

Alternative hypothesis: H_a: A least two of the seven stimuli differ in the distribution of their family income.

Friedman's test statistics is:

$$\chi_r^2 = \frac{12}{np(p+1)} \Sigma R^2 - 3n(p+1)$$

$$\chi_r^2 = \frac{12}{(14)(7)(7+1)}(24{,}572) - 3(14)(7+1) = 40.1076$$

where the sum of squares of the rank is

$$\Sigma R^2 = 23^2 + 36^2 + 53^2 + 57^2 + 70^2 + 70^2 + 57^2 + 83^2 = 24{,}572$$

We reject the null hypothesis if the Friedman test statistic exceeds the values of the Chi Square Distribution at a critical level. We calculated the Friedman test statistic as 40.1076. "The probability of a value greater than 40 is .000001. There can thus be little question that the observed mean ranks differ significantly, i.e., that the standard deviation is related to the income level" (Friedman, 1932: 679). The Friedman test is used in the literature, and is included in standard statistical packages such as SPSS, SYSTAT, and MINITAB. Our survey touches on all of Friedman's major work, except for his views on Auction Theory.

To conclude, my personal recollection of gratitude is in place. In the early 1970s at the American Economic Association Convention in New Orleans, at the John Commons Session, Friedman conferred upon me the Irving Fisher Award for the dissertation *Economics of the Israeli Diamond Industry,* which was subsequently published (Szenberg, 1973). Samuelson, when asked for the secret of receiving so many awards, remarked that the most important thing is to get the first one. Then the others follow. Friedman contributed an insightful anecdote of his interaction with Samuelson to our biography, *Paul A. Samuelson: On Being an Economist* (Szenberg, Gottesman, and Ramrattan, 2005) and expressed readiness to pen a Foreword to our volume (Szenberg, Ramrattan, and Gottesman, 2006) honoring Samuelson's ninetieth birthday, but his failing health prevented him from accomplishing it. In his articles, lectures, and books he advanced his views with extraordinary vigor, conviction, and rhetorical flourish. With his passing, he leaves a legacy of creative thought to which we may turn for answers to the economic and social questions of the twenty-first century.

Notes

In modal logic, first order logic (FOL) is concerned with individuals, economies, or nations (Nolt et al., 1991: 280). Second order logic is concerned with the properties of the individuals. But propositional logic (PL) is concerned with sentences that are either true or false (Stebbing, 1961: 33).

References

Barro, R. J., & Gordon, D. B. (1983). Rules, discretion, and reputation in a model of monetary policy. *Journal of Monetary Economics*, 12, 101-120.

Blanchard, O. J., & Fischer, S. (1990). *Lectures on macroeconomics*. Cambridge, MA: MIT Press.

Boaz, D. (1997a). *The libertarian reader*. New York: The Free Press.

———. (1997b). *Libertarianism: A primer*. New York: The Free Press.

Bernoulli, D. (1954). Exposition of a new theory on the measurement of risk. (1738). (L. Sommers, Trans.). *Econometrica*, 22, 23-36.

Bradley, R., & Swartz, N. (1979). *Possible worlds: An introduction to logic and its philosophy*. Oxford: Blackwell.

Cagan, P. (1956). The monetary dynamics of hyperinflation. In M. Friedman (Ed.), *Studies in the quantity theory of money* (25-117). Chicago: University of Chicago Press.

Chambernowne, D. G. (1969). *Uncertainty and estimation in economics* (vol. 3). San Francisco: Holden Day.

Chari, V. V., & Kehoe, P. J. (2006). Modern macroeconomics in practice: How theory is shaping policy. *The Journal of Economic Perspectives*, 20(4), 3-28.

Dixon, K. (1985). *Freedom and equality: The moral basis of democratic socialism*. London: Routledge & Kegan Paul.

Frazer, W. (1997). *The Friedman system: Economic analysis of time series*. Westport, CT: Praeger.

Friedman, M. (1977). Time perspective in demand for money. *Scandinavian Journal of Economics*, 79(4), 397-416.

———. (1976). *Price theory*. Chicago: Aldine Publishing.

———. (1969). *The optimum quantity of money and other essays*. Chicago: Aldine Publishing.

———. (1968, Jan.). The role of monetary policy. *American Economic Review*, 58, 1-17.

———. (1968). Money: Quantity theory. In D. L. Sills (Ed.), *International encyclopedia of the social sciences* (432-447). New York: The Macmillan Company and The Free Press.

———. (1957). *A theory of the consumption function*. Princeton: Princeton University Press.

———. (1956). The quantity theory of money—A restatement. In M. Friedman (Ed.), *Studies in the quantity theory of money* (3-21). Chicago: University of Chicago Press.

———. (1953). *Essays in positive economics*. Chicago: University of Chicago Press.

———. (1948). A monetary and fiscal framework for economic stabilization. *American Economic Review*, 38, 245-264.

———. (1940, Mar.). A comparison of alternative tests of significance for the problem of m rankings. *Annals of Mathematical Statistics*, 11, 82-92.

———. (1937, Dec.). The use of ranks to avoid the assumption of normality implicit in the analysis of variance. *Journal of the American Statistical Association*, 32, 675-701.

Friedman, M., & Schwartz, A. J. (1963). *A monetary history of the United States, 1867-1960*. Princeton: Princeton University Press for the National Bureau of Economic Research.

———. (1982, Feb.). The effect of term structure of interest rates on the demand for money in the United States. *The Journal of Political Economy*, 90(1), 201-221.

Friedman, M., & Friedman, R. (1962). *Capitalism and freedom*. Chicago: University of Chicago Press.

———. (1979). *Free to choose*. New York: Harcourt, Brace and Jovanovich.

———. (1984). *Tyranny of the status quo*. New York: Harcourt Brace Jovanovich.

———. (1998). *Two lucky people*. Chicago: University of Chicago Press.

Gilboa, I., & Schmeidler, D. (2001). *A theory of case-based decisions*. Cambridge: Cambridge University Press.

Gray, J. (1986). *Concepts of social thought: Liberalism*. Minneapolis: University of Minnesota Press.

Hayek, F. A. (1992). *The collected works of F. A. Hayek* (vol. 4). P. G. Klein (Ed.). Chicago: University of Chicago Press.

———. (1960). *The constitution of Liberty*. Chicago: A Gateway Edition.

Heller, H. R., & Khan, M. S. (1979, Feb.). The demand for money and the term structure of interest rates." *The Journal of Political Economy*, 87(1), 109-129.

Heyne, P., Boettke, P., & Prychitko, D. (2003). *The economic way of thinking*. Englewood Cliffs, NJ: Prentice Hall.

Hicks, J. R. (1984). *The economics of John Hicks*. D. Helm (Ed.). Oxford: Basil Blackwell.

———. (1946). *Value and capital*, (2nd ed.). Oxford: Clarendon Press.

Keynes, J. M. (1955). *The scope and method of political economy* (4th ed.). New York: Kelley and Millman.

Krugman, P. (2007, Feb. 15). Who was Milton Friedman? *The New York Review of Books*, 27-30.

Kydland, F. E., & Prescott, E. C. (1977). Rules rather than discretion: The inconsistency of optimal plans. *Journal of Political Economy*, 85(3), 473-492.

Modigliani, F. (1986). *Collected papers* (vol. 1). Cambridge, MA: MIT Press.

Modigliani, F., & Papademos, L. (1980). Optimal demand policies against stagflation. In A. Andrew (Ed.), *The collected papers of Franco Modigliani* (vol. 3, 198-219). Cambridge, MA: MIT Press.

———. (1989). Monetary policy for the coming quarters: The conflicting views. In S. Johnson (Ed.), *The collected papers of Franco Modigliani* (vol. 4, 155-201). Cambridge, MA: MIT Press.

Nolt, H., Rohatyn, D., & Varzi, A. (1991). *Theory and problems of logic* (2nd ed.). *Schaum's Outline Series*. New York: McGraw-Hill.

Papademos, L., & Modigliani, F. (1990). The supply of money and the control of nominal income. In B. M. Friedman & F. H. Hahn (Eds.), *Handbook of monetary economics* (vol. I, 399-494). Amsterdam: Elsevier.

Phelps, E. S. (1967, Aug.). Phillips curves, expectations of inflation, and optimal unemployment over time. *Economica*, 34, 254-281.

Rothbard, M. N. (1973). Praxeology as the method of economics. In Ma. Natanson (Ed.), *Phenomenology and the social sciences* (vol. 2, 311-339). Evanston, IL: Northwestern University Press, 1973.

———. (1970). *Man, economy, and state: A treatise on economic principles.* Los Angeles: Nash Publishing.

———. (1951, Dec.). Praxeology: Reply to Mr. Schuller. *American Economic Review*, 41(5), 943-946.

Samuelson, P. A. (1986). *The collected scientific papers of Paul A. Samuelson* (vol. 5). K. Crowley (Ed.). Cambridge, MA: MIT Press.

———. (2007). An interview with Paul A. Samuelson. In P. A. Samuelson & W. A. Barnett (Eds.), *Inside the economist's mind: Conversations with eminent economists* (143-164). Oxford: Blackwell Publishing.

Savage, L. J. (1972). *The foundation of statistics.* New York: Dover Publications.

Simons, H. C. (1936). Rules versus authorities in monetary olicy. *The Journal of Political Economy*, 44(1), 1-30.

Stebbing, L. S. (1961). *A modern introduction to logic.* New York: Harper TorchBooks.

Szenberg, M. (1973). *Economics of the Israeli diamond industry.* With an Introduction by M. Friedman. New York: Basic Books.

Szenberg, M., Gottesman, A. A., & Ramrattan, L. (2005). *Paul Samuelson, on being an economist.* Foreword by J. E. Stiglitz. New York: Jorge Pinto Books.

Szenberg, M., Ramrattan, L., & Gottesman, A. (Eds.). (2006). *Samuelsonian economics and the twenty-first century.* Foreword by K. J. Arrow. Oxford: Oxford University Press.

Von Mises, L. (1963 [1949]). *Human action* (3rd ed.). Chicago: Contemporary Books, Inc.

PART IV

INSTITUTIONALISTS

John Kenneth Galbraith

John Kenneth Galbraith

This section attempts to address the essential legacy of John Kenneth Galbraith (1908-2006), spread over a broad range of subjects. Galbraith is a forerunner of the most popular, imaginative, and idea-creating economic writers of the last century. His economic eyes were the first to discern the historic and institutional forces behind the countervailing powers of big business and big unions, the culmination of techno structure in the land-capital dominance of the evolution of factors of production, the pairing of buyers and sellers for market clearance in disequilibrium, and as Milton Friedman stated, the only person who has made a serious attempt to justify price and wage controls.

Introduction

John Kenneth Galbraith was born on October 15, 1908, at Iona Station in Ontario, Canada, the son of William and Catherine Galbraith. His father was a schoolteacher and a politician of Canada's Liberal party, holding various offices in the county. Galbraith attended local schools, graduating from Ontario Agricultural College in 1931, and then moved to the United States. He did his graduate studies at the University of California at Berkeley in agricultural economics, gaining a PhD in 1934 for his dissertation on *California County Expenditures*. In 1934 he became an instructor at Harvard, where some of his colleagues included Joseph Schumpeter, Alvin Hansen, and Seymour Harris. At Harvard, Galbraith broadened his economic perspectives to include macroeconomics and industrial organization.

In the 1930s, when the world was suffering from the Great Depression, when unemployment was rampant and governments were struggling with policy measures to steer the economy back to growth, Galbraith published an influential paper titled *Monopoly Power and Price Rigidity* (1936) to address the problem. It was a landmark year because John Maynard Keynes, who brought macroeconomics into being, had published his *General Theory* the same year, dealing with similar concepts of price rigidy. After receiving a social science research fellowship in 1937, Galbraith went to Trinity College in Cambridge, where he met distinguished economists such as Michael Kalecki, Joan Robinson, Richard Kahn, and Piero Sraffa. At that time, Keynes had suffered a heart attack, so Galbraith did not meet him, but got the gist of his macroeconomics from Keynes' colleagues. He did study with Keynes, however, in 1937-1938 (Dimand, 1988: 146), and impressed him, who viewed Galbraith "as an engaged and politically purposive intellectual" (Parker, 2005: 96).

From that time onwards, Galbraith stayed in the public arena. He served on the National Defense Advisory Committee from 1940 to 1941. In 1942 he was appointed as deputy administrator of the Office of Price Administration, where he served until May 1943. He was co-director of the United States Strategic Bombing Survey after WWII, and served as an ambassador to India from 1961 to 1963 under the Kennedy administration.

As we review Galbraith's main contributions, we provide a preamble of what others think about his works. In the area of price theory, he was praised by his adversary, Milton Friedman, who wrote: "of price and wage control, Kenneth Galbraith has the company of many other people—but so far as I know, he is the only person who has made a serious attempt to present a theoretical analysis to justify his position" (Friedman, 1977: 12).

In industrial organization, Galbraith propounded the virtues of Schumpeter's theory that large firms are "almost perfect instruments for inducing technical change" (Galbraith, 1956: 91), and formulated his own theory of Countervailing Power, which states that if sellers develop market power through concentration, then buyers will also develop market power through concentration giving rise to big business and big unions. This Countervailing Power ideology is comparable to the Classical Capitalist, Managerial, People's Capitalism, and Enterprise Democracy ideologies of capitalism (Samuelson, 1972: vol. 3, 613). The place of this idea in the economic literature stands opposite to Karl Marx's prediction of the demise of capitalism. The rivalry of "giants against giants," in Galbraith's Countervailing Power view, is not “decadence but rather . . . ruthless efficiency and dynamic expansion” (Samuelson, 1973: vol. 3, 707).

Galbraith criticized growth for its own sake as wasteful. What is still carried in modern textbooks is his argument that firms use advertising to create demand. In growth theory proper, Galbraith stands against Marx’s self-destruction prognosis for capitalism. He sees growth in capitalism through a neoclassical lens, looking “forward to continued real progress, rather widely shared among the various income classes, the rich and the poor” (Samuelson, 1972: vol. 3, 705). While this growth would require technological progress to transcend limited resources, government participation will be necessary to address fair distribution of the gains.

In macroeconomics, Galbraith echoed the works of Keynes, R.H. Tawney and Alvin Hansen (Samuelson, 1966: vol. 2, 1504-1505). An important thread that links these authors is their “emphasis upon the importance of programs in the public sector in comparison with the expansions of private spending” (Samuelson, 1977: vol. 4, 875). One implication here is that the “public sector is too small compared to the private sector” (Samuelson, 1972: vol. 3, 509). On the fiscal policy side, his mantra on the income policy was “permanent governmental controls of prices and wage rates,” which works in the very short run (Samuelson, 1986: vol. 5, 966). Galbraith was “against the use of restrictive monetary policy” since monetary policy may not be able to lower interest rates enough to offset the decline of investment demand functions (Samuelson, 1972: vol. 3, 569). Inflation was not quite as much of a monetary phenomenon for Galbraith as for Friedman. Galbraith was credited for early views on administered price inflation (Stigler, 1968: 236-238). The increased monetary spending, like controls, is most potent in the short run, where it is found to have influence on production and employment, when full employment and production is not achieved (Samuelson, 1977: vol. 5, 966).

In a review of Galbraith’s *Age of Uncertainty*, George Stigler summarized some of Galbraith’s views at that time. On the economic side, the list started with “Adam Smith preached a narrow doctrine of self-interest,” and ended with the need to confront the anxiety of the age, namely nuclear warfare (Stigler, 1985). In a review of Galbraith’s *The Affluent Society*, F. A. Hayek identified Galbraith’s main argument to be that “in our affluent society the important private needs are already satisfied and the urgent need is therefore no longer to further expansion of the output of commodities but an increase of those services, which are supplied (and presumably can be supplied only) by government" (Hayek, 1961: 21). All in all Paul Samuelson, Stigler, Hayek, and Friedman have paid attention, and valued Galbraith's contributions, albeit to varying degrees.

On Economics

The economics of Galbraith is liberal, a departure from the classical market theory. The justification of this departure; its consequences; the successful attempt to elevate this departure from the view point of logic and reason, and the final arrival of a liberal market structure to build economics for the future is the roadmap of Galbraith's work in economics.

Galbraith's Definition and Methodology of Economics

Following Alfred Marshall, Galbraith accepts, with some modification, that "economics is a study of men as they live and move and think in the ordinary business of life. But it concerns itself chiefly with those motives which affect, most powerfully and most steadily, man's conduct in the business part of his life" (Marshall, 1920: 14). Galbraith had studied Marshall's *Principles* during graduate school, but he was also influenced by Thorstein Veblen and Marx (Gambs, 1975: 28). Galbraith does not seem to have any problem with Marshall's definition, although he adds: "a reference to organization for economic tasks by corporations, by trade unions and by government. Also of how and when and to what extent organizations serve their own purpose as opposed to those of the people at large. And of how the public purpose can be made to prevail" (Galbraith, 1980: 1).

More modern definitions claim scientific grounds for economics. Economic agents engage in choice behavior, which economists study from a scientific point of view. This was particularly the case for Lionel Robbins' definition, to the effect that economics is a science, which studies how scarce resources, which have alternate uses, are channeled to a certain end by consumers and producers (Robbins, 1935: 16). Galbraith examined the image that this definition creates for economics.

As one economist put it, "Galbraith believes that men orientate themselves not to phenomena but to the images of those phenomena which they have formed in their minds; and that ideologies and belief-systems are of particular value as a map of the somewhat forbidding world of economic and social reality" (Reisman, 1980: 1). Galbraith explicitly noted that "economics provides (people) with their image of economic society. That image notably affects their behavior—and how they regard the organizations that comprise the economic system" (Galbraith, 1973: 5). On the producer's side, the term "scarcity" represents an image that attaches great importance to organizations of production. On the consumer side, the "imagery of choice" in the aggregate is the controlling mechanism of the economic system. As for corporations, "nearly all study of the corporation has been concerned with its derivation from its legal or formal image" (Galbraith, 1967: 73).

Galbraith stands on the shoulders of Keynes. Keynes thought that "the ideas of economists and political philosophers, both when they are right and when they are wrong, are more powerful than is commonly understood. . . . I am sure that the power of vested interest is vastly exaggerated compared with the gradual encroachment of ideas" (Keynes, 1936: 383). Although Galbraith believed that "ideas may be superior to vested interest," he added that "they are also very often the children of vested interest" (Galbraith, 1967: 73). But the duality of ideas and vested interests is not complete for Galbraith. We are still missing one element. Galbraith wrote "in economic affairs, decisions are influenced not only by ideas and by vested economic interest. They are also subject to the tyranny of circumstance" (ibid.: 74). In other words, we are forced to rewind and consider that circumstances may "close in and force the same action on all," whether we are to the right or left, liberals or conservatives, capitalists or socialists. In times of crisis, the choice of what to do is very limited, and there are not many options for the different believers to follow.

In Galbraith's methodology, we see a movement from images, ideas, and vested interests to circumstances. The latter can be seen in light of the word "events" used in *The Affluent Society*, where we find that "the first requirement for an understanding of contemporary economic and social lives is a clear view of the relation between events and ideas which interpret them" (Galbraith, 1958: 35). In this view, Galbraith is building on the works of giants. Since the time of John Locke and David Hume, the terms "image" and "ideas" have been centerpieces for the study of thought. Locke took great pains to prove that all our ideas have their source in experience, sensation, and reflection (Osler, 1970: 11). With Locke, however, we did not come to a clear understanding of "ideas." It can be either simple or complex. It is intentional in that it is an idea of something. Apparent objects are ideas, attributes and partial ideas. Ideas are tied up with intuition, reason, sensation, and perception (Husserl, 1900: 355; Russell, 1945: Ch. XIII). For David Hume, ideas are mental images. He declares that all of our sensations, passions, and emotions under impressions and ideas are "faint images of these in thinking and reasoning" (Flew, 1961: 22).

In the applications of images and ideas, Galbraith accorded more freedom to the interpreter of economic phenomena than to the interpreter of physical phenomena. In economics this freedom leads to the belief of what is more acceptable, than what is more relevant. We "associate truth with convenience," and "we adhere, as though to a raft, to those ideas which represent our understanding. This is a prime manifestation of vested interest." Further, "familiarity may breed contempt in some areas of human behavior, but in the field of social ideas it is the touchstone of acceptability." Familiarity bestows on acceptable ideas great stability, which yield predictable results. The stable, acceptable ideas for a time period have the element of predictability Galbraith called "conventional wisdom" (Galbraith, 1958: 36-38).

Events are the enemy of conventional wisdom. The view we hold of the world is challenged as new events in the real world occur. For instance, Galbraith explained that people are caught in the vision of a liberal state dating from the time "traders and merchants in England . . . had learned that they were served best by a minimum of government restriction rather than, as in the conventional wisdom, by a maximum of government guidance and protection. . . . These views were finally crystallized by Adam Smith" (ibid.: 40). The theory of David Ricardo pointed out the core economic roots of the social imbalance. "Labour and capital increased in productivity; the land supply remained constant in quality and amount. Rents, as a result, increased more than proportionately and made the landlords the undeserving beneficiaries of advance" (ibid.: 69). "Ricardo's case for leaving everything to the market . . . was essentially functional. Idleness not being subsidized and substance not being wasted, ore was produced and the general well-being would thus be raised" (ibid.: 69, 73). The prediction of this acceptable view is what Kenneth Boulding (1959) called "social imbalance." He argued "that the conventional wisdom resists the expansion of public goods because it still judges the sacrifice in terms of an earlier age when private goods were scarce. This devil therefore consigns us to a peculiarly appropriate hell in which we drive increasingly elaborate (private) cars on increasingly inadequate (public roads) in search of ever more evanescent (public) parking places, and in which we picnic with ever more elegant (private) equipment on (public) site ever more befouled by both biological and economic excreta" (Boulding, 1959: 81). The solution in this case would be an appropriate mix of sales taxes and poverty policies. Further methodological development of Galbraith's thoughts can be examined through the lenses of Institutionalism, and of economics in general.

Galbraith as an Institutionalist

Galbraith was a modern institutionalist, who emphasized the importance of the open-system of production and consumption, evolution in technological progress and circular cumulative causation, social planning, and the normative aspects of science (Tsuru, 1993: 73). Galbraith's concept of countervailing power "goes beyond the closed-system character of neoclassical economics. . . . The concept of 'dependence effect' is also an example of the open-system character of consumption where the consumers' sovereignty is circumscribed by the aggressive policies of suppliers" (ibid.: 78).

Galbraith self-identifies as an institutionalist by his emphasis of the evolutionary character of technology. Technology is the driver of change. But modern changes require the lengthening of the time required for production. For example, the Model-T was produced in a much shorter time span than a modern car. As the time to complete a task increases, more capital has to be committed to it, which in turn requires more skilled labor. As the production process becomes more specialized, its counterpart, the organizational structure, must improve. Furthermore, all these operations need planning.

Planning is needed by firms to harmonize the production process in the face of advanced technology, but also at the state level to redress any social imbalance. For Galbraith, "the productive society . . . provides an opulent supply of some things and a niggardly yield of other[s] . . . the line which divides our area of wealth from our area of poverty is roughly that which divides privately produced and marketed goods and services from publicly rendered services" (Galbraith, 1958: 207). He also states: "Failure to keep public services in minimal relation to private production and use of goods is a cause of social disorder or impairs economic performance" (ibid.: 213).

In his review of Veblen, Galbraith gave more credit to his theory of leisure class for its equating of human behavior to that of the savages. He wrote:

> The rich have often been attacked by the less rich because they have a superior social position that is based on assets and not on moral or intellectual worth. . . . These attacks the rich can endure. That is because the assailants conceded them their superior power and position; they only deny their rights to that position or to behave as they do therein. . . . Here is Veblen's supreme literary and polemical achievement. He concedes the rich and the well-to-do nothing. . . . Veblen calmly identified the manners and behavior of these so-called gentlemen with the manners and behavior of the people of the bush. (Galbraith, 1979: 136-137)

In a more modern work, Galbraith has further echoed the work of Veblen. He wrote about work that "those who least need compensation for their effort, could best survive without it, are paid the most. The wages, or more precisely the salaries, bonuses and stock options, are the most munificent at the top, where work is a pleasure. This evokes no seriously adverse response. Not until recently did the inflated compensation and extensive perquisites of functional or nonfunctional executives lead to critical comment" (Galbraith, 2004: 18-19).

Galbraith does not find much science in Veblen's economics. He noted that "Raymond Aron argues that Veblen was better in his social than in his economic perception. With this I agree" (Galbraith, 1979: 144). He reflected on his reading of Veblen's *The Theory of Business Enterprise* when he was at Berkeley:

> There is a conflict between the ordered rationality of the machine process as developed by the engineers and the technicians and the moneymaking context in which it operates. . . . The money makers . . . sabotage the rich possibilities inherent in the machine process . . . the idea has been a blind alley. Organization and management are greater tasks than Veblen implies; so is the problem of accommodating production to social need. (ibid.: 144)

Galbraith went on to take these ideas in different directions. For instance, he wrote: "There is no name for all who participate in group decision-making or the organization which they form, I propose to call this organization the Technostructure" (Galbraith, 1967: 71).

Galbraith's General Economic Model

Galbraith's education is anchored to classical economic theory. Galbraith departed from the classics by painting some "alternative picture of the structure of modern economic society" (Galbraith, 1979: 3). He summarized his thoughts under two distorting factors. The first is the great inclination to think in static terms, as in the physical sciences. This image is distorting because of "the very high rate of movement that has been occurring in the basic economic institutions." The second distorting factor is a "not valid" image of the modern industrial economy. That image includes such propositions as: the market dominates; firms are numerous; firms are competitive; firms submit to the will of the consumers; consumer's decision is sovereign; prices are profits determined by the market; diseconomies reflect "higher preference of people for the goods being produced as opposed to the protection of air, water or landscape," and that "an organic relationship between the business firm and the state does not exist" (ibid.: 4-7).

He modified the classics as he saw fit for *The Good Society*. The good society has both "utopian" and "achievable" worlds in it (Galbraith, 1996: 3). It is also characterized by "human" and "institutional" characteristics in the sense that "human beings are human beings wherever they live," and "there is fixed instructional structure of the economy—the corporations and the other business enterprises, large and small, and the limits they impose" (ibid.: 6). Within that view of society, people are committed to consumer goods "as the primary source of human satisfaction and enjoyment and as the most visible measure of social achievement. Among these achievable or accessible institutional attainments are personal liberty, basic well-being, racial and ethnic equality, and opportunities for a rewarding life (ibid.: 2-4).

Galbraith categorized traditional economics as having a unimodal image. He wrote that "The presently accepted image of this economy is of course, of numerous entrepreneurial firms distributed as between consumer- and producer-good industries, all subordinate to their market and thus, ultimately, to the instruction of the consumer. Being numerous, the firms are competitive; any tendency to overprice a product by one firm is corrected by the undercutting of a competitor. . . . In one exception, the firm has influence over prices and output; that is the case of monopoly or oligopoly" (Galbraith, 1979: 5). He added that "the valid image of the economic system is not, in fact, of a single competitive and entrepreneurial system. It is a double of a bimodal system" (ibid.: 7). By bimodality he meant that concentrated large firms account for approximately half of the market activity, while the dispersed sector accounts for the other half.

As a test to his bimodal hypothesis, Galbraith pointed to the combination of severe unemployment and severe inflation. Fiscal and monetary policies will fail to stop the demand for goods and services from falling if inflation exists. Galbraith speculated that only an income and price policy can arrest unemployment, as it did in Germany, Austria, Switzerland, and Scandinavia, where "implicit incomes policy . . . considers the effect of wage concessions on both domestic inflation rates and external competitive position" (ibid.: 14).

For Galbraith, income and price policies rested on a cost-push inflation. As C. G. F. Simkin pointed out, the possibility "of using controls over wages, if these can be applied, obviously depends upon the extent to which prices are cost-determined and upon the extent to which wages are influenced by other factors than demand for labour" (Simkin, 1968: 170). Galbraith has advanced such a possibility. The argument is that trade unions have power over wages and corporations have power over prices. While the old-fashioned wage-price spiral argument is no longer prevalent, unions and management can collectively bargain and pass price increases to the public. "Complaints over the cost of wage settlements now rarely come from employers. Almost invariably they come from the government, which is concerned over the inflationary effects, or from the public, which has to pay the higher price" (Galbraith, 1979: 12).

According to Galbraith, acceptance of the bimodal model creates more unequal developments. The corporate sector is able to convince the government and consumers of the need for their product. It achieves this goal by employing technical skills, advance organizations, and large amounts of capital. On the other hand, the competitive sector has less adequate means. This bimodality explains why products such as adequate housing and health care are usually undersupplied even in developed countries. A correlate to this unequal development is inequality of opportunity and income. It is not easy for the unemployed to move into a unionized job, and movement in the competitive sector is associated with lower paying jobs. This process augments the unemployment that is associated with the inability of fiscal and monetary policy to control inflation.

Galbraith's socio-economic views appear as a research program. For over seventy years, he moved between "approved belief... conventional wisdom... and the reality." His research revealed that "reality is more obscured by social or habitual preference and personal or group pecuniary advantage in economics and politics than in any other subject" (Galbraith, 2004: ix). He continued: "economics and larger economic and political systems cultivate their own version of truth.... It is what serves, or is not adverse to influential economic, political and social interest.... Most progenitors ... are not deliberately in its service. They are unaware of how their views are shaped, how they are had." In this new reality, "Managers... not the owners of capital, are the effective power in the modern enterprise... the term 'capitalism' is in decline.... Management having full authority in the modern great corporation, it was natural that it would extend its role to politics and government.... The blurring of the difference between the private and corporate sector and the diminishing public sector proceeds . . ."; and "the institution and its leader are the ordained answer to both boom and inflation and recession" (ibid.: 3, 35-36, 43).

Galbraith's Propositions of Economics

We turn now to some propositions in Galbraith's works that form the premises of the bulk of his arguments.

Theorem I (Galbraith: Power):

"... if choice by the public is the source of power, the organizations that comprise the economic system cannot have power" (Galbraith, 1973: 5 [italics added]). This proposition established the dichotomy between the market system and the planning system. "Power is the ability of an individual or a group to impose its purposes on others.... In the planning system, the economy of the large corporation, the power is possessed by the technostructure" (ibid.: 99). "In the neoclassical mode the firm is ultimately subordinate to the market and thus to the consumer" (ibid.: 105).

Galbraith argued that "the neoclassical system is not a description of reality" (ibid.: 28). Power resides with the control of the factors of production. Galbraith asked "why power is associated with some factors and not with others" (Galbraith, 1967: 47).

An examination of history indicates that "power over the productive enterprise . . . has shifted radically between the factors of production" (ibid.: 50-51). For centuries after the discovery of America, land was given a strategic power role. For instance, the physiocratic school held that land was the source of value. For Ricardo, diminishing returns were a result of lack of arable land for cultivation at the margin, and the source of Malthus' dismal prediction can be traced to the lack of land to grow the needed food supply for the geometrically growing population. With the coming of the Industrial Revolution and new technological innovations, the role of capital became elevated (ibid.: 54).

It is interesting to note that power did not pass to labor or to the classical entrepreneur as a factor of production. "Labor has won limited authority over its pay and working conditions but none over the enterprise" (ibid.: 58). The entrepreneur's "principal qualifications were imagination, capacity for decision and courage in risking money. . . . None of these qualifications are especially important for organizing intelligence or effective in competing with it" (ibid.: 68).

For Galbraith, Theorem I is equivalent to an "either or" proposition: either the market system in which "consumer behavior, costs, the response of suppliers, the behavior of the state, are all beyond the reach of the individual firm" or a planning system where "firm seeks and wins power or influence over all of these things. . . . It is not to individuals but to organizations that power in the business enterprise and power in the society has passed" (ibid.: 60). With this passing of power to the organization, "there is, *a priori*, no reason to believe that it will maximize the return to capital. More plausible it will maximize its success as an organization" (ibid., 121). That is not to say that an organization has no goals in regards to returns. "The first concern of the technostructure . . . is to protect the minimum level of return which secures its autonomy and hence its survival" (ibid.: 192). This security resides with stable prices and control of demand through the management of how income is spent. "The purpose of demand management is to insure that people buy what is produced" (ibid.: 203).

Several corollaries follow from Theorem I.

Corollary 1 to Theorem I:

Organizations "are merely instruments in the ultimate service of that choice" (Galbraith, 1993: 5). Galbraith thinks that "if we know the goals of the society we will have guidance to the goals of the organizations that serve it and the individuals that comprise these organizations" (Galbraith, 1967: 159). He therefore, finds it "necessary to summarize and reaffirm a rule. The relationship between society at large and the organization must be consistent with the relation of the organization to the individual. There must be consistency in the goals of the society, the organization and the individual" (Ibid.: 160).

Members of the technostructure have goals. The technostructure refers to all the participants "in group decision-making or the organization which they form" (ibid.: 71). Their goals are reflected in the corporation. The goals of the corporation are in turn a reflection of the goals of society (ibid.: 161).

Corollary 2 to Theorem I:

"Persuasion . . . becomes the basic instrument for the exercise of power" (Galbraith, 1973: 7). Corporations can assure themselves of a minimum return for survival if they manage the demand for their product. The kind of management required includes persuasive advertising and other sales effort. "Product design, model change, packaging and even performance reflect the need to provide what [are] called strong selling points" (Galbraith, 1967: 203). As the goal of a firm is to expand sales, the technostructure must be aggressive in its sales promotion, advertising, and marketing efforts. In other words, "if sales are slipping, a new selling formula can be found that will correct the situation. By and large this assumption is justified, which is to say that means can almost always be found to keep exercise of consumer discretion within workable limits" (ibid.: 207). The development of advertising media—radio, television, magazines, newspaper, etc.—have enabled and facilitated "mass persuasion."

Corollary 3 to Theorem I:

(Galbraith: Countervailing Power) *"Power on one side of the market creates both the need for, and the prospect of reward to, the exercise of countervailing power from the other side"* (Galbraith, 1956: 113). Big unions are said to countervail the power of big corporations. With the shift of power from capital to the technostructure, the power of unions has been diminished. "Labor relations, naturally enough, are conducted in accordance with the goals of the technostructure.... This means that the technostructure may readily trade profits for protection against such an undirected event with such an unpredictable outcome as a strike" (Galbraith, 1967: 265). A negotiated wage increase does not come out of the pocket of the union negotiator. It need not come out of profits either, as "the mature firm does not maximize profits, its negotiated wage can come out of increased prices" (ibid.: 265).

Corollary 4 to Theorem I:

(Galbraith: Firms vs. State) "*Technological compulsions, and not ideology or political wile, will require the firm to seek the help and protection of the state*" (Galbraith, 1967: 20). The education and technology on which the technostructure depends is mostly provided by the public sector (ibid.: 296). The firm depends on the state in matters of patenting, regulation, wage-price control, and antitrust. "Thus the state, through the tariff, could accord the entrepreneur protection from foreign competition; it also had railroad, power or other public utility franchises to grant; it possessed land, mineral rights, forests and other natural resources for private exploitation; it could offer exemption or mitigation of taxes; and it could provide moral or armed support in managing refractory workers" (ibid.: 298).

To summarize:

> The mature corporation ... depends on the state for trained manpower, the regulation of aggregate demand, for stability in wages and prices. All are essential to the planning with which it replaces the market. The state, through military and other technical procurement, underwrites the corporation's largest capital commitments in its area of most advanced technology. The mature corporation cannot buy political power. Yet, obviously, it would seem to require it. (Ibid.: 308)

The consequences of Theorem 1 and its corollaries have been controversial. The corporations, along with government, wield a lot of power, although not in its absolute form. As a step toward recognizing the reality of this power, Galbraith advocated a revision of standard Keynesian and neoclassical economics. His model shifts power of the production from land, labor, capital, and the entrepreneur to the technostructure of the modern corporation. Once such an amendment is in place, the incentive mechanism of the firm is adjusted from profit maximization toward sales maximization. This leads to another theorem. According to Harold Demsetz, "There does exist in Galbraith's work one concisely stated hypothesis. . . . This hypothesis states that technostructure-oriented firms sacrifice profits in order to accelerate growth of sales" (Demsetz, 1974: 1).

We now state these conditions as Theorem II and its corollary below:

Theorem II (Galbraith and Baumol):

The objective of the technostructure is *"to achieve the greatest possible rate of corporate growth as measured in sales"* (Galbraith, 1967: 17). This sales hypothesis was first advocated by William J. Baumol but Galbraith has brought it under the arms of his technostructure model.

Corollary 1 to Theory II:

Management desires to "prevent the disruption of the firm's plan" (Demsetz, 1974: 3). As Demsetz explains, the control of prices and/or output allows the technostructure to plan. The technostructure needs stable prices for its maintenance, and consumers should not refuse to buy at those stable prices. We see that "intimately intertwined with the need to control prices is the need to control what is sold at that price" (Galbraith, 1967: 199). This second theorem and its corollary prompted a characterization of the technostructure firm as one that engages in "capital intensive production methods, extensive use of advertising, oligopolistic industry structure, large firm size, and orientation toward military production" (Demsetz, 1974: 2-3). However, Demsetz is careful to add that "Galbraith never instructs his readers explicitly as to a method by which it can be ascertained which firms are most closely bound by the demand of modern technology" (ibid.: 2). Others have given mathematical and game theory characterization to this theorem.

Galbraith's Mathematical and Game Theory Model Justifications

Galbraith has not given us any mathematical model, but what he says about economics has led economists to formulate such models. On the mathematical side, the model of "price maker" as opposed to "price taker" can be adopted to represent Galbraith's position, as he is well-known for his views on price control. We therefore examine this position before we present any model.

Galbraith on Price Fixing

Traditional classical economics advocates a "price takers" point of view where the market mechanism will determine prices. The question arises as to whether it is wise and possible to fix prices and wages, as is customary to fix taxes and interest. For Galbraith, "when the number of buyers is relatively small, or the number of sellers relatively small, or both conditions obtain, the market as an abstract entity disappears" (Galbraith, 1954: 11). More bluntly put, "a market system in which wages and prices are set by the state is a market system no more. Only the blithely obtuse can reconcile 'this Free Enterprise System' with the enforcement of wage and price controls" (Galbraith, 1973: 339).

If prices are fixed, say below equilibrium, sellers will give preference to some buyers they favor, which in the ideal case will eliminate excess supply."When the government fixes prices, it delegates to sellers in imperfect markets the responsibility of rationing their customers which they, in turn, have the power to undertake" (Galbraith. 1954: 11). This method assumes that buyers are paired with sellers. It worked well in the primary metal markets during the Office of the Price Administration in the early 1940s, but not so well in the market for fresh vegetables (ibid.: 12).

Another challenge to price control occurs when "it is technically possible for sellers in such imperfect markets to ration their customers at the fixed prices. . . . The more profitable course, the sanction aside, is to raise prices and break the law. Historically, the consequences of such violation—recalling always that it occurs under circumstances when sellers can charge and buyers will pay more—has been considerable more disastrous for the price-fixing authority than for those it sought to regulate." Price-fixing requires "effort to adapt regulation to existing practice rather than to force the adaptation of price to regulation" (ibid.: 13). It would require policing, which is easier in imperfect markets where the players are few.

In some cases, "it is relatively easy to fix prices that are already fixed" (ibid.: 15). Where market power exists, firms are known to fix prices, and may for any one of a number of reasons seek to minimize the frequency of price changes.

Such markets use discounts, special deals, and other non-price weapons in preference to price changes because buyers have become accustomed to them. Sellers, therefore, are required by this rule and not regulation to maintain stable prices. Galbraith observed that such stability of prices facilitates control.

Retailers tend to follow a customary method of pricing. "That many sellers neglect the opportunities for profit maximization in setting prices cannot be doubted. They follow the easy rule of charging what they have charged before or what someone else is charging. Pricing by custom, in this case, represents, no doubt, an atrophy of market motivation; the seller is opting for a habitual rather than a profitable pattern of behavior" (ibid.: 18). Such pricing is characterized in terms of markup, or rule-of-thumb pricing. Price controls in such markets are only a continuation of such rules.

Galbraith's price control is opposed to the classical and neoclassical model. "In the neoclassical model, prices are primary; they are the intelligence network of the economic system. . . . It is through prices that the neoclassical monopoly or oligopoly exploits the power that goes with being one, or one of the few, sellers in the market. . . . In the planning system, the role of prices is greatly diminished, they are much more effectively under the control of the firm. . . . The control of prices by the firm in the planning system, like the other uses of its power, is governed by the protective and affirmative purposes of the technostructure" (ibid.: 119-121).

A Mathematical Model of Galbraith's Price Makers

John H. Hotson, George Lermer, and Hamid Habibagahi (1976) presented a model for Galbraith that overshadows the classical picture.

$$\dot{P} - (S_A P_0)(C(x,r) - P_0)$$

$$X = I(X, r, T) + G$$

$$L(X,r) = \frac{M}{P+T}$$

where $\dot{P}$ is the rate of change of price with respect to exogenous variables G for government, M for money, and T for taxes. P_0 is initial equilibrium prices, S_A is speed of adjustment, I is an aggregate demand function, C is marginal cost, L is for real balance, X is real output, and r is the nominal interest rate.

In their price maker model, output reacts to excess demand, and prices react to cost-price differential. The complete model also has a real balance effect. The model predicts a correlation between firms and government behavior, and sales. "Price makers are seen as responding to increased government spending by running down inventory and increasing output at initially constant prices. If expanded sales raise their costs . . . they subsequently raise their prices" (ibid.: 183). The authors are cognizant of the discretionary nature of prices in a planning situation, stating that "firms may not raise prices when cost increases . . . they may not lower prices merely because costs have fallen" (ibid.).

A Game Theory Model of Countervailing Power

The game theory confirmation of Galbraith's hypothesis takes on a firm's behavior directly. A biographer of Galbraith wrote:

> In the 1980[s] . . . economists sought new ways of looking at theoretical issues. . . . They used game theory, for example, to suggest that claims like Galbraith's about "countervailing power" might not be so implausible after all, by concentrating on situation of "uncertainty" and "interaction," in which traditional economics' rules for "rational actors" were not clear. A new understanding of "information" and its costs in economic transactions also seemed to support *American Capitalism*'s insistence that orthodox notions of "competition" were flawed. (Parker, 2005: 250)

Such a game theory model involves negotiations between an employer and a labor union. The model of perfect competition by Cournot can be of use. These models can be shown to have Nash bargaining solutions. Broadly speaking, in cooperative games with convex payoff regions, all the possible payoffs are contained in that region. Within that region some payoffs are better than others. One particular payoff point, the status quo point, is achieved without negotiations. It is the payoff that the players can assure themselves, their security level payoff, which represents the maximum a player can get regardless of what its opponent does. If preplay negotiations are allowed in the game, a player may threaten to play a particular strategy all the time. The payoff to this threat strategy may be worse than the payoff of the status quo point. The aim of negotiation, therefore, is to yield a better payoff than the status quo point, or the payoff associated with the threat strategy.

Take two players, M and L, who want to decide how to split C = \$1,000 royalty from a joint book project they have done. The book publisher suggested 2/3 and 1/3 split, but that was rejected. Player M, being spiritual, prefers the *parable of the vineyard* solution, where each receives half of the royalties regardless of their effort. Player L will accept the parable outcome as well. Assume that the players' utility functions are the same: $U(M) = C$; $U(L) = C$. Assume that if they fight, M wins with a probability of 0.8. The Treat Point (TP) gives the expected utility of the players: $E(M) = 0.8(1000) = 800$, and $E(L) = 0.2(1000) = 200$. We note that a 50:50 split solution, without recontract, gives each player \$500, which is Pareto Optimal since one can gain more only at the expense of the other. In order to find the Nash Bargaining solution, we maximize the following equation, which yields \$500 as the maximum after setting the first derivative to zero.

$$Max[(U(M) - TP(M)(U(L - TP(L)] = Max[(C - 800)(C - 200)]$$

$$Max(C^2 - 200C - 800C + 160{,}000) = Max(C^2 - 1000C + 160{,}000)$$

In an article in the *International Journal of Industrial Organization*, Thomas von Ungern-Sternberg revisited Galbraith's countervailing power hypothesis from the Nash Bargaining point of view. For the purpose of that test, countervailing power meant "to compare the results of a large producer selling to a large number of small retailers with a situation where he is faced with a smaller number of large retailers . . . the ability of these retailers to extract lower prices from their supplier was more important than any negative effect due to the increase in concentration at the distribution level" (von Ungern-Sternberg, 1996: 508).

The justification of this hypothesis can be found in Galbraith's work. He wrote: "One of the seemingly harmless simplifications of formal economic theory has been the assumption that producers of consumers' goods sell their products directly to consumers. . . . In fact goods pass to consumers by way of retailers and other intermediaries and this is a circumstance of first importance. Retailers are required by their situation to develop countervailing power on the consumer's behavior" (Galbraith, 1956: 117). The retailer can use a variety of strategies to exact a low price. Such strategies include developing "their own source of supply," concentrating their "entire patronage on a single supplier," and "keeping the seller in a state of uncertainty" (ibid.: 120-121).

Galbraith, however, does not rest the whole foundation of countervailing power on retailing. Countervailing power is most visible in the labor market. "The labor market serves admirable to illustrate the incentives to the development of countervailing power and it is of great importance in this market . . . ; Countervailing power also manifests itself, although less visible, in producers' goods markets. For many years the power of the automobile companies, as purchasers of steel, has sharply curbed the power of the steel mills as sellers" (ibid.: 117). Galbraith points to the residential-building industry as an instance where countervailing power is absent because of the existence of many thousands of small individual firms that build houses. Even if the little restraints in the form of alliances with each other, unions, and politicians were removed, "the typical builder would still be a small and powerless figure buying his building materials in small quantities at high cost from suppliers with effective market power" (ibid.: 125).

The literature has examined the Countervailing Power hypothesis, as it should, from the retailing point of view where the hypothesis is more pervasive. Frederic Scherer and David Ross (1990) presented the industrial organization side of the hypothesis through bilateral monopoly and oligopoly. Earlier, Joe Bain anchored Galbraith's thought in the domain of "bilateral monopoly or bilateral oligopoly, which is then pasted on the whole industrial economy" (Bain, 1972: 220). This bilateral domain of economic theory is noted for its indeterminism of output and prices. Nevertheless, Scherer and Ross concluded that "countervailing power is most likely to benefit consumers when three conditions hold simultaneously: when upstream supply functions are highly elastic, when buyers can bring substantial power to bear on the pricing of monopolistic suppliers, and when those same buyers face substantial price competition in their end product markets" (Scherer and Ross, 1990: 528). Observing these conclusions, von Ungern-Sternberg (1996) introduced a game theory model to further improve the bilateral foundation of the countervailing power model. The following is a summary of his model.

We assume N retailers, each buying from the producer at some input price, c_n, and selling to the consumers the quantity x_n. Profits for each will be $\pi_n = x_n(p_n - c_n)$. p_n is the second stage price. If a retailer refuses to buy the input for price c_n, then his profits will be equal zero. We assume M producers, with costs c_m, each selling to all N retailers, with profits: $\pi_p^N = N x_n(c_n - c_m)$. In the case of one producer facing all retailers, we can express the Nash Bargaining problem as follows:

$$Max_{c_i} = \left[\pi_N(C_i) - \pi_{0\ P}^{N} \right]^{\beta} \left[\pi_P(C_i) - \pi_0^P \right]^{(1-\beta)}$$

The terms in the first bracket are profits less treat point payoff to the retailer. Similarly, the terms in the second bracket represent profits less treat point payoff to the producer.

Among other expressions, the results of the maximization yield a degree of bargaining power, $\alpha = \beta / (1 - \beta)$. The change in the N retailers relative to the producer is equal to the degree of bargaining power to the ratio of their respective derivative, i.e. $\Delta\pi_N / \Delta\pi_p = \alpha\,[\pi'_N / \pi'_N]$. The assumption about the results is that "if any one retailer does obtain a lower input price than his competitors, he obtains this lower input price only for the equilibrium quantity he would normally sell in the second stage, and not for any greater quantity" (ibid.: 512).

The interpretation of the results turned on the relationship between bargaining power and the number of retailers, α vs. N, assuming that the consumers have a linear demand: $P = a - bx$. The author concluded that "these theoretical models suggest that to find results in support of Galbraith's theory one must have good reasons to suppose that the retailer's bargaining power (as defined in the Nash bargaining solution) increases as their number decreases, i.e. their bargaining power increases more than proportionately with the losses they can inflict on the producer" (ibid.: 518).

Modal Elements in Galbraith's Work

Because much controversy surrounds Galbraith's ideas, we wish to explore his thought from a logical point of view. His works resonate modes of what is necessary and what is possible in the world of economics. The "necessary" and the "possible" are foundational terms in modal logic. first order logic (FOL), a branch of logic that goes back to Aristotle, is concerned with individuals, which can be defined as people or nations (Holt et al., 1998: 280). A second order logic (SOL) is concerned with the properties of the individuals and propositional logic (PL) is concerned with sentences that are either true or false (Stebbing, 1961: 33). For our purpose, "it is sounder to view modal logic as the indispensable core of logic, to view truth-functional logic as one of its fragments, and to view 'other' logics—epistemic, deontic, temporal, and the like—as accretions either upon modal logic . . . or upon its truth-functional components" (Bradley and Swartz, 1979: 219).

Logic of Necessity and Possibility

Galbraith's thought on economic matters is modal in many senses. Economic expressions have many different moods. In normative economics, we make statements about policies that takes the mood that we "should" take a certain policy. In positive economics, we use the expression that something "is" the case. In instrumental economics, we use statements such as that we "ought to" increase or decrease the rate of interest. Modal logic studies what implications those moods have for economic reality.

The difference between ordinary propositional logic, and the modal logic lies precisely with the concept of implications. Bertrand Russell and Alfred North Whitehead (1910) gave us the concept of material implication when they introduce implications in PL. That method relied on the true (T) and false (F) values of sub-sentences for validation. For instance, when we say of the two sub-sentences A and B that A implies B, we can construct a truth table to show that the argument has validity. The elements of the table hold that 1) if A is true, then B is true; 2) if A is false then B is false; and 3) if A is false then B is true.

The inference that B is true when A is false implies a weak implication for the logicians C. I. Lewis and Cooper Langford (1932), who prefer to deal with "strict" implications of various degrees, which they labeled S1 to S5. By adding the concepts of necessary and possible, their system has laid the foundation of modern modal logic (ML).

Logicians have been busy evolving the methods of reasoning in ML. They use terms such as "necessary" or "possible" to avoid being self-contradictory in their expressions. All of Galbraith's works, for instance, are consistent in that they "describe a set of possible situations that are possible together. The story may or may not be true. The actual world is the story that's true—the description of how things in fact are" (Gensler, 2002: 145).

Corresponding to Kurt Godel's investigation of completeness theorem for PL, Saul Kripke studies completeness theorem for ML. A simple meaning of completeness is that the axioms and rules of a system of logic do not allow one to infer or deduce a conclusion that both B and not B are valid. (For a discussion of Godel, see Szenberg et al., 2005.) Here we describe Kripke's system for modal logic (ML) for our purpose of expounding Galbraith's methodology.

In Kripke's terminology, we have an actual world that belongs to the set of all the possible worlds that could have existed. He explained: "Intuitively, we look at matters thus: *K* is the set of all 'possible worlds'; *G* is the 'real world'. If H_1 and H_2 are two worlds, $H_1 R H_2$ means intuitively that H_2 is 'possible relate to' H_1, i.e., that every proposition true in H_2 is possible in H_1" (Kripke, 1963: 86).

The model structure (*G*, *K*, *R*) is a model that assigns T or F to the propositional variables for each world, *H*, in all the possible worlds, *K*. Essentially, we can now consider the true values of the relationship.

When the facts are overwhelming, and can be applied in all states of affairs, the argument from necessity is obtained. However, when the facts are only partial, and therefore apply to only some of our state of affairs, the argument is from possibility. In propositional logic, the operators ∀ and ∃ are used respectively to indicate necessity and possibility. They may be used to say that an economic proposition is true for all, or true for some cases, respectively. In modal logic, the respective operators □ and ◊ are added.

Both necessary and possible arguments occur in a sphere of influence. We therefore first define what that sphere of influence or state of affairs, is for Galbraith. The logicians suggest alternative ways of doing this. We follow the simple way suggested by Lewis (1973: 6-7). A ball represents a set of worlds, S_i. The ball itself contains worlds, i, that can access the set of worlds in S_i.

What might Galbraith's "sphere of influence" be? One candidate is his definition of "The Good Society," S_i (Galbraith, 1996). The Good Society contains both "utopian" and "achievable" worlds within it (ibid.: 3). It is also characterized by "human" and "institutional" characteristics in the sense that "Human beings are human beings wherever they live," and "there is fixed instructional structure of the economy—the corporations and the other business enterprises, large and small, and the limits they impose" (ibid.: 2-3). Among the achievable or accessible human activities in his "sphere of influence" is the commitment to have consumer goods "as the primary source of human satisfaction and enjoyment and as the most visible measure of social achievement. Among the achievable or accessible intuitional attainments are personal liberty, basic well-being, racial and ethnic equality, and opportunities for a rewarding life (ibid.: 4). Necessity and possibility limit the scope of the sphere of influence. We can make simple ML and PL statements about Galbraith as follows.

Major Premise: "Economics, like other social life, does not conform to a simple and coherent pattern" (Galbraith, 1970: 35). Where E is economics, and C is a coherent pattern, the ML and PL expressions for this premise are respectively:

$$E\Box \rightarrow {\sim}C \text{ or}$$

$$\text{All } x\ (E(x) \rightarrow {\sim}C(x))$$

"But one must have an explanation or interpretation of economic behavior . . . ; Within a considerable range he (the individual) is permitted to believe what he pleases. He may hold whatever view of this world he finds most agreeable or otherwise to his taste" (ibid.: 35). It is possible to accept conventional wisdom when it is convenient to do so, for "truth ultimately serves to create a consensus, so in the short run does acceptability" (ibid.: 34), and we largely "associate truth with convenience" (ibid.: 36). This leads to the notion that there exists a view, an opinion for all persons. If P is a person then P has a view. These possible expressions may take the following ML and PL forms respectively:

$$P\Diamond \rightarrow V \text{ or}$$

$$\text{All } x\ (P(x) \rightarrow V(x))$$

In the *New Industrial State,* Galbraith stated the necessity of planning this way:

> From the time and capital that must be committed, the inflexibility of this commitment, the needs of large organization[s] and the problems of market performance under conditions of advanced technology, comes the *necessity for planning* . . . The need for planning, it has been said, arises from the long period of time that elapses during the production process, the high investment that is involved and the inflexible commitment of that investment in the particular task. (Galbraith, 1967: 16 [italics added])

The planning system that Galbraith advocates is of the nature of "collective intelligence" involving organizations. "ORGANIZATION is an arrangement for substituting the more specialized effort or knowledge of several or many individuals for that of one. For numerous economic tasks organization is both *possible* and *necessary*" (Galbraith, 1973: 87 [italics added]).

In these arguments, the necessity for planning comes out of technological process. Galbraith pinned this necessity of planning to the technological process because technology translates organized or scientific knowledge into practical outcomes (Galbraith, 1967: 12). Investment requires the firms to tie up capital for a time during which the anticipated demand may fail to occur. During that time, the firm will have to anticipate that the inputs will be available in a way that cost is compatible with the expected price (ibid.: 24). Technology is both a cause and a consequence of change, which modern corporations are always undergoing (ibid.: 20), and following Schumpeter, technology is in the hands of big corporations.

In summing up the necessary and possible, let *QcG* represent the inclusion of the government sphere. *G* is government, and *c* is a member of all government activities. Similarly, let *RdM* represent the inclusion of the private market sector. *M* is the market, and *d* is a member of all private market activities. Galbraith's model can now be represented as:

$$\text{QcG \& RdM} \tag{1}$$

Equation 1 represents dummy variables, which we can use as operators to make decisions. One can expand the equation to represent countervailing power by adding C for countervailing power by unions and making e the inclusion operator. The equation will then become:

$$\text{QcG \& RdM \& SeC} \tag{2}$$

The necessity and possibility operators can now be called upon to validate statements.

Large corporations necessitate large unions, implying countervailing power. Sharply deteriorating economic conditions, such as the Great Depression, or budget deficits, necessitate government intervention, implying control by economic agents.

Conclusion

Samuelson states that Galbraith belongs to that group of economists who believe in the "big picture theory" of the economy (Samuelson, 1972: vol. 3, 275). In this generalist view of economics, power is essential. In the historic evolution of society, economics has witnessed the evolution of power of the factors of production from land to capital, and labor being left behind. Galbraith advanced the view that capital is no longer central to economics as the classical and neoclassical economists thought. The role of capital in the power structure is superseded by the technostructure. This model stands along the classical, neoclassical, and Keynesian models as a viable alternative explanation of the capitalist economic system.

Although Galbraith does not use mathematical language, his model is adaptable to mathematics. In our exposition we have given examples of such exposition in terms of theorems, price maker theory, game theory, and modal logic.

References

Bain, J. S. (1972). *Essays on price theory and industrial organization.* Boston: Little Brown.

Boulding, K. (1959, Feb.). Book review of *The Affluent Society. The Review of Economics and Statistics,* 41(1), 81.

Bradley, R., & Swartz, N. (1979). *Possible worlds: An introduction to logic and its philosophy.* Oxford: Blackwell.

Demsetz, H. (1974, March). Where is the new industrial state? *Economic Inquiry,* 7(1), 1-12.

Flew, A. (1971). *Hume's philosophy of belief.* London: Routledge and Kegan Paul.

Friedman, M. (1977). *Friedman and Galbraith.* Vancouver, Canada: The Fraser Insitute.

Galbraith, J. K. (2004). *The economics of innocent fraud: Truth for our time.* New York: Houghton Mifflin.

———. (1996). *The good society: The humane agenda.* Boston: Houghton Mifflin.

———. (1979). *Annals of an abiding liberal.* Andrea D. Williams (Ed.). Boston: Houghton Mifflin.

———. (1973). *Economics and the public purpose.* Boston: Houghton Mifflin.

———. (1970 [1958]). *The affluent society.* London: Pelican.
———. (1970, May). Economics as a system of belief. *American Economic Review,* 60(2), 469-478.
———. (1967). *The new industrial state.* Boston: Houghton Mifflin.
———. (1954 [1952]). *A theory of price control.* Cambridge, MA: Harvard University Press.
———. (1956 [1952]). *American capitalism.* Boston: Houghton Mifflin.
———. (1954). *The great crash 1929.* New York: Time.
Galbraith, J. K. & Salinger, N. (1980). *Almost everyone's guide to economics.* Boston: Bantam Books.
Gambs, J. S. (1975). *John Kenneth Galbraith.* Boston: Twayne.
Gensler, H. J. (2002). *Introduction to logic.* London: Routledge.
Hayek, F. A. (1961, April). The non sequitur of the "dependence effect." *Southern Economic Journal,* 27.
Holt, J., Rohatyan, D., & Varzi, A. (1998). *Logic: Schaum's outlines* (2nd ed.). New York: McGraw Hill.
Hotson, J. H., Lenmer, G., &Habibaghi, H. (1976). Some dynamics of Harrod's and Galbraith's dichotomies. In John H. Hotson, *Stagflation and the bastard Keynesians.* Waterloo, Ontario: University of Waterloo Press.
Husserl, E. (1970). *Logical investigations.* Vol. 1, (1900). Translated by J. N. Findlay. London: Routledge & Kegan Paul.
Keynes, J. M. (1936 [1970]). *The general theory of employment interest and money.* London: Macmillan St. Martin's Press.
Kripke, S. (1963). Semantical considerations of modal logic. *Acta Philosophica Fennica,* 16, 83-94.
Lewis, D. (1973). *Counterfactuals.* Cambridge, MA: Harvard University Press.
Lewis, C. I., & Langford, C. H. (1959). *Symbolic logic* (2nd ed.). New York: Dover Publications.
Marshall, A. (1920). *Principals of economics* (8th ed.). London: Macmillan.
Parker, R. (2005). *John Kenneth Galbraith: His life, his politics, his economics.* New York: Farrar, Strauss and Giroux.
Reisman, D. (1980). *Galbraith and market capitalism.* New York: New York University Press.

Robbins, L. (1935). *An essay on the nature and significance of economic science* (2nd ed.). London: Macmillan.

Russell, B. (1945). *A history of western philosophy.* New York: Simon and Schuster.

Russell, B., & Whitehead, A. (1910-1913). *Principia mathematica.* 3 vols. Cambridge: Cambridge University Press.

Simkin, C. G. F. (1968). *Economics at large: An advanced textbook on macro-economics.* London: Weidenfeld and Nicholson.

Stebbing, L. S. (1961). *A modern introduction to logic.* New York: Harper Torchbooks.

Stigler, G. J. (1985, May 27). John Kenneth Galbraith's marathon television series: A certain Galbraith in an uncertain age. Reprinted in K. R. Leube & T. Gale (Eds.), *The essence of Stigler.* Stanford: Hoover Institution Press, 1986. pp. 352-258.

———. (1968). *The Organization of Industry.* Chicago: University of Chicago Press.

Szenberg, M., Ramrattan, L., & Gottesman, A. A. (2005). Paul A. Samuelson: Philosopher and theorist. *International Journal of Social Economics,* 32(4), 325-338.

Tsuru, S. (1993). *Institutional economics revisited.* Cambridge: Cambridge University Press.

von Ungern-Sternberg, T. (1996). Countervailing power revisited. *International Journal of Industrial Organization,* 14, 507-520.

PART V

MARXIAN ECONOMICS

Adolph Lowe

Adolph Lowe

As a professor of economics at the New School, Adolph Lowe had a reputation for being stingy with grades. It is well known that he flunked the dissertation of his best student and friend, Robert Heilbroner—and that *The Worldly Philosophers* went on to become an all-time bestseller. Students would rather audit Lowe's courses than be graded on his curve, and all agreed that they had best avoid having him evaluate their PhD dissertations. As a student of Lowe's, I (Lall) remember that before he let you audit his course, he required you to "go down to the registrar and pay," as he would say.

Despite this, Adolph Lowe was my greatest teacher. He reflected the time-honored tradition of coming in early to write down the essentials on the chalkboard and having students transcribe them as notes that formed the core of their learning. Lowe's toughness was a result of the strong grounding in economic methodology that forms the core of his work.

Education

Adolph Lowe was born in Stuttgart, Germany in 1893. His father was a merchant, so the young Lowe absorbed the lessons of a business environment. Lowe graduated from gymnasium in Stuttgart and studied at several universities in Munich, Berlin, and Tübingen between 1911 and 1915, receiving his doctorate in Law from the University of Tübingen in 1918. From 1918 to1931 he worked for the Weimar government, and from 1924-1926 he also worked for the German Bureau of Statistics. His academic career flourished at the University of Kiel (1925-31), where he was known for research on business cycles. From 1931 to 1933, he taught economics and political economy at the University of Frankfurt.

The remainder of Lowe's academic life was spent in the West. He was the first professor of social sciences to be dismissed by the Nazi government, in 1933. A few months later, he and his wife decided to emigrate after their daughters were dismissed from school because of their "race." The family left for Britain just before the German government revoked the passports of those it defined as Jewish.

In the UK, Lowe lectured at the University of Manchester and was a Rockefeller Foundation fellow from 1933 until 1938. In 1935, he published his first book, *Economics and Sociology: A Plea for Co-Operation in the Social Sciences*. In 1939 he moved to New York City to help found The New School, where he spent the rest of his academic career until retirement. During that tenure, in 1953, he held a one-year appointment at the Hebrew University in Jerusalem.

Lowe On Economic Methodology

Lowe's methodology is associated with the concept of instrumental analysis. His ideas are different from work in pragmatism and John Neville Keynes' tri-party characterization of economics as positive, normative, or practical (see Machlup, 1978: 506). Instrumental analysis is an approach for deriving one or more paths that society or the economy can take. The problem is to find the suitable path, given the micro behavior and motivations, as well as political control appropriate for the attainment of that path. This solution lies in the broad domain of political economy.

Lowe's work at the University of Kiel was focused on the dynamic aspects of growth and cycles in the economy. His approach was a feedback mechanism wherein economic goals are likened to the process of filling a glass with water. Through observation (with the eye), a control mechanism (the hand) regulates the path of growth (the flow) to obtain balanced growth in the different sectors of the economy (see Hagemannn and Kurtz, 1998: 23). Lowe is on the critical side of this mechanism. The orthodox side "bears all the characteristics of a negative feedback mechanism, which automatically corrects any deviation from stability. The critics, on the other hand . . . are alleged to produce positive feedbacks amplifying partial distortions into general disequilibrium" (Lowe, 1987: 238).

Lowe's methodology is found operational in economic growth. An economy is driven by flows of inputs such as labor and capital, which are subject to human behavior. Society's desires should dictate the path of its economy. The agents of society pull on a set of prescribed incentives, stimuli, or instruments that steer the economy toward the desired path. In that sense, Lowe's methodology is characterized as instrumental, involving a spectrum of means or interventions to be determined by political consent, and therefore not merely positive economics (Heilbroner, Hagemann, and Kurtz, 1998: 11).

Lowe's methodology is not without its detractors. Fritz Machlup raised questions about whether it can be truly differentiated from Keynes' tri-party apparatus, whether preference can truly be overlooked in selecting the "different types of measures capable of steering behavior along suitable paths," and whether "different aspirations of goal-setters are mutually compatible and can be translated into a consistent and realizable set of targets" (Machlup, 1978: 509-510). Machlup also asked whether one can truly separate "goal setting" and "policy-choosing," and whether instrumental analysis should need to cross the critical boundary. Machlup likens the latter point to crossing an immigration boundary between countries. A traveler can only declare all the things (norms and customs) it has at the time, but not things that will be developed later. Therefore, Machlup questions whether an honest declaration for instrumental analysis is possible (ibid.: 511).

Lowe on Business Cycles

Lowe's 1926 contributions center on a methodological model for assessing the business cycle empirically. Lowe is particular about defining scientific economics. His system of variables feed back on itself negatively, and he enumerates between constants and variables. He uses theoretical, empirical, historical, and political methods in his arguments. He talks of an "intra-systemic process" as well as a "reciprocal causation" (Lowe, 1975: 415).

The methodological tug-of-war Lowe underscored is that equilibrium theory is static, while business cycle theory is dynamic. Economists tend to use the "*ceteris paribus* clause of the variation method [which] acquires complete and exclusive validity in the closed, interdependent system" (Lowe, 1977: 250). "All the systems of economics since the Physiocrats have centered around the concept of equilibrium. From the trivial idea of the balancing of supply and demand to the differential equations of the mathematical school and the entire theory of price, all are based on the idea of tendencies to equilibrium" (ibid.: 252). Analysis with that equilibrium tool is what Lowe dubbed a "closed, interdependent system" or a "static system." Basically, the methodology of the static view conforms to a system because "they explicitly set out to deduce the cycle from an equilibrium position" (Ibid.: 257). Some of the theories Lowe analyzed and rejected are displayed in Table 1.

Nobel laureate and empirical growth economics expert Simon Kuznets has assessed Lowe's view on business cycle theory, and classifies the works of Albert Aftalion and Gustav Cassel into the group of circular reasoning. The others in Table 1 fall under the group of generalizing theories. Into the anti-theoretical category, Kuznets places Arthur Pigou, and in the group of time discrepancy, he places Irving Fisher. There is also yet another group that believes in theories of independent variables. The general result is that the postulate of equilibrium is blocking the light of what causes cycles (Kuznets, 1953: 8-12).

Nobel laureate Frederic Hayek was also influenced by Lowe's model; he seems to accept the notion that cycles should be analyzed for an "open system" rather than a closed system point of view (Hayek, 2012: vol. 7, 12-13).

TABLE 1: Famous Static Business Cycle Theories

Description	Reason for Crisis	Solution for Crisis	Page number (Lowe, 1977)
Aftalion, A.	Shortage of consumption goods	Price rise will induce production	254
Cassel, G.	High interest rates and participating movements in wages and prices	Low interest rates and participating movements in wages and prices	255-256.
Spiethoff	Isolation between the production and consumption spheres	New markets and technological progress	256.
Sombart and Schumpeter	Overproduction due to technical circumstances. Technical efficiency drives competitors out of the market.	Those activities caused by business leaders are cancelled by "opposite change in some other part of the system." (Kuznets, 1953: 9)	257.

Sources: Lowe, 1977; Kuznets, 1953.

Lowe on Economic Growth

One cannot clearly distinguish Lowe's contribution of growth from his contribution to business cycles. In his magnum opus, *The Path of Economic Growth*, Lowe explains that he was in search of a model of "cyclical growth," an obvious attempt to merge cycle theory with growth (Lowe 1976: ix). This is a significant point for modern growth theory because as recently as 2001, the Nobel Laureate and growth theorist Robert Solow had this to say about the fusion of growth and cycle theory:

> if you pick up an article today with the words "business cycle" in the title... the underlying model will be... a slightly dressed up version of the neoclassical growth model. The question I want to circle around is: How did that happen.... My interest is in the formal assumptions of the informal background presumptions or perhaps the judgments of fact that encouraged this transformation of a theory without business cycles into a theory of business cycles. (Solow, 2001: 19)

Lowe's contribution to economic growth is traceable to his 1955 article for the National Bureau of Economic Research. Lowe focused on real capital formation without regard for finance or business organization. For Lowe, "arriving at valid generalizations of all the determinants of the level of output—is so difficult to accomplish. The reason is that almost all these determinants are themselves the result of forces which operate outside the economic realm" (Lowe, 1965: 286) Lowe chose real capital as a source of growth because "being an output as well as an input, the size and variation of the capital stock are intra-economic phenomena, open to the discovery of 'dependable uniformities'" (ibid.: 286). The term "dependable uniformities" refers to structurally stable characteristics that cause the level and growth in output. They include a complex of things such as natural, psychological, and institutional characteristics, and the changes in social structures themselves. Economic growth seems to rely more on historical factors, which are hard to ascertain. In synthesizing these characteristics, Lowe said that "The economic theory of growth thus largely coincides with the theory of capital formation" (ibid.: 287).

Lowe built a structural model on an *a priori* basis, that is, without attempting statistical or descriptive validation. His structural model is essentially fluid. As the editor of the National Bureau of Economic Research article put it, Lowe argued that "if resources are not utterly fluid, a level of investment that adequately offsets desired saving may be out of adjustment with the capacity of the capital-goods industries in equipment and trained labor. Or the rate of increase in investment required to maintain steady growth may be out of adjustment with the capacity of the machine-tool and related industries to expand the capacity of the capital-goods industries. These states of imbalance, he shows, threaten our stability and limit our ability to progress" (Abramowitz, 1955: 15). Lowe therefore set out to study only the real or physical aspects of growth, ignoring monetary conditions.

Lowe chose to work with Karl Marx's simple and expanded reproduction schema. A Walrasian-type structure, reflected in the well-known Wassily Leontief's input-output type of analysis, would not do because it focused only on values. Marx's model brings out physical-technical relationships, which is what Lowe sought (Lowe, 1955: 586). According to Paul Samuelson, Lowe was aware that the Marxian Schema was more sophisticated than the Austrian "earliness or lateness" production models (Samuelson, 1966: vol. 1, 385). In any case, one can infer from Lowe's business cycle methodology that a model with equilibrium as a reference point will not capture the dynamic features that his model allows.

In spite of this, Lowe set out to expand the capital department of the Marxian Schema to represent his view. In the first place, he said:

> Marx's schema seems to be suited especially well to the study of real capital formation. There is an *a priori* presumption that the theoretical problems associated with the building up and wearing down of the capital stock, the relation between capital stock and output flow, the processes of "widening" and "deepening," and the effects of innovations upon capital formation are basically the same in every industry. But their solutions are bound to differ according to whether we study "capital-producing" or "capital using" processes, a distinction which is central for the Marxian schema. I speak of an "attempt," because in its original form the schema is defective in at least three respects: (Lowe 1955: 586)

1. Marxian Schema are meaningful for describing flow.
2. Working capital concepts need to be integrated, and the vertical stages of how natural resources are transformed into consumption and capital goods need addressing.
3. More essential circularity is needed in the capital goods sector to show production of capital goods for the capital sector, as well as for the consumption sector.

On the Flow Concept:

Lowe's model starts by transferring fixed capital into flows. An example of this is illustrated by the concept of depreciation, which shows how the fixed capital changes over the production cycle. So, from fixed capital, *F*, one gets depreciated capital by multiplying *F* by a depreciation rate, *d*. Given productivity of capital, we need to ascertain the flow of capital as input, which is not the physical size of capital, *F*, but the rate at which it is depreciated. It is worthwhile to lay out some of the quantitative flow assumptions of Lowe's model at this point. They are:

1. ***k*** **= value of fixed capital to output**. For instance, ***k*** can take the value of 2.
2. ***d*** **= rate of depreciation**. For instance, ***d*** can take the value of 10 percent.
3. Lowe assumes equal ***k*** and ***d*** ratios for all three sectors.
4. $\frac{k^2d^2}{1-kd}$ **= Sum of an infinite series with multiplier kd.**
5. $W = \frac{\text{Input}}{2} = \frac{\text{Output}}{2} =$ **average period of maturation.**
6. ϕ **= average density of a stationary flow, allows to write. W =** ϕ**.input =** ϕ**.Output. (Lowe, 1967:43 – 51)**

Using these assumptions, one can construct a physical system for the sectors based on the depreciated capital-output ratio. One key to this construction is to recognize that the output in each of the three sectors is a linear combination of the flow of depreciated capital-output ratios as inputs. For instance, since Sector Ia produces all the capital goods in the equipment sector, if ***kd*** amount of that capital is retained in Ia, then (**1** – ***kd***) is used in Ib, so that Sector Ia's output can be written as OIa = ***kd.Ia*** + (**1** – ***kd***)***.Ib***. Similarly, we can get the linear combination of the outputs in the other two sectors (Lowe, 1976: 46).

Another key point is to note that Lowe uses fixed over smooth coefficients in his sectors. Edward Nell's (1976: 290) exposition of Lowe's model was directed at an audience of fixed-coefficient modelers of the von Neumann, Leontief, and Sraffa models. However, there are differences between those models that can be made compatible. According to Dorfman, Samuelson and Solow, the von Neumann technology can be made consistent with the Leontief technology by suppressing some of its activities (Dorfman, Samuelson and Solow, 1958: 364).

Ian Steedman set out to reach an audience of Samuelson, John Hicks, and Luigi Spaventa modelers. In Hicks's view, a fixed coefficient is not taken in the sense that we need a fixed ratio of inputs, such as two hydrogen atoms and one oxygen atom to make a molecule of water. The ratios are quantities that are needed in equilibrium. We can have more than 1,000 units of output from a capital stock that is appropriate for 1,000 units of output (Hicks, 1972: 137).

These fixed coefficient models resemble Leon Walras' "'coefficient of production,' that is to say, the quantities of each of the productive services . . . which enter into the production of one unit of each of the products" (Walras, 1969: 239). Walras goes on to show that "the selling prices of the products are equal to the cost of the productive services employed in their manufacture" (ibid.: 240). Although Pierro Sraffa (1960) avoids concepts such as cost of production and capital, we can begin to understand Lowe's model in terms of comparing price and cost in each sector using fixed-coefficients following Micho Morishima (1969). One has two options in such a layout—a physical or quantity system, or a value or price system.

On Working Capital

Points 5 and 6 in the section above give the assumption of working capital. One aspect of the quantitative (physical) system, which will be illustrated below, is the way it takes stock quantities and distributes them in the three sectors. This is done for one unit of consumption goods. One can then introduce multiples of goods as goals, and see, instrumentally, what capital flow is required in the equipment sector to achieve that goal. The goals need further adjustments to account for work-in-progress, which is ascertained by using the factors in points 5 and 6 in the section above.

One More Point on Circularity

The last point for the modification of the Marxian Schema is a signature feature of Lowe's contributions to growth economics. One can find the need for a Sector Ia in Volume I of Lenin's work, "On the So-Called Market Question." Lenin has indicated that:

> the conclusion cannot be drawn that department I predominates over department II: both develop on parallel lines. But that scheme does not take technical progress into consideration. As Marx proved in Volume I of

> *Capital,* technical progress is expressed by the gradual decrease of the ratio of variable capital to constant capital (v/c), whereas in the scheme it is taken as unchanged. . . . It goes without saying that if this change is made in the scheme, there will be a relatively more rapid increase in means of production than in articles of consumption [in the Marxian model]. (Lenin, 1894: 85)

Lenin subdivided the capital goods sector into two parts: one that produces fixed-capital goods used in the capital goods sector, and the other which produces fixed-capital goods used in the consumer goods sector. Like Lenin and other writers of that era who opposed underconsumptionist arguments, Lowe stresses the structure of production—the technological relationships inherent in the production process.

Lenin found that

> growth in the production of means of production as means of production is the most rapid, then comes the production of means of production as means of consumption, and the slowest rate of growth is in the production of means of consumption. That conclusion could have been arrived at without Marx's investigation in Volume II of *Capital* on the basis of the law that constant capital tends to grow faster than variable: the proposition that means of production grow faster is merely a paraphrase of this law as applied to social production as a whole. (Lenin, 1894: 87)

One can see similarities between Lowe's diagram in Figure 2 above and Lenin's A (economy) mapping to >W (output) diagram (ibid.: 90).

Nell (1976) opened up a discussion by communicating Lowe's schema in modern sectorial mathematical analysis. Subsequent analysis of Lowe's schema was performed by Joseph Halevi in 1983, and Harald Hagemann and Albert Jeck in 1984. Halevi emphasized that the model was found useful for Choice of Technique analysis. This technique is a throwback to the Ricardian corn model unearthed by Maurice Dobb and Sraffa in their editing of David Ricardo's *Collected Works,* which shows the rental and wage rates expressed by revenue less cost weighted by corn input in each sector (see Mainwaring, 1984: 8). We should mention also the work of Steedman (in Hagemann and Kurtz, 1978) in the technical direction initiated by Nell.

Lowe's Three-Sector Model

Lowe's growth model is based on the production side of the economy. Production converts the stock of an economy into flows. Stocks are of two kinds: 1) original—labor and natural resources; and 2) manufacturing—equipment (plants, machines, and residential buildings), and commodities. Production combines these stocks into finished consumer and equipment products (Lowe, 1952: section 3).

Lowe postulated two main sectors: I. equipment goods and II. consumption goods. He subdivided the equipment sector into Subsector Ia, which produces equipment to be used as inputs in both Sectors Ia and Ib, and Subsector Ib, which supplies only Sector II, the consumption goods sector (Lowe, 1976).

Now we are ready for production flows. A straightforward representation of the order of production can be represented as follows:

Growth in Table 2 takes place in a hierarchical (vertical) system. The order signifies input on the left and output on the right in a serial manner. The dynamics of the process are brought out by studying the "technical conditions of 'resource replacement'" (Lowe, 1976: 37). In this analysis, the data in the Natural Resource column in Table 2 is not used.

Figure 1 below is Lowe's first illustration demonstrating how the three sectors of the model interact. The shaded area illustrates how capital-output ratio flows. We first explain the realism of the data in the model, and then its stationary and dynamic states.

TABLE 2: Stocks and Flow in Hierarchal Growth

	Stocks and Inputs in Production					Output
States of Production	Labor	Fixed Capital	Natural Resource	Combine Flows	Produces	Flows
1.	N_1	F_1	R_1	0	→	w_1= cotton
2.	N_2	F_2	R_2	w_1	→	w_2= yarn
3.	N_3	F_3	R_3	w_2	→	w_3= cloth
4.	N_4	F_4	R_4	w_3	→	w_4= c = dress

Sources: Adapted from Lowe, 1952: 146.

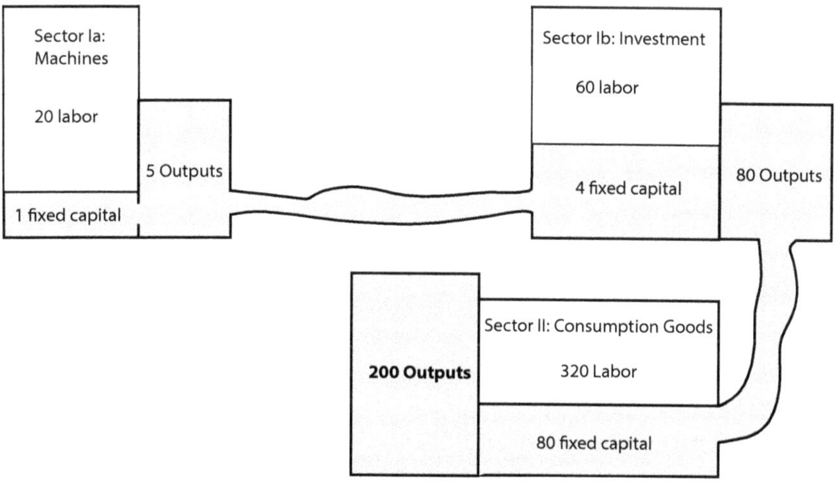

Figure 1 Capital and Output Flows in a Stationary State. Instead of arrows, we used circularity as in the sense of a river with tributaries flowing.

Sector 1a produced 5 Output units, keeps one and exports 4 to Sector Ib. Sector Ib makes 80 Outputs units, and exports them as capital to Sector II.

Sources: Data are from Lowe 1976,p. 38. River flow is adoped from: J.Marcus Fleming, "The Period of Production and Derived Concepts,"RES, Vol.3, No. 1 (Oct., 1935), pp. 1-17.Boxes are adopted from: Ragnar Nurkse,"The Schematic Representation of the Structure of Production," RES, Vol. 2,No.3(Jun., 1935), pp. 232 244.

Realism of the Data in Figure 1

Sectoral Ratios

Lowe's assumptions about the labor-capital, output-capital, and output-labor ratio are the same in the three sectors. As Nell explained, because "each sector has only one capital good, the ratios cannot be compared dimensionally unless they are expressed in value terms" (Nell, 1976: 303). The problem is that the capital-labor ratios Sector Ia and Ib are consistent with each other, but they are inconsistent with capital-labor ratio Sector II (Hagemann and Jeck, 1984: 172).

In Figure 1, Lowe used the following constant ratios:

1. $\frac{Output}{Labor}=1.25$. (Productivity of Labor).

2. $\frac{Output}{Capital}=5$. (Productivity of Capital).

3. $\dfrac{Capital}{Labor} = 0.25$. (Constant to Variable Capital).

4. $\dfrac{Capital - Good\,Ia}{Consumption - Good\,Ib} = \dfrac{Total Capital - Good}{Total Consumption - Good} = 1:4$

Labor Productivity:

The output-labor ratio, measured in terms of employed capital to man-hours, was around that number during the post-World War II period. For the years 1945 to 1949, the average was (1.296 + 1.215 + 1.194 + 1.221 + 1.275)/5 = 1.24 (Solow, 1957: 315).

Those were years of rapid growth. During the years of the Great Depression, the average was consistently lower, less than unity from 1939 to 1937.

From 1899-1953, John Kendrick reported the annual change as 1.9 for Output-Labor (Kendrick, 1956: 9). For the period of 1948–1952, the growth in labor input appeared fairly constant, averaging 1.46 annually, compared with 1.45 percent annually between 1929-1948 (Gordon, 1990: 377). Lowe's labor productivity data therefore appear realistic.

Capital Productivity:

The output-capital ratio can be derived from Solow's data by dividing the given "GNP per man-hour" by "employed capita per man-hour." For the period 1945-1949, the average was 0.48 (Solow, 1957: 315). For 1899-1953, Kendrick's number for annual change was 1.1 for Output-Capital.

While in both cases Lowe's estimate of 5 percent appears much too high, forces were set up in the economy for more rapid input of capital and its productivity. From 1948-1973, the annual growth in capital input increased by 0.77, exactly 7 times higher than the annual average of 0.11 to 0.77 (Gordon, 1990: 377). Not all of this increase is capital productivity, for the index of labor productivity almost doubled in that time frame, moving from 52.8 to 96.4 (ibid.: A2-A3). The reason for the increase in capital input appears to be a catch-up effect following the fall of demand for capital during the Great Depression, and the diversion of investments to war production during World War II (ibid.: 388). However, opposite trends began in the 1970s, a period of double-digit inflation that increased the tax rates on capital income and decreased private investment incentives.

Capital-Labor Ratio:

This ratio, also called the technique of production, is critical for growth analysis. For instance, in countries where labor is abundant, preference is given to labor-intensive techniques (Dobb, 1960: 34; Sen, 1968: 9). There, the ratio is important for the choice of technique analysis. Lowe used it in the Marxian sense of the "organic composition of capital" defined as constant (*c*) to variable capital (*v*) (Dobb, 1967: 39). The Marxian context has a well-known implication for capitalism that states that over time the constant capital will grow greater than variable capital (Dobb, 1967: 119). Such a change will be important for traverse analysis in growth. There are two types of influences. In Type I, where the *c* / *v* remains constant, accumulation will rise at a faster rate than labor supply, bidding up real wages, lowering profits, and slowing down accumulation. In Type II, where the *c* / *v* ratio rises, labor displaces technical progress. Increasing output will lower price and benefit the laborers. If *c* rises faster than *v*, more *c* will be needed to re-employ the displaced, and employment and profits will fall. Some counteracting tendency may be at work.

From the equation capital-output = (capital-labor)/(output-labor) ratios, the capital-labor ratio can be derived using two ratios already discussed (1.25/5 = 0.25) (see Dobb, 1963: 38). The level of the capital-labor ratio depends on the other two ratios. An easy comparative statics exercise is that if we double the capital-labor rate, say because of innovation, and labor productivity also doubles because of better machines, then the capital-output rate will remain constant. From 1955 to 1995, the capital-labor ratio approximately doubled (Federal Reserve Bank of Cleveland, 1998: 16). Labor productivity has kept pace with that increase, from 64.8 in 1955 to 110.6 in 1988 (Gordon, 1990: A3), lending some credence to the view that the capital-output ratio or the naïve accelerator is constant.

Ratio of Goods between Sectors:

Dobb stated that "the net output ratio between consumer goods industries and capital goods industries" was between 4 and 5 around the beginning of the nineteenth century for Britain, Belgium, and France (Dobb, 1967: 41). While the US ratio was between 2.3 and 2.4 in the prior half-century, it fell to about unity in the 1920s. This fall indicates that more capital goods were being produced as developed countries were exporting to less developed countries.

Lowe's factor of 4 split is therefore on the high side. As the global economy advanced, FDI flows were observed to be concentrated in the Triad regions of Asia, North America, and Europe.

Ratio of Capital between the Sectors: Kuznets has provided some percentage split of national income for the net formation of capital. Over a long period, 1869-1948, the percentage shares of capital formation in National Product remained fairly stable: 20 percent at the gross level, and 13.5 percent at the net level. Even when overlapping sub-periods are taken into account, the data remains stable (Kuznets, 1952: 514). Trend-wise, the share increased from 1869 to 1878, and fell afterwards.

During the go-go years of 1919-1928, consumption goods prevailed and the share of capital, therefore, began to decline even before the early phase of the Great Depression. From 1919-1928 the net percent was 10.9; it declined to 6.7 in 1924-1933, and 2 percent in 1929-1938 (Kuznets, 1946: 53).

Solving the Sectoral Model

Lowe's three-sector model can be solved for price (values) or quantity (physical). In fact, Lowe worked in both modes. But taking a slow-motion approach, he solved the physical system first, and then applied prices to the physical solutions.

Physical System

From convex combinations of the inputs of each sector above, Lowe gives the following input-output system, using **a**, **b**, and **z** for output of the three sectors, respectively (Lowe: 1976: 46).

$$kd.a + kd.b = a$$

$$kd.z = b$$

$$(1 - kd)(a + b + c) = z$$

In an attempt to solve this model, we use the output of the consumer goods from the last equation as the numeraire. The commodity of sectors Ia and Ib are expressed in terms of the commodity of the consumption goods sector with the value $z = 1$. We get $b = kd$ from the second equation, and substitute into the first equation to get a value for a (see Nell, 1976: 294).

Price System

The simple idea that the price of goods must be equal to or greater than the cost of production is a reasonable starting point. Not all analysts, however, choose to work in terms "cost of production" and "capital," because of the idea that quantities are separate and determined before the prices of products are determined (Harcourt, 1972: 132). Lowe's model may take form as follows:

> Price of Sector Ia machine-goods ≥ Cost of any process available to the investment-goods sector
>
> Price of Sector Ib investment-goods ≥ Cost of any process available to the investment-goods sector.
>
> Price of Sector II consumption-goods ≥ Cost of any process available to the consumption-goods sector.

Following Nell and Steedman (in Hagemann and Kurtz, 1998), we can frame these price equations into symbolic forms. Interest and depreciation on capital are omitted for now. We assume one machine can produce one output. Also, we can suggest how to use the numbers in the Flow diagram, Figure 2 above, to derive the coefficients for Sector Ia, following Luigi Pasinetti (1977: 37, 51). In the symbolic formulation below, $\mathbf{a}_1$ and $\mathbf{n}_1$ are the coefficients for capital and labor in Sector 1a. Similarly, $\mathbf{a}_2$ and $\mathbf{n}_2$ are the coefficients for capital and labor in Sector 1b, and $\mathbf{a}_3$ and $\mathbf{n}_3$ are the coefficients for capital and labor in sector II.

$$a_1 p_1 + n_1 w = p_1 \; [5p_1 + 20w = p_1] \cdots \textit{Sector Ia}$$

$$a_2 p_1 + n_2 w = p_2 \; [4p_1 + 60w = p_2] \cdots \textit{Sector Ib}$$

$$a_3 p_2 + n_3 w = w \; [80p_2 + 320w = w] \cdots \textit{Sector II}$$

Where the coefficients can therefore be interpreted as follows:

a_1: Sector Ia produced 5 units of capital goods, and used a fifth of them (.2 x 5) in Sector Ia.

a_2: The remaining 4/5 of the capital goods were produced in Sector Ia but used in sector Ib.

a_3: The amount of capital in Sector Ib used to produce 1 unit of consumption goods in Sector II.

n_1; n_2; n_3: The amount of labor needed in the respective Sectors Ia, Ib, and II to produce a unit of their respective commodity.

Again, we solve three equations following the medium of a numeraire system. This will make the price W = 1. Now we can solve for the subsistence level prices. We assume a subsistence standard of living, which is a special case of a stationary economy where more goods are produced for sustenance (Nell, 1976: 205). Following the procedure of Nell (ibid.: 295), we can derive prices symbolically as follows:

We are given w =1. From Ia, $p_1 = \frac{n_1}{1-a_1}$. Substituting these values in Ib yields

$$p_2 = a_2\left(\frac{n_1}{1-a_1}\right) + n_2 = \frac{a_2 n_1 + (1-a_1)n_2}{1-a_1}.$$

Simulating Lowe's Model

Lowe's Stationary State

Lowe used his structural model of production to explain how an economy can sustain itself. By adding some assumptions about behavior and motivation, the model can be extended to explain human actions in society. The structural model can be made to sustain itself and so remain stationary in time. The time period of the state is the life of the physical capital stock. A prerequisite is that the model must follow Marx in the sense that "all capital is circulating capital" (Marx, 1973: 620). Lowe stated that Adam Smith and Ricardo both tried to find a distinction between "fixed" and "circulating" capital, and "the latter concept became more and more identified with the "wage fund" and, thus, with one of the most dubious constructs of classical economics" (Lowe, 1976: 48). So, it appears that according to Lowe, "fixed capital is circulating capital of a special kind (the circulation of which requires a longer period of time) (ee Meacci, in Hagemann and Kurtz, 1998: 80).

To simulate stationary equilibrium, the flow of the capital-output net of depreciation (*kd*) and sector ratio are used. Lowe wrote that "it is possible to translate all stock and flow variables defining stationary equilibrium into multiples of *kd* and 1 – *kd*" (Lowe, 1976: 45) We used the following steps for the simulation.

Step 1: Lay out the basic accounting for output in terms of the sectors (Lowe, 1955: 596).

a. The sum of the output for the three sectors is denoted as small letter o.

b. Since **k** = ***Fd* / *o*, *okd*** is total capital.

c. The sectors Ia and Ib produce the output of capital. So ***Iao*** + ***Ibo*** = ***okd***.

Now we can express the output in each sector in *okd* form, as follows:

Output of Sector II = $o - (Iao + Ibo) = o - okd = o(1 - kd)$.

Output of Sector Ib is the depreciated capital going to Sector II = $o(1 - kd)\,kd$.

Output of Sector Ia = $o - o(1 - kd) - o(1 - kd)kd = o(1 - 1 + kd - kd + (kd * dk) = o(kd)2$.

Step 2: We set up the output for each sector using the ratio of 1 to 4, for one unit of output o = 1.

a. Input a value for ***k*** and ***d***. Say ***k*** = **2**, and ***d*** = **1**.

b. Find the value of ***kd*** = **2 * .1** = **.2** for the givens.

c. The output coefficient for Sector II will be **1** – ***kd*** = **1** – **0.2** = **.8**.

d. Using a similar analysis, we find the output coefficient to be 0.04 for Ia, and 0.16 for Ib.

e. Notice: the ratio is 1:4 for the sectors, namely: $\mathbf{0.4 : 0.16 : \sqrt[2]{0.16^2}}$.

Step 3: Calculate the capital in each sector:

a. For ***F*** = fixed capital, multiply the output of each sector by ***k***.

b. For ***f*** = flow capital, multiply the output of each sector by ***kd***.

c. For the flow of labor, multiply the output of each sector by **1** – ***kd***, following a 1 machine, 1 worker assumption.

d. Now we have the coefficient for each sector for 1 unit of output shown in Table 3 below:

TABLE 3: Stationary Coefficients for Lowe's Three Sector Model for 1 Unit of Output

	F		F		n		0
Ia	0.08		0.008		0.032		0.04
1b	0.32		0.032		0.128		0.16
II	16		0.16		0.64		0.8

Since the coefficients are for units of output, $o = 1$, if we make $o = 2$, the coefficient will double. For $o = 3$, they will triple, and so on. We can use an application in Lowe's instrumental sense to see how much investment in the machine Sector Ia is necessary to attain the full potential Gross Domestic Product (GDP). Table 4 shows these calculations. The shortfall was highest in

TABLE 4: Simulating Investment Short-Fall in the Machine Sector

GDP Data			Sector Is Output					
Stationary Simulation in billion of 1982 Dollars						Work-in-Progress (WIP)		
	Actual	Natural	Ia Actual	Ia Natural	Inv.	WIP	WIP	Net
Year	Real GDP	Real GDP	Inv. Mach.	Inv. Mach	Gap	Actual GDP	Nat. GDP	WIP
1928	666.7	664.7	250.9	250.2	-0.8	66.7	66.5	-0.2
1929	709.6	681.8	267.1	256.6	-10.5	71	68.2	-2.8
1930	642.8	699.3	241.9	263.2	21.3	64.3	69.9	5.7
1931	588.1	717.2	221.3	269.9	48.6	58.8	71.7	12.9
1932	509.2	735.7	191.7	276.9	85.2	50.9	73.6	22.7
1933	498.5	754.6	187.6	284	96.4	49.9	75.5	25.6
1934	536.7	773.9	202	291.3	89.3	53.7	77.4	23.7
1935	580.2	793.8	218.4	298.8	80.4	58	79.4	21.4
1936	662.2	814.2	249.2	306.4	57.2	66.2	81.4	15.2
1937	694.3	835.1	261.3	314.3	53	69.4	83.5	14.1
1938	664.2	856.6	250	322.4	72.4	66.4	85.7	19.2
1939	716.6	878.6	269.7	330.7	61	71.7	87.9	16.2
1940	772.9	901.2	290.9	339.2	48.3	77.3	90.1	12.8
1941	909.4	924.3	342.3	347.9	5.6	90.9	92.4	1.5
1942	1080.3	948.1	406.6	356.8	-49.8	108	94.8	-13.2
1943	1276.2	942.4	480.3	354.7	-125.6	127.6	94.2	-33.4
1944	1380.6	997.4	519.6	375.4	-144.2	138.1	99.7	-38.3
1945	1354.8	1023	509.9	385	-124.9	135.5	102.3	-33.2
Input	k=k/o	d	0/L	0/K	K/L	Kg/Cg	kIa/kIb	WIP
Ratios:	5	0.12	1.25	1.026898	0.9738	0.629999	1.587304	0.1

Source: GDP from Gordon, 1990: A2

1933 (10.1) and was fully made up by the end of the decade. (Recall that Sector Ib is 4 times Ia, and II is 4 times Ib, so it is not necessary to do the tabulations for them.)

To add more realism to the situation, we can open up the model to bring in the government and the international sector. Lowe intended his model to work under "collectivism" as well as under a "free-market system" (Lowe, 1976: 63-64). Under the latter, the government did intervene, but mostly in public machinery such as roads and bridges. International policy was reserved mainly for the reparation of loans abroad.

Step 4. Lowe proceeded to account for working capital or unfinished goods in his model. Unfinished goods become finished in stages, for which a uniform density of completion is assumed. The parameters of such a density function are the maturation period, and the period of observation following inputs and outputs.

The uniform density function, say W = 0.5, acts as a growth factor for the output column in Table 3. Taking half of the output columns of Table 3 yields 0.02, 0.08, and 0.4, respectively, of the sectors. It means that we have enhanced the calculated output by that percentage of output. But in this case, the proportion of output and working capital remains proportional over the sectors.

Reconciliation of the Data and Ratios for Simulation

Regarding the ratio of consumption goods to capital goods, we follow the empirical findings of Walter G. Hoffmann's application of Lowe's model to the processes of economic development. Hoffmann's purpose was to show that "predominantly agricultural economy becomes industrialized" (Hoffmann, 1970: 114). He specified consumption-goods output to capital-goods for different stages of the industrialized process. The ratio moves from 5:1, to 2.5:1, to 1:1, from early to later stages. In the last stages, there is a continuing tendency for the output of the capital sector to be greater than the output for the consumption sector. Using Lowe's output-capital ratio of 5 as stipulated above brings the ratio of output between the sectors to the final stage of the development process to 1:1, in line with Hoffmann's findings.

For the purpose of simulation, we need to ascertain how to classify industries into capital and consumption goods sectors. If one uses final demand goods for households or firms, as is done in input-output tables, then the classification is straightforward (Hoffmann, 1970:113). Using Leontief

Input-Output tables, one can get an estimate for final demand for the years 1919, 1929, and 1939. The ratios of consumption goods to capital goods were 0.627, 0.643, and 0.623 for those years, respectively (Hoffmann, 1970: 115; Leontief, 1953: Tables). These ratios appear stable, and therefore, we will use the average of those values, 0.63. Since we already pointed out that Lowe's $k = 5$ is on the high side, we should only change the $d = 0.1$ input. It turns out that we only need $d = 0.12$ to achieve the 0.63 average consumption to capital goods ratio. This seems reasonable since during the Great Depression, capacity utilization rate was low.

One needs to ascertain one other factor to make a first operational model of Lowe. That is, in addition to k and d, we need a value for work-in-progress density (W) ratio. Lowe suggests the use of $W = 0.5$. Since production was low during the Great Depression, we lower the pipeline activities to $W = 0.1$.

One objective we can set for instrumental activities is to decide what the driver should be to close the gap between actual and natural GDP in the time period. Table 4, below, indicates a simulated run to help solve that problem. Considering Sector Ia as the driver of GDP growth, Table 4 shows Investment in short-fall in that sector starting in 1930, the first year year after the Great Depression.

The short-fall peaked in 1930 at $96.4 billion. Full recovery of this sector's inputs occurred in 1942. The estimates show that from 1930 to 1941, some works-in-progress were going on that should be added to the actual GDP. But in no case would the addition close about half of the gap of investment needed in Sector Ia.

Dynamic Considerations

We can look at growth from two perspectives. The first and easier way is to grow all the sectors by the same proportion, but this requires a growth rate. Lowe introduced the symbol G to represent growth in the labor force, α, and labor productivity, π, where $G = \alpha + \pi$. Under collectivism, a planner stipulates the rate of growth. But under a free market system, the "macrosaving" ratio is the driver, which is defined as $G = \frac{s(1-kd)}{k}$.

With the introduction of the saving growth rate, the sectoral variables become receipt and expenditure flows. On the receipt side: *f* is amortized (*am*); *n* is payroll (*pay*); output is sales receipts (*sal rec*); profits, *P*, now appears as a receipt from payroll as amortization is fixed. On the expenditure side, *f* = demand for replacement (*d recp*); *n* = demand for consumer goods (*d co*); *a* and *b* are supply of equipment goods (*S equ*); *z* is supply of consumer goods (*S co*); profits becomes net savings (*Sa*); and net demand for equipment goods or net investment (*I*).

Simulation of Growth for Intersectoral and Intertemporal Models

In order to demonstrate Lowe's sectoral growth process, we need to gather some assumptions. Looking at the US economy just before the Great Depression, from 1928 to 1929, nominal GDP grew by 6.8 percent, but from 1929 to 1930 it fell by 12.2 percent. As GDP rates fell, people saved less. Further, the liquidity crises removed saving from the financial institutions, further diminishing the amount of savings.

We can assume with Keynes the MPC was between 60 and 70 percent in boom times. (Keynes, 1973 [1936]: 128). Those percentages place the MPS between 0.4 and 0.3. We can therefore use an average of s = 0.35 just before the Depression, in 1928.

We also need some statistics on depreciation rates. Keynes provides depreciation data which are based on current dollars only (ibid.: 388-389). Solomon Fabricant supplies some estimates based on historical costs ranging from 4 to 6 percent for current and original costs, respectively. Since the upper end of Fabricant's number is close to the 10 percent Lowe suggested in his model, we will use 10 percent for the purpose of this illustration.

At this stage with given sectorial ratios, one can apply some ratios to simulate the base period growth. The vector of inputs required to do this for the stationary coefficients in Table 3 for the data in Figure 2 is $[k, d, s] = [2, 0.1, 0.35]$ Such a vector of values yields a growth rate of 14 percent. For simplicity, we can determine that profits and investments will also grow at 14 percent. We can simulate the base period (t = 0) and one period ahead (t = 1) by applying the growth rates in Model 1 below. A lower growth occasioned by the decrease in the MPS is used in Model 2.

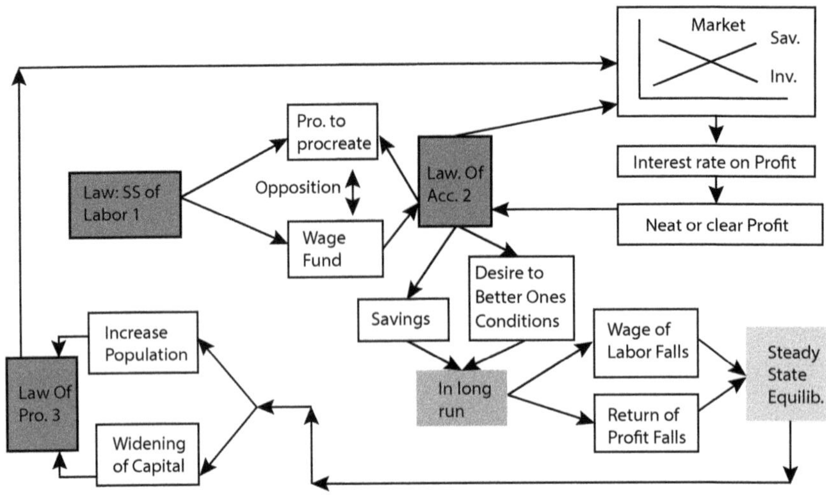

Figure 2 Adolph Lowe's Model of Adam Smith Growth Process.

Table 5 gives the equilibrium condition for Models 1 and 2. In the first model, parts 1 and 2 are for the time periods t = 0 and t = 1, respectively, using the inputs vector $[k, d, s] = [2, 0.1, 0.35]$ Model 2 reduced only the savings rate from 0.35 to 0.1. The equilibrium values are then calculated using the input of 1929 nominal GDP value given by Gordon as $103.9 billion (1990: A2). The growth rate of capital, $= \frac{s(1 - kd)}{k} = 0.14$, is kept in period 2 of Models 1 and 2 for some comparisons.

Looking at the top and bottom outputs of Table 5, we see that the decrease of the saving rates from 0.35 to 0.1 has caused some distortion in the equipment sector. Sector Ib has an excess of capital of $2.05 billion, namely, the difference of the original amount of $25.93 billion at the top of the table, less what has been used, $23.88 billion at the bottom of the table. Meanwhile, Sector 1a had its original capital growing at a rate of 0.14 percent in model 1 and 0.04 in model 2, which also created excess capital in Sector 1 of approximately $18.25 billion.

To summarize, we have converted the constant flow in the stationary case to changing flows. Such a dynamic is occasioned by savings, which are used to increase the equipment sectors (Ia and Ib) relative to the consumption sector (II). As the saving ratio changes, the need for redistribution of proportional inputs may arise between the capital and consumption sectors.

TABLE 5: Fall in Equilibrium Values for 1929 to 1930 Nominal GDP Model I Period Equilibrium

Model 1 Period 1($ Billions) [k, d, s] = [2, 0.1, 0.35]				
Agg Pay	54.03	equals	Agg Out Ib	54.03
Out Ia + Ib	49.87	equals	Am + P	49.87
Out Ib	25.93	equals	Am + I in II	25.93
Model 1 Period 2:				
Agg Pay	61.59	equals	Agg Out Ib	61.59
Out Ia + Ib	56.85	equals	Am + P	56.85
Out Ib	29.56	equals	Am + I in II	29.56
Model 2 Period 1: [k, d, s] = [2, 0.1, 0.1]				
Agg Pay	74.81	equals	Agg Out Ib	74.81
Out Ia + Ib	29.09	equals	Am + P	29.09
Out Ib	20.95	equals	Am + I in II	20.95
Model 2 Period 2				
Agg Pay	85.28	equals	Agg Out Ib	85.28
Out Ia + Ib	33.17	equals	Am + P	33.17
Out Ib	23.88	equals	Am + I in II	23.88

A logical step for further analysis would require us to change the ratio of k, which takes us into the domain of "traverse" analysis. The term "traverse" was introduced by Hicks to describe the adjustment path of "an economy which has in the past been in equilibrium in one set of conditions, and . . . then a new set of conditions is imposed" (Hicks, 1972: 184). If an economy is at equilibrium at state g_0, then that rate must correspond to a capital-labor ratio, say k_0. If the growth rate changes to Δg_0, holding k_0 constant will be an inconsistency, because a new capital-labor ratio, Δk_0, would be appropriate for a new equilibrium. This might not be a problem for some countries embarking on development without a choice of techniques.

Traverse is relevant to Lowe's model because he was concerned with the "Path of Growth." Normally, when the initial condition of growth is specified, traverse becomes relevant, and when it is not specified, golden growth becomes relevant (Wan, 1971: 272). Markets would not give the proper signals on the traverse because growth would require the two capital sectors to move in opposite directions. As an example, "a lower rate of growth requires a higher level of consumption, to maintain full employment, so the subsector producing capital goods for the consumer-goods sector will have to expand, while the basic capital-goods subsector contracts—and conversely for a higher rate of growth" (Nell, in Hagemann and Kurtz, 1998: 132).

We can now underscore some conditions for traverse analysis. In Lowe's model, the capital stock is reconstituted each period. The capital in Sector Ia is depreciated capital stock in period t + 1 plus increment to output in Ia. The capital in Sector Ib is depreciated capital stock in period t + 1 plus increment to output in Ia. To determine how the incremental stock should be divided between Ia and Ib, we can assume a ratio of $\sigma = 0.2$ $(0 < \sigma < 1)$.

In the literature, the capital-output ratio is constant, usually denoted as v (but Lowe used k instead). With the value of v constant, the growth rate of capital stock in each sector can be determined by $G = -d + \frac{\sigma}{v}$. The Japanese economist Taniguchi Kazuhisa has made some suggestions on how to simulate Lowe's traverse using the difference equation.

Lowe as an Expositor of Economic Systems

Lowe's exposition of Smith's growth model is a student's dream come true. Lowe's model presented Smith on a scientific basis, predicting that output or income for the economy will increase on a "hitchless" basis. The path of such growth is like a spiral, showing outward expansion each time period for the wealth of a nation. The term "hitchless" is Joseph Schumpeter's (1954) way of saying that nothing is standing in the way of continuous expansion of productivity. Like a true model builder, Lowe laid out the assumptions of Smith's model upfront. These are assumptions as categorized into natural, psychological, and institutional groups. Then Lowe laid out the laws that would set the system into motion, as shown in Figure 2 below.

Figure 2 may be likened to a dialectic process of a growth model, where opposition rather than causal forces are at play. Lowe's argument starts in Figure 2 with the Law of Supply of Labor. Two arrows show the dialectic positions of the propensity to create and the wage fund, which gave rise to the

Law of Accumulation. The Law of Accumulation shows a mini-bifurcation where the supply of savings interplays with the demand for investment, which can lead to "neat or clear profit." But the main bifurcation of the Law of Accumulation opposes savings to the desire to better one's conditions, where the first internal hitch can present itself.

Heilbroner was the first to point out an internal hitch in Smith's model. He quotes Smith to the effect that when a country has achieved the full complement of riches it can acquire, "the wage of labour and the profits on stocks would probably be very low" (Heilbroner, 1975: 527). This quote, however, was known to Lowe, who quoted it in its entirety in his early exposition of Smith's growth process (Lowe, 1954: 134). We show its place in the process between the Law of Accumulation and, to use a modern term, steady state equilibrium. To get out of that steady state situation, one needs to widen capital, because the concept of deepening capital was a later development.

It is customary to appeal to Ricardo's diminishing return, both at the external and internal margin as other hitches to Lowe's presentation of Smith's model. Of course, the arguments of Rev. T. R. Malthus and Marx are strong versions of Smith's model that can be considered death hitches.

Conclusion

In 1982, after the death of his wife Beatrice Lowe, Lowe went to live with his daughter Hannah in Germany. He died on June 4, 1995 in Wolfenbüttel, Germany. Lowe has left enough of a research program to occupy the capable minds in economics, particularly in the area of growth and cycles, for a long time to come. Anyone who had him as a teacher is forever grateful to him for his groundbreaking insights into the science of economics.

References

Abramovitz, M. (1955). *Capital formation and economic growth.* Princeton: NBER.

Dobb, M. (1967). *Capitalism, development, and planning.* New York: International Publishers.

———. (1963). *Economic growth and underdeveloped countries.* New York: International Publishers.

———. (1960). *An essay on economic growth and planning.* New York: Monthly Review Press.

Dorfman, R., Samuelson, P. A., & Solow, R. (1958). *Linear programming and economic analysis.* New York: Dover Publications.

Federal Reserve Bank of Cleveland. (1998, Feb.). Economic trends. The Research Department of the Federal Reserve Bank of Cleveland. Retrieved from https://www.clevelandfed.org/research/trends.

Gordon, R. J. (1990). *Macroeconomics.* Glenview, IL: Scott Foresman and Company.

Hagemannn, H., & Kurtz, H. D. (Eds.). (1998). *Political economics in retrospect: Essays in memory of Adolph Lowe.* Northampton, MA: Edward Elgar.

Hagemann, H., & Jeck, A. (1984, Apr.-Jun.). Lowe and the Marx-Friedman-Dobb model: Structural analysis of a growing economy. *Eastern Economic Journal,* 10(2), 169-186.

Halevi, J. (1984, Apr.-Jun.). Lowe, Dobb and Hicks. *Eastern Economic Journal,* 10(2), 157-167.

———. (1983, Summer). Employment and planning. *Social Research,* 50(2), 345-358.

Harcourt, G. C. (1972). *Some Cambridge controversies in the theory of capital.* Cambridge: Cambridge University Press.

Hayek, F. A. (2012). *The collected works of F. A. Hayek* (vol. 7, part I). H. Klausinger (Ed.). Chicago: University of Chicago Press.

Heilbroner, R. (1975). The paradox of progress: Decline and decay in *The wealth of nations.* In A. Skinner & T. Wilson (Eds.), *Essays on Adam Smith* (424-539). Oxford: Clarendon Press.

Hicks, J. (1983). *Collected essay on economic theory, volume III: Classics and moderns.* Cambridge, MA: Harvard University Press.

———. (1972 [1965]). *Capital and growth.* Oxford: Oxford University Press.

Hoffmann, W. G. (1970). The growth of industrial economies. *Hitotsubashi Journal of Economics,* 11(1), 113-116.

———. (1958). *The growth of industrial economics.* Manchester: University of Manchester Press.

Kendrick, J. (1956). Productivity trends: Capital and labor. Retrieved from http://www.nber.org/chapters/c5596.

Kuznets, S. (1953). *Economic change: Selected essays in business cycles, national income and economic growth*. New York: W. W. Norton and Company, Inc..

———. (1952, May). "Proportion of Capital Formation to National Product," *The American Economic Review*, Vol. 42, No. 2, *Papers and Proceedings of the Sixty-fourth Annual Meeting of the American Economic Association*, 507-526.

———. (1946). Long-term changes, 1869-1938. in *National Income: A Summary of Findings* (31-72). Cambridge, MA: National Bureau of Economic Research, Inc.

Lenin, V. I. (1893-1894). On the so-called market question. In *V. I. Lenin collected works* (vol. 1, 75-122). Moscow: Progress Publishers.

Leontief, W. W. (1953). *The structure of American economy, 1919-1939* (2nd ed.). Oxford: Oxford University Press.

Lowe, A. (1952, Jun.). A structural model of production. *Social Research*, 19(2), 135-176.

———. (1954). The classical theory of economic growth. *Social Research*, 21(1), 127-158.

———. (1955). Structural analysis of real capital formation. In M. Abramowitz (Ed.), *Capital formation and economic growth* (581-634). Princeton: NBER.

———. (1965). *On economic knowledge: Toward a science of political economics*. New York: Harper and Row.

———. (1975). Adam Smith's system of equilibrium growth. In A. Skinner & T. Wilson (Ed.), *Essays on Adam Smith* (415-425). Oxford: Clarendon Press, 1975.

———. (1976). *The path of economic growth*. Cambridge: Cambridge University Press.

———. (1977, Jun.). How is business cycle theory possible at all? *Structural Change and Economic Dynamics*, 8, 245-270.

Machlup, F. (1978). *Methodology of economics and other social sciences*. New York: Academic Press.

Mainwarning, L. (1984). *Value and distribution in capitalist economies: An introduction to Sraffian economics*. Cambridge: Cambridge University Press.

Marx, K. (1973). *Grundrisses*. Harmondsworth: Penguin Books.

McFarlane, B. (1984, Apr.-Jun.). Economic planning and Adolph Lowe's economic perspective. *Eastern Economic Journal*, 10(2), 187-202.

Morishima, M. (1969). *Theory of economic growth*. Oxford: Clarendon Press.

Nell, E. J. (1976). An alternative presentation of Lowe's basic model. In A. Lowe, *The path of economic growth* (289-325). Cambridge: Cambridge University Press.

Pasinetti, L. L. (1977). *Lectures on the theory of production*. New York: Columbia University Press.

Samuelson, P. A. (1986)., *The collected scientific papers of Paul A. Samuelson*, (vol. 5). K. Crowley (Ed.). Cambridge, MA: MIT Press.

———. (1966). *The collected scientific papers of Paul A. Samuelson* (vol. 1). J. E. Stiglitz (Ed.). Cambridge, MA: MIT Press.

Sen, A. K. (1968). *Choice of techniques* (3rd ed.). Oxford: Basil Blackwell.

Solow, R. M. (2001). From neoclassical growth theory to new classical macroeconomics. In J. Dreze (Ed.), *Advances in macroeconomic theory* (19-29). New York and London: Palgrave Macmillan.

———. (1957, Aug.). Technical change and the aggregate production function. *The Review of Economics and Statistics*, 39(3), 312-320.

Spaventa, L. (1970, Jul.). Rate of profit, rate of growth, and capital intensity in a simple production model. *Oxford Economic Papers, New Series*, 22(2), 129-147.

Taniguchi, K. (2004). Lowe's traverse and the numerical examples. Working Paper No E-2, School of Economics, Kenki University, Osaka, Japan. Retrieved from http://www.eco-kindai.ac.jp/tani/index-eg.html.

Walras, L. (1969). *Elements of pure economics*. (W. Jaffe, Trans.). New York: Augustus M. Kelley Publishers.

Wan, H. Y., Jr. (1971). *Economic growth*. New York: Harcourt Brace Jovanovich, Inc..

PART VI

ECONOMETRICS

Lawrence Klein

Lawrence Klein

Lawrence Klein was born in Omaha, Nebraska in 1920. He attended Los Angeles City College, and received his BA in economics from University of California, Berkeley in 1942 and a PhD in economics from MIT in 1944. His was the first PhD in economics granted by MIT. Another first for Klein is that while Ragnar Frisch, Jan Tinbergen, and Michael Kalecki used the term macrodynamics, Klein was the first to use the term macroeconomics as contrasted to microeconomics in a Keynesian system. While Tinbergen was the first to have a Keynesian econometric model, Klein was the first to have a large scale one.

Klein is famous for his contributions in the area of econometrics, which include model building, specification, estimation, forecasting, and policy analysis. He received the Nobel Memorial Prize in Economic Sciences in 1980 for "the creation of economic models and their application to the analysis of economic fluctuations and economic policies." Other awards include the John Bates Clark Medal of the American Economic Association (1959) and the William Butler Award of the New York Association of Businessmen (1975).

After graduating from MIT, Klein worked for the Cowles Commission, then attached to the University of Chicago, where the environment was conducive for econometric innovative ideas. He was advised by Jacob Marschak at an Econometric Society meeting that "what this country needs—meaning the United States—is a new Tinbergen model, a fresher approach to it" (Klein, 1987: 412). The result was the birth of Klein Model I, which by 1947 merged Keynesian and Marxian elements of income and capital and appeared in a book form (Klein, 1950). For a time, it was the paradigm of a small model for a dynamic economy engulfing the world of simultaneous estimates. It included specification for consumption, investment, private wages, equilibrium demand, private profits, and capital stock. Exogenous variables included government spending, taxes and net exports, and the government wage bill. Predetermined variables for forecasting purposes included lagged values of capital stock, private profits, and total demand (Greene, 2000: 656-657). Subsequently, Klein Model I was modified and enlarged.

The theoretical foundation for Klein's empirical works was his PhD dissertation, *The Keynesian Revolution*, which later became a bestselling book. Essentially, Klein sourced the Keynesian revolution to the replacement of "the classical saving-investment theory of interest by the Keynesian savings-investment theory of effective demand or employment" (Klein, 1942: iii). He was motivated by his mentor, Paul Samuelson, into a research program that "the identification problem in saving-investment analysis is an exact mathematical analogue of the identification problem in supply and demand analysis" (Klein, 1987: 411). The identification process involves placing restrictions of zero on the coefficients of an equation in a simultaneous equation model, eliminating the variable from the equation (Ramrattan and Szenberg, 2008a). Klein's theoretical basis for the Keynesian system was unique in showing that rigidities in a system would create involuntary rather than stable equilibrium (Samuelson, 1986: vol. 5, 343).

Klein's positions at various institutions can be mapped to the various stages in the development of his model. From the Cowles Commission, he went to Ottawa, Canada in 1947, where he built an econometric model for Canada. In October 1947, he went to Norway, where he worked with the famed economists Frisch and Trygve Haavelmo. In 1948, he met Tinbergen, who was to share the first Nobel Prize in economics, given in 1969, with Frisch. In the autumn of 1948, he worked at the National Bureau of Economic Research, which was linked to the Survey Research Center at the University of Michigan. It was there that he met his student Arthur Goldberger and formulated the Klein-Goldberger Model.

After four years at the University of Michigan, Klein spent the next four years at Oxford University, where he reflected on conditioning and improving the variance-covariance matrix of regression analysis and hence the error of the model. He thought of Hans Theil's 2SLQ model in terms of the instrumental variable approach of which he was aware of in the Cowles Commission. At Oxford, he met A. Phillips, whose model would play a big role in adaptive and rational expectation models that dominated macroeconomics in the latter half of the twentieth century. Klein thought that he and Tinbergen had incorporated elements of Phillips' analysis in their models through wage-price specifications. "In fact, the Phillips curve is very close to ideas that I had used in order to close the Keynesian system for the determination of absolute prices and wages. It was also very close to the wage determination equations in Tinbergen's models of the 1930s. I think Phillips put the idea very interestingly, but in many respects it was a complete analogy of what Tinbergen had done and what I had done in terms of determining wage rates and the price level in Keynesian type systems" (Klein, 1987: 425).

In 1976, Klein coordinated Jimmy Carter's economic task force prior to the US presidential election and advanced a detailed analysis of economic issues for Carter's presidential campaign on such matters as inflation, farm income and prices, welfare, housing, and consumer protection (Berson, 1976: 39). Klein later declined an offer to join Carter's administration. The historic records show that the Carter administration was daunted by the shock of stagflation, which led to his repudiation for a second presidential term (Samuelson, 1986: vol. 5, 337).

Finally, in 1958, Klein settled at the University of Pennsylvania, where he founded the Wharton Model. That model formed the basis for large scale application of econometrics to both developed and developing countries, such as Japan, Israel, and Mexico. While his original model had only twelve equations, it expanded to 200 equations in the Wharton version (Evans and Klein, 1967), representing the interests of various American corporations such as IBM, Deere, Bethlehem Steel, Standard Oil, and General Electric. This version was later extended to the Brookings model, the DRI model, and the FRB-Penn-SSR model (Klein, 1987: 430). In 1968, a LINK model was developed to compare the US to the rest of the World. LINK was later modified to reflect the changes resulting from the Bretton Woods system and also OPEC's driven crisis in the1970s. It considered international policy coordination, protectionism, and telecommunication problems (ibid.: 438). The essence of these models is that they use instruments to attain goals as suggested by Tinbergen (1952), conduct social welfare analysis as suggested by Theil (1961), or simulate and forecast probable outcomes in a stochastic way (Ramrattan and Szenberg, 2008b).

The issues with Klein's models that dominated econometric research from the 1940s through the 1960s are manifold. Criticism surfaced in the 1970s in the face of stagflation. One problem relates to its system models and its identification aspects, and another relates to expectations (Ramrattan and Szenberg, 2008a, 2008c). The identification system emerged when Christopher Sims raised the question: "Is there statistical evidence that money is 'exogenous' in some sense in the money income relationship?" (Sims, 1972: 540). This was an attack on the identification system model that classifies variables in terms of whether they are exogenous, given to the system, or endogenous, determined within the system. Sims' intention was to have only endogenous variables. This is tantamount to having no system, as in the methodology of Vector Autoregression (VAR), where all dependent variables are regressed on their lagged form. It also meant the purging of restrictions on coefficients that was at the heart of the identification problem. In a large macro system all variables are subject to change, so none can be left out.

Klein was skeptical about those types of innovation in econometrics, which he felt represent "Measurement without Theory" (Klein, 1987: 417). He thought that autoregression, autoregressive integrated moving average (ARIMA), and VAR were resting on the naive concept either that today's outcomes were based on yesterday's outcomes, or that their changes are related. To disregard the system of models is to throw away information particularly about agents' behavior in the economy. In this context, Klein declared, "I prefer the large-scale system because it has more informational content" (1987: 418). The system models can be easily adapted to predict complex situations such as the OPEC and the Iranian crisis of the 1970s. Klein thought VAR was promising but found the use of only endogenous variables "bothersome" and, on the identification side, he noticed that "not all the terms in the vector autoregression are used, and some zeros are, on a judgmental basis, placed here and there until the model is fine-tuned" (ibid.).

Analysts of modern co-integration of time series data are grateful for Klein's early work on the great ratios in economics. The ratios include the savings-income ratio, the capital-output ratio, labor's share of income,

income velocity of circulation, and capital-labor ratio (Klein and Kosobud, 1961: 173). Without any differentiation, such ratios display remarkable stability over time. In this sense, Klein is said to have founded the I(0) stationary co-integration series. "Klein (1953) discusses various great ratios of economics, implicitly assuming a stationary, of I(0), world . . . given that the components of these relations are I(1) . . . Klein's ratios are early examples of co-integration hypothesis" (Banerjee et al., 1997; 310). In the term I(0), the letter "I" means integration, and the figure in the bracket tells the order of differencing that would make the series stationary. For great ratios, no differencing is needed for stationarity. When combining stationary series, usually the higher order of series that are integrated dominates. For instance, if x is of order I(1), and y is of order I(3), then their linear combination would be I(3), but some exceptions may prevail in long term co-integration (ibid.: 415, 427).

When Klein's models were in their peak performance in the 1960s, rational expectation models were making their debut by explaining business fluctuations. Robert Lucas, a proponent of rational expectation models, thought that while the scholastic terminology "rational expectation school" can "displace technocratic languages suggesting that economics can affect policy solely through the engineering of scientific consensus. It is not, however, a useful terminology in discussing research on business cycles" (Lucas, 1994: 1). We find on the one hand, that Lucas explained business cycles based on the information content on which decisions are made. On the other hand, Klein's model recognized the Keynesian prescription that people have varying degrees of information. Volatility, such as we find in the stock market and in modern variations in the exchange rates, creates an uncertainty that makes people prefer "to make money out of mugs than . . . to sink an oil well" (Samuelson, 1986: vol. 5, 297).

Klein agreed with Samuelson's view that although the rational expectation approach is different from the Keynesian approach, "the qualification to rational expectation that Lucas, for example, had to make in order to explain business cycles" was not different from the Keynesians (ibid.: 297). What really makes rational expectation different from Keynes' model is the formation of expectation. Rational expectations form from a probability distribution that is exogenous to the economic system, such as shocks. This involves uncertainties that are associated with phenomena such as earthquakes, which are not expectations about people's decisions found in a rival oligopolistic situation of the Cournot or Nash type of equilibrium. It purges the behavior assumption that makes such competition deterministic, assumptions that are permanent in Keynesian systems of equations, such as the consumption function. Samuelson found that the latter version of rational expectation that makes "public policy" react to "public opinion" was "favorable to Keynesian policies" (ibid.: 298).

In terms of econometric specifications, the rational expectation approach separates variables into actual and expected, which creates a measurement error, while the Kleinian approach separates variables into anticipated and non-anticipated, which does not rely on how accurately the variables are measured. Klein prefers to confront expectation variables with what people say their expectations are. The Wharton Model handles expectations by including "consumer-purchase expectations, business-investment expectations, housing starts, and other kinds of anticipatory data directly into the models" (Klein, 1987: 420). Given people's stated expectations, the method is to relate them to the state of the economy as defined by the "state of the stock market, the state of the bond market, the movement of inflation rates, and the movement of monetary instruments" (ibid.: 420-421). In essence, "we have feedback from market conditions to the expectations and from the expectations to those indicators, so they can be fully endogenized. We have something that many investigators are neglecting: we have observations on people's statements of what their expectations are" (ibid.: 420).

Nevertheless, Klein saw in the early stages some strength in the VAR model for forecasting, particularly in the short run. A detailed review of this issue reveals that the FRB/US model incorporated some of these features (Szenberg and Ramrattan, 2008: Ch. 6). The more recent question is how Klein's econometric exercise performs in the face of asset bubbles and crisis situations even though it has exhibited flexibility in modeling such situations (Klein and Shabbir, 2006). Writing about Asia before and after the financial crisis of 1997-1998 in the first chapter of their 2006 book, they concluded that econometric predictive models must be jettisoned in the aftermath of the crisis with regards to its impact on income distribution and other social welfare effects. In his 2006 book, Klein and others used modified econometric models for capital control, financial crises, and cures for

Malaysia, which validated capital control as a solution against the contrasting views that rely solely on market mechanisms. He backed up this approach with a system of 438 equations and 607 variables. For the Chinese economy, he modified his Keynesian-Neoclassical IS-LM model to a two-gap specification, namely the savings-investment gap and the export-import gap (Liang and Klein, 1989: 2).

Klein weighs in on the forecasting side of the current economic crisis by advancing a premise that the "global recession has proved that no country or group of countries . . . is immune to adverse developments in other countries. The costs of these developments in production and employment are immense and bring up the question of the predictability of such drops in economic activity and the usefulness of those forecasts for decision makers" (Klein and Özmucur, 2010: 1453). Starting at the data gathering stage, forecasts suffer from not having real-time data to match the available real-time financial data. Klein thinks that the use of survey data is necessary to synchronize real and financial data. He postulates a simple autoregressive model of order 12, augmented with one to ten other variables to make a prediction. He overrides adaptive and rational expectation models by directly including expectation variables for production, price, and employment, which are of major concern in the current long, drawn-out recovery. Although the US is not included in the sample of countries used, we can relate to the finding that the expectation indicator is a significant predictor variable.

Klein has definitive views on some of the problems in the current recession, such as the debt crisis, infrastructure investments, and the emergence of new growth centers in the world. He offers plausible evidence that the center of gravity of economic activities has shifted from the Atlantic to the Asian Pacific areas based on "overall economic activity, national economic accounts, demographics, sexual specifics, education, health, life expectancy, and energy output" (Klein, 2009: 492). He spotlights the major role of public infrastructure as an input for growth in the 1970s and 1980s. Those effects show up in models where private and government capital disaggregated to the IT level and fitted to a transcendental production function show significant effect on output. The findings "indicate that both IT capital and public infrastructure make significant contributions to technological progress" (Duggal, Saltzman, and Klein, 2007: 500-501).

Klein (1997) lays out a three-pronged approach. As for future research in econometric modeling, he alerts us to consider the impact of the information age. He advises to incorporate more high-frequency data which involves using daily and weekly data for linked and unlinked models in the global economy. Another step is to incorporate more countries and information as they become available into his LINK model. A third step would be to include military activities as they impact the performance of the economy. He has done so for World War II, as well as for the Korean, Vietnam and Gulf Wars (ibid.: xxxv).

Conclusion

Samuelson once said that "We are all in Klein's debt. . . . For in plain truth every judgment of the modern age rides piggyback on the output of hundreds of operating computers . . . by knowledge of what is being said by Klein's Wharton model" (Samuelson, 1986: vol. 5, 833). Klein believes in tailoring an econometrics model for a specific economy, which explains the variety of models he has developed. He does not cling to a rigid specification, but is willing to incorporate changes dictated by the predictive performance of the model, as he demonstrated with the FBR/US model, as well as with the models for the Asian economy.

In the face of an uncertain future, Klein econometric models for the US and other economies have enabled policy prescriptions and solutions to economic crises. His passion for econometrics seems to be driven by the lesson learned during the Great Depression, when he decided to specify the first large scale Keynesian econometric model for the US. Some of the special cases of the Keynesian model, such as liquidity trap, deflation, wage-rigidity, and interest inelasticity, are still with us in the current Great Recession, and as the aftermath unfolds we may find solutions under a revised econometric specification in line with Klein's view.

References

Banerjee, A., Dolado, J., Galbraith, J. W., & Henry, D. F. (1997). *Co-integration, error-correction, and the econometric analysis of non-stationary data.* New York: Oxford University Press.

Berson, L. (1976, Aug. 16). Economics Prof. Lawrence Klein has a bright new pupil—Jimmy Carter. *People*, 6(7).

Duggal, V. G., Saltzman, C., & Klein, L. R. (2007). Infrastructure and productivity: An extension to private infrastructure and its productivity. *Journal of Econometrics*, 140, 485–502.

Evans, H. K., and Klein, L. R. (1967). *The Wharton econometric forecasting model.* Philadelphia: Economics Research Unit, University of Pennsylvania.

Greene, W. H. (2000). *Econometric analysis* (4th ed.) Englewood Cliffs, NJ: Prentice-Hall.

Klein, L. R. (2011, Mar. 21). Autobiography. *Official Nobel Prize website.* Retrieved from http://nobelprize.org/nobel_prizes/economics/laureates/1980/klein-autobio.html.

———. (2006). Issues posed by chronic US deficits. *Journal of Policy Modeling*, 28, 673–677.

———. (1997). *Selected papers of Lawrence R. Klein: Theoretical reflections and econometric applications* (vol. 1). K. Marwah (Ed.). River Edge, NJ: World Scientific Publishing.

———. (1992). My professional life philosophy. In M. Szenberg (Ed.), *Eminent economists* (180-190). New York: Cambridge University Press.

———. (1974 [1953]). *A textbook of econometrics* (2nd ed.), Evanston, IL: Row, Peterson, and (Originally Englewood Cliffs, NJ: Prentice-Hall).

———. (1971). *An essay on the theory of economic prediction.* Chicago: Markham Publishing Company.

———. (1966 [1947]). *The Keynesian revolution* (Ed.). New York: Macmillan.

———. (1962). *An introduction to econometrics.* Englewood Cliffs, NJ: Prentice-Hall.

———. (1950). *Economic Fluctuation in the United States, 1921-1941.* New York: John Wiley.

———. (1942). *The Keynesian revolution* (unpublished doctoral dissertation). MIT, Cambridge, MA.

Klein, L. R., and Özmucur, S. (2010). The use of consumer and business surveys in forecasting. *Economic Modelling*, 27, 1453–1462.

Klein, L. R. and Shabbir, T. (Eds.). (2006). *Recent financial crises: Analysis, challenges and implications.* Northampton, MA: Edward Elgar Publishing.

Klein, L. R., and Mariano, R. S. (1987). The ET interview: Professor L. R. Klein. *Econometric Theory*, 3(3), 409-460.

Klein, L. R., & Kosobud, R. F. (1961, May). Some econometrics of growth: Great ratios of economics. *The Quarterly Journal of Economics*, 75(2), 173-198.

Klein, L. R, & Goldberger, A. S. (1955). *An econometric model of the United States, 1929-1952*. Amsterdam: Elsevier.

Liang, Y., & Klein, L. R. (1989). The two-gap paradigm in the Chinese case: A pedagogical exercise. *China Economic Review*, I(1), 1-8.

Lucas, R. E., Jr. (1994) [1981]. *Studies in business-cycle theory*. Cambridge, MA: MIT Press.

Ramrattan, L., & Szenberg, M. (2008a). Identification problem. In *International encyclopedia of the social sciences* (2nd ed.) (vol. 3, 550-551). London and New York: Macmillan.

———. (2008b). Econometrics. *International encyclopedia of the social sciences* (vol. 2, 2nd ed.). London and New York: Macmillan.

———. (2008c). Expectation. *International Encyclopedia of the Social Sciences* (vol. 3, 2nd ed.). London and New York: Macmillan.

Samuelson, P. A. (1986). *The collected scientific papers of Paul A. Samuelson* (vol. 5). K. Crowley (Ed.). Cambridge, MA: MIT Press.

Sargent, T. J., & Wallace, N. (1975). "Rational" expectations, the optimal monetary instrument and the optimal money supply rule. *Journal of Political Economy*, 83(2), 241-254.

Sims, C. A. (1972). Money, income and causality. *American Economic Review*, 62(4), 540-552. Reprinted in R. E. Lucas, Jr. & T. J. Sargent (Ed.), *Rational expectations and econometric practice* (387-403). Minneapolis: University of Minnesota Press, 1981.

Szenberg, M., & Ramrattan, L. (2008). *Franco Modigliani, a mind that never rests*. Foreword by R. M. Solow. New York: Palgrave Macmillan.

Thiel, H. (1961). *Economic forecasts and policy* (2nd ed.). Amsterdam: Elsevier.

Tinbergen, J. (1952). *On the theory of economic policy*. Amsterdam: Elsevier.

PART VII

GENERAL EQUILIBRIUM

Gerard Debreu, John Hicks, and Maurice Allais

Gerard Debreu

Introduction and Background

The world-renowned Nobel Laureate and mathematical economist Gerard Debreu passed away on December 31, 2004, at the age of 83. The economic profession will long grieve the loss of a genius of his caliber, who was well known for bringing the rigor of mathematics to economics.

Debreu, the son of Camille and Fernande (née Decharne) Debreu, was born on July 4, 1921, in Calais, France. In 1941, he attended the Ecole Normale Superieure, where he studied and lived until the spring of 1944. He studied mathematics under the famous Henri Cartan and became attracted to Walrasian economics through the 1943 work of the future Nobel Laureate Maurice Allais, *A la Recherche d'une Discipline Économique*. In the summer of 1948 he was further influenced by a seminar given by another future Nobel Laureate Wassily Leontief. In 1949, he visited Harvard, Berkeley, Chicago, and Columbia Universities on a Rockefeller Fellowship. In the same year, he joined the Cowles Commission, which was attached to the University of Chicago at the time, where he gained a decade of experience working on Pareto Optima, existence of a general economic equilibrium, and utility theory. He followed the Commission when it moved to Yale University in 1955. He spent 1960-1961 at Stanford University, and then moved to UC Berkeley in 1962, where he remained until his retirement in 1991. In 1975, he became a citizen of the US, with all the credits and renown of a learned person. While at Berkeley, Debreu lived in Walnut Creek, California. He is survived by his wife, Francoise Debreu of Walnut Creek, and his two daughters, Chantal De Soto of Aptos, California, and Florence Tetrault of Vancouver, British Columbia.

Debreu's fame began when he turned his critical mind from pure mathematics toward its application to economics. The area where he made his mark is called General Equilibrium (GE), which, according to several modern economic methodologists, is "the most prestigious economics of all and it has absorbed an entire generation of some of the finest minds in modern economics" (Marchi and Blaug, 1991: 508–509). GE models come in different versions, but we will focus on the popular Arrow-Debreu model. Debreu's work on that model earned him the Nobel Prize in Economics in 1983 for introducing analytical and mathematical rigor in the reformulation of the theory of General Equilibrium.

The determination of price and output for the economy goes back to Adam Smith, who did not give his system a mathematical treatment. Many well-known mathematical economists have tried their hands at a GE system that would determine price and output. The best known mathematical treatment occurred around the marginal revolution in 1870, with the works of Carl Menger, the least mathematical of the marginal school; Leon Walras, the most mathematical; and Stanley Jevons, who proposed that "economics, if it is to be a science at all must be a mathematical science" (Jevons, 1970: 78). For Walras, "*Pure economics* is, in essence, the theory of the determination of prices under a hypothetical regime of perfectly free competition" (Walras, 1954: 40). He held that "this whole theory is mathematical . . . we cannot understand without mathematics why or how current equilibrium prices are arrived at not only in exchange, but also in production" (ibid.: 43).

Debreu improved upon the old Walrasian approach. Walras' system had total demand and total supply of factors (2m variables), and the demand for commodities and their prices (2n variables), for a total of 2n+2m variables and equations. Walras used a numeraire system, setting the price of one commodity equal to one. He also estimated the value of one variable from what is called Walras' Law. In the end, he had 2m+2n–1 independent equations and variables. We know that a "theory would be determinate if its equilibria could be expressed as the zeroes of a system having the same number of equations as of unknowns" (Mas-Colell, 1989: 175). Paul A. Samuelson illustrated this with a system in which many individuals each have one apple and three oranges, and a taste that dictates they spend half their income on apples and half on oranges.

> Having lived as a scholar in both the pre- and post-Debreu era, I can testify that the modern proofs are better than what used to pass muster for demonstration of determinate economic equilibrium. Here is how our wave-of-the-hand expositions used to go. We used to count our number of unknowns—in this case one unknown price ratio. And then we counted our number of independent equations—in this case the function for p_a/p_o representing aggregate supply of apples be equated to the function representing aggregate demand for apples. (Samuelson, 1986: 839)

The Walrasian system had all the necessary conditions for a solution, ruling out the trivial solution of zero. However, it could lead to negative values, which do not have any meaning in economics. Also, Walras relied on a *tâtonnement* (search) process to eliminate excess demand and supply by at least three ways—through an auctioneer, through contracting and re-contracting, and through the nullification of old contracts (Negishi, 1989: 281). According to Knut Wicksell, "he clothed in a mathematical formula the very arguments which he considered insufficient when they were expressed in ordinary language" (Robinson, 1964: 55-56). Mathematics began to have a bad name in the profession. "[Alfred] Marshall in his own way also rather pooh-poohed the use of mathematics. But he regarded it as a way of arriving at the truths, but not as a good way of communicating such truths" (Samuelson, 1966: 1755). In the 1930s, however, mathematics started to make a comeback in the hands of stalwarts such as John Hicks, Samuelson, and others.

In his Nobel Laureate lecture and other sources, Debreu said: "To somebody trained in the uncompromising rigor of Bourbaki, counting equations and unknowns in the Walrasian system could not be satisfactory, and the nagging question of existence was posed" (Debreu, 1992: 89). Then, "in the summer of 1950, [Kenneth] Arrow, at the Second Berkeley Symposium on Mathematical Statistics and Probability, and I, at a meeting of the Econometric Society at Harvard, separately treated the same problem by means of the theory of convex sets" (ibid.).

Debreu's Description of the GE Model

A GE model starts with proper care in the definition of a commodity. A commodity has spatio-temporal and physically differentiated characteristics, which can be represented by a symbol, l, in a Euclidian space, R^l. As Debreu puts it, "by focusing attention on changes of dates one obtains . . . a theory of savings, investment, capital, and interest. Similarly by focusing attention on changes of locations one obtains . . . a theory of location, transportation, international trade and exchange" (Debreu, 1959: 32). He later explained that Arrow's uncertainty assumption has shifted the paradigm away "from a simple reinterpretation of a primitive concept" to "a novel interpretation of the same primitive concept" that allows for "unknown choices that nature will make from the set of possible states of the world" (Hildenbrand, 1989: 5).

Debreu then specified the agents, consumers and producers, and characteristics. "For any economic *agent* a complete plan of action . . . is a specification for each commodity of the quantity that he will make available or that will be made available to him, i.e., a complete listing of the quantities of his inputs and of his outputs" (Debreu, 1959: 32). "A complete description of an *economy* . . . consists of: For each consumer, his consumption set . . . and his preference ordering . . . For each producer, his production set . . . the total resources" (ibid.: 75). A state of the economy is "a specification of the action of each agent," and net demand is formed from canceling out "all commodity transfers between agents of the economy" (ibid.). If one also subtracts the agent's resources from net demand, one gets excess demand.

"A state is called a *market equilibrium* if its excess demand is 0" (ibid.: 76 [italics original]). More generally, equilibrium exists if "(a) . . . every consumer has chosen in his consumption set a consumption that satisfies his preferences best under his budget constraint . . . [b] every producer has maximized his profit in his production set . . . [c] for every commodity the excess of demand over supply is zero. The equilibrium defined by conditions (a), (b), and (c) is competitive in the sense that every agent behaves as if he had no influence on prices and considers them as given when choosing his own action" (Debreu, 1982: 704).

Existence of Equilibrium

In one of his frequent surveys, Debreu noted:

> Four distinct, but closely related, approaches to the existence problem can be recognized. (1) At first, proofs of existence of an economic equilibrium were uniformly obtained by application of a fixed-point theorem of the Brouwer type or of the Kakutani type or by analogous arguments . . . (2) In the last decade, efficient algorithms of a combinatorial nature for the computation of an approximate economic equilibrium were developed . . . (3)

More recently, the theory of the fixed-point index of a map and the degree theory of maps were used... (4) Finally, in 1976 Smale proposed a differential process whose generic convergence to an economics equilibrium provides an alternative constructive solution of the existence problem. (Debreu, 1982: 677–678)

A discussion with Professor Robert Anderson, UC Berkeley Mathematical Economics Department, underscores that these four stages have more or less remained intact, covering the popular areas of existence of equilibrium—fixed points, core theory, Debreu-Scarf works, and welfare theorems. We will be concerned with mainly the first one, for, to paraphrase Professor Anderson, Debreu's work progressed from undergraduate level to more entrenched graduate level research. Even with this restriction, Professor Anderson warns us about the difficulty of entering the dimensions higher than two.

Debreu explained how he got into the fixed-point solution from the mathematical side, including game theory.

I learned about the Lemma in [John] von Neumann's article of 1937 on growth theory that Shizuo Kakutani reformulated in 1941 as a fixed point theorem. I also learned about the applications of Kakutani's theorem made by John Nash in his one-page note of 1950 on "Equilibrium Points in N-Person Games" and by Morton Slater in his unpublished paper, also of 1950, on Lagrange multipliers. Again there was an ideal tool, this time Kakutani's theorem, for the proof that I gave in 1952 of the existence of a social equilibrium generalizing Nash's result. Since the transposition from the case of two agents to the case of n agents is immediate, we shall consider only the former which lends itself to a diagrammatic representation. Let the first agent choose an action a_1 in the *a priori* given set A_1, and the second agent choose an action a_2 in the *a priori* given set A_2. Knowing a_2, the first agent has a set $\mu_1(a_2)$ of equivalent reactions. Similarly, knowing a_1, the second agent has a set $\mu_2(a_1)$ of equivalent reactions. $\mu_1(a_2)$ and $\mu_2(a_1)$ may be one-element sets, but in the important case of an economy with some producers operating under constant returns to scale, they will not be. The state $a = (a_1, a_2)$ is an equilibrium if and only if $a_1 \in \mu_1(a_2)$ and as $a_2 \in \mu_2(a_1)$, that is if and only if $a \in \mu(a) = \mu_1(a_2) \times \mu_2(a_1)$. (Debreu, 1983: 90–91).

In our article of 1954, Arrow and I cast a competitive economy in the form of a social system of the preceding type.... In this manner a proof of existence, resting ultimately on Kakutani's theorem, was obtained for an equilibrium of an economy made up of interacting consumers and

> producers . . . . In the early fifties, the time had undoubtedly come for solutions of the existence problem. In addition to the work of Arrow and me, begun independently and completed jointly, Lionel McKenzie at Duke University proved the existence of an "Equilibrium in Graham's Model of World Trade and Other Competitive Systems" [1954], also using Kakutani's theorem. A different approach taken independently by David Gale . . . in Copenhagen, Hukukane Nikaido [1956] in Tokyo, and Debreu [1956] in Chicago permitted the substantial simplification given in my *Theory of Value* [1959] of the complex proof of Arrow and Debreu. (ibid.: 91)

It is clear that a substantial mastery of mathematical tools is needed before one can get a feel for Debreu's contribution to GE. In order to lay out that road for the readers to get an intuitive feeling of Debreu's contribution, we take the following approach in the rest of this memoriam: Part IV takes up some disagreements over GE and Part V speculates about the future of GE.

Debreu's Tools of the Trade

In his presentation of the Nobel Laureate speech, Professor Karl-Göran Mäler of the Royal Academy of Sciences said:

> In the development of the general equilibrium theory, Professor Debreu has not merely given us information about the price mechanism, but also introduced new analytical techniques, new tools in the toolbox of economists. Gerard Debreu symbolizes the use of a new mathematical apparatus, an apparatus comprehended by most economists only abstractly. Nevertheless, his work has given us an improved intuitive understanding of the underlying economic relevance. His clarity and analytical rigor, as well as the distinction drawn by him between an economic theory and its interpretation, have given his work important bearing on the choice of methods and analytical techniques within economic theory on a par with any other living economist. (Mäler, 1992)

Samuelson has said that "Debreu is known for his unpretentious no-nonsense approach to the subject" (Weintraub, 2002: 113). It is common to mention that Debreu is from the Bourbaki school of mathematics, and that sends a shiver down the spine of any aspiring economist. Debreu revealed in an interview to E. Roy Weintraub that his early high school education in geometry "called for imagination, intuition, experimentation, and I think that it gave me an excellent education, and a very good preparation for the geometric viewpoint that I have often taken up in my work since" (ibid.: 127). In 1990, at public lecture, one of the present authors asked Debreu what is his contribution to the tools of his trade had been, what his unique mathematical contribution was. He replied that he mainly relied on other people's tools. It is difficult to list them all, but his early works are sprinkled with convex set theory, fixed point theorem, and partial ordering; and his later works made use of topology, measure theory, and non-standard analysis. We present in this section some of the intuitive tools that are unique to him, tools that he contributed to economics and that are understandable at an undergraduate level.

Convex Sets

A cursory check of the literature reveals that convex analysis goes back to ancient Greece: "This is what Archimedes said (Werke, 1963) 'I give the name convex on one side of those surfaces for which the line joining any two of its points . . . will lie on one side of the surface.' This definition has remained virtually unchanged up to the present day" (Gamkrelidze, 1980: 3). A popularization of this concept states that "a convex set has the property that a collection that contains two items also contains an average of these two items" (Kay, 2004: 179). This is not an unrealistic assumption. "It probably isn't an exaggeration to say that the behavior of market economies depends on how convex the world is. To get a sense of why this is so, imagine dropping a ball into a bowl: it circles round, slows down, and eventually arrives at some sort of equilibrium" because the bowl is convex. Now if the bowl is turned upside down, the points in the bowl are no longer convex, and the position of the ball is unpredictable (ibid.: 180).

The space we live in (3-dimensional) is convex because you can join any two points in it by a line. By the same logic, a plane (2-dimensional), such as a sheet of paper, can be separated into two halves, two convex sets, and we can join any two points in each half plane by a line. From that point, it is easy to show that the intersection of convex sets are convex, and to define other convex properties such as convex hull, one-dimensional convex figures which can be a line, a line segment, or a ray.

Consumption Set

An example of a convex set is the consumption set. If X is a set of all possible consumption, then X is not zero, and it lives in the space R^l, mentioned above.

One concern is to represent a utility function that takes on many variables by a number: $U(x_1,x_2) = x_1.x_2$. Or more formally: $U:X \rightarrow R$, where R represents a real number. We can build our intuition of such a utility function by asking a person to rank their preference of a bundle of one commodity over a bundle of another. An example of a bundle is x_1 = (2 grapes, 1 banana), and other would be x_2 = (5 grapes, 4 bananas). Normally these bundles can be plotted on a (grapes, banana, utility), i.e. (x_1, x_2, U) coordinate system, and utilities are ranked in an ordinal way. Our objective is to assign a number to those rankings, which would make the ranking of utility cardinal. Originally, the concept of utility was first thought out cardinally. For example, when we eat an apple we say we get so many utils. This way we can add up all the utils we get from consuming many different commodities. Debreu, therefore, is standing on the shoulders of giants in wanting to strengthen the foundation of the old cardinal utility concept. Such a concept is useful, for instance, in mathematical programming (Mas-Colell et al., 1995: 46).

The cardinal utility concept is born out of a preference relationship. On X, the commodity space, we want a binary relation. A binary relation allows a pair-wise comparison of commodities. To get a feel for this, if we wish to say that the weight of Albert, w(A), is not greater than the weight of Ben, w(B), then we can write $w(A) \leq w(B)$. This would imply that Albert, A, is not heavier than Ben, B. Consumers are therefore comparing (ordering or ranking) their bundles, x_1 and x_2, in a pair-wise or binary manner. If x_1 is "at least as good as" x2, we will use the symbol $\succsim$, and if they are indifferent, we will use the symbol $\sim$. A utility function $U:X \rightarrow R$, where R represents real numbers, represents a preference relation of the set X if certain conditions hold, i.e. $x_1,x_2 \in R$, $x_1 \succsim x_2 \Leftrightarrow U(x_1) \geq U(x_2)$. What do we need to construct such a utility function? First, on the preference side we require that the agents be rational, which means that the consumers should make a *complete* ranking of all bundles, and the ranking should be *transitive*. Additionally, because it was found that lexicographic preference relations are discontinuous, it is necessary to add that the utility function be *continuous* as well. Continuity means that if we are told that a series of consumption bundles are "at least as good as" a given consumption, then the limit of the sequence will have that property. For convenience, we can make some more assumptions: (1) that "more is better"; this will imply that people are non-satiated, (2) free disposal, i.e. consumers can get rid of goods costlessly, and (3) convexity, implying that a mixture of two extreme bundles is preferred to the extremes, and that consumption is divisible. With these assumptions, we can have an intuitive feel of how to construct a utility function.

The feel goes like this: let us decide to assign utility to only bundles that are on an indifferent curve. We can find these indifferent curves by traveling on a line from the origin of a diagram, 0, or the worst case consumption set, outward to meet the an indifference curve. If we do not use the convexity assumption, then the indifference curve can be winding, but that is not germane to the proof.

Take a two dimensional coordinate system (x_1, x_2). Plot the point $e = (1, 1)$, a point on the diagonal. Now, we can move on the diagonal by multiplying e by a number, say t, to get t.e. The number t can be less than or greater than one, which will make us move on the diagonal line e. Now draw in an indifference curve to meet the t.e line. We have decided to call this meeting our utility function, i.e. $U(x) = t.e$.

We need to check that the preference assumption holds. Given that $t(x_1) \geq t(x_2)$ iff $x_1 \succsim x_2$. First, we can substitute $t(x_1).e$ and $t(x_2).e$ for $t(x_1)$ and $t(x_2)$. Second, since $t(x_1).e \sim x_1$ and $t(x_2).e \sim x_2$, we can substitute x_1, and x_2 in to get $x_1 \succsim x_2$.

Conversely, let's start with $x_1 \succsim x_2$. First, since $t(x_1).e \sim x_1$ and $t(x_2).e \sim x_2$, substitute $t(x_1).e$ and $t(x_2).e$ for x_1 and x_2. Second, dropping the e in the expressions yields $t(x_1) \geq t(x_2)$. So, we have shown that $t(x_1) \geq t(x_2)$ iff $x_1 \succsim x_2$.

Check that the continuity assumption holds. This is much more difficult to do. But, intuitively, we need to show that distance is a continuous concept. We indicate distance from the origin to t.e by the bi-directional arrow in Figure 1. In symbolic form, we can write $||t(x).e||$ for distance. So, $U(x) = ||t(x).e||$. We need to show that a series of x and distances converge to the same point x on the indifference curve. Since points above and below the indifference curve includes the indifference curve, then the distance on the ray is closed. Therefore, the limit points of the series are closed. Closeness and limit points of the sequences, therefore, imply continuity.

Separating Planes

In economics, we encounter disjointed convex sets, such as consumption and production sets, to be separated by a plane, representing the budget line in 2-dimension. Debreu defined separation of planes as follows: "A hyperplane H

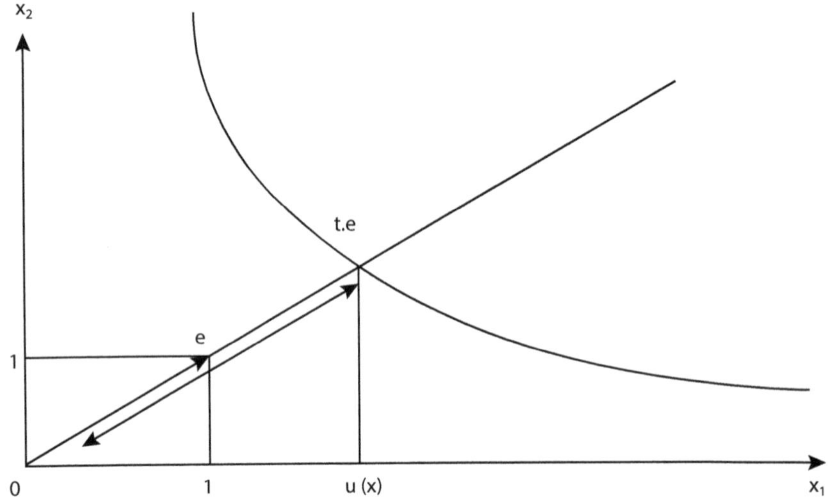

Figure 1 Construction of a Utility Map.

is separating for two sets A, B if A is contained in one of the closed halfspaces determined by H and B in the other" (Debreu, 1959a: 95). Debreu proceeded to give an intuitive proof of separation using Figure 2.

Our intuitive explanation of Debreu's diagram, while not fit for a mathematician, may be worthwhile for a learner. Figure 2 uses the technique of proof by contradiction. The hyperplane H separates the halfplane A, above, from the halfplane B, below. Keep in mind that we want to prove that "the hyperplane H through x', perpendicular to $x^o x'$, is separating for A and x^o" (Debreu, 1959a: 95).

We start out with the assumption that the distance from x^o to x', $d(x^o,x')$, is the shortest distance you can find from of all points x in A, to x^o in B. Thus defined, any other point, x, in A will be further from x^o in B than x' in A. Lets make the argument that there is a point x" in A, but that it lies below H, i.e., it lies on the same side of H with x^o. Another way of saying this is that the distance from x^o to x," $d(x^o,x'')$, is greater than or equal to, ≥, the distance from x^o to x', $d(x^o,x')$. How would this be a contradiction to the assumption that x' is the closest point in A to x^o in B? It is a contradiction because we can now see that $\overline{x}$ would be in A and closer to x^0 than x' is away from x^o. In other words, $d(x^o,x') \geq d(x^o,\overline{x})$. As we have started with the assumption that $d(x^o,x')$ is the shortest distance from x^0 in B to x' in A, we have reached a contradiction.

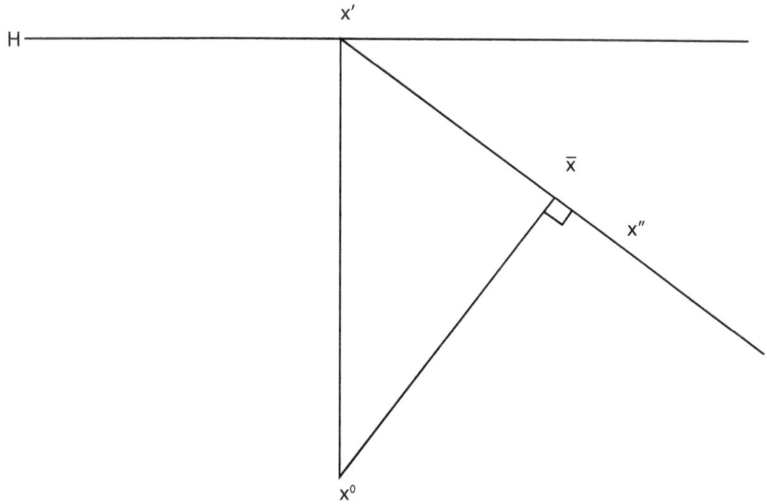

Figure 2 Debreu's Intuitive Diagram.

What is Debreu's proof intuitive to? It is intuitive to, for instance, an earlier proof, still prevalent in textbooks, that was introduced by John von Neumann and Oskar Morgenstern (von Neumann et al., 1944). Neumann et al. state that "we must find a correspondence between utilities and numbers which carries the relation u > v and the operations $\alpha u + (1-\alpha)v$ for utilities into the synonymous concepts for numbers.... denote the correspondence by... $u \rightarrow \rho = v(u)$ ... u being the utility and v(u) the number which the correspondence attaches to it. Our requirements are then: ... u > v implies v(u) > v(v)" (ibid.: 24).

A modern attempt to generalize this intuitive concept of Debreu's goes as follows: Consider the stick person in Figure 3. The head (H) is compact, i.e. closed and bounded. The body (B) is closed. Let the minimum point in H at the arrowhead be h', and the maximum point in B at the arrow tail be b'. The separation theorem says, for instance, that there is a vector orthogonal to the point b' on the arm, such that for any h in H, ph' ≤ ph, and for any b in B, pb'≥ pb. If we denote the length of the neck by p = h'-b', the distance of the neck from the head to where it meets the shoulder, then we get p.p = p(h'-b'). This yields ph' > pb' because distance is positive. We want to show that for any point b in B, pb' ≥ pb, and for any point h in H, ph' ≤ ph. Because the head and body are convex, we can join any points in them by a line. In the case of the body, join b and b' this way: b* = (1-a)b' + ab, where a is a percent between

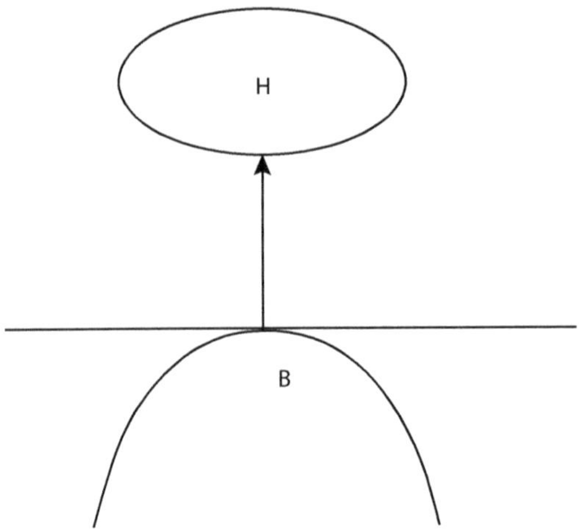

Figure 3 Plane-Separation.

0 and 1. This line will be contained in the body by the convexity assumption. Now, if you form $|h'-b^*|^2$, then, with some manipulation, you get $pb' \geq pb$. A similar analysis will yield $ph' \leq ph$ in the head area. Then it is possible to slip a hyperplane between these sets.

Fixed Point Theorems

Sir Karl Popper told a story to show that absolute truth exists. Popper was in the company of Alfred Tarski, and they were on a mountain-climbing mission. The day was foggy, with the fog completely covering the mountain peak. Tarski took advantage of the situation to indicate the existence of absolute truth, at least his brand of it. He said that just because you cannot see the peak, you nevertheless feel intuitively that the peak exists. Similarly, Debreu has used Brouwer's and Kakutani's fixed point theorems to show that GE prices exist. This was a fruitful exercise because, later on, researchers such as Herbert E. Scarf developed algorithms to compute those prices. Today, by the method of complementarity, the world is swamped with computational general equilibrium (CGE) analysis. For instance, the International Trade Council has develop a CGE model, which it used to advise President Clinton about the welfare gains from trade to be attained from the US joining NAFTA. Also, the WTO has its brand of CGE models to determine the potential benefits from forming the FTAA on world economies. Private researchers and institutions have developed databases and computer softwares to make this kind of analysis routine, even though GE models are still being pursued in a rigorous manner.

Debreu, in one of his last lectures, explained fixed point this way: we are concerned with mapping points on a rubber sheet to other points on the rubber sheet. Stretching the rubber sheet, thereby pulling points from where they were to other positions, can do this but we should not pull in a manner that would tear the rubber sheet. The idea of a fixed point is that, in the process of stretching the rubber sheet, one point will not move. It will be mapped onto itself. For those of you familiar with demand and supply curves, here is another intuitive feel: imagine the demand and supply curves are two separate graphs. Mark off two quantities, a supply quantity, Q_s, and a demand quantity, Q_d. Then trace up from the two quantity axes to the demand and the supply curves to find two prices, a supply price, Ps, and a demand price, Pd. If we can find a function, a map, of $f(P_s) = P_d$ or $f(Q_s) = Qd$, then we have a fixed point mapping for the equilibrium problem (Baumol, 1965: 494). (Baumol claimed that this is the direction Lionel Mckenzie took when he originally proposed his contribution in 1954.) For higher dimensions, the concept of the "hairy-ball" problem gives a similar intuition. Loosely speaking, try to move every hair on your head from its current position to the position of another hair. The fixed-point theorems say that one hair cannot be so moved. It will have to stay fixed.

In writing about Debreu, Samuelson was drawn into the fixed point solution from the two dimensions point-of-view as well. From a simple function, Samuelson explained the intuitive concept of a fixed point as follows:

> Draw a square and pencil in the 45-degree diagonal connecting its southwest and northeast corners. Is there any way to draw a curve that goes from the square's east side to its west side without taking pencil off the paper, such that the curve and the diagonal have no single point in common? Brouwer's fixed-point theorem in one dimension proves that there is indeed no possible way. Similarly, under specified conditions about people's tastes and goods endowments, there is no way for curves of supply and demand to be drawn without having at least one intersection point in common. (Samuelson, 1986: 839)

Continuity

Continuity is generally defined from the point of view that $f(x) \to f(x_0)$ as $x \to x_0$. This method is used for Brouwer's fixed point theorem, which is defined as follows: if a theorem says that if $f(x)$ is a continuous point-to-point mapping of a closed set, S into itself, then there exists a point x in S such that $x = f(x)$. However, we will be dealing with point-to-set mapping where $f(x)$ and $f(x_0)$ take on sets of values, as in the Kakutani fixed point theorem, which generalizes Brouwer's theorem to a point-to-set mapping. Kakutani's theorem states that if S is closed, and φ is an upper semicontinuous mapping from within S to a closed convex subset of x, then there exists a point x in S such that x is in $\varphi(x)$ (Karlin, 1959: 408–409).

In order to get a feel for upper semicontinuity, let us consider the point-to-set mapping: $Y = \{y|\ 1/3x \leq y \leq x\}$. We are pulling elements of x from a domain set, say B, and they go to a subset of image points y in A. If we restrict the mapping to the interval [0, 1], we can imagine the image of the mapping to be the area between the equation $y = x$, that is the diagonal example that Samuelson used above, and the equation $y = 1/3\,x$. Now, our focus is on what happens as $x \to x_0$. There will be an image set $Y(x_0)$, and a set S of limit points indicating all the approach paths of sequences in the image set as $x \to x_0$. If S is a subset of $Y(x_0)$, the mapping is upper semicontinuous (Lancaster, 1968: 347).

Existence of Equilibrium

Werner Hildenbrand wrote that "when Debreu began to write his *Theory of Value* in 1954 he based the existence proof on a result that today is called the 'fundamental lemma.' . . . It was proved independently of Debreu by D. Gale . . . and H. Nikaido" (Hildenbrand, 1989: 20). The description we now give is from Hukukane Nikaido (1956). Start with a referee setting the price, P. Consumers will maximize their utility, $U_i(x)$, subject to PX = PA, where A is endowment and goods X is in space $E = \{X \mid 0 \leq X \leq C)$, C being an arbitrary bundle such that C > A. All acceptable bundles with respect to P are labeled $\varphi_i(P)$, the ith individual demand function. Its sum is just $\varphi(P)$. If total demand, X, does not match total available bundles, A, the referee must make an adjustment. The difference is X-A. Its value is P(X-A). The referee's objective is to pay a person a value PX that is greater than the endowment value PA. In other words, choose a price, Q, that will maximize the price-manipulating function: $\theta X = \{P \mid P(X\text{-}A) = \max Q(X\text{-}A) \text{ for all } Q \text{ in } S^k\}$, where X is total demand lying in Γ.

We now have a demand function and a price-adjustment function.

$S^k \ni P \rightarrow \varphi(P) \subset \Gamma$ (Demand function)
$\Gamma \ni X \rightarrow \theta(X) \subset S^k$ (Price-manipulating function)

We want to choose (X, P) in this Demand and Price adjustment space, $\Gamma \times S^k$, so that $\varphi(P) \times \theta(X)$ is contained in $\Gamma \times S^k$. This is possible because the mapping is upper semicontinuous. Therefore, the equilibrium price exists.

Upper semicontinuity is easy to show for $\theta(X)$. Given $P_n \rightarrow P$ in S^k, $X_n \rightarrow X$ in Γ and $P_n \in \theta(X_n)$, then $P \in \theta(X)$. The proof is that, for any Q price-constellation, $P_n (X_n - A) \geq Q(X_n - A)$, and, for the whole sequence, $n \rightarrow \infty$, $P(X - A) \geq Q(X - A)$. Therefore, $P \in \theta(X)$. The reader can check the original source for the rest of the continuous tests.

A Concrete Example

We wish to end this section with a concrete example of how GE is entering the modern textbooks of economics. We illustrate this with the following two-dimensional model that is now widely used in many textbooks to build a feeling for Debreu's solution (Aliprantis et al., 1990). The economy has three agents: 1, 2, 3, and two commodities: x, y, with endowment $(w_1, w_2, w_3)=\{(1, 2), (1, 1), (2, 3)\}$, and utility functions $U_1 = xy$, $U_2 = x^2y$, and $U_3 = (xy^2)$. Using the Lagrange multiplier for agent 1 yields: $y = \lambda p_1$, $x = \lambda p_2$, and $p_1x + p_2y = p_1 + 2p_2$ (Aliprantis et al., 1990: 34–36). We can now find demand for agent 1: $x_1(p) = \{(p_1 + 2p_2)/2p_1, (p_1 + 2p_2)/2p_2\}$. Repeat the procedure to find $x_2(p)$ and $x_3(p)$. If we add the three demands, we get total demand, z(p), and by subtracting the total endowment, (4, 6), we get excess demand. The equilibrium price will be $p^e = (0.45, 0.55)$, approximately.

S is a price simplex. P represents a vector of prices. The market would not be clear. We would call on the price adjustment referee to change prices so as to move in the direction P = (0.45, 0.55). This is equivalent to rotating the whole orthogonal Price and Z(p) contraption towards the P_1 axis, which is done by mapping $f(p) = p + z^+(p)$ (Mas-Colell et al., 1995: 588).

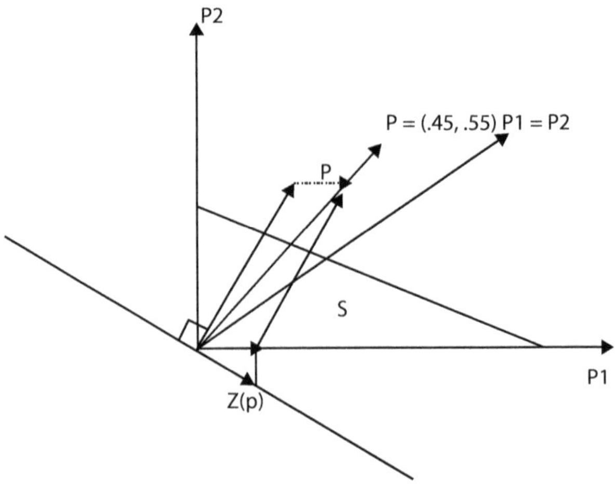

Figure 4 Equilibrium Price Simplex.

Disagreement about GE

Disagreements range from complete rejection of GE models to pointing out damning criticisms with the scientifically honest view of making the model a progressive research program. We look at the latter.

Paradigm vs. Theory

From a methodological perspective, Mark Blaug views Debreu's place in the mathematical schema somewhat differently. For him, Arrow and Frank Hahn have committed a "category mistake" by saying that Walras wanted to make precise the Smithian doctrine (Marchi and Blaug, 1991: 508). Walras' contribution is a "framework" or "paradigm" rather than a "theory." It does not have empirical testable propositions. It was almost still-born: it "went into decline almost as soon as Walras had formulated it" (ibid.: 507). It started to come out of oblivion through the works of Hicks, Samuelson, and Oskar Lange in the 1930s and "came to the very forefront of economic theorizing in the famous Arrow/Debreu articles of the 1950s" (ibid.: 507). One of the hallmarks of that framework is that it could be turned into operationally meaningful theorems, which can make it testable, falsifiable, or verifiable in the form of, say, CGE models, Leontief's input-output form, or John Maynard Keynes' IS-LM models (ibid.: 506). It is said that "Debreu and others have made significant contributions to the understanding of Keynesian economies just by describing so precisely what would have to be the case if there were to be not Keynesian problems" (Hahn, 1984: 65).

The Aim of General Equilibrium

What GE is about is not without controversy. Some say it is about the finding of a set of equilibrium prices that are stable and unique, given the smallest set of assumptions. But "an Arrow-Debreu equilibrium may exist when there are increasing returns . . . it is perfectly possible for an Arrow-Debreu equilibrium to exist even though the axioms of the theory are violated" (ibid.: 51). In other words, one needs the "absence of significant economies of scale in production" to show that "equilibrium prices can indeed be found" (ibid.: 74). Joseph Stiglitz, for instance, evolved a parallel GE universe where information is central. He steered the research from a competitive to an information paradigm (Stiglitz, 2004: 35). Others have tried to accommodate risk, irrationality, and cooperation rather than competition (Kay, 2004: 207). The big question is how does one decide to give up a theory? By the realism of its assumption? By a fixed number of times that it fails? By its lack of operationally meaningful theorems? When one of its additional assumptions fails? We do not have a definitive answer. Like sophisticated falsificationists, Debreu and others have continued to work with the GE model to answer new and anomalous questions. We give a brief review of some of these attempts below.

Weakness of General Equilibrium

Hahn stated that it is incorrect to "claim that Debreu was looking for the 'minimum basic assumptions for establishing the existence of an equilibrium set of prices which is (a) unique, (b) stable.' Debreu did not concern himself with either" (Hahn, 1984: 48). Hahn's overarching point seems to be that "it is undesirable to have an equilibrium notion in which information is a perfect and as costless as it is in Arrow-Debreu" (ibid.: 53). He mentioned works that were done to (1) accommodate available information, (2) examine the extent that prices are efficient information signals, (3) study transaction possibilities that may be costly in a sequential economy, (4) recognize stochastic equilibrium, (5) differentiate random preferences and endowments, and (6) to analyze multivalued short-period equilibrium (ibid.: 53–55).

An early criticism of the socialists includes problems with distribution. Hahn adds that "distribution of preferences of agents is not God-given, and is different for different societies . . . what is needed is . . . a theory of preference formation and of the way endowments come to be what they are" (Hahn, 1991: 67–68). If we take the days of typewriters as an example, people who learned to type developed that type of 'human capital'; and, when technology changed, it was not adopted because of the cost of retraining. Therefore, if equilibrium were defined to ignore what happened in the past, it would not be a true equilibrium. Again, take increasing returns to scale. Suppose one of two techniques with equal possibilities were chosen by chance and yielded increasing returns perhaps by specialization. Then one technique that was not chosen would be rendered inferior only because it was not chosen.

Hahn's criticism seems to have mellowed. In his 1984 article, he stated that "the theory itself, however, is likely to recede and be superseded" (Hahn, 1984: 86–87). In the1991 version of his article, he seems to take a cautionary view: "I am keen to end on a cautionary note. It is not my view that current economic theorizing is totally misdirected or useless. Rather the reverse. I think economists have probably attained a durable understanding of many important phenomena. . . . To the practical economists they are not of deep concern. . . . What I am proposing is that theorists should catch up with them" (Hahn, 1991: 74).

Another unsettled notion of the Arrow-Debreu model resides in the area of core theory. Core theory can be traced back to the Edgeworth's contract curve. The issue is how to generalize the core for large economies. One way to do so is to make replica economies by grouping or replicating similar preferences and endowments. A measurable achievement here is that a price system for a decentralized core allocation exists. The topic of equilibrium for large economies was a springboard for continuation of agents' models.

Future of GE

Current research seems to have balked at the point of showing the comparative static properties of GE. As Samuelson has pointed out, this is a necessary condition to move the development above the childish level of parroting demand and supply analysis. As a refresher, such analysis requires one to check that the excess demand function have certain properties. Those properties are that it (1) is single valued and bounded from below, (2) is continuous, (3) is homogenous, and (4) obeys Walras' Law. Under conditions of gross substitutability, it is possible to demonstrate comparative static properties in the sense of Hicks and Samuelson. Hicks' model predicts that prices that exceed demand will be higher for those goods whose price changes are smaller. Samuelson predicted that excess demand will be more positive when only one good in the *ceteris paribus* set of goods changes, and less positive if the price of a second one in the set changes, showing the Le Chatelier principle at work. Debreu, however, did not think that the excess demand functions lack the structure to answer this problem. This area is now receiving much attention in the literature (Hildrenbrand, 1989: 26–27).

If we add some operational content to this theorem, we can perform CGE estimates for an economy or the world. The International Trade Centre (ITC) and the World Trade Organization (WTO), for instance, use CGE models to predict the effect that freer trade among integrated areas such as NAFTA and the EU will have on the welfare of a country. CGE is a simulation type of model. Given empirical estimates of import elasticities, substitution among commodities, and inputs on the one hand, and specification for utility and production functions on the other hand, it computes benchmark prices. Counterfactual assumptions can be made to obtain effects of policy measures. In short, CGE is a way to do GE with numbers, and it is made possible by the revival of GE analysis.

Conclusion

In this memoriam, we show our appreciation for a few intuitive concepts Debreu has bequeathed to us, but we have just begun to scratch the surface of the fruits of his erudition on GE. Today, the ideas of convexity can be found in most popular introductory textbooks at the undergraduate level. However, research is continually being done, from questioning the basic assumptions of GE models to expanding the horizon of their application. Being armed with a few of the intuitive insights, a modern student can begin to penetrate the all-pervasive subject of GE, knowing that it will be a long journey.

We have covered several important simple areas, only briefly commenting on game theory and welfare economics. Game theory was mentioned by Debreu in his prize lecture, but got to the heart of the problem very quickly. His way of teaching game theory is more gentle, starting with simple parlor games, going through the proofs of minimax theorem, and ending with correspondence mapping. His way of teaching the welfare side starts with simple proofs that are available for the first welfare theorem, and ends with the theory that the Walrasian equilibrium is in its core a complex subject.

In general, Debreu's teaching style was comprehensive from the simple to the abstract. It is clear that he preferred the mathematical to the economics side. You can hear him take pride and delight in saying that a certain conclusion has been reached from a purely mathematical point of view, without the use of economics, underscoring that economic concepts formulated in the language of mathematics help us to grasp things that would ordinarily not be possible. He was fond of saying that mathematicians tend to do well when they are young, while economists do well when they are old. He clinched this tale with the notion that students of mathematical economics are very lucky, for they get the best of both the mathematical and economic worlds.

Professor Debreu was very considerate to the young and budding mathematical economist. Students could interrupt his lecture to clarify problem areas. When students asked unclear questions, a typical response was that he did not quite understand the question. As the student tried again, he would say "I am beginning to see your point." He would sometimes pump-prime his students, saying "I would like to see more of this diagram in the literature." Once, when one of the authors met him on the streets of Berkeley campus, he exclaimed in a reprimanding tone: "What have you been doing?" This was his way of encouraging the student to do more by way of contributing to the literature. Mathematical economists never had a greater ambassador than Professor Gerard Debreu.

References

Aliprantis, C. D., Brown, D. J., & Burkinshaw, O. (1990). *Existence and optimality of competitive equilibria*. Berlin: Springer-Verlag.

Baumol, W. J. (1965). *Economic theory and operation analysis* (2nd ed.). Englewood Cliffs, NJ: Prentice-Hall, Inc.

Debreu, G. (1959, Jul. 1). Separation theorem for convex sets. *Selected Topics in Economics Involving Mathematical Reasoning* (95-98). SIAM Review.

———. (1959). *Theory of value.* New York: John Wiley and Sons, Inc.

———. (1982). Existence of competitive equilibrium. In K. J. Arrow & M. D. Itriligator (Eds.), *Handbook of mathematical economics* (vol. 2, 677–743). Amsterdam: Elsevier Science Publisher.

———. (1983, December 8). Economic theory in the mathematical mode: Nobel memorial lecture. *Economic Science*: 87–102.

———. (1993). Random walk and life philosophy. In M. Szenberg (Ed.), *Eminent economists: Their life philosophies* (107–114). London and New York: Cambridge University Press.

De Marchi, Neil, & Blaug, M. (1991). *Appraising economic theories: Studies in the methodology of research programs.* Cheltenham: Edward Elgar.

Gamkrelidze, R. V. (1980). *Encyclopaedia of mathematical sciences: Analysis II*, Vol. 14. New York: Springer-Verlag.

Hahn, F. (1984). *Equilibrium and macroeconomics.* Cambridge, MA: MIT Press.

———. (1991). History and economic theory. In K. Arrow (Ed.), *Issues in contemporary economics, vol. 1: Markets and welfare* (67-74). New York: New York University Press.

Hildenbrand, W. (1989). Introduction. In *Mathematical economics: Twenty papers of Gerard Debreu.* London: Cambridge University Press.

Jevons, W. S. (1970). *The theory of political economics.* London: Penguin Books.

Karlin, S. (1959). *Mathematical methods and theory in games, programming and economics* (vol. 1). Reading, MA: Addison-Wesley, Inc.

Kay, J. (2004). *Culture and prosperity: The truth about markets.* New York: Harper-Collins.

Lancaster, K. (1968). *Mathematical economics.* New York: Dover Publications, Inc.

Mäler, K.-G. (Ed.). (1992). *Nobel lectures, economics 1981-1990.* Singapore: World Scientific Publishing Co.

Mas-Colell, A. (1989). *The theory of general equilibrium: A differentiable approach.* London: Cambridge University Press.

Mas-Colell, A., Whinston, M. D., & Green, J. R. (1995). *Microeconomic theory.* Oxford: Oxford University Press.

Negishi, T. (1989). Tatonnement and recontracting. In J. Eatwell, M. Milgate, & P. Newman (Eds.), *General equilibrium* (vol. 4, 589-596). London and New York: Macmillan.

Nikaido, H. (1956). On the classical multilateral exchange problem. *Metroeconomica* 8, 135–145.

———. (1970). *Introduction to sets and mappings in modern economics.* (K. Sato, Trans.). Amsterdam: North-Holland Publishing Company.

Robinson, J. (1964). *Economic philosophy.* New York: Doubleday & Company, Inc..

Rothbard, M. N. (1962). *Man, economy, and state: A treatise on economic principles,* Vol. 1. Los Angeles: Nash Publishing.

———. (1973). Praxeology as the method of economics. In M. Natanson (Ed.), *Phenomenology and the social sciences* (vol. 2, 311–339). Evanston, IL: Nothwestern University Press.

Samuelson, P. A. (1966). *The collected scientific papers of Paul A. Samuelson* (vol. 2). J. E. Stiglitz (Ed.). Cambridge, MA: MIT Press.

———. (1972) *The collected scientific papers of Paul A. Samuelson* (vol. 3). R. C. Merton (Ed.). Cambridge, MA: MIT Press.

———. (1986). *The collected scientific papers of Paul A. Samuelson* (vol. 5). K. Crowley (Ed.). Cambridge, MA: MIT Press.

Stiglitz, J. E. (2004). Information and the change in the paradigm of economics. In M. Szenberg & L. Ramrattan (Eds.), *New frontiers in economics* (27-67). London: Cambridge University Press.

Von Neumann, J., & Morgenstern, O. (1944). *Theory of games and economic behavior.* Princeton: Princeton University Press.

Walras, L. (1954). *Elements of pure economics or the theory of social wealth.* New York: Augustus M. Kelley

Weintraub, E. R. (2002). *How economics became a mathematical science.* Durham, NC: Duke University Press.

John Hicks

Sir John R. Hicks was born in England on April 8, 1904. He was the author of twenty books on economics, was knighted in 1964 and received the 1972 Nobel Prize for his contributions to general equilibrium theory and welfare economics. After graduating from Oxford University in 1925 he taught at the London School of Economics (LSE), where he formulated concepts on the elasticity of substitution, relative income shares of labor and capital, and liquidity. At LSE, Hicks came under the influence of Lionel Robbins and Friedrich Hayek but broke away from their thought in his book *The Theory of Wages*, where he considered unions monopolies in the sense of rigid wages in a wage discrimination setting. He joined Cambridge University (1935-1938), where he was swayed by Keynes' writings. Afterward, Hicks was chair of political economy at the University of Manchester. He became a fellow at Nuffield College, Oxford, in 1946 and was the Drummond Professor of Political Economy from 1952 until his retirement in 1965. Hicks continued his work in the areas of fixprice and flexprice markets, liquidity, and inventions. He died on May 20, 1989.

Hicks' contributions stand out in the areas of applied economics, Keynesian economics, value theory, and technological progress. His method was to modify a theory to fit the facts. Facts are linked to events of the day and have a history that can become dramatic at times. According to Hicks, these dramatic facts are like blinkers waiting to be simplifed, theorized, and selected to explain topical events. Hicks continuously revised his theories because economic facts are less permanent and less repeatable than facts of the natural sciences.

Hicks viewed welfare economics as an application of demand theory, focusing on efficient and optimal cost and use of the social product. An efficiency test for welfare benefits tells us how to acquire more of one thing without having less of another thing. Demand theory makes sure that what we are getting more of is not detrimental. A welfare optimum may not be attained in a market with uniform prices, making room for cost-benefit analysis.

Hicks's IS and LL curves represent Keynes' ideas of equilibrium in the goods and money markets, respectively. Alvin Hansen later suggested the label LM (liquidity preference–money supply) instead of LL (Hansen, 1953: 144). Darity and Young (1995: 1-14, 26-27) clarified that Hansen's contribution emphasized one sector, while Hicks' contribution emphasized two sectors. Hicks developed a four equation system representing liquidity preference $M = L(r, Y)$, investment $I = I(r, Y)$, savings $S = S(r, Y)$, and saving-investment equilibrium $S = I$, where M is money, I is investment, S is savings, Y is income, and r is the rate of interest. The first equation yields the LM. If the interest rate rises, the alternative cost of holding money relative to other assets becomes more expensive, lowering the demand for money. A rise in income will increase the demand for money. The other three equations yield the IS curve, which shows how income and interest rates adjust to make savings equal to investments. By making unsold inventories depend on the future, the model accommodates short-period expectations. In the short term, such as a day, expectations do not change, so the condition for saving to equal investment in the model is achieved. The IS-LM curves can take on special shapes that would prevent automatic adjustments from occurring. Hicks later thought that the IS curve represents a flow concept, and the LM curve, a stock concept. In his *Capital and Growth,* he proceeded to show that a stock equilibrium over a period would require a flow equilibrium over that period.

Hicks argued against the cardinal view, where utility is added, and for the ordinal view of value, where consumers rank their tastes and preferences. Alfred Marshall and the founders of the marginal revolution examined value with a given utility function. They required a utility surface for consumer maximization. Hicks' value theory examined "what adjustments in the statement of the marginal theory of value are made necessary by Pareto's discovery" (Hicks, 1981: 7). Vilfredo Pareto postulated a scale of preferences concept, which represented value only by indifference curves. Hicks transformed the cardinal concept of total utility to the marginal rate of substitution between two commodities on an indifference curve. Similarly, he transformed the idea of diminishing marginal utility to diminishing marginal rate of substitution measured by the convex shape of the indifference curve. Following Hicks' work, comparative static analysis that allows prediction from demand analysis can be performed. One of his predictions states that if demand shifts from good 1 to good 2, then the relative price of 2 in terms of 1 would increase, except if 2 is a free good.

On the technology side, Hicks classified inventions as neutral, labor-saving, or capital-saving. When inventions change the marginal productivity of labor and capital in the same proportion, the invention is called neutral. Hicks predicted that if wages increased, labor's share of output would rise, and that would encourage inventions to replace labor, making them labor-saving. In an analogous manner, the same can be argued for capital-saving inventions. In general, when changes in relative prices of factors occur, they induce inventions; otherwise inventions are autonomous. Autonomous inventions are likely to be randomly distributed, while induced inventions are likely to be labor-saving.

References

Darity, W., & Young, W. (1995). IS-LM: An inquest. *History of Political Economy*, 27(1), 1-41.

Hansen, A. H. (1953). *A guide to Keynes*. New York: McGraw-Hill.

Hicks, John R., and R.G.D. Allen,."A Reconsideration of the Theory of Value," *Economica*. 1934.

Hicks, J. (1937). Mr. Keynes and the classics: A suggested simplification. *Econometrica*, 5(2), 147-159.

———. (1956). *A revision of demand theory*. Oxford: Clarendon.

———. (1965). *Capital and growth*. Oxford: Clarendon.

———. (1980). IS-LM: An Explanation. *Journal of Post Keynesian Economics*, 3(2), 139-154.

———. (1981). *Collected essays in economic theory, Vol. I: Wealth and welfare.* Oxford: Basil Blackwell.

———. (1982). *Collected essays in economic theory, Vol. II: Money, interest and wages.* Oxford: Basil Blackwell.

———. (1983). *Collected essays in economic theory, Vol III: Classics and moderns.* Oxford: Basil Blackwell.

Hicks, J. R., & Allen, R. G. D. (1934). A reconsideration of the theory of value. *Economica*, 1(2), 196-219.

Maurice Allais

Introduction

Maurice Félix Charles Allais was a French economist, engineer, historian, and physicist. According to Paul Samuelson, "he was a fountain of original and independent discoveries" and a "part of a Paris renaissance in economic theory. Had Allais' earliest writings been in English, a generation of economic theory would have taken a different course" (Samuelson, 1986: vol. 5, 83-85). Indeed, a large portion of his work is still not available in English. Nevertheless, Allais' translated literature is more than enough to paint a portrait of his genius.

In this memoriam, we focus on the work for which he won the Nobel Memorial Prize in economics in 1988, "for his pioneering contributions to the theory of markets and efficient utilization of resources." Allais interprets this contribution in a way that is synonymous with the popular definition of the economic problem: "I should like to interpret this motivation in its broadest sense, that is to say, as relating to all those conditions which may ensure that the economy satisfies with maximum efficiency the needs of men given the limited resources they have at their disposal" (Allais, 1997: 3). He identified his fundamental contribution to economics in five areas: "the theory of economic evolution and general equilibrium, of maximum efficiency, and of the foundations of 'economic calculus'; the theory of intertemporal processes and maximum capitalistic efficiency; the theory of choices under uncertainty and the criteria to be considered for rational economic decisions; the theory of money, credit, and monetary dynamics; and probability theory, as well as the analysis of time series and their exogenous components" (ibid.: 4).

Allais came to economics with a strong background in physics and history. For experiments in physics he received the Galabert Prize from the French Astronautical Society, and a laureate prize from the Gravity Research Foundation of the US, both in 1959. In the area of history, he authored a book entitled *Rise and Fall of Civilizations—Economic Factors,* which he continued to revise and develop over a period of 40 years. From 1933 to 1987, he received fourteen scientific prizes, the most distinguished being the Gold Medal from the National Center for Scientific Research in 1978 (Allais, 1992: 20-21).

Methodology

Allais had a broad methodological approach to economics. "Analysis of societies obviously requires a synthesis of all the social sciences: political economics, law, sociology, history, geography, and political science," he wrote (ibid.: 31). In his economic writings, he took inspiration from the philosophy of Alexis de Tocqueville, Walras, Irving Fisher, Pareto, and Keynes. He pursued theory with facts, maintaining that his goals were "first, to constantly found [theories] on in-depth theoretical investigations; second, to always provide accompanying quantitative estimates" (ibid.: 29).

One manifestation of Allais' methodological approach can be illustrated by his well-known paradox. Peter Fishburn (1991: 28) classified its place in decision theory as "experiments that refute expected utility's ability to describe actual behavior" and as "non-linear alternatives to expected utility." Allais (1990: 8) claimed that it was not a mere counter-example, but that it was based on a general theory of random choice. Generally, examples show either that something makes sense or that something does not make sense (Gelbaum and Olmsted, 1964: v). Allais believed that a fundamental theory about the psychology of risk is missing in the expected utility hypothesis. It was a reaction also to an axiomatic theory—something that is accepted without proof and allows us to make logical (deductive) conclusions. Allais stated that "mathematics is merely a tool for transforming statements. Real importance attaches only to the discussion of the premises adopted and the result obtained" (Allais, 1979: 37).

In his counter-example, Allais did not treat the axiomatic method as a dead science (Samuelson, 1972: vol. 3, 316). He organized his early works into five axioms—probability, ordered field of choice, absolute preference, composition, and an index of psychological values (ibid.: 457, 460). After revisiting his early studies, he added two more axioms—homogeneity and invariance of the index of psychological value, and cardinal isovariations (Allais, 1979: 480-481). He also incorporated an axiom of Ole Hagen to the effect that "a constant increase in the utility of every outcome increases the utility of the entire prospect by the same amount" (Fishburn, 1987: 835).

In terms of mathematical tools, Allais indicated a partiality for the calculus over set theoretic approaches in economics. In developing his market economy concept, he wrote, "*from an economic point of view, reasoning based on marginal equivalences and surpluses is very fruitful; it provides a better understanding of the underlying nature of economic phenomena than the demonstration, under very restrictive conditions, of the existence of a price vector sufficient for the equilibrium of a market economy*" (Allais, 1978: 150 [italics original]). Overall, his view of mathematics in economics is that "formal rigor is of little value if it is accompanied by a serious distortion of the true nature of reality, and it is better to have an approximative theory that corresponds to actual reality than a formally rigorous theory that can only be built by seriously distorting the facts" (ibid.: 149). Furthermore, "every theory is necessarily approximative, and the approximative nature of a theory is not a defect in itself. The only imperative that can justifiably be demanded of a theory is that it should not distort reality sufficiently to modify its nature" (ibid.: 148).

In his discussions on market economy, Allais changed the DNA, so to speak, of general equilibrium. Just as scientists found that argon can replace carbon at the core of DNA structure, Allais found that the pressure of free competition on human beings can replace price taking. Only in a stable state are input prices uniquely defined, because efficiency results from the pressure that free competition puts on human beings rather than on the price system (Munier, 1995: 20-21).

Major Works

Allais' first major book, *In Quest of an Economic Discipline* (1943), enunciated an equivalence theorem about any state of equilibrium and any state of maximum efficiency. He defined four new concepts relating to "the surface of maximum possibilities in the hyperspace of preference indices of the consumption units; the concept of distributable surplus corresponding to a feasible modification of the economy from a given situation; the concept of loss, defined as the maximum distributable surplus for all feasible modifications of the economy which leave the preference indices unchanged; and the related concept of surfaces of equal loss in the hyperspace of preference indices" (Allais, 1997: 4).

In his second major book, *Economy and Interest* (1947), we find precursors to many well-known models in modern economics. His intergenerational model was an extension of his notion of maximum efficiency. He touched on the theory of productivity of capital, which foreshadowed the modern contribution of the golden rule of optimal growth theory. We also find discussions on the transaction demand for money, behavioral economics, and his famous Allais paradox. What follows is a sample of some of his major theories.

The Allais Paradox

This paradox relates to utility, preference, and probability. Allais was reacting to the axiomatic expected utility hypothesis that started with the Swiss mathematician and physicist Daniel Bernoulli (1700-1782). If one is offered an equal [50:50] chance of getting 0 or 20,000 ducats, the mathematical expectation theory yields a value of: 0.5(0) + 0.5(20,000) = 10,000 ducats. In general, if x_i is the amount, and p_i is the probability, the expected value is the average outcome, $E(x_i) = \overline{x}$, and so, $E(x_i - \overline{x}) = 0$ is considered a fair price for the lottery. Let P be the person's expectation of profits. We can then compare P with $\overline{x}$. If $E(x_i - P) > 0$, the lottery will be favorable, and if $E(x_i - P) < 0$, then the lottery will be unfavorable (Jensen, 1967: 164).

Bernoulli (1954: 24) pointed out that "all men cannot use the same rule to evaluate the gamble . . . the determination of the value of an item must not be based on its price, but rather on the utility it yields. The price of the item is dependent only on the thing itself and is equal for everyone; the utility, however, is dependent on the particular circumstances of the person making the estimate. Thus there is no doubt that a gain of one thousand ducats is more significant to a pauper than to a rich man though both gain the same amount."

Essential to the Bernoulli doctrine is the distinction between a physical fortune, x, and a moral fortune or utility, y. A change in utility dy is not only proportional to changes in physical fortune, dx but inversely proportional to x as well. We can therefore write $dy = k(dx/x)$, where k is the proportional constant. Integrating that equation yields:$y = klog(x) + C$ The constant of integration depends on a person's initial wealth defined as $\alpha = x_0$, which is estimated as $C = -klog(\alpha)$ by setting $y = 0$ According to Marshall (1982: 693), Bernoulli thought of α as the "income which affords the barest necessaries of life." Utility is therefore represented by a log arithmetic function: $y = k\ log(x) - k\ log(\alpha) = k\ log(x/\alpha)$ (Keynes, 1973: 350). This equation describes a curve that shows diminishing marginal utility of money and that people do not have linear utility (Samuelson, 1986: vol. 5, 135). As the marginal utility of money declines, "it follows that the mathematical expectation of utility (rather than of money) in the game was finite, so that the individual Daniel Bernoulli put his expected utility hypothesis to the task of explaining the St. Petersburg paradox, proposed by his cousin, Nicholas Bernoulli. The paradox is: "Peter tosses a coin and continues to do so until it should land 'heads' when it comes to the ground. He agrees to give Paul one ducat if he gets 'heads' on the very first throw, two ducats if he gets it on the second, four if on the third, eight if on the fourth, and so on, so that with each additional throw the number of ducats he must pay is doubled" (Bernoulli, 1954: 31). The payoff for the nth toss is 2^n. The mathematical expectation is $\sum_{n=1}^{\infty}(2^n)(1/2^n)$, which represents an infinite amount of money. To help illuminate this solution, we use the equivalent relation proposed by Allais, namely, cardinal utility function, $V \sim a + [log\,C / log\,2]$, where V is the psychological monetary value of the prospect, a is a proportional constant, and C is the player's capital (Allais, 1990: 3). We recall that ½ and etc 2/4. belong to the same equivalent class of rational numbers. We test their equivalence by setting them as equal and cross multiplying. Similarly, we can have u, v, w etc. as equivalent classes in U. An equivalent, say v in U, is defined by a set of events The events x_1, x_2 belong to an equivalent class if the agent is indifferent between them, i.e. $x_1\ I\ x_2$ (Malinvaud, 1952: 679). With the Allais formulation, $V \sim \$18$ when $a = 0.942$, and $C = \$100{,}000$, indicating that a player is not willing to pay much for the coin toss prospect (Allais, 1990: 3).

The Bernoulli model is concerned with risks, using objective probability such as the tossing of a coin to find the value of an outcome. His model can be looked at as an objective expected hypothesis (OEH) that preserves the mathematical expectation by introducing a non-linear utility function which was extended by von Neumann and Morgenstern (1944). Thomas Bayes (1763) seems to have reversed the process, defining probability in terms of mathematical expectation, which is described as the inverse probability problem (Keynes, 1973: 192, 413-414). It is similar to F. P. Ramsey's development of the subjective expected utility (SEU) model, which was later expanded by Leonard Savage (von Neumann, 1990: 191). Ramsey started with measuring a person's degree of belief by proposing "a bet, and [seeing what were] the lowest odds which he [would] accept" (Ramsey, 1960: 172). The difference is that the OEH was probability based and therefore espoused risk analysis, whereas the SEU model was concerned with uncertainty as well as risk (Machina, 2005: 2-3; von Neumann, 1990: 190).

The axiomatic literature on utility theory is vast. We need to specify some objectives to navigate our way through it. First, we need to show that the logarithmic function is not necessarily bounded as Bernoulli thought. Second, we need to develop the theory to a level that is clearly axiomatic. Third, we need to distinguish between a risk measure of a random toss of a fair coin, and uncertainty, such as a state of nature where the coin is bent, for instance. Fourth, we need to show the axiomatic formulation in a form that is illustrative of the Allais paradox. Then some implication and discussion of Allais' positions would be necessary. The rest of this section discusses those objectives in turn.

Objective 1: Bounded vs. Unbounded Utility Function

Carl Menger argued that the addition to wealth formula, *dy*, described above "implies that the subjective expectation in the Petersburg Game is finite, but by changing the game slightly, one can stipulate a similar game for which not only the mathematical but also the subject expectation based on the logarithmic value function is infinite and yet no one in his right mind would risk a substantial amount" (Menger, 1967: 217). For example, Jensen (1967: 168) has shown that if the reward to the coin toss was 2^{2^n} instead of just 2^n, then the payoff would be $Ln2(1 + 1 + \ldots)$, an infinite sum. Menger's position is stated in a general theorem:

Carl Menger (Unbounded Utility Theorem):

For any evaluation of additions to a fortune by an unbounded function, there exists a game related to the Petersburg Game in which subjective expectation of the risk-taker on the basis of that value function is infinity. (Menger, 1967: 218 [italics original]).

Following Menger's insight, one hope is to obtain a bound for the utility function. Intuitively, Menger followed the suggestion that money wealth, W can be thought of as bounded if its value does not increase beyond a certain amount. For instance, "the subjective value $f(W)$ of an amount of money W is equal to if W is smaller than $10 million and is equal to $10 million whenever Wexceeds that amount" (ibid.: 219). The aim here is to obtain a bounded function $f(W) < M < \infty$, such that $\lim_{W \to \infty} f(W) = M$, otherwise we will open a Mengerian Super Petersburg Paradox (Samuelson, 1986: vol. 5, 135, 141). If the utility function is not bounded, then problems arise with the axioms, such as transitivity and continuity, which are necessary for the axiomatic formulation of the utility function. For instance, two prospects might both have $E[f(w)] = \infty$ while being non-indifferent, undermining the transitive argument (ibid.: 145).

David Blackwell and Meyer Abraham Girshick (1954) have extended the *NM* utility function to consider conditions that bound the utility function from above and below. Consider two lotteries, $p_1 \dots, p_u, \dots; q_1 \dots, q_u, \dots$ with probabilities $\alpha_1, \dots, \alpha_u, \dots$. If $I.\ \alpha_1 q_1 + \alpha_2 q_2 + \dots$, and $II.\ \alpha_1 p_1 + \alpha_2 p_2 + \dots$, then for all u's $q_u \geq p_u$ implies $II \geq I$. Also if for some u, $q_u > p_u$ and $\alpha_u > 0$ then $II > I$. Blackwell and Girschik (1954: ch. 4) built a utility function in this way that is order-preserving, linear in the probabilities, and bounded (ibid.: 109-110).

Objectives 2 and 3: Axiomatic Works on the Bernoullian Utility Model in terms of Risk and Uncertainty

The works of Ramsey (1960), von Neumann and Morgenstern (1944) (NM), and Savage (1954) continue the axiomatization of the Bernoulli expected utility hypothesis, while alternating between their consideration of risk and uncertainty. Ramsey, whose model includes uncertainty, added to our degree of belief, proper guide to conduct, and the finite number of alternatives to random gains (Ramsey, 1960: 183). He expounded the first axiomatic bases of the expected utility hypothesis based on moral propositions where full belief is represented by a probability of 1, the opposite probability being 0, and equal belief in the two is represented by the probability of 0.5 (ibid.: 175). Ramsey's model, as summarized by Fishburn (1989: 388), considers events, E, denoted by A and B; outcomes of events denoted by x, y, z, w; utility denoted by u; and probabilities denoted by π. The Ramsey axioms model is as follows:

> RM1: $\{x \text{ if } A, y \text{ if not } A\}$ is preferred to $\{z \text{ if } B, w \text{ if not } B\}$ implies and is implied by
>
> RM2: $\pi(A)u(x) + [1 - \pi(A)]u(y) > \pi(B)u(z) + [1 - \pi(B)]u(w)$.

The interpretation of his model has four steps. "First identify an 'ethically neutral' event E with $\pi(E) = 1/2$. Second, use E to assess u on outcomes, largely by indifference comparisons between acts of the form $\{x \text{ if } E, y \text{ if not } E\}$. Third, use u to measure $\pi(A)$, the person's degree of belief that A obtains, as follows: if x is preferred to y, and y to z, and if y is indifferent to $\{x \text{ if } A, z \text{ if not } A\}$, then $\pi(A) = [u(y) - u(z)]/[u(x) - u(z)]$. The final step extends the third to assess conditional probabilities" (ibid.: 388).

Von Neumann and Morgenstern (NM) were concerned with the measurability of utility only in the second edition of their book in 1947. They approached economics through the lenses of rational behavior, particularly from the belief that a numerical approach to utility will supersede the ordinal approach to utility. They "proved that the Bernoulli principle can be derived as a theorem from a few simple assumptions" (Borch, 1967: 197). They characterized their contribution this way: "We have assumed only one thing . . . that imagined events can be combined with probabilities" (NM, 1953: 20). They call the event imagined because they locate it in the future, mainly because they did not want to complicate their analysis by dealing with the past, present, and future. The probability number that combines the events is a real number between 0 and 1. Events or entities, objects or abstract utilities, when combined with probabilities are also events or entities, objects or abstract utilities.

For the measurability of utility, von Neumann and Morgenstern wanted "a correspondence between utilities and numbers" (ibid.: 24). In other words, the goal is that a preference relation between two events, and a probability operation on two events should correspond to a number. To achieve that goal, some properties of the relationship and operation must be postulated. These postulates are of three types—complete ordering, ordering and combining, and the algebra of combining, which is a purely mathematical task (ibid.: 26).

The hypothesis of completeness is necessary because if "the preferences of the individual are not all comparable, the indifference curves do not exist" (ibid.: 19-20). An individual should be able to rank his preference in a trichotomous way using the signs <, >, and =, and also be consistent in his ranking by following the transitive rule. Such ordering allows a combination of the form that if an event is preferable to another, then even a chance of the event is preferred to the other. Combination of this sort implies that the indifference curve would be linear and parallel (MasColell, 1995: 178). The algebra of combining appeals to continuity: "However desirable [an event] may be in itself, one can make its influence as weak as desired by giving it a sufficiently small chance. This is a plausible 'continuity' assumption" (NM, 1953: 27). The algebra does not require an order in which events are combined, and allowed for combinations to occur in steps as well. The three types of postulates allowed NM to form the following two major axioms:

NM1: $x \succsim y \Leftrightarrow u(x) \geq u(y)$.

NM2: $u[(1-\pi)x + \pi y] = (1-\pi)u(x) + \pi u(y)$.

The convention followed in the interpretation of these axioms is that the right-hand side of the equations corresponds to utilities, and the left-hand side to numbers, because "utilities are numerically measurable quantities" (ibid.: 16). NM1 says that if event x is preferred to event y, then the utility which is a number for x is at least greater than the utility for y. NM2 says that one can distribute the utility over a mixture of the events.

How do the NM axioms work? NM1 and NM2 determine the utility of x and y. To find the utility of another event, z, we will consider $u(1-\pi)u(x) + \pi u(y)$ as a standard lottery. We would then have to determine the probability, either through an interview or behavioral observations, which would make us indifferent between the standard lottery and the new event, z, namely: $u(z) = (1-\pi)u(x) + \pi u(y)$ (Baumol, 1965: 518; Dixon, 1980: 207-212). In other words, given our preference for a glass of tea to a cup of coffee, if we introduce a third object, such as a glass of milk, a person must now decide whether "he prefers a cup of coffee to a glass, the content of which will be determined by a 50%-50% chance device as tea or milk" (NM, 1953. 18).

The two NM axioms are equivalent to a complete and transitive preference relationship that satisfies the Archimedean and the independence axioms

(Kani and Schmeidler, 1991: 1770). Samuelson was the first to show that the NM axioms satisfy the independence axiom. The independence axiom holds that "whether heads or tails come up, the A lottery ticket is better than the B lottery ticket; hence, it is reasonable to say that the compound (A) ticket is definitely better than the compound (B) . . . This is simply a version of what Dr. Savage calls the 'sure-thing principle'" (Samuelson, 1966: vol. 1, 139). Savage uses this principle to establish probabilities and utility functions (Kani and Schmeidler, 1991: 1767). The Archimedean property is a standard mathematical concept which states that if x is preferred to y, then a multiple of x is preferred to y, namely $nx > y$. We demonstrate how the Archimedean and independence axioms strengthened the axiomatic method of expected utility following I. N. Herstein and John Milnor's work (1953).

Because of the lengthiness of their presentation, practitioners choose simpler systems such as the Herstein-Milnor axioms discussed below to demonstrate NM axioms. Herstein and Milnor (HM) axioms are necessary for the existence for the von Neumann and Morgenstern (1944) utility on a mixture space S. Mixture refers to probability weighting, order means preference, and mixture space is a set of prospects. As an example, they gave us $a, b \in S$; $\lambda, \mu \in [0,1]$. We can mix a, b to get $\mu a + (1 - u)b \in S$. This operation is possible because of three mixture axioms (Herstein and Milnor, 1953: 265):

$$\text{I. } 1a + (1-1)b = a, \Leftrightarrow (1-0)a + 0b = a,$$

$$\text{II. } \mu a + (1-\mu)b = (1-\mu)b + \mu a,$$

$$\text{III. } \lambda[\mu a + (1-\mu)b] + (1-\lambda)b = (\lambda u)a + (1-\lambda u)b.$$

With these mixtures, we can show that $\lambda a + (1-\lambda)a = a$. This is proven by putting $a = b$; $\mu = 0$ in III to get: $\lambda[0a + (1-0)a] + (1-\lambda)a$. By I, the square bracket items $= a$, and by II we can switch terms around, yielding: $\lambda a + (1-\lambda)a = a$. More complicated examples can be done, but it is more interesting to point out that the HM axioms are "at least necessary conditions" for the existence of an NM utility (ibid.: 266). Their assumptions are featured as follows:

HM1: (Completeness). The space of lotteries, S, is completely ordered by the preference relation $\succsim$. For lotteries a, b, complete ordering means that 1. either $a \succsim b$, or $b \succsim a$; 2. the reflective property is $a \succsim a$; and 3. For lotteries a, b, c, the transitive property: $a \succsim b$, and $b \succsim c$ implies $a \succsim c$.

HM2: (Continuity). For some elements in S, a, b, $c \in S$, there exists a probability $\alpha \in [0.1]$, such that a mixture of a, b will be preferred to c and vice versa. This is expressed as $(A).\{\alpha | \alpha a + (1-\alpha)b \succsim c\}$ and $(B).\{\alpha | c \succsim \alpha a + (1-\alpha)b\}$.

Using NM1 and NM2 we can apply the utility concept to get $(A').\{\alpha \mid \alpha u(a) + (1-\alpha)u(b) \geq u(c)\}$ and $(B').\{\alpha \mid u(c) \geq \alpha u(a) + (1-\alpha)u(b)\}$, respectively. These are closed sets as the probability α lies in the $[0, 1]$ closed interval. From (A'), we can find $\alpha \geq [u(c) - u(b)]/[u(a) - u(b)]$ for $u(a) > u(b)$, and $\alpha \leq [u(c) - u(b)]/[u(a) - u(b)]$ for $u(a) < u(b)$. If we set $u(a) = u(b)$ we get zero or the whole interval.

The idea of continuity implies that we can perturb the probability α without changing the ranking of the lotteries. Herstein and Milnor (1953: 267) preserved continuity by the limiting concept: $\lim \alpha_{i \to \infty} = \alpha$. If we are given two sequences of points such as p_n, q_n, then for all n we can state that $p_n \succsim q_n \Leftrightarrow \lim p_n \succsim \lim q_n$ (Mas-Colell et al., 1995: 46). Continuity helps us avoid such phenomena as infinitely favorable or unfavorable outcomes of a lottery. We want to purge such outcomes because they would create a lexicographical ordering which would make the indifference curve non-existent (ibid.: 171).

HM3: Given a, $a' \in S$, $a \sim a'$, then for every $b \in S, \frac{1}{2}a + \frac{1}{2}b \sim \frac{1}{2}a' + \frac{1}{2}b$.

If one is indifferent between a and a', then one is indifferent between a 50:50 chance of getting a or b, and a 50:50 chance of getting a' or b. This is the Herstein-Milnor way of simplifying the independence axiom (Fishburn, 1983: 303).

Originally, the NM axioms did not explicitly show the independent axiom. They used abstract operations or an abstract utility concept (Karni and Schmeidler, 1770). HM generalized the outcome to a mixture set using a weaker independence axiom (HM3) and a stronger mixed continuity axiom than what traditionally is called an Archimedean axiom. It is a traditional student exercise to show that the HM axioms are necessary for the NM utility. HM1 follows from the well-ordering of the real line, HM2 follows from NM1 and NM2. HM3 follows from $a \sim a' \Leftrightarrow u(a) = u(a')$. This is a mathematical venture, but the steps in the march toward a NM utility function are worth noting. The completeness axiom gives the best and worst outcomes. The continuous axiom allows us to get an indifference curve.

It tells us that there exists a probability $\alpha \in [0.1]$ such that for the lottery c, we can write $u(c) = \alpha$, which is a construction of the utility function (Jehle, 1991: 198; Laffront, 1989: 11). We will describe this function to a greater extent later. For now, it is worth noting also that the utility function is better described as a "kind of function, with certain specific mathematical property," rather than a function that represents preference in the ordinal senses. It is a mapping from the gamble to the real line possessing the expected utility property (Jehle, 1991: 197).

Objective 4: Allais' Reaction to the Axiomatic Model

Using the standard NM example, $u(z) = (1 - \pi)u(x) + \pi u(y)$, we can show indifference with an example such as $u(\$40) = 1/2u(\$100) + 1/2u(0)$, indicating "indifference between a \$40 gain with certainty and an even-chance gamble between a gain of \$100 and no gain. The same algebraic expression, rewritten as $u(\$40) - u(\$0) = u(\$100) - u(\$40)$, has the Bernoullian interpretation that, apart from any consideration of chance, the individual's degrees of preference for \$40 over \$0 and for \$100 over \$40 are equal" (Fishburn, 1989: 390).

Table I below illustrates the Allais paradox. Since $U(A) = U(100)$, $U(B) = .89U(100) + .1U(500) + .01U(0)$, $U(C) = .89U(0) + .11U(100)$, and $U(D) = .9U(0) + .1U(500)$, then $U(A) - U(B) = U(C) - U(D)$ by simple arithmetic.

If one prefers A to B, then $U(A) > U(B)$. Doing the arithmetic, we get: $U(100) > 0.89U(100) + 0.1U(500) + 0.01U(0)$ or $U(100) - 0.89U(100) > 0.1U(500) + 0.01U(0)$ or $0.11U(100) > 0.1U(500) + 0.01U(0)$.

TABLE 1: The Allais Paradox (in Millions of Dollars)

First Pairs of Offers				Second Pairs of Offers			
Situation A		Situation B		Situation C		Situation D	
Win	Prob.	Win	Prob.	Win	Prob.	Win	Prob.
\$100	1	\$100	0.89	Nothing	0.89	Nothing	0.9
		\$500	0.1	\$100	0.11	\$500	0.1
		Nothing	0.01				

Source: Allais, 1990: 5.

Similarly if one prefers D to C as Allais found, then $U(D) > U(C)$. Doing the math yields: $0.9U(0) + 0.1U(500) > 0.89U(0) + 0.11U(100)$ or $0.9U(0) - 0.89U(0) + 0.1U(500) > 0.11U(100)$ or $0.11U(100) < 0.01U(0) + 0.1U(500)$, where the < sign contradicts the above > sign (Machina, 2003: 24; Munier, 1995a: 192; Resnik, 1987: 104). Allais (1990, 5), therefore, found through experimentation that the preference of A to B is matched with the preference of D to C, which contradicts the NM axioms.

An attempt to cope with the Allais paradox was provided by Savage, who participated in Allais' experiment and agreed at first with his conclusion. After further reflection, particularly on the logic of the independence axiom or the sure-thing principle, he saw a flaw in his original decision and opted to make a correction to his original choice. Such a reflection is obtained from an experiment that asks us to draw tickets labeled 1 to 100 at random. This is given as the heading in Table 2 below.

The first column of Table 2 corresponds with the four situations given by Allais in Table I. Situation A in the first row in Table 2 indicated a guaranteed $100M payoff irrespective of any drawing of a ticket. Situations B, C, and D are gambles. To interpret Situation B in Table 2, we note that the probability of $0 is given as 0.01 in Table 1 for Situation B, which means 1 ticket in 100; therefore, we place the $0 under Ticket 1. Similarly we place $500 under Tickets 2-11 for Situation B, because Table 1 shows its probability is 0.1, which is 10 of 100. The same logic makes us place $100 for Situation B under Tickets 12-100, for its probability in Table 1 is 0.89, or 89 of 100. The rest of Table 2 is filled in the same manner.

Savage reflected that payoffs of Tickets 12-100 would not have any influence in choosing A over B or C over D and can therefore be omitted in the

TABLE 2: The Allais Data in Savage Format (in Millions of Dollars)

	Ticket: 1 Allais (p=0.01)	Tickets: 2-11 Allais (p=0.10)	Tickets: 12-100 Allais (p=0.89)
Situation A	$100	$100	$100
Situation B	$0+F1	$500	$100
Situation C	$100	$100	$0
Situation D	$0+F2	$500	$0

Source: Adapted from Savage, 1972: 103.

decision making. This observation is referred to as the "common effect." Now, the matrix of payoff in section A is the same as the matrix of payoff in section B for Tickets 1-11. Upon reflection, Savage now is willing to state that the original choice he made, which was inconsistent with the NM axioms, was an error. The preference of 3 to 4 can be reversed only if one makes an error in choice. Such errors are normative and can be corrected should it be pointed out to the person.

Allais rejoined the debate by pointing out that Savage's experiment had destroyed the certainty part of his own experiment. We get the inputs for Row A in Table 2 by breaking up a certainty of winning \$100M into three probabilities: 0.01 + 0.11 + 0.89 = 1 (Sugden, 2004: 696). This procedure had eliminated the "complementarity effect operating in the neighborhood of certainty" (Allais, 1979: 535). In other words, the certainty of \$100M cannot be so factored. This is the general argument Allais made against the independence axiom, where a third prospect is put in complementary relations with two others. When two events are mixed under the independence axiom, they are considered mutually exclusive, that is, complementarity is not allowed. Another way of looking at it is to observe that one can have only one of the two events, one with a probability of α, and the other with a probability of $(1 - \alpha)$, but the two events do not occur together (ibid.: 141). Students who learn choices of bundles in consumer theory can appreciate that two commodities in a bundle can be jointly consumed, which contrasts with two outcomes in choice under risk where the outcomes are mutually exclusive.

Allais claims that the independence axiom will fall apart if we can "*find case in which the complementarity relations . . . may change the order of preference*" (Allais, 1979: 90 [italics original]). Fishburn (1988: 85-86) feels that it is in the nature of empirical analysis that such findings may occur. "The empirical fact is that the nature of r and the size of λ can make a difference in the preference between $\lambda p + (1 - \lambda)r$ and $\lambda q + (1 - \lambda)r$, and it is hard to ignore this in assessing the normative adequacy of independence. . . . The point is that there are certain patterns of preferences, held by reasonable people for good reasons, that simply do not agree with the axioms of expected utility theory."

To clinch the complementarity argument, we adapt Fishburn's tabular illustration (1979: 248-249). If one chooses the first row, a chance device will determine that his payoff will be $\lambda p(x)$ or $(1 - \lambda)r(x)$. Traditionally, we can argue that if the payoffs of the first row dominate the payoffs of the second row, *p* will be chosen over *q*, and *r* will be chosen over *S*. But "Allais' criticism lies in the assertion that . . . an individual's preference judgment . . . is properly based on a comparison of these two gambles in their full perspectives and not on a comparison of separate parts such as *p* versus *q* and *r* versus *S*" (ibid.).

The techniques we use to reason out our choices "involve a combination of the three basic techniques, namely, rule-based decision, probabilistic inference, and analogies" (Gilboa and Schmeidler, 2001: 2). John Conlisk (1989) was concerned with three tests that lay bare the independence axiom. Kenneth R. MacCrimmon and Stig Larsson (1979: 349-351) listed 23 rules. Rule 6, for instance, states that when one alternative is certain, you should select it even if you are giving up a chance of winning a bigger amount with a lower probability. Rule 6 can be seen as a composite of two other rules—Rule 10, which takes the prospect with the higher probability when two prospects have payoffs that are desirable, and Rule 2, which takes the prospect with the larger payoff when their probabilities are similar.

In responding to the Allais paradox, Morgenstern (1979: 178) pointed out that the domain of axioms should be restricted, meaning that the probabilities used should not "go to 0.01 or even less than 0.001 . . . a normal individual would have some intuition of what 50:50 or 25:75 means." On the theoretical side, "if our preferences are only partially ordered—which means, grossly speaking, that they are in considerable disarray—then there is no presently known guiding principle for optimal allocation" (ibid.: 182).

Experiments revealed other causes of violation of the expected utility hypothesis beside the common effect cited above. According to Michael Weber (1978: 100) even when one disregards the effect of the last column in

TABLE 3: Combination of Gambles via Chance Device

	Gambles	Chance Device	
		λ	$1-\lambda$
You Chose:	$\lambda p+(1-\lambda)r$	p	r
	$\lambda p+(1-\lambda)r$	q	s

Source: Adapted from Fishburn, 1979: 248.

Table 2, one is likely to experience more negativity in choosing B over A and losing, than in choosing D over C and losing. In Table 2, $F1 < F2 < 0$, analogous to $-12 < -5 < 0$, indicates such negativity. The reason for the terrible feeling of $F1$ is that A is certain, and to lose something one has for certain would create more negativity than losing something one is not sure about. As explained by Daniel Kahneman and Amos Tversky, "people underweigh outcomes that are merely probable in comparison with outcomes that are obtained with certainty. This tendency, called the certainty effect, contributes to risk aversion in choices involving sure gains and to risk seeking in choices involving sure losses. In addition, people generally discard components that are shared by all prospects under consideration. This tendency, called the isolation effect, leads to inconsistent preferences when the same choice is presented in different forms" (Kahneman and Tversky, 1979: 263). Only when such feelings are taken into account would the paradox be in line with the prediction of the expected utility theory. The problem becomes more complicated when disappointment and regrets are considered, making the Allais paradox resilient (Weber, 1998).

Analysts frequently use the simplex method to demonstrate violations of the expected utility hypothesis. Here we illustrate the common effects and the fanning-out process. It involves the construction of two types of indifference curves, one for the expected utility hypothesis and one for the mathematical expectation hypothesis, and to show that the latter is steeper than the former. This concept is best explained by a rectangular isosceles triangle, first presented by Jacob Marschak (1950) and popularized by Mark Machina (1990).

Figure 1 is a simplex representing the Allais payoffs and probabilities on the three axes. The rectangular box at the origin shows the coordinate of points such as (p_1, p_2, p_3). Points such as A and B can be similarly coordinated by other boxes. The prizes are $x_3 = \$500M$ representing the best outcome, $x_2 = \$100M$ the second best outcome, and $x_1 = \$0M$ \$0 the worst. These outcomes form a set $W = x_3 \succ x_2 \succ x_1$. The probability set is $D = [0, M]$, which is represented in this case as a set with three probability elements, $D = \{p_1, p_2, p_3\}$, that sums to 1. We write A as preferred to or indifferent to B as $A \succsim B$. By the NM axioms, the ordering yields a utility function $A \succsim B \Leftrightarrow U(A) \geq U(B)$. Although we show the payoff amount on the axes, it is common practice to scale the axes to unity for analysis (Mas-Collel et al., 1995: 169).

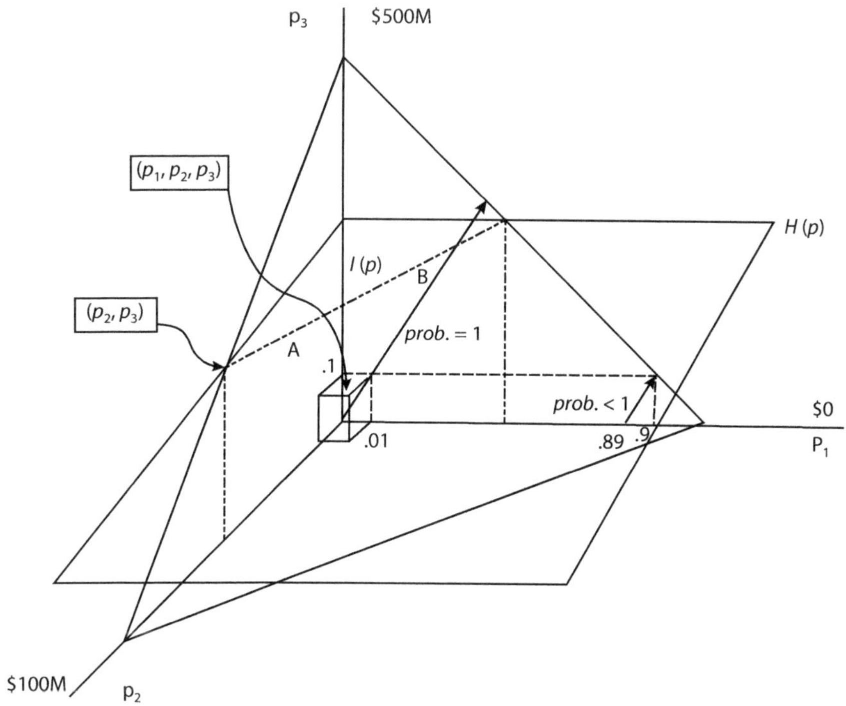

Figure 1 Simplex view of the Allais Paradox.

The next step is to obtain indifference curves by cutting the simplex with a hyperplane, $H(p)$ (Conlon, 1995: 637). These cuts yield triangle figures such as $I(p)$, which are the indifference curves for this simplex configuration. The indifference curve will increase upward, as the best outcome is measured upward, which is analogous to the three dimensional representation of consumer choice over bundles of commodities in standard microeconomics. Abusing the geometry of simplex somewhat, we can think to the linear indifference curves in a two dimensional surface by collapsing the intermediate payoff between the best and worse payoff. Linear indifference curves and the Iso-value curves, respectively, can be drawn for a constant level of satisfaction, as in K and L: $p_1U(x_1) + p_2U(x_2) + p_3U(x_3) = K$; $p_1(x_1) + p_2(x_2) + p_3(x_3) = L$. Taking the derivative of the indifference and Iso-value curves allows us to find their slopes. Whenever the slope of the Iso-value curves exceeds the slope of the indifferent curve, fanning-out is present.

Fanning-out occurs as the probability in the D-distribution of probabilities changes. "Intuitively, if the distribution . . . involves very high outcomes, I may prefer not to bear further risk in the unlucky event that I don't receive it. . . . But if (the distribution) . . . involves very low outcomes, I may be more willing to bear risk in the event that I don't receive it" (Machina, 1987: 129–130). Fanning-out is more pronounced at the outer edges of the collapsed triangle, and can exhibit linear as well as nonlinear utility curves. The curvature is captured by the Arrow-Pratt ratio that shows changes in the slope of the curve measured by the ratio of their second partial to first partial derivative. The "nonlinearity in a preference functional is to specify how the derivative (i.e. the local utility function) of the functional varies as we move about the domain $D[0, M]$. Our formal hypothesis . . . as we move from one probability distribution in $D[0, M]$ to another . . . [is that] the local utility function becomes more concave at each point x . . . in terms of the Arrow-Pratt ratio" (Machina, 1983: 282).

As mentioned above, the two dimensional representation on the unit triangle, the side of p_2, will collapse to the origin. Following Chris Starmer (2000: 340), two parallel lines that would represent Allais' A, B and C, D prospects can be indicated by arrows in the best vs. worst plane as shown in Figure 1. With p_2 now collapsed to the origin, the origin will represent situation A, and situation B is given by the probability coordinates (0.01, 0.1). In a similar way, the second arrow in the parallelogram would represent situations C and D. The common consequence criterion requires that the slopes of the two arrows be the same.

The arrow labeled prob. = 1 is a multiple of the arrow labeled prob. < 1, and suggest what is known as the common ratio effect. As the former arrow decreases, we will move toward the right on lower indifference curves. This ratio will also show inconsistent choices.

Such linear and parallel lines would reflect the predictions of the independence axiom (Sugden, 2004: 695). But we will find that "the individual is most sensitive to changes in the probability of x_1 relative to changes in the probabilities of x_2 and x_3 (i.e. $\text{MRS}[x_2 \to x_3, x_2 \to x_1; F]$) is the highest near the left edge of the triangle, or in other words precisely when x_1 is a low probability event (i.e. p_1 is low)" (ibid.: 285).

In 1988, Allais presented an expansion of his model, which accentuated the difference and illustrated how to reconcile his position with the expected utility model. He introduced a special probability distorting function, θ(•), and a utility of a sure monetary payoff function, *u*(•) (Munier, 1995: 38; Stigum, 2003: 464). The former function measures attitude toward risks. The latter function can have any shape, such as convex or concave. Both functions can be continuous and strictly increasing. The distorted function representing the utility of a prospect can be written as:

$$Z(P) = u_1 + \theta(1 - p_1)[u(x_2) - u(x_1)] + \theta(1 - p_1 - p_2)[u(x_2) - u(x_1)] + \ldots + \theta(p_n)[u(x_n) - (x_{n-1})].$$

When there is no probability distortion represented by θ, then the model reverts back to the expected utility hypothesis. This extended formulation allows a variety of utility models. Gathered "under the heading of the 'anticipated utility' hypothesis. . . . This could be the ultimate result of Allais' contribution to decision under risk" (Munier, 1995: 39).

Besides Allais' generalized model, Machina (1995b) has attempted another generalization that has sparked some controversy. His articles on two errors in Allais' impossibility theory starts the problem. In his 1982 and 1983 articles, Machina discussed the impossibility of local and generalized utility functions. The controversy is about defining a Bernoullian index that simultaneously satisfies three conditions. As Allais puts it: "This *Impossibility Theorem* shows the *impossibility of simultaneously meeting the three following conditions: definition of the local neo-Bernoullian index in the discrete case* . . . its validity *over the whole interval* (0, *M*) . . . and its definition *up to within a linear transformation*" (Allais, 1995: 264 [italics original]). Disagreement centers on the appropriate definition of a local discrete utility function.

By way of summary, the Allais paradox picked up on the marginal valuation of income/wealth in the original Bernoulli specification, and added a person's attitude toward risk to it. While attitudes toward risk are built into the curvature of a person's utility function in the NM axiomatic model, it appears as different only between one person and another. In the Allais model, however, attitude toward risk is generalized to account for changes in the same person. This change is said to be systematic, and not due to mere randomness or illusion. The Allais paradox holds, therefore, that "*attitudes towards risk change not only from an individual to another, but also for a given individual between different patterns of risk.*" (Munier, 1995: 36 [italics original]).

Allais (1990: 8) demonstrated that his paradox has some novelty, which he posits to "basic psychological realities" that would not identify monetary with psychological values, and the distribution of risks in valuing cardinal utilities. Risks show up in the standard NM lottery described above, where expected utility hypothesis will yield the same values for many combinations of two prospects.

Overlapping Generation Model (OLG)

In his *Economy and Interest*, Allais presented a model of consumption for individuals in time periods that overlap for successive generations. This model is said to precede Samuelson's 1958 popularization of the subject by 11 years (Malinvaud, 1995: 111). Some differences need to be pointed out between the two models. Allais studied interaction between the production and consumption sectors, while Samuelson studied trade between different generations. While the data that Allais used for production and preferences were not sufficient to determine the rate of interest and allocation of resources, Samuelson developed a demographic theory of the interest rate equal to the rate of increase of the population. Yet another difference is that Allais used two time periods, and Samuelson used three. We have discussed Samuelson's contribution in this area elsewhere (Szenberg et al., 2006). In Allais, however, government intervention leads to different interest rates (Malinvaud, 1994: 126-127).

In Allais' framework, consumers provide a fixed quantity of labor in the first period, and do not work in the second period. Consumers are of the same type and they consume in both periods. One can write the production functions using Q for consumption goods, K for production goods, L_1 for employment in the production goods sector, L_2 for employment in the consumption goods sector, U for land, α as a constant, and all values are equal to or greater than zero. The two production functions and their employment restrictions are:

$$Q = \sqrt{L_2}(\sqrt{K + U}) \tag{1}$$

$$K = \alpha L_1 \tag{2}$$

$$L = L_1 + L_2 \tag{3}$$

Considerable degrees of freedom are allowed in the model. Edmond Malinvaud distinguishes three typical cases where the young consumers' wealth is either their labor income, or the national income, or the sum of rent and labor income (Malinvaud, 1987: 104-105). A golden rule condition requires a maximum output of consumer goods at a zero interest rate. A stationary equilibrium condition would require specification of consumer choices to work with the production plans in the two-period setting.

The predictions of Allais' OLG model are not unique because of the numerous degrees of freedom required for a stationary equilibrium. Some important variables to be specified include distribution rights, technical feasibility, psychological preferences, and consumption plans. Consumption plans have resource restriction discounted at the youthful stage. Distribution rights have to be specified intergenerationally. Malinvaud shows different predictions for resources as an exogenous datum, work only revenues, aggregate income, rents distributed to the young, and rents distributed to the old (Malinvaud, 1995: 121-125).

Allias' OLG is an alternative to traditional general equilibrium models. Practitioners have tried to reconcile differences between the Allais and Samuelson models, on the one hand, and the Arrow-Debreu GE model on the other. The works of Allais and Samuelson "would have complemented each other, because they brought to light different effects of the overlapping generation's structure" (Malinvaud, 1987: 105).

Attempts to reconcile OLG with other Walrasian general equilibrium models are still being studied (Geanakoplos, 1987; Geanakoplos and Polemarchakis, 1991). Extensions of the Allais-Samuelson model "permit generations to live longer, and even be immortal, include many commodities in each period and introduce uncertainty" (Geanakoplos, 1991). We find that "Walras' law need not hold for economies of overlapping generations . . . and . . . the model of overlapping generations has been interpreted as 'lack of market clearing at infinity'" (ibid.: 1901). In general, to get market clearing for OLG models, we may require that consumption bundles exceed initial endowment, that prices do not signal aggregate scarcity, and that competitive allocations are not Pareto Optimal (ibid.: 1902).

On the empirical side, the OLG model is "a workhorse of macroeconomics, monetary theory, and public finance" (Mas-Collel, 1995: 769). For instance, Laurence Kotlikoff's work has given rise to a new term in the expansion and articulation of the OLG model particularly in generational accounting. Both Kotlikoff and Peter Diamond take up current and future concerns of the Social Security problem, a good indication of the relevance of the model for the twenty-first century.

Monetary Theory

The quantity theory of money has a long history. We find Keynes turning it into a demand for money function, based on transaction, speculation, and precautionary motive (Keynes, 1936: Ch. 15). We can then write the demand for money function in an operational way, representing a liquidity preference function that varies with wealth, income, and expected returns, and the expected return from the broad spectrum of assets that can be held as wealth. In the post-World War II period, accelerating prices were the sole determinant of inflation. As one researcher in the monetarist school puts it, "the astronomical increases in prices and money dwarf the changes in real income and other real factors" (Cagan, 1956: 25).

In the early 1950s, Cagan and Allais were simultaneously evolving demand for cash balance models that would make the quantity theory falsifiable in situations of rapidly increasing prices. As Allais explained, "Cagan's research was brought to my attention by Friedman in a discussion we had in July 1954 when I described to him the interesting results I had reached . . . in my research on the theory of the business cycle" (Allais, 1966: 1123).

The predictions of Allais' and Cagan's models are essentially the same, namely that the demand for cash balances depends on the rate of change in prices. Allais made a correspondence of the variables, showing that the different choices lead to the same goal (ibid.). He explained his unique approach this way:

> My theory of monetary dynamics is based on the introduction of new concepts which have no equivalent in the earlier literature; the concepts of the psychological rate of interest, the rate of forgetfulness, and the

> reaction time, whose values vary according to the economic situation; the concept of the coefficient of psychological expansion which represents the average appraisal of the economic situation by all economic agents; the concept of psychological time, the referential of psychological time being such that the laws of monetary dynamics remain invariant therein. (Allais, 1997: 6)

In this formulation, heredity makes the present depend on the past and relativity makes the dependent relation unchanging or invariant when we use the psychological time in place of physical time.

Model of a Market Economy

Basically, Allais forged a general equilibrium model that depends on the efficient use of surplus in the economy. In this model, economic agents make transactions that generate surplus and distribute them in the economy to reflect optimality and stability. In outlining his contributions, Allais stated, "My work on economic evolution and general equilibrium, maximum efficiency, and the foundations of economic calculus has developed in two successive phases, from 1941 to 1966, and from 1967 to the present day" (Allais, 1997: 4). Allais thought that through the effective distribution of surplus, the economy would tend toward a state of maximum efficiency.

Allais' concept of surplus dominates the role of prices in traditional GE.

> A surplus can be realized when the marginal equivalences of consumption and production units differs. (Allais, 1977: 122)

> The maximum distributable surplus of a given good is the largest quantity of that good that can be made available by a better organization of the economy which leaves all preference indexes unchanged. (Ibid.: 133)

Allais' concern for the market economy has created two research programs in literature. The programs are in the direction of probing Pareto Optimal conditions, and stability of equilibrium. Pareto optimality means "a situation where any one preference index is maximal for given values of the other preference indexes" (ibid.: 134). Allais asserts a concept of general equilibrium where "there is no potential surplus for any good" (ibid.: 131). Allais' concept of equilibrium differs from the Walrasian concept where the overall demand is equal to the overall supply, and from Edgeworth's concept where one preference index is maximal for given values of the other preference indexes. His definition, however, still depends on multiple, convergent, and stable equilibrium.

In developing the Pareto and stability conditions for the economy, Allais shows a partiality for the calculus-based approach and eschews concerns with topology and convex sets. Some extensions of his model in modern literature, however, use both tools. We discuss the two aspects of his model further as follows.

Pareto Optimal Conditions

In his article "Economic Surplus and the Equimarginal Principle" in the *The New Palgrave Dictionary of Economics* (2nd ed., 2008), Allais gave a utility frontier illustration of the Pareto Optimal conditions. "A situation of maximum efficiency can be defined as a situation in which it is impossible to improve the situation of some people without undermining that of others." Allais' illustration corresponds to points on the utility frontier, which demarcates points above that are impossible, and points below that are possible. Allais emphasized that this definition of maximum efficiency is made independent of the assumptions of continuity, differentiability, or convexity, except for a common (nummaire) good. Following Allais' 2008 presentation, this can be fleshed out using a function $f_i(U_i, V_i, \ldots W_i)$ for consumers, and $f_j(U_j, V_j, \ldots W_j)$ for producers. The goods U vary continuously, and it enters all the production and consumption functions. The utility frontier is defined to represent a state where the producer index is equal to zero, i.e. $f_j(U_j, V_j, \ldots W_j) = 0$.

Modern researchers have been able to estimate this optimal condition with the use of a benefit function. Following David Luenberger, a benefit function that measures changes from the utility function in a reference bundle, g, can be made. The benefit function has three elements, $b(g; x, u)$, which "measure the amount that an individual is willing to trade, in terms of a specific reference commodity bundle g, for the opportunity to move from utility level u to a consumption bundle x" (Luenberger, 1992b: 461). "The concept of a benefit equilibrium is a natural modification of that of a competitive equilibrium. Utility is just replaced by individual benefit" (Luenberger, 1992a: 234).

In Allais' model, "a necessary and sufficient condition for X* to be Pareto efficient is that the distributable surplus be negative or zero for all feasible X (i.e., X* is zero maximal), and his statement is correct, in general, except for edge pathologies" (ibid.: 232). One can picture values of X* as points on the Allais utility frontier, and all feasible points, X, as points below the frontier. Like the production possibility curve one observes in elementary economics, the challenge is to find correspondence between the points of X and points of X*. We have adapted the standard consumer maximization and Edgeworth Box following Bertrand Munier (1995: 21-22) and others in Figures 2a and 2b below to illustrate the Allais equilibrium conditions.

Figure 2a shows paths from the feasible point X approaching the Allais utility frontier, which is non-convex. One can imagine a series of allocations starting from X and converging to different utility points, such as X_1 and X_2. The allocation vector is thought of as a series of points $\{x\}_n = \{x_1, x_2, \ldots, x_n\}$, and on the utility frontier are a series of utility functions, $U_i(X)$, which is also a series $\{U\}n = \{u_1, u_2, \ldots, u_n\}$. Allocations are consumption bundles of commodities. The allocation set is usually assumed to be convex, closed, and bounded from below (Luenberger, 1995: 161). A set of feasible allocations is defined as the situation where the sum of the allocation is equal to the sum of the traders' endowments (Courtault and Tallon, 2000: 478).

For equilibrium, we want to know if the utility sequence will converge to a maximum as each allocation sequence converges. The optimal point X* is such an equilibrium point in standard analysis where the price line is tangent to a convex utility curve. Extending the argument to a general benefit function would make the oval-shaped benefit region tangent to X* as demonstrated by Briec and Garderes (2004: 106).

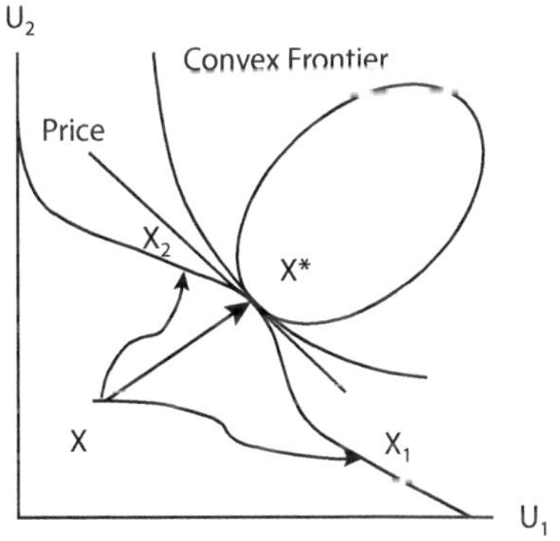

Figure 2a Utility Frontier.

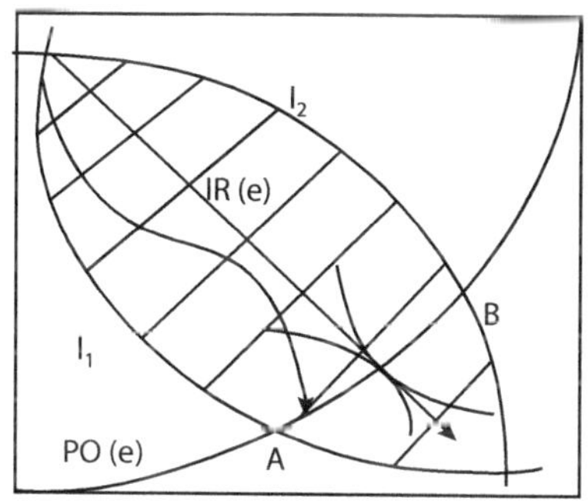

Figure 2b Edgeworth Box.

Figure 2b shows the feasible set of allocation, IR, as the hatched lense-shaped area in the Edgeworth Box. The core is the segment AB of the Pareto Optimal (PO) curve. Both IR and PO are determined by the endowment, *e*, of the traders. Allais' equilibrium is indicated by the curved arrow on the core. Walrasian equilibrium is attained where the straight arrow intersects the core. While both equilibrium conditions are in the core, Allias' equilibrium arises from many paths leaving an initial state, while only one equilibrium arises in the Walrasian model.

Allais' Stable States

The initial state of the economy, E_1, is characterized by the consumer and producer functions. A finite change in E_1, designated by δE_1 comes about by finite changes in the variables of the functions. A new state $E_2 = E_1 + \delta E_1$ will emerge from such changes. A third state E_3 that is made "isohedonous" with the state E_1 accounts for changes that return the preference indices to their initial values.

Commenting on Allais' model, Munier asserted that the set of stable states of the economy include the set of Walrasian equilibria of that economy. This condition is likened to the core concept of the Edgeworth Box with two traders. Traditional research that emphasizes a given price system establishes a unique Walrasian state in the core. For Allais, however, the stable state in the core need not be unique, and when more than two traders are involved, it may take on a larger core. Only in the stable states are input prices uniquely defined, because efficiency results from the pressure that free competition puts on human beings rather than on the price system (Munier, 1995: 20-21).

Conclusions

We found major precursors to modern theory in the works of Maurice Allais. We have touched on his paradox, overlapping generation model, and the market economy in this review. His paradox has steered research in a new direction in the economic literature, embracing psychological experiments of a highly scientific nature. It was a springboard for leading research to diverge from the traditional expected utility model toward a more psychological paradigm.

Allais' market model has turned the core elements of the Walrasian or Edgeworthian general equilibrium research program from price toward the effect of competition on humans. As we showed in Figures 2a and 2b, more general equilibrium results are included, and uniqueness based on convex analysis or convergence of the core is not the main object of general equilibrium analysis.

Michael Szenberg has a personal recollection of gratitude to express. Allais was a member of the Committee that conferred upon him the Irving Fisher Award for the Economics of the Israeli Diamond Industry (Szenberg, 1973).

The other members included Kenneth Boulding, Friedman, Egon Neuberger, and Samuelson. The volume *Eminent Economists: Their Life Philosophies* by Szenberg included the opening essay "The Passion for Research" by Allais, which provides lofty lessons in scholarship. Getting the final version of Allais' essay took about eight submitted drafts, fifty letters and cables, and numerous [overseas] telephone calls. As mentioned in the volume (p. 25), "this is meticulousness of the highest order on part of the contributor. Students are meant to understand that 'Inspiration,' in the words of Tchaikovsky, 'is a guest that does not visit lazy people.'" How appropriate and timely to conclude this memoriam with Allais' quote: "... without any exaggeration, the current mechanism of money creation through credit is certainly the 'cancer' that's irretrievably eroding market economies of private property" (1999: 74).

References

Allais, M. (1999). *La crise mondiale d'aujourd'hui. Pour de profondes réformes des institutions financières et monétaires*. Paris: Clement Juglar.

———. (1997, Dec.). *Nobel lecture, December 9, 1988*. Reprinted as An outline of my main contributions to economic science. *The American Economic Review*, 87(6), 3-12.

———. (1995). The real foundation of the alleged errors in the Allais impossibility theorem: Unceasingly repeated errors or contradictions of Mark Machina. *Theory and Decision*, 38, 251-299.

———. (1992). The passion for research. In M. Szenberg (Ed.), *Eminent economists: Their life philosophies* (17-41). Cambridge: Cambridge University Press.

———. (1990 [1987]). Allais Paradox. In J. Eatwell, M. Milgate, & P. Newman (Eds.), *The new Palgrave: Utility and probability* (3-9). New York: W. W. Norton and Company.

———. (1988). The general theory of random choices in relation to the invariant cardinal utility function and the specific probability function. In B. R. Munier (Ed.), *Risk, decision and rationality* (231-290). Dordrecht: D. Reidel Publishing Company.

———. (1978). Theories of general equilibrium and maximum efficiency. In G. Schwödiauer (Ed.), *Equilibrium and disequilibrium in economic theory* (129-201). Dordrecht: D. Reidel Publishing Company.

———. (1972, Feb.) Forgetfulness and interest. *Journal of Money, Credit and Banking*, 4(1), Part 1, 40-73.

———. (1966, Dec.). A restatement of the quantity theory of money. *American Economic Review*, 56, 1123-1157.

———. (1962, Oct.). The influence of the capital-output ratio on real national income. *Econometrica*, 30(4), 700-728.

———. (1953, Oct.). Le comportement de l'homme rationnel devant le risque: Critique des postulats et axiomesde. *Econometrica*, 21(4), 503-546.

Arrow, K. J. (1984). *Collected papers of Kenneth Arrow: Individual choice under certainty and uncertainty* (vol. 3). Cambridge, MA: Belknap Press.

Baumol, W. J. (1965). *Economic theory and operations analysis* (2nd ed.). Englewood Cliffs, NJ: Prentice Hall, Inc.

Bayes, T. (1763). An essay towards solving a problem in the doctrine of chance. *Philosophical Transactions of the Royal Society*, 53, 370-418. Reprinted in *Biometrika*, 45 (1958), 293-315.

Bernoulli, D. (1954, Jan.). Exposition of a new theory on the measurement of risk. *Econometrica*, 22(1), 23-36.

Blackwell, D., & Girshick, M. A. (1979 [1954]). *Theory of games and statistical decision*. New York: Dover Publication.

Borch, K. (1967). The economics of uncertainty. In M. Shubik (Ed.), *Essays in mathematical economics: In honor of Oskar Morgenstern* (197-210). Princeton: Princeton University Press.

Briec, W., & Garderes, P. (2004). Generalized benefit functions and measurement. *Mathematical Methods of Operations Research*, 60, 101–123.

Bryant, V. (1990). *Yet another introduction to analysis*. Cambridge: Cambridge University Press.

Cagan, P. (1956). The monetary dynamics of hyperinflation. In M. Friedman (Ed.), *Studies in the quantity theory of money* (25-117). Chicago: University of Chicago Press.

Champernowne, D. G. (1969). *Uncertainty and estimation* (vol. 3). San Francisco: Holden Day.

Conlisk, J. (1989, Jun.). Three variants on the Allais. *The American Economic Review* 79(3), 392-407.

Conlon, J. R. (1995). A simple proof of a basic result in nonexpected utility theory. *Journal of Economic Theory*, 65, 635-639.

Courtault, J. M., & Tallon, J.-M. (2000). Allais' trading process and the dynamic evolution of a market economy, economic theory. *Economic Theory*, 16, 477–481.

De Montbrial, T. (1995). Maurice Allais, a belatedly recognized genius. In B. R. Munier (Ed.), *Markets, risk and money: Essays in honor of Maurice Allais* (50-58). Boston: Kluwer Academic Publishers.

Dixon, P. B., Bowles, S., & Kendrick, D., with L. Taylor & M. Roberts. (1980). *Notes and problems in microeconomic theory*. Amsterdam: North-Holland Publishing Company.

Fishburn, P. C. (1991, Jan.). Decision theory: The next 100 years? *The Economic Journal*, 101(404), 27-32.

———. (1989). Foundations of decision analysis. *Management Science*, 35(4), 387-405.

———. (1988). Normative theories of decision making under risk and under uncertainty. In D. E. Bell, H. Raiffa, & A. Tversky (Eds.), *Decision making: Descriptive, normative and prescriptive interactions* (78-98). Cambridge: Cambridge University Press.

———. (1987, Dec.). Reconsiderations in the foundations of decision under uncertainty. *The Economic Journal*, 97(388), 825-841.

———. (1983). Transitive Measurable Utility. *Journal of Economic Theory*, 31, 293-317.

———. (1982). Nontransitive measurable utility. *Journal of Mathematical Psychology*, 26, 31-67.

———. (1979). On the nature of expected utility. In M. Allais & O. Hagen (Eds.), *Expected utility hypotheses and the Allais paradox* (243-257). Dordrecht: D. Reidel Publishing Company.

Gelbaum B. R., & Olmsted, J. M. H. (1965). *Counter examples in analysis*. San Francisco: Holden-Day Inc.

Geanakoplos, J. D., & Polemarchakis, H. M. (1991). Overlapping generations. In W. Heldenbrand & H. Sonnenschein (Eds.), *Handbook of mathematical economics* (vol. 4, 1899-1960). Amsterdam: Elsevier Science Publisher.

Genakoplos, J. D. (1987). Overlapping generations models in general equilibrium. In J. Eatwell , M. Milgate, & P. Newman (Eds.), *The new Palgrave: A dictionary of economics* (767-779). New York: Macmillan.

Gilboa, I., & Schmeidler, D. (2001). *A theory of case-based decision.* Cambridge: Cambridge University Press.

Hahn, F., & Solow, R. (1995). *A critical essay on modern macroeconomic theory.* Cambridge, MA: MIT Press.

Herstein, I. N., & Milnor, J. (1953). An axiomatic approach to measureable utility. *Econometrica,* 21, 291-297.

Huntington, E. V., (1921). *The continuum and other types of serial order* (2nd ed.). Cambridge, MA: MIT Press.

Jehle, G. (1991). *Advanced microeconomic theory.* Englewood Cliffs, NJ: Prentice Hall.

Jensen, N. E. (1967, Sept.). An introduction to Bernoullian utility theory: I. utility functions. *The Swedish Journal of Economics,* 69(3), 163-183.

Kahneman, D., & Tversky, A. (1984). Choices, values, and frames. *American Psychologist,* 39, 341-350.

———. (1979). Prospect theory: An analysis of decisions under risk. *Econometrica,* 47, 313-317.

Karni, E. & Schmeidler, D. (1991). Utility theory with uncertainty. In W. Hildenbrand & H. Sonnenchein (Eds.), *Handbook of mathematical economics* (vol. 4, 1831-1961). Amsterdam: Elsevier Science Publishers.

Keynes, J. M. (1970, [1936]). *The collected writings of John Maynard Keynes: The general theory of employment, interest and money, Vol. VII.* London: Macmillan and St. Martin's Press.

———. (1973 [1921]) *Collected writings of John Maynard Keynes, Volume VIII: Treatise on probability* (3rd ed.). Royal Economic Society.

Laffont, J.-J. (1989). *The economics of uncertainty and information.* (J. P. Bonin & H. Bonin, Trans.). Cambridge, MA: MIT Press.

Luenberger, D. G. (1995). Externalities and benefits. *Journal of Mathematical Economics,* 24, 159-177.

———. (1992a, Nov.). New optimality principles for economic efficiency and equilibrium. *Journal of Optimization Theory and Applications*, 75(2), 221-264.

———. (1992b. Benefit functions and duality. *Journal of Mathematical Economics*, 21, 461-481.

MacCrimmon, K. R., & Larsson, S. (1979). Utility theory: Axioms versus "paradoxes." In M. Allais & O. Hagen (Ed.), *Expected utility hypotheses and the Allais paradox* (333-403). Dordrecht: D. Reidel Publishing Company.

Machina, M. J. (2005, Jun.) Expected utility/subjective probability analysis without the sure-thing principle or probabilistic sophistication. *Economic Theory*, 26(1), 1-62.

———. (2003). States of the world and the state of decision theory. In D. J. Meyer (Ed.), *The economics of risk* (17-49). Kalamazoo, MI: W. E. Upjohn Institute for Employment Research.

———. (1995a). On Maurice Allais's and Ole Hagen's expected utility hypotheses and the Allias paradox. In B. R. Munier (Ed.), *Markets, risk and money: Essays in honor of Maurice Allais* (179-194). Boston: Kluwer Academic Publishers.

———. (1995b). Two errors in the "Allais Impossibility Theorem." *Theory and Decision*, 38, 231-250.

———. (1990). Expected utility hypothesis. In J. Eatwell, M. Milgate, & P. Newman (Ed.), *The new Palgrave: Utility and probability* (79-95). New York: W. W. Norton and Company.

———. (1987). Choice under uncertainty: Problems solved and unsolved. *Journal of Economic Perspectives*, 1, 121–154.

———. (1983). Generalized expected utility analysis and the nature of observed violation of the independence axiom. In B. P. Stigum & F. Wenstop (Ed.), *Foundations of utility and risk theory with applications.* (263-293). Dordrecht: D. Reidel Publishing Company.

Malinvaud, E. (1995). Maurice Allais, unrecognized pioneer of overlapping generation models. In B. R. Munier (Ed.), *Markets, risk and money: Essays in honor of Maurice Allais* (111 128). Boston: Kluwer Academic Publishers.

———. (1987, Mar.). The overlapping generation model in 1947. *Journal of Economic Literature*, 25(1), 103-105.

———. (1952). A note on von Neumann-Morgenstern's strong independence axiom. *Econometrica*, 20, 679.

Marschak, J. (1950, Apr.). Rational behavior, uncertain prospects, and measurable utility. *Econometrica*, 18(2), 111-141.

Marshall, A. (1982 [1890]). *Principles of economics* (8th ed.). Landers: The Macmillan Press, Ltd.

Mas-Colell, A., Whinston, M. D., & Green, J. R. (1995). *Microeconomic theory*. New York: Oxford University Press.

Menger, C. (1967 [1934]). The role of uncertainty in economics. In M. Shubik (Ed.), *Essays in mathematical economics: In honor of Oskar Morgenstern* (211-231). Princeton: Princeton University Press.

Morgenstern, O. (1979). Some reflections on utility. In M. Allais & O. Hagen (Eds.), *Expected utility hypotheses and the Allais paradox* (55-78). Dordrecht: D. Reidel Publishing Company.

Munier, B. R. (1995). Fifty years of Maurice Allais's economic writings: Seeds for renewal in contemporary economic thought. In B. R. Munier (Ed.), *Markets, risk and money: Essays in honor of Maurice Allais* (1-50). Boston: Kluwer Academic Publishers.

———. (1991, Spring). Nobel laureate: The many other Allais paradoxes. *The Journal of Economic Perspectives*, 5(2), 179-199.

Newman, P. (1990). Frank Plumpton Ramsey. In J. Eatwell, M. Milgate, & P. Newman (Eds.), *The new Palgrave: Utility and probability* (186-197). New York: W. W. Norton and Company.

Ramsey, F. P. (1960, [1931]). *The foundation of mathematics*. Paterson, NJ: Littlefield, Adams and Co.

Resnik, M. D. (1987). *Choices: An introduction to decision theory*. Minneapolis: University of Minnesota Press.

Samuelson, P. A. (1986). *The collected scientific papers of Paul A. Samuelson* (vol. 5). K. Crowley (Ed.). Cambridge, MA: MIT Press.

———. (1958, Dec.). An exact consumption-loan model of interest with or without the social contrivance of money. *The Journal of Political Economy*, 67(6), 467-482.

Savage, L. J. (1972 [1954]). *The foundation of statistics*. New York: Dover Publication, Inc.

Sen, A. (2002). *Rationality and freedom.* Cambridge, MA: Belknap Press.

Sheysin, O. B. (1977). D. Bernoulli's works on probability. In M. Kendall & R. L. Plackett (Eds.), *Studies in the history of statistics and probability* (vol. II, 105-132). London: Macmillan.

Starmer, C. (2000, Jun.). Developments in non-expected utility theory: The hunt for a descriptive theory of choice under risk. *Journal of Economic Literature,* 38(2), 332-382.

Stigum, B. P. (2003). *Econometrics and the philosophy of economics.* Princeton: Princeton University Press.

Sugden, R. (2004). Alternatives to expected utility: Foundation. In S. Barberá, P. J. Hammond, & C. Seidl (Eds.), *Handbook of utility theory, vol. 2: Extensions* (685-756). Boston: Kluwer Academic Publishers.

Szenberg, M., Ramrattan, L., & Gottesman, A. A. (Eds.). (2006). *Samuelsonian economics and the twenty-first century.* New York: Oxford University Press.

———. (1973). *The economics of the Israeli diamond industry.* With an Introduction by M. Friedman. New York: Basic Books.

———. (1992). *Eminent economists: Their life philosophies.* Cambridge: Cambridge University Press.

Von Neumann, J., & Morgenstern, O. (1953 [1944]). *Theory of games and economic behavior* (3rd ed.). Princeton: Princeton University Press.

Weber, M. (1998, Oct.). The resilience of the Allais paradox. *Ethics,* 109(1), 94-118.

Wu, G., & Gonzales, R. (1998). Common consequence conditions in decision making under risk. *Journal of Risk and Uncertainty,* 16, 115–139.

PART VIII

SOCIOLOGY AND ECONOMICS

Gary Becker

Gary Becker

Gary Stanley Becker was born in Pottsville, Pennsylvania in 1930. His family moved to Brooklyn, New York when he was a child. His father was a small business owner and was becoming blind, so young Becker used to read him the stock market and financial news. At age 16, Becker attended James Madison High School, where he took a liking to mathematics. He earned his BA from Princeton University in 1951 and went on to do graduate studies at the University of Chicago, earning a PhD in 1955. He was a professor of economics at Columbia University (1957-1968), and then at the University of Chicago. He received the John Bates Clark Medal in 1967, followed by the Nobel Prize in Economics in 1992 and the National Medal of Science in 2000.

In addition to teaching and conducting research, Becker wrote a conservative column for *Business Week* from 1985 to 2004. He started the Becker-Posner Blog in December 2004 with notable legal economist and Judge Richard Posner. He was also affiliated with the Hoover Institute.

Becker married Doria Slote in 1954 and had two children, Catherine and Judy Becker. Ten years after Doria's passing in 1970, Becker married Guity Nashat.

Becker's Methodology

Becker said, "I took a lot of heat over my career from people who thought my work was silly or irrelevant or not economics" (Levitt and Dubner, 2005: 206). Becker contended that "what most distinguishes economics as a discipline from other disciplines in the social sciences is not its subject matter but its approach . . . the economic approach is uniquely powerful because it can integrate a wide range of human behavior" (Becker, 1976: 5) As one economist, Yoram Ben-Porath, put it: "The fact that a unified set of concepts is being used to describe and analyze human behavior in education, health, fertility, marriage, allocation of time, bequests, and income distribution is no minor achievement" (Ben-Porath, 1982: 58-59).

Becker built his methodology on a standard micro- to macroeconomic foundation. He adhered to the rule that a model should be simple but still explain a lot. Complexity is introduced as needed in a process that tries to get a lot out of a simple model. For example, Becker took a standard ordinal utility function where utility is a function of two goods, $\boldsymbol{x}$ and $\boldsymbol{y}$, and inserted a variable called social capital into it to get: $\boldsymbol{U} = \boldsymbol{U}(\boldsymbol{x}, \boldsymbol{y}; \boldsymbol{S})$. Without the insertion of **S**, the standard utility function would shift about as **S** changes. With the insertion, the standard function will not shift, but rather utility will rise or fall when S changes (Becker and Murphy, 2000: 9).

In expanding the standard micro model, Becker was standing on the shoulders of giants such as Jeremy Bentham, Alfred Marshall, Arthur C. Pigou, Irving Fisher, and Thorstein Veblen (Becker, 1976: 254-255). Students of economics may recall that Bentham was concerned with minimizing pain and maximizing pleasure, and Veblen was concerned with conspicuous consumption. The standard marginal theory of Leon Walras, Carl Menger, and Stanley Jevons, and to some extent Marshall, restricted utility maximization only to basic determinants of wants.

But Becker would draw further distinction between his methodology and orthodox microeconomics. In his Nobel laureate address, he stated: "I have tried to pry economists away from narrow assumptions about self-interest. Behavior is driven by a much richer set of values and preferences . . . individuals maximize welfare as they conceive it, whether they be selfish, altruistic, loyal, spiteful, or masochistic. . . . Actions are constrained by income, time, imperfect memory and calculating capacities, and other limited resources, and also by the opportunities available in the economy and elsewhere" (Becker, 1993: 385-386). As one of his colleagues, the Nobelist George Stigler, preached, "Economic logic centers on utility-maximizing behavior by individuals. . . . Gary Becker has analyzed it with striking results in areas such as crime, marriage and divorce, fertility, and altruistic behavior" (Stigler, 1982: 21).

Becker has explicitly stated that "all human behavior can be viewed as involving participants who maximize their utility from a stable set of preferences and accumulate an optimal amount of information and other inputs in a variety of markets" (Becker, 1976: 14). His brand of utility maximization is not self-centered but includes concerns for others. According to Amartya Sen's evaluation, Becker rejects self-centered welfare where one is concerned only with his own consumption and the richness of his life (Sen, 2002: 33-34).

A View of Becker's Generalized Model

In his Nobel speech, Becker illustrated his methodology in an appendix for the general audience. This is an overlapping generational model with a parent being altruistic by paying for his child's education. The model contains three periods: young, middle, and old age. Becker provided an even simpler version to his economics class. It is a simple two-period model, with one sector where parents either choose to invest in their child or consume their income. The parents have a child in a time, t, and the parent dies in the next period, $t+1$. This implies that parents do not live to recoup their investments. When the children are adults, the parents are dead. So no contractual relations can be made between children and parents for repayment.

At time t, the parent has a given income. They have to choose between consuming all their income or investing some in their child's education. The parent utility function can be made to represent this as follows:

$$\boldsymbol{Max\ U_p(w_p) = u(c_p) + aV(w_c)} \qquad (1)$$

$$\text{s.t. } \boldsymbol{c_p = w_p + y_p} \qquad (2)$$

where: w_p = parental income; y_p = goods spent on children;
w_c – earnings of children when adults; c_p = parental consumption;
$V(w_c)$ = children's utility when they become adults, and a = degree of altruism; e.g. $a = 0$ if parents are selfish.

Human capital enters the model in the form of $H_c = f(y_c)$, household production function for human capital, where the first derivative is assumed to be zero or positive, implying that more investment in the child increases human capital. The second derivative can be negative, implying diminishing returns, or zero (as in the case $H_c = ky_c$, where k is a constant), or positive yielding increasing returns. For example, if we take the brain capacity as fixed for learning, making f(y, Brain), then $f'(y_c)$ is positive, and $f''(y_c)$ can be negative or zero. The idea is that with the brain capacity fixed, you can invest a lot in the child and still get diminishing returns.

A further concern is what determines earnings. We need to convert human capital into earnings by specifying a proportional constant between them, such as $w_c = rH_c$. Such a specification will convert a unit of human capital into monetary values. The proportional constant is influenced by the following variables:

$$r = \psi(\sum \textit{Human Capital of Everyone, Technology, Physical Capital})$$

The market is competitive. One person investing in becoming a doctor does not affect others investing in becoming doctors. So a parent can take *r* as given by market forces.

Given the above simple specifications, we can now proceed like a student to maximize the parent's utility function with the given constraint in equations 1 and 2 above. The solution is in the following form:

$Lagrange : Up - \lambda(c_p + y_p - w_p)$ which yields

$$1.\ u'(c_p) = \lambda \text{ and}$$

$$2.\ \frac{a\partial V(w_c)}{\partial y_c} \leq \lambda.$$

One ready implication is that if the parent is not altruistic, a =-, and the left side of 2 is zero. Then, according to the constraint, the parents will not invest in the child. Another, more traditional implication is seen from the decomposition of 2 to get: (a∂V(w_c))/(∂y_c) ≤ λ. This expression takes the following form:

$$a\frac{\partial V}{\partial w_c}\cdot\frac{\partial w_c}{\partial H_c}\cdot\frac{\partial H_c}{\partial y}=aV'_c rf_y \leq \lambda. \text{ But since } rf_y=\frac{\partial w}{\partial y_c}=1+r=R_y$$

we get: $aV'_c R_y \leq \lambda = u'(c_p)$ and so $R_y = \frac{u'(c_p)}{aV'_c}$.

The implication is that the marginal rate of substitution from the parent's consumption and what they get from investing in their kids (a today versus tomorrow paradigm) is the interest rate, a classical result.

Continuing with his methodology, Becker added a plateful of theorems and metaphors to the economist's lexicon. We make a brief summary of the following Becker theorems:

1. Rotten-Kid Theorem, in which the metaphor of a child as a durable good is used.
2. "Crime Would Not Pay": L or loss function for crime.
3. A Theory of the Allocation of Time, in which time is a commodity.
4. The Theory of Marriage, in which emotions and love are treated as commodities.

On The Rotten Kid Theorem

Becker wrote: "The Rotten Kid Theorem implies that for '. . . rotten kids to act rotten, they must have rotten parents, and . . . rotten wives must have rotten husbands.' Even selfish and envious children or wives act as if they are altruistic towards their parents or husbands if their parents or husbands are altruistic towards them, and act as if they are envious towards their parents or husbands if these persons are envious towards them" (Becker, 1981: 8).

One can demonstrate this by writing out the utility function for a husband, ***h***, and two kids, Jane, ***j***, and Tom, ***t***. Suppose Tom is considering an action that will affect Jane's utility, then their choices can be joined in a utility function, $\boldsymbol{\Psi} = \boldsymbol{\Psi}(\boldsymbol{Z}_t,\boldsymbol{Z}_j)$ where the partial derivative $\boldsymbol{\Psi}_j < 0$. Now embed Tom and Jane's utility function in their father's utility function: $\boldsymbol{U}_h = \boldsymbol{U}(\boldsymbol{Z}_{h,}; \Psi(\boldsymbol{Z}_t, \boldsymbol{Z}_j), \boldsymbol{Z}_j)$. The last term represents that Jane's utility benefits the father. The middle expression picks up what we said about Tom's action lowering Jane's utility. For the father to benefit, therefore, the effect of the positive last term must outweigh the negative effect of the middle term (ibid.: 8).

The Rotten Kid Theorem can be demonstrated in the form of a game. Let the child start the game with action ***A***. The consequence is for both the child and parents to benefit or lose from the action. Suppose both gain income $\boldsymbol{C}(\boldsymbol{A})$ and $\boldsymbol{P}(\boldsymbol{A})$, respectively. Now we look at the parent's response. The parents can exhibit altruistic behavior by leaving a bequest, ***B***, for the child. Summing up, the child's utility is $\boldsymbol{UC}(\boldsymbol{C}(\boldsymbol{A}) + \boldsymbol{B})$ The parent's utility is $\boldsymbol{UP}[(\boldsymbol{P}(\boldsymbol{A}) - \boldsymbol{B}) + \boldsymbol{aUC}(\boldsymbol{C}(\boldsymbol{A}) + \boldsymbol{B})]$. In this case, we want to maximize the family income, that is, the parent and child income, C(A) + P(A). We see that the child's action maximizes the family income (Gibbons, 1992: 30).

"Crime Would Not Pay"

In his crime and punishment framework, Becker wrote that the "conclusion that 'Crime would not pay' is an optimality condition and not an implication about the efficiency of the police or courts" (Becker, 1976: 78). He concentrated "almost entirely on determining optimal policies to combat illegal behavior and paid little attention to actual policies." The framework of his model assumes (ibid.: 77):

- Public expenditure on police and courts.
- The probability, p, that an offender will be detained and convicted.
- The size of the punishment, f, for the convicted.
- The number of offenses, O.
- The cost of achieving p.
- The effect of changes in p and f on O

The net cost to society of a crime can be given by an equation: $\boldsymbol{D(O) = H(O) - G(O)}$, where $\boldsymbol{H_i = H_i (O_i)}$ specifies harm from the ith activity, and $\boldsymbol{G = G(O)}$ represents the gain to offenders.

The activities of the courts, A, is a production function f, which takes inputs such as manpower, material, and capital. So, one can write $\boldsymbol{A = f(m, r, c)}$. Increasing activities can be determined by the relation $\mathbf{C = C(A)}$.

The number of offenses is determined by a function also: $\boldsymbol{O = O\ (p, f, u)}$. The new symbol, $\boldsymbol{u}$, is an error term that picks up other omitted variables. While this function may differ for the jth person, we can work with the average of all persons. An offender uses the expected utility paradigm to weigh its income from an offense. This model would use values of $\boldsymbol{p}$ in the calculation rather than $\boldsymbol{f}$. Risky activities would weigh the income down, and less risky choices would imply higher income. This has led Becker to the conclusion that "whether 'crime pays' is then an implication of the attitudes offenders have towards risk and is not directly related to the efficiency of the police or the amount spent on combating crime . . . social loss from illegal activities is usually minimized by selecting p and f in regions where risk is preferred, that is, in regions where 'crime does not pay'" (Becker, 1976: 49).

One more piece of information allows Becker to specify a loss function to society. The relation postulates a coefficient $\boldsymbol{b}$ so that $\boldsymbol{bf}$ ascertains the social cost '$\boldsymbol{f}$'. One can now specify a welfare function that measures losses from social offenses. That function is: $\mathbf{L = L\ (D, C, }\boldsymbol{bf}\mathbf{, O)}$.

Assuming that the losses are measured in terms of income, the loss function becomes: = $D(O) + C(p, O) + bpfO$, where the partial derivatives with respect to D, C, and bf are positive. Taking the partial derivatives with respect to p and f yields marginal costs, MC_p and MC_f, which can be set equal to marginal revenues, MR_p and MR_f, respectively, to find equilibrium values.

To see the implication of this model for the situation that "crime does not pay," we take the two partials:

$$\frac{\partial L}{\partial f} = -bpf\left(1 - \frac{1}{e_f}\right) = MC_f = MR_f, \text{ where elasticity } e_f = -\frac{f}{o}O_f \quad (3)$$

$$\frac{\partial L}{\partial p} = -bpf\left(1 - \frac{1}{e_p}\right) = MC_p = MR_p, \text{ where elasticity } e_p = -\frac{f}{o}O_p \quad (4)$$

The partial derivatives in Equations 3 and 4 indicate that MR_p would be less than MR_f only if $e_p > e_f$. This condition is "precisely the condition indicating that offenders have preference for risk and thus that 'crime does not pay'" (Becker, 1976: 53).

On Allocation of Time

In the traditional utility model, each household has a utility function, $U(Z_i)$, where $i = 1, 2, 3, \ldots, m$ commodities. A person takes time, T, along with goods, x, to produce commodities, using a production function $Z_i = f_i(x_i, T_i)$. For instance, to produce a good night's sleep may require commodities such as a bed, sleeping pills, and time (ibid.: 91). The inputs are vector bundles. A vector for time can mean that

$T = \{daytime, nighttime, weekdays, weekends, and\ holidays\}$.

Perhaps the first thing to recognize in Becker's time allocation model is that a household functions as both a producer, like a small factory, and a consumer. While they maximize utility, households are also combining goods and time to produce the commodities Z_i that yield utilities when consumed.

One approach to the optimal allocation of time is to maximize $U(Z_i)$ for separate constraints for each commodity, x_i, and each time, T_i. Different activities will require different mixes of commodities and time. Taking the wage rate as a measure of the opportunity cost of time, a change in the wage rate will change the relative costs of an activity. To illustrate, suppose you are deciding whether to prepare a meal or buy it from a restaurant. Let us weigh the two options.

1. You earn \$10 an hour, and the meal costs \$15 from the restaurant and takes one hour to purchase and eat. Your cost for this option is \$25.
2. Let the cost of inputs for the meal be \$1.50, and it takes you half an hour to prepare it, and one hour to eat it. \$1.50 + \$5 +10 = \$16.50. Comparing the two options, you should make the meal at home rather than buy it from the restaurant. Now, our choices between these two activities can be affected by changes in the wage rate. If the wage rate increases, one has to attend to substitution and income effects. More income will be gained from working an extra hour, making labor spent on making the meal (non-market activity) less attractive (see Meza and Osbourne, 1980: 215-216).

Rather than separating the constraints for time and commodities, treating them as independent, Becker saw that the constraints are related. The two constraints are related because "time can be converted into goods by using less time at consumption and more at work" (Becker, 92-93). The aggregated constraint is then derived as the expenditure on goods plus the expenditure of time. Each commodity is translated into values by multiplying them by their respective prices, $\boldsymbol{p}$, and summing them, and similarly, each element in the vector of time is multiplied by the wage rate, $\overline{w}$ and summed. The problem then becomes the following, where V is the household nonwage income:

$$\textit{Maximize } U(Z_i) = U(f_i) = U(x_i, T_i)$$

$$s.t \sum p_i x_i + \sum T_i \overline{w} = V + T\overline{w} = S$$

One can then set up the usual Lagrangian maximization problem as:

$$L = \left(Z_i\right) - \left(\sum p_i x_i + \sum T_i \overline{w} - S\right)$$

Taking the partial derivatives of L with respect to the Z_i shows that the ratio of their marginal utilities must be equal to the ratio of their costs. Taking the partial derivatives with respect to the factors, goods and time, one understands that the ratio of marginal products must equal the ratio of prices, providing that both factors are used in the same production function (Becker, 1976: 136).

Empirical applications of Becker's allocation of time theory include: 1) areas where the use of time is a large component, such as passenger transportation, and areas where time is a scarce resource: the service of a professor in school, medical advisor, or auto mechanic; 2) human capital raises the market value of time and its productivity lowers prices; 3) In the areas of marriage and fertility, timing of marriage and divorce can be important (ibid.: 141-143).

A Theory of Marriage

A first view of marriage is that of two persons sharing a household. Since each member of the household can now produce commodities such as children, prestige, recreation, companionship, love, and health status, the household utility function can be increased (ibid.: 207). One can create an aggregate demand and production function for these commodities, **Z**. Each household member wants to maximize the utility of **Z** that he or she receives.

The theory of marriage is concerned with: 1) gains from marriage versus remaining single; 2) how people sort themselves using characteristics such as IQ, education, attractiveness, skin color, etc. This sorting allows for positive and negative correlation in the traits of the married couple; and 3) how the couple shares their output. Becker deals with the problem in two phases, 1) Optimal Sorting, and 2) Assortive Mating, which we describe below.

In Optimal Sorting, Becker states the necessary condition for gains from a marriage. The utility and production function are similar to those we discussed in regard to the allocation of time. Time is now divided into male time, t_m, and female time, t_f. Using Z_{mo} and Z_{of} to identify male and female maximum output, and m_{mf} and f_{mf} to identify male and female married income, we can postulate a necessary condition for marriage to be: $m_{mf} + f_{mf} = Z_{mf} \geq Z_{mo} + Z_{of}$

Complementarity and substitutes play a significant role in the economics of marriage. We use the example of putting social and environmental variables, along with goods and services, into a utility function, such as in $U = U(x, y; S)$, mentioned above. Becker allows complementarity arguments such as that an increase in **S** can increase the utility of x, say by raising the demand for x. The power of strong complementarity is tyrannical in that "individuals are 'forced' to conform to social norms . . . strong complementarities between social capital and individual behavior appears to leave little room for individual choice" (Becker and Murphy, 2000: 9).

One can look at complementarity from the production side as well. If I desire to produce the output, say "driving effectively to reach a destination," then I create a production function with $\boldsymbol{Z} = f(\boldsymbol{x}, \boldsymbol{y}, \boldsymbol{S})$. We can think of $\boldsymbol{x}$ as the side of the road I like to drive on, left or right. Let $\boldsymbol{S}$ be the convention that society specifies, namely, the right-hand side. I can produce my desired output if I follow the convention. That output can now be placed in the utility function above as $\boldsymbol{Z}$. Similar complementarities exist with regard to the adoption of units of measurement—metric, decimal, computer operating systems, and network standards.

One consequence of complementarity is that it can cause multiple equilibria. For instance, a society can adopt two opposing conventions for driving: left- or right-hand side, as they do in the UK and US, respectively. Similarly, different systems of weight and measurement can be adopted by convention. The resulting multiple equilibria are not problematic as long as one does not shift constantly between them. One becomes habituated into one equilibrium over time. Here a distinction is made between social norms, $\boldsymbol{S}$, and habits, $\boldsymbol{H}$. We can have $\boldsymbol{H} = \boldsymbol{H}(\textbf{\textit{past selves}})$, while $\boldsymbol{S} = \boldsymbol{S}(\textbf{\textit{other selves}})$. So they enter the utility function as two separate variables (ibid.: 15-17).

The source of gains assumes complementarity between the couple's time. This concept is illustrated by a Cobb-Douglas production function where both time inputs of the couple are needed in the function, such as in $\boldsymbol{Z} = \boldsymbol{k}\boldsymbol{x}^{a}\boldsymbol{t}_{m}^{b}\boldsymbol{t}_{f}^{c}$. If we make either time input zero, then the output on the right-hand side will be zero. Therefore, the two times must somehow complement each other, even though male time is an imperfect substitute for female time and vice versa.

Sorting Equilibrium in Marriage

The sorting of the characteristics of the couple also contributes to the gains of the marriage. Each potential partner in a marriage, $\boldsymbol{i}$, has an output to offer to another potential partner, $\boldsymbol{j}$. Each male or female will search for the partner who brings the maximum income to the marriage. One can think of the marriage problem as a coalition game in game theory, where each potential partner attaches a utility value to being single, and a value to a potential marriage they can form. The problem is to determine how many marriages will be formed, and how the partners will divide up the gains of the households formed by marriage (Davis, 1993: 180).

In an example that Becker gave, the values for males and females staying alone are: $\boldsymbol{m}_{11} = \mathbf{3}$; $\boldsymbol{m}_{22} = 5$; $\boldsymbol{f}_{11} = \mathbf{5}$; $\boldsymbol{f}_{22} = \mathbf{2}$, where $\boldsymbol{m}$ is for male, $\boldsymbol{f}$ is for female, the first subscript identifies the player, and the second subscript identifies who the player selects. If the players form a marriage, the utilities they expect to receive are given in the matrix as:

	f_1	f_2
m_1	8	4
m_2	9	7

It is tempting to state that 9 is the optimal value, and therefore the marriage or coalition $\boldsymbol{m}_2\boldsymbol{f}_1$ should be formed. While 9 is the maximum value, it is not the optimal value. To see this we note that if the individuals stayed single, $\boldsymbol{m}_{22} + \boldsymbol{f}_{11} = \mathbf{10}$. So if they were to form a marriage and then divide up the 9, one of them stands to lose because however they divide up 9, the parts will never add up to 10. One should have as a condition for the solution that: condition 1) $\boldsymbol{m}_{ii} + \boldsymbol{f}_{ii} \geq \boldsymbol{Z}_{ij}$. Using this rule, we find that the values of 9 and 4 are ruled out from forming a partnership because: $\boldsymbol{m}_{22} + \boldsymbol{f}_{11} = \mathbf{5} + \mathbf{5} = \mathbf{10} > \mathbf{9}$; $\boldsymbol{m}_{11} + \boldsymbol{f}_{22} = \mathbf{3} + \mathbf{2} = \mathbf{5} > \mathbf{4}$. Another condition relating to how the product is distributed is implied, namely, that the total output is the sum of the output each mate gets from the marriage, condition 2) $\boldsymbol{m}_{ij} + \boldsymbol{f}_{ij} = \boldsymbol{Z}_{ij}$.

After ruling out the off-diagonal elements, 9 and 4, one can see that the partnership formed from the main-diagonal elements are equalities, namely: $\boldsymbol{m}_{11} + \boldsymbol{f}_{11} = \mathbf{3} + \mathbf{5} = \mathbf{8}$; $\boldsymbol{m}_{22} + \boldsymbol{f}_{22} = \mathbf{5} + \mathbf{2} = 7$. In the language of game theory, we can say that the main-diagonal entries are in the Core, and therefore are optimal solutions.

In a more general setting, we can proceed to find a solution in steps. First, both males and females should agree on a system for ranking the characteristics. For women, we may have a ranking $\boldsymbol{W} = \boldsymbol{W}_1 \ldots \boldsymbol{W}_N$, and for males, a ranking $\boldsymbol{M} = \boldsymbol{M}_1 \ldots \boldsymbol{M}_k$. Then we examine factors such as 1) flexible prices, 2) altruism and love, and 3) falling out of love (Becker and Murphy, 2000: ch. 4).

Market equilibrium with flexible prices assumes an equal number of men and women. Each person's utility depends on his or her own income, and only monogamous relationships are allowed. On the one hand, complementarity dictates one possible solution under perfect positive sorting: "the 'best' woman marries the 'best' man, the next-best woman marries the next-best man, and so on until the worst woman marries the worst man" (ibid.: 32). On the other hand, substitution dictates that "the 'best' of one sex would be matched with the 'worst' of the other if their characteristics are substitutes in the production of marital output." If the market has more women than men, then the demand for men will increase, bidding up their income.

Distortion occurs when non-market characteristics such as altruism and love are considered. They introduce idiosyncratic factors into the model. Becker concludes that "even when characteristics are substitutes rather than complements, love induces positive sorting." Falling out of love is most likely in mismatched marriages. Becker also investigates the efficiency of positive and negative sorting. They are efficient when the second derivative of the production function I are positive and negative, respectively (ibid.: 43-46).

Marriage games have always been looked at from the perspective of coalition games, which were popularized by David Gale and Lloyd Shapley (1962). While we described Becker's solution to the marriage problem in coalition game theory terminologies, he was following an assignment perspective developed by Tjalling Koopman and Martin Beckman (1957). They did not position the problem as an assignment, but rather as a cooperative game (Shubik, 1984: 214).

Basically, the solution will be optimal for the individuals who start the proposal. In the first round, all males make proposals to their favorite females. A female receiving more than one proposal keeps her favorite proposal on a string: she does not make a decision yet, in case she gets a better proposal from someone else. Meanwhile, she rejects her non-favorite proposals. In the second round, the rejected males will propose to their second choices, and the same procedure continues as in the first round. When all the females have received proposals, each girl will marry the person she kept on a string. The solution reached is equivalent to reaching a point in the Core of a game (ibid.: 215). It is also stable in that each female prefers her husband to any other male, whom she has rejected at some point in the game.

In summary, Becker's theory of marriage treats marriage as a firm. In this firm, males and females can hire each other profitably. Rather than market prices, the theory deals with shadow or imaginary prices for the nonmarket variables such as altruism, love, care, and so on. Market solutions, therefore, are not the ones we expect from "institutions for trading, negotiations, contract-making, and enforcement of contracts" in the Walrasian market process (Sen, 1984: 373).

On the Economics of Discrimination

Becker is well-known for his economics of discrimination. His 1955 PhD dissertation was a study of racial discrimination, and two years later he published the first edition of *The Economics of Discrimination* (1971 [1957]). Becker stated that the work developed "a theory of discrimination in the marketplace that supplements the psychologists' and sociologists' analysis of causes with an analysis of economic consequences" (1971 [1957]: 11).

Becker's theory is now well-established in modern labor economics textbooks from the perspective of the demand for labor curve. For neoclassical theory, one can use, say, a Cobb-Douglas production function to construct the labor demand curve. Such a construction of the labor demand curve is given in Figure 1 as the Marginal Product of Labor (MPL) curve.

From Figure 1, if we take the equilibrium wage rate, we can make the argument that where it equals the marginal product of labor (MPL) is equilibrium. For if $w > MPL$, then long queues will form at that firm's employment office, leading to lower w. If $w < MPL$, workers will tend to leave that firm.

Now, Becker built into the framework above what he calls "taste for discrimination," which he measured by a coefficient of discrimination (Becker, 1971: 14). One can look at d from several viewpoints.

- An employer is willing to pay a higher wage, $w(1 + d_i)$, to exclude someone from employment.
- An employee is willing to accept a lower wage, $w_j * (1 - d_j)$, to avoid working near to someone.
- A consumer is willing to pay a higher price, $p(1 + d_k)$, not to be served by someone.

The case for the first viewpoint is illustrated in Figure 1. The discrimination wage is higher than the equilibrium wage, $w(1 + d_i) > w$. The result is a fall in employment of persons discriminated against. Because a colorblind employer can get the job done at the equilibrium wage, an employer who discriminates is likely to make less profit. One is tempted to add to the well-known aphorism on crime: discrimination also does not pay.

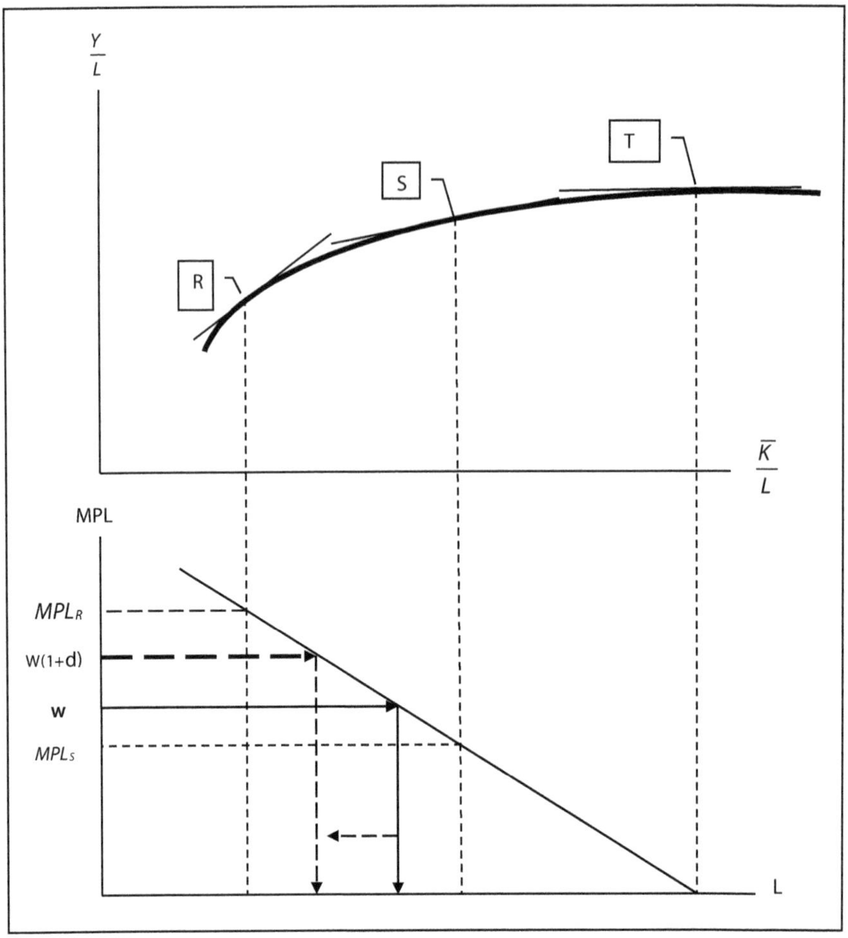

Figure 1 Construction of the MPL Curve.

Upper Diagram show a part of the Total Production Function. With capital K fixed, indicated by a bar of K, labor varies, and the tangent to the curve assume lower slopes as at points R,S, and T, plotted in the diagram below. Given w = MPL, Employment is determined. With discrimination, at w(1+d), the discimination coefficient allows employment to fall.

Human Capital

According to Deirdre McCloskey (1985: 77), the term "human capital" was invented at the University of Chicago by the 1979 Nobel Laureate Theodore Schultz. According to Paul Samuelson, the concept of Human Capital was first pioneered at the University of Chicago by Milton Friedman and

Simon Kuznets (Samuelson, 2011: vol. 7, 863) A major finding in that study was that physician salaries were high because physicians were scarce due to the high level of certification required (ibid.: 863). It was "Becker who laid the full conceptual foundations for the theory of human capital" (Coleman, 1993: 171).

Becker clarified essentially that human capital "cannot be separated from their [humans'] knowledge, skills, health, or values in the way they can be separated from their financial and physical assets" (Becker, 2008). Human Capital theory studies have explained that:

1. High school and college education greatly increases people's income.
2. The opportunity cost of having an education outweighs that of not being educated.
3. Human Capital theory explains the fall in black high school graduates in the 1980s. Such students are mostly from low-income families, and the cut in federal subsidies in that timeframe dissuaded their enrollment.
4. Human Capital theory explains the surge in women's enrollment in college. As women entered the labor force, the demand for varied and higher-level skills led to an increase in their college enrollment.
5. A significant part of Human Capital is on-the-job training.
6. Human Capital increases the influence of families on children in the areas of knowledge, skills, health, values, and behavior, which in turn have a positive influence in broad areas of education, marriage, etc. Statistically, the correlation of the years of schooling between parents and students follows a "regression to the mean" model, where if a parent earns above 20 percent of the mean in his generation, his child may earn 8-10 percent above the mean of his/her generation.

Some anomalous findings about Human Capital in Becker's view include:

- A lack of correlation between the earnings of parents and children. This is surprising since we find a relationship between years of schooling of parents and their children. It was found that if a father earns x percent above the mean of his generation, his son, at a similar age, will earn about half of that percentage above the mean for his own generation.

- There is no relationship between the earnings of grandparents and grandchildren at comparable ages. Earnings relation lives for only three generations. While there may be upward mobility for the first poor generation, there is a downward mobility for the higher up in the third generation.

In general, Human Capital is a broad concept. It includes the impacts of major social variables such as education, health, information, and on-the-job training on a person's utility or well-being. Becker's approach is to look at utility and earnings, costs, inequality, family, growth of the economy, and mortality through the link between parents and children, and then build up effects on the macro level.

By studying Human Capital as a durable good, one can embed it in an extended view of the standard utility and production function of microeconomics and make predictions about utility and output. Much of the productivity of the modern economy cannot be explained in standard neoclassical growth models by the use of only physical inputs of labor and capital. The contribution of Human Capital to productivity is about 3 to 4 percent higher than the contribution of non-human capital. Human Capital explains the residual growth of income in the United States after the contribution of physical capital and labor are taken into account.

Human Capital also underscores the importance of education in economic development (Becker, 1993: xxi). Education, training, skills, and health are capital embodied in humans. This capital is mobile as labor is mobile, that is, it cannot be separated from the owner. Capital and labor are subject to diminishing returns. Therefore, a nation that wants continuous growth should pursue "expansion of scientific and technical knowledge that raises the productivity of labor and other inputs in production." For instance, from 1929 to 1982, increased schooling for the average worker accounted for approximately 25 percent of the rise in per capita income in the US (ibid.: 16-24).

In his 1964 study of Human Capital, Becker discussed returns to specific training costs (see Akerlof, 2005: 291). This required some kind of bargaining between employer and employee—a game theory. Consider a repeated bargaining situation between a worker and a firm. Let's say they reach an agreement where $\boldsymbol{I}$ is the general level of training, $\boldsymbol{c}(\boldsymbol{I})$ is the cost to the firm for the general training provided, $\boldsymbol{f}(\boldsymbol{I})$ is the output to be produced from such an agreement, and $v(I)$ is the wage the worker can get if he quits and begins working for another firm. The first-best level of general training will be the ***maximum of*** $f(I) - c(I)$, which will be less than the efficient level of general training provided under the competition (Muthoo, 1999: 320).

Much of Human Capital is produced in the family and not in the firm. A theoretical difference between family and firm regarding Human Capital is that children grow up and parents may or may not get a return on their investment in the child, unlike profits accruing on an investment in a firm.

On the whole, wealthier parents will help children to invest in Human Capital directly. They tend to teach their kids when they are young, or they can afford to hire teachers to teach them. Children from poor families are less likely to go to college. That may help explain their poorer schooling or lower IQs, and associated low earnings. With Becker's model, one can begin to analyze these phenomena using a production function and utility function for the family.

One question about Becker's contribution for the future relates to Barbara Bergmann's skepticism about Becker's theory on the persistence of race and sex discrimination (Szenberg and Ramrattan, 2004). Becker's theory predicts that employers who discriminate would not survive among those who do not discriminate. Competition will drive the discriminators out because they will overpay their employees, which will show up in higher prices for their products. Bergmann asserted that wage setting is determined by status.

In conclusion, Becker has extended the standard microeconomics paradigm to include social capital apart from the usual market quantities and prices. While this expansion of the micro-apparatus is welcomed by some, others greet it with much skepticism. We have already mentioned Sen's concern with "self" goals. We may also question the metaphor of treating children as durable capital. From the moral point of view, McCloskey (1997: 115) wrote that Becker singles out only Prudence for analysis from among the sets of variables that Adam Smith advocated for moral economic analysis, which were Courage, Temperance, Prudence, Justice, and Love.

References

Becker, Gary S. (2004). *Lectures on human capital.* Retrieved from https://www.youtube.com/watch?v=QajILZ3S2RE&list=PL9334868E7A821E2A.

———. (2014, Jul. 26). Human capital. *The concise encyclopedia of economics.* 2008. Library of Economics and Liberty. Retrieved from http://www.econlib.org/library/Enc/HumanCapital.html.

———. (1993, Jun.). Nobel lecture: The economic way of looking at behavior. *The Journal of Political Economy,* 101(3), 385-409.

———. (1992, Fall). Habits, addictions, and traditions. *Kyklos,* 45(3), 327-345.

———. (1996). *Accounting for tastes.* Cambridge, MA: Harvard University Press.

———. (1981, Feb.). Altruism in the family and selfishness in the market place. *Economica, New Series,* 48(189), 1-15.

———. (1976). *The economic approach to human behavior.* Chicago: University of Chicago Press.

———. (1993). *Human capital: A theoretical and empirical analysis with special reference to education* (3rd ed.). Chicago: University of Chicago Press.

———. (1971). *The economics of discrimination* (2nd ed.). Chicago: University of Chicago Press.

Ben-Porath, Y. (1982). Economics and the family: Match or mismatch? A review of Becker's *A Treatise on the Family. Journal of Economic Literature,* 20, 52-64.

Coleman, J. S. (1993). The impact of Gary Becker's work on sociology. *Acta Sociologica,* 36, 169-178.

Davis, M. D. (1993). *Game theory: A nontechnical introduction* (revised ed.). New York: Basic Books.

Friedman, M., & Kuznets, S. (1945). *Income from independent professional practice.* New York: National Bureau of Economic Research.

Gale, D., & Shapley, L. S. (1962). College admission and the stability of marriage. *American Mathematical Monthly,* 69, 9-15.

Gibbons, R. (1992). *Game theory for applied economists.* Princeton: Princeton University Press.

Koopman, T. C., & Beckmann, M. (1956, Jan.). Assignment problems and the location of economic activities. *Econometrica,* 25(1), 53-76.

Levitt, S. D., & Dubner, S. J. (2005). *Freakonomics.* New York: Harper Collins.

McCloskey, D. (1997, Winter). One small step for Gary. *Eastern Economic Journal,* 23(1), 113-116.

———. (1985). *The rhetoric of economics.* Madison: University of Wisconsin Press.

Meza, D., & Osborne, M. (1980). *Problems in price theory.* Chicago: University of Chicago Press.

Muthoo, A. (1999). *Bargaining theory with applications.* Cambridge: Cambridge University Press.

Ramrattan, L., & Szenberg, M. (2007). Discrimination, wage, by race. In *International encyclopedia of social sciences* (2nd ed.). London and New York: Macmillan Reference.

Samuelson, P. A. (2011). *The collected scientific papers of Paul A. Samuelson.* J. Murray (Ed.). Cambridge, MA: MIT Press.

Sen, A. (2002). *Rationality and freedom.* Cambridge, MA: Harvard University Press.

———. (1984). *Resources, values and development.* Cambridge, MA: Harvard University Press.

Shubik, M. (1984). *A game-theoretic approach to political economy* (vol. II). Cambridge, MA: MIT Press.

Stigler, G. J. (1982). *The economist as preacher and other essays.* Chicago: University of Chicago Press.

Szenberg, M., & Ramrattan, L. (Eds.). (2004). *Reflections of eminent economists.* Foreword by K. Arrow. Northampton, MA: Edward Elgar Publishers.

PART IX

GAME THEORISTS

Robert Aumann

Robert Aumann

Introduction

Fragments of Robert Aumann's life and work philosophy have already taken form in various biography pieces and interviews in the literature. In this paper, we bring some unity to those sketches that are already in the public domain. Some of the major sources of information include the materials that were offered to the Nobel Committee, an interview with *Macroeconomic Dynamics,* information contained in his two volumes of collected papers published by MIT Press (which contain his work on game theory up to 1995), and sketches of his background in different places including his website.

Background

Aumann was born in Frankfurt am Main, Germany, in 1930. Like many Jewish families, his emigrated to New York in 1938, fleeing Nazi persecution. Leaving everything behind, his parents were still able to educate Aumann and his brother at Yeshiva elementary and high schools in New York City. Aumann proceeded to earn a bachelor's degree in mathematics from the City College of New York in 1950 and a PhD in mathematics from MIT in 1955. His doctoral dissertation was a specialization on Knot theory, entitled *Asphericity of Alternating Linkages,* under the supervision of George Whitehead, Jr., an algebraic topologist.

Aumann's interest in mathematics began in high school—the Rabbi Jacob Joseph Yeshiva on the lower East Side of New York City, where a teacher named Joseph Gansler used to gather the students around his desk and expound on geometry, theorems, and proofs.

Aumann did a bit of soul-searching when finishing high school, contemplating whether to become a Talmudic scholar or to study secular subjects at a university. For a while he did both: rising at 6:15 a.m. to take the subway for more than an hour to college, studying calculus for an hour, then returning to the yeshiva for most of the morning, only to go back up to City College at 139th Street and study there until 10 p.m. After a semester of this, he made the hard decision to quit the Yeshiva and study mathematics.

City College in the late 1940s boasted a very active group of mathematics students, who had their own "mathematics table" in the cafeteria. Between classes, the students would sit and have ice cream and discuss things like the topology of bagels. Aumann took a course on functions of real variables—measure, integration, etc.—with the famous logician Emil Post, which consisted entirely of Post assigning exercises and then calling on the students to present the solutions on the blackboard.

As an undergraduate, Aumann read a lot about analytic and algebraic number theory. He has said that number theory is fascinating because it uses very deep methods to attack problems that are in some sense very "natural" and simple to formulate. A schoolchild can understand Fermat's last theorem, but it took extremely deep methods to prove it. A schoolchild can understand what a prime number is, but understanding the distribution of prime numbers requires the theory of functions of a complex variable; it is closely related to the Riemann hypothesis, whose very formulation requires at least two or three years of university mathematics, and which remains unproven to this day. Another interesting aspect of number theory was that it was absolutely useless—mathematics at its purest.

Aumann did his dissertation on knots, which he has described as similar to number theory in the simplicity of the problems. Knot theory was attractive to Aumann because it is very difficult to prove anything at all about knots; it requires very deep methods of algebraic topology. And, like number theory, knot theory was "totally, totally useless."

Aumann has said that his dissertation had no connection with game theory. But while there is no direct connection, "there is a sort of allegorical connection. In Hebrew, the word for knot (*kesher*) is the same as that for relationship—as in the relationship between people. In English, too, we refer to 'ties' between individuals, companies, and nations" (Aumann, 1995: 161-162).

In his autobiography, Aumann tells the story of how fifty years after he published his dissertation:

> The phone in my flat rings. My grandson Yakov Rosen, who is in the second year of medical school, is on the line. "Grandpa," he says, "can I pick your brain? We are studying knots. I don't understand the material, and think that our lecturer does not understand it either. For example, what exactly are 'linking numbers'?" I asked him why he was studying knots. And what did knots have to do with medicine? "Well," he said, "sometimes the DNA in a cell gets knotted up. Depending on the characteristics of the knot, this may lead to cancer. So, we have to understand knots." I was completely bowled over. Fifty years later, the "absolutely useless"—the "purest of the pure"—is taught in the second year of medical school, and my grandson is studying it. (2010)

After graduating from MIT in 1955, Aumann did his postdoctoral study at Princeton, where he gained an interest in game theory while working with a group of operational research specialists.

Aumann's life was also heavily influenced by a strong spiritual desire to return to Israel. In his biographical sketch for the Nobel committee, Aumann wrote: "In our central prayer, which we recite three times a day, we ask the Lord to 'return to Jerusalem, your city in mercy, and rebuild it and dwell therein.'" When the State of Israel was established in 1948, Aumann and his brother committed to eventually resettling there. In 1953 Aumann met an Israeli girl, Esther Schlesinger, who was visiting the United States. They were married in Brooklyn in April 1955. The following fall, Aumann took up a position as instructor of mathematics at the Hebrew University of Jerusalem, and has been there ever since. He and Esther enjoyed forty-four years of marriage before Esther's death from ovarian cancer in October 1998. In November 2005, about a week before being awarded the Nobel Prize in Economics, Aumann married Esther's widowed sister, Batya Cohn.

In 1990, Aumann helped found the Center for Rationality at the Hebrew University, an interdisciplinary research center focused on game theory, with members from over a dozen different departments within the university. Today, he is professor emeritus at the Center for Rationality.

Aumann has discussed the two major aspects of his life—academic and religious—and explained that they are not contradictory, but rather orthogonal. In a 2005 interview in *Macroeconomic Dynamics*, he said that "belief is an important part of religion, certainly; but in science we have certain ways of thinking about the world, and in religion we have different ways of thinking about the world. Those two things coexist side by side without conflict."

Economic Contributions

Aumann stepped into economics through game theory and continuum analysis. He received the Nobel Memorial Prize in Economic Sciences in 2005 for "having enhanced our understanding of conflict and cooperation through game-theory analysis." Game theory is of interest to economists because traditional economic tools, such as minimizing costs or maximizing profits, do not yield unique solutions, such as in cases of oligopoly, where rivalry among participants is of paramount importance. The attempt at solutions started with Augustin Cournot, whose work appeared in 1838 and was first translated into English in 1897. Cournot introduced a behavioral assumption for the solution of the oligopoly model, which John Nash was able to improve upon for game theory. In his article *What is Game Theory Trying to Accomplish?*, Aumann elaborated upon "four of the most important solution concepts of game theory—the Nash equilibrium, the core, the N-M stable set (or 'solution') and the Shapley value" (Aumann, 2000: vol. 1, 18).

In a joint paper in 1985 with Michael Maschler, Aumann was able to answer a difficult passage in the Babylonian Talmud, Ketubot 93a, applying the concept of *nucleolus* to a bankruptcy problem. The problem was to account for the distribution of debt in a bankruptcy situation from the given value of the estate. "When E = 100, the estate equals the smallest debt . . . equal division then makes good sense. The case E = 300 appears based on the different—and inconsistent principle of proportional division. The figures for E = 200 look mysterious. . . . We obtain . . . an explicit characterization of the nucleolus of the coalitional game that is naturally associated with this problem" (ibid.: vol. 2, 136). The table below illustrates the case.

TABLE 1: Distribution of Debt in Bankruptcy

			Debt	
		100	200	300
	100	33.5	33.5	33.5
Estate	200	50	75	75
	300	50	100	150

Three broad areas of game theory characterize Aumann's work: repeated games; knowledge, rationality, and equilibrium; and perfect competition (Hart, 2006: 185). In the remainder of this paper, we will provide the gist of the three areas for which Aumann is mostly cited.

On Repeated Games

Repeated games model the psychological, informational side of ongoing relationships. The theory predicts phenomena like cooperation, altruism, trust, punishment, and revenge. Repetition is a kind of enforcement mechanism; agreements are enforced by "punishing" deviators in subsequent stages.

In the background of repeated games is an *n*-person game in strategic form, *G* This game can be played for a finite or infinite sequence. In a finite sequence, the players will play their dominant strategy in the last (n^{th}) game, and recursively, they will use their dominant strategy for the n-1, n-2, games etc. If the game is played infinitely, however, there is no last game, and a player may start playing strategies early in the game to influence future outcomes (see Waldman and Jensen, 2006: 214).

We can collect an infinite series of play of the game *G* under the label G^*, called a supergame. To this supergame, Aumann attributes Theorem I: *The payoff vectors to Nash equilibrium points in the supergame G^* are the feasible individually rational payoffs in the game G.* (Aumann, 2000: vol. 1, 412-413 [italics original]).

In his Nobel laureate lecture, entitled *War and Peace,* Aumann discussed his contributions to repeated games and their relation to wars and other conflicts such as strikes. In a prisoners' dilemma situation, we usually find that a cooperate-cooperate strategy is mutually beneficial to the players. This outcome can be made stable if each player believes that if he or she cheats on that cooperation, the alternative outcome will be inferior.

Cooperative outcomes are achievable through agreement (contracts that are enforceable). Their relation to repeated games is that repetition serves as an enforcement mechanism.

> People are much more cooperative in a long-term relationship. They know that there is a tomorrow, in which inappropriate behavior will be punished (in the future). A businessman who cheats his customers may make a short-term profit, but he will not stay in business long.... What is maintaining the equilibrium in these games is the *threat of punishment*. If you like, call it

> "MAD"—mutually assured destruction, the motto of the cold war. One caveat is necessary to make this work. The discount rate must not be too high. Even if it is anything over 10%—if $1 in a year is worth less than 90 cents today—then cooperation is impossible. . . . I don't mean just the monetary discount rate, what you get in the bank, I mean the personal, subjective discount rate. For repetition to engender cooperation, the players must not be too eager for immediate results. The present, the now, must not be too important. If you want peace now, you may well never get peace. But if you have time—if you can wait—that changes the whole picture; *then* you may get peace now. It's one of those paradoxical, upside-down insights of game theory, and indeed much of science. (Aumann, 2005)

Knowledge, Rationality, and Equilibrium

Since the time of Plato, people have equivocated about the epistemology of knowledge and belief. Aumann probed how "common knowledge" can provide the information we need to solve a game. In his 1976 article "Agreeing to Disagree," he wrote that "when we say that an event is 'common knowledge,' we mean more than just that both 1 and 2 know it; we require also that 1 knows that 2 knows it, 2 knows that 1 knows it, 1 knows that 2 knows that 1 knows it, and so on" (Aumann, 2000: vol 1, 593-596). In this article, Aumann focused on the "common knowledge" of strategies, information, and preferences players possess when they make economic choices. It seemed to him that if two players have "common knowledge" about, say, the probability assessment of an event, then the assessment should be the same.

"A person's behavior is rational if it is in his best interests, given his information" (Aumann, 2005: 351). In this sense, war can be rational. "In the long years of the cold war between the US and the Soviet Union, what prevented 'hot' war was that bombers carrying nuclear weapons were in the air 24 hours a day, 365 days a year. Disarming would have led to war" (ibid.: 353). In general, "Rationality is just one of the relevant factors affecting human behavior; no theory based on this one factor alone can be expected to yield reliable predictions. . . . If our theory appears not to work, we don't lose any sleep . . . we say blandly 'here something else was at work'" (Aumann, 2000: vol. 1, 12-13). In the case of war, "the bottom line is—again—that we should start studying war, from all viewpoints, for its own sake. Try to understand what makes it happen. Pure, basic science. That may lead, eventually, to peace. The piecemeal, case-based approach has not worked too well up to now" (Aumann, 2005: 352).

Aumann made various contributions on equilibrium solutions. The common knowledge solution based on the agreement arrangement has found application in the financial literature. Aumann refined the successful Nash equilibrium to the concepts of a strong equilibrium, and correlated equilibrium: "a strong equilibrium of a strategic game as a profile of strategies for which there is no coalition S whose players can, by changing their strategies, raise the payoffs of all the members of S, while the players outside S do not change their strategies" (ibid.: 322).

People can base the choices they make on weather conditions, information in the news, and other random variables. A correlated equilibrium gives the optimal choices under those conditions, and decision rules. "A correlated strategy vector is a probability distribution on the set of all pure strategy *vectors,* just as a mixed strategy is a probability distribution on individual strategies" (Aumann, 2000: vol. 1, 322).

Perfect Competition

Perfect competition is the market structure that idealizes the way the market mechanism works. It works best when no economic agent exercises market power in the sense that he or she can influence the equilibrium price or output. The assumption of a large number of economic agents guards against such market power, and since the time of Adam Smith, the father of perfect competition, mathematical economists have been trying to model such market outcomes.

Two early mathematical models of perfect competition are credited to Cournot (1838) and Leon Walras (1874). Cournot used the calculus of functions to explain competition between two sellers. He was concerned with increasing the number of the agents to achieve perfect competition. Walras built on Cournot's work to establish a state of general equilibrium for the economy (Walras, 1874: 372). While Cournot generalizes his results from monopoly through duopoly to unlimited competition, Walras starts with "unlimited competition as a general case, and then . . . [works] toward monopoly as a special case" (ibid.: 440).

The next pertinent development was by Francis Ysidro Edgeworth (1881), who developed the Edgeworth Box to analyze competition. His model is characterized by two traders with given preferences and endowments. In a process of re-contracting, the traders will eliminate areas inside the box that each can block, such as areas below their indifference curves. This process will bring them to a lens-shaped area formed by their indifference curves going through the coordinate points of their endowment. If agents are willing to rearrange trade in the lens-shaped area by giving up some of one commodity for the other agent's commodity, then unblocked points of equilibrium can be reached. Such unblocked points in the lens shape form the core. They are tangent points of the two players' indifference curves through which we can pass a hyper-plane of prices to achieve Walrasian equilibrium.

Based on the work of Martin Shubik, Gerard Debreu and Herbert Scarf were able to capitalize on Edgeworth's expanded economy, which consists of "2n consumers divided into two types; everyone of the same type having identical preferences and identical resources . . . as n becomes larger more and more allocations are ruled out, and eventually only the competitive allocations remain" (Debreau, 1983: 152). Their economy consists of m-types of individuals and r-replications, i.e., different individuals of the same type. For a typical replication, q, and the ith, an allocation would be $x_{q,i}$. Individuals will have insignificant influence on market outcome and the sense that their endowment e_i would be small relative to the total endowment $r\left[\sum_{i=1}^{m}(e_i)\right]$. In terms of demand and supply, we will have $\sum_{\substack{q=1\ldots r\\ i=1..m}} x_{q,i} = r\left[\sum_{i=1}^{m}(e_i)\right]$. The key to Debreu and Scarf's theory lies in their equal treatment assumption, namely that identical agents will have the same allocation, i. e., $x_{q,i} = x_{q',i}$ for all q and q'. In a situation where the allocations are not equal, a coalition of m-individuals with the worse allocations will block the allocations. In the Walrasian case, each consumer of type i will face the same price and receive the same endowment and the same allocation. We will have an allocation in the l-commodity and m-type of consumer space, an allocation vector that is in the core, C'. Also, the coalition in the core for $r + 1$is contained in the core for r because a blocking coalition in the r-replicated economy will be available for blocking in an economy with $r + 1$ replicated economy. As the number of replication increases, the intersection of the ontologically decreasing cores will be equal to the Walrasian system. In set theory terms, the Hausdorff distance between the Walrasian equilibrium and the core will then tend to zero as r tends to infinity.

The above description of perfect competition in the literature serves as a background for Aumann's contributions. He broke away from the tradition of a replicated economy toward a continuum of players, introducing a new paradigm for looking at perfect competition. This approach harks back to a paper by John Milnor and Lloyd Shapley entitled "Oceanic Games," published in 1978. The theory dealt with "a small number of relatively 'large' players, who swim in an 'ocean'—or continuum—of tiny, individually insignificant players. An example is a corporation with a few large stockholders and an 'ocean' of small ones" (Aumann, 2000: vol. 2, 167). "The idea of a continuum of traders may seem outlandish to the reader. Actually, it is no stranger than a continuum of prices or of strategies or a continuum of 'particles.' In fluid mechanics . . . the purpose of adopting the continuous approximation is to make available the powerful and elegant methods of the branch of mathematics called 'analysis,' in a situation where treatment by finite methods would be much more difficult or even hopeless" (ibid.: 161).

The continuum model takes measure theory as its basis, which is not possible to develop in this forum of communication. Rather, Aumann gave an intuitive difference between the traditional approach and the continuum. The traditional approach described above starts out with a finite set of agents, numbered from 1, 2, $\cdots$, n while the latter will use a closed interval or real numbers denoted by [0, 1]. While the traditional approach will deal with the sum of economic concepts such as endowment and allocations, the continuum approach will replace the sum with the integral. Technically, instead of doing analysis "for all" agents, we do analysis for "almost every" agent in the continuum model.

In 1964, Aumann published the "Markets with a Continuum of Traders" in *Econometrica* (1964: 39–50). The set of traders, T, is the closed unit interval, [0, 1]. Each trader has preferences, $\succ_i$, an initial assignment (endowment), i, and an allocation, x. For a non-atomic economy the traders must be uncountable or infinite to result in a continuum of traders. Non-atomic means there is a "continuum of sides, a large number of players" (ibid.: 42). In other words, there are only small players. This is in contrast with the Atoms result, where we find some large players called atoms. "An example of a non-atomic game is a large economy, consisting of small consumers and small businesses only, without large corporations or government interference. Another example is an election, modeled as a situation where no individual can affect the outcome. Even the 2000 US presidential election is a non-atomic game—no single voter, even in Florida, could have affected the outcome. (The people who did affect the outcome were the Supreme Court judges.) In a non-atomic game, large coalitions can affect the outcome, but individual players cannot" (ibid.: 45).

If for the set of traders, T, we make set, a, of all subsets, S_i, in a, that is $S_i \supset a$, then the union of all S_i is also in a, that is $\bigcup_i S_i \supset a$. Let $v(S) = \# S / \# A > 0$, the fraction of the number of coalitions in a, therefore, $v(A) = \# A / \# = 1$. Analogous to the previous results, we now have $\int_T x = \int_T i$ for unblocked coalitions. If a coalition can block an allocation, then that coalition can take its own resources, $\int_S i$ and redistribute them among its members, say $\int_S y$, in such a way that almost everywhere in S_i, $x_a \prec_a y_a$. The set of unblocked allocations forms the core. Aumann's theorem makes the core of the equilibrium allocations equivalent in the sense that *the core coincides with the set of equilibrium allocations.* The equilibrium allocation is "a pair of price vectors p and an allocation x, such that for almost every trader t, x(t) is maximal with respect to (the agents' preference) . . . An equilibrium allocation is an allocation x for which there exists a price vector p such that (p, x) is a competitive equilibrium" (ibid.: 48).

The research encapsulated in "Existence of Competitive Equilibria in Markets with a Continuum of Traders" (1966) indicates that "all markets with a continuum of traders possess competitive equilibria." His 1975 article "Values of Markets with a Continuum of Traders" demonstrates the equivalence of competitive outcomes with Shapley values, which is different from the competitive versus core equivalence concept. This value equivalence theorem holds that "in a non-atomic market with uniform smoother preferences, the set of value allocations coincide with the set of competitive allocations" (Aumann, 2000: 222).

Conclusion

From abstract Knot theory to applied game theory, Aumann's contributions have furthered research into the problem of economic solutions to the ordinary business of life. Many researchers have built on his models to address problems not only about war and peace, but how to calculate reactions among different players where behavioral assumptions and norms can facilitate conflict or rival solutions.

In his scientific work, Aumann strove for understanding and not for the absolute truth. His studies focused mainly on relations "between different ideas, relations between different phenomena; relations between ideas and phenomena. Rather than asking 'How does this phenomenon work?' we ask, 'How does this phenomenon resemble others with which we are familiar?' Rather than asking 'Does this idea make sense?' we ask, 'How does this idea resemble other ideas?'" (Aumann, 2005: 736).

References

Allen, G. G. D., & Bowley, A. L. (1935). *Family expenditure: A study of its variations*. London: Staples Press.

Aumann, R. J. (2010, Aug. 5). Autobiography. Nobelprize.org. Retrieved from http://nobelprize.org/nobel_prizes/economics/laureates/2005/aumann.ht.

———. (2005, Dec. 8). War and peace. Nobel Prize lecture.

———. (2000). *Collected Papers* (vol. 1-2). Cambridge, MA: MIT Press.

———. (1987). Correlated equilibrium as an extension of Bayesian rationality. *Econometrica*, 55, 1-18.

———. (1974). Subjectivity and correlation in randomized strategies. *Journal of Mathematical Economics*, 1, 67-96

Cournot, A. (1963 [1938]). *Researches into the mathematical principles of the theory of wealth*. Homewood, IL: Richard D. Irwin.

Davis, M., & Maschler, M. (1965). The kernel of a cooperative game. *Naval Research Logistics Quarterly*, 12, 223-259.

Debreu, G., & Scarf, H. (1963). A limit theorem of the core of an economy. *International Economic Review*, 4, 235-236. Reprinted in G. Debreu, (1983). *Mathematical economics* (151-162). Cambridge: Cambridge University Press.

Edgeworth, F. Y. (1967 [1881]). *Mathematical psychics*. New York: Augustus M. Kelley Publishers.

Hart, S. (2006). Robert Aumann's game and economic theory. *Scandinavian Journal of Economics*, 108(2), 185–211.

———. (2005). An interview with Robert Aumann. *Macroeconomic Dynamics,* 9, 683–740.

Milgrom, P., & Stokey, N. (1982). Information, trade and common knowledge. *Journal of Economic Theory,* 26, 177-227.

Milnor, J. W., & Shapley, L. S. (1978). Values of large games II: Ocean games. *Mathematics of Operation Research,* 3, 290-307.

O'Neill, B. (1982). A problem of rights arbitration from the Talmud. *Mathematical Social Science,* 2, 345-371.

Shapley, L. S. (1953). Stochastic games. *Proceedings of the National Academy of Sciences,* 39, 327-332.

Shubik, M. (1959). Edgeworth market games. In A. W. Tucker & R. D. Luce (Eds.), *Contributions to the theory of games IV* (267-278). Princeton: Princeton University Press.

Waldman, D. E., & Jensen, E. J. (2006). *Industrial organization: Theory and practice* (3rd ed.). New York: Pearson-Addison Wesley.

Walras, L. (1969 [1874]). *Elements of pure economics.* New York: Augustus M. Kelley Publishers.

PART X

SOCIO-ECONOMIC THEORISTS

Robert Heilbroner

Robert Heilbroner

Introduction

Robert Heilbroner, best known for taking a dismal science and making it come to life, died on January 4, 2005, at the age of 85. He was professor emeritus of the New School University in New York City.

Heilbroner went to Harvard University in 1936, where he intended to study writing, but came under the influence of Joseph Schumpeter, Alvin Hansen, Edward Mason, Wassily Leontief, and other economists. At Harvard, Paul Sweezy was his tutor, of whom he later wrote: "I rather doubt that Paul was ever aware of his voice within my head, but I am certain he knew of such a connection with many others, like himself in search of a perspective from which one could better grasp the world" (Heilbroner, 2000: 53). Heilbroner graduated in 1940, *summa cum laude*, in economics, history, and government.

Heilbroner later did his graduate work at the New School under the unwavering mind of Adolph Lowe. He was clear about Lowe's influence on his thought, and has dedicated almost all of his work to him. Lowe held the view that, 1) traditional economics has lost the predictive power it once had under simple conditions; and 2) traditional economics must be replaced by political economy with an "instrumental" twist, i.e. "laws and rules which permit us to predict what means are suitable for the attainment of a given end" (Hutchison, 1970: 445). Although Heilbroner admitted Lowe's influence on him, he remained an independent thinker. For instance, he told of how Lowe advised against starting work on *The Worldly Philosophers*, but later encouraged him after he had seen a few chapters (Heilbroner, 1999: 8).

Heilbroner came to perceive economics broadly. In his discussion of capitalism, he wrote: "I cover a wide range of material: anthropological investigations into early civilization; psychologically based speculations with regard to 'human nature'; various aspects of political and sociological theory; and of course a good deal of general and sometimes quite specific history" (Heilbroner, 1985: 19). According to Edward Nell, "Heilbroner falls clearly into that set of economists, mostly classical, but including the leading American institutionalists, who see economics as the analysis of the engine that drives the progress of history. . . . Economics therefore has two tasks, both prefigured in Adam Smith: to understand the logic of capital accumulation, and to comprehend the nature of markets" (Nell, 1993: 2). Therefore, we find that in his PhD dissertation from the New School, *The Making of Economic Society* (1963), he went beyond the traditional exposition of micro- and macroeconomics, expounding on the APPSH (anthropology, psychology, politics, sociology, and history) forces behind capitalism. His famous book *The Worldly Philosophers,* documenting the life and work of major economists, including Karl Marx, was a best seller, selling approximately 4 million copies. The fruits of his erudition came out in W. W. Rostow's review of his book *The Nature and Logic of Capitalism,* in which he wrote that Heilbroner's ideas belong "at the center of political economy in the century and a half from David Hume to Alfred Marshall" (Rostow, 1986: 577). Only a few people can claim such stature in that classical span.

What Heilbroner gained from the classics, he transmitted to us in palatable doses in 20 books and over 100 articles. Yet, he did not feel that he had to commit to the belief of a particular school of thought. He read every work—neoclassical, classical, Marxian—and showed interest in both their literary and mathematical forms. In his popular seminar on Adam Smith, he wanted all the current theories discussed, and no limit was placed on the time to get it done. In an oral PhD defense, he asked that the mathematical forms of Smith's, David Ricardo's, and Lowe's growth models be presented, and he asked questions to make sure that the verbal content of their exposition was adequately represented. Heilbroner perceived capitalism as a research program punctuated by progressive and degenerative phases. At times, he talked as if a paradigmatic shift has taken place. This is the point of view we wish to take as we examine his major works, starting with methodology.

Heilbroner on Methodology

Heilbroner's methodological thought is latent in *The Worldly Philosophers,* and made explicit in his subsequent works, especially his 1973 *Social Research* article. We will lay out his methodology as a prelude to his other contributions to the literature.

The Worldly Philosophers

The Worldly Philosophers was first published in 1953. Heilbroner explained that the title could have been "The Money Philosophers" or "The Great Economists" (Heilbroner, 1999: 8). It is a sample of economists who "embrace in a scheme of philosophy the most worldly of all of man's activities—his drive for wealth" (ibid.: 16). The central theme of the book is the "search for the order and meaning of social history that lies at the heart of economics" (ibid.: 16). We study not "principles" but "history-shaping ideas," for the great economists have discovered a "welter of social patterns" from which we find and trace "the roots of our own society" (ibid.: 16–17). The sample of great economists we meet starts with Smith and ends with Schumpeter.

The methodological view of *The Worldly Philosophers* is not about Smith's maximization of individuals in society, Marx's dialectical materialism, or John Maynard Keynes' government role in capitalistic society. The works of Smith, Marx, and Keynes are central in the book, but the underlying methodological view builds on Schumpeter's view of a "vision" in the history of economics. Methodologically, the word "vision" conveys a "virtually identical" idea as Imre Lakatos' idea of the "hard core" (Blaug, 1983: 37). The "hard core" is composed of ideas that scientists are not willing to give up. They are much like one's cherished beliefs. Schumpeter distinguished "vision" from "analysis." Vision is "preanalytic." It precedes logic. It is necessary in that it is "a process from which we cannot escape." It is on the "value" side as opposed to the "positive" side of thought because it deals with the way in which we "wish" to see things, whereas "analytic work . . . embodies in the picture of things as we see them" (Heilbroner, 1999: 308).

Heilbroner developed the notion of Schumpeter's "vision" in a unique direction. His first step gives "an illustration of which Schumpeter himself was almost certainly unaware," which relates to a distinction between consumption and investment output (ibid.: 308). Keynes attracted attention away from Schumpeter by this distinction, dominating economic thought in the first half of the twentieth century. Heilbroner's second and more fundamental step from Schumpeter's vision downplayed the prominence of the marginal revolution, in the sense that the names of Stanley Jevons, Leon Walras, and Carl Menger do not have a central place among *The Worldly Philosophers*. Here we can use John Hicks' term "catallactic" to mark the difference. It means a "vision" of economic life out of the theory of exchange, as the classics had done out of the social product (Hicks, 1983: 10).

> Schumpeter . . . judges economists by their contribution to economics in the catallactic sense. It is the great catallactists (Jevons, Walras, and Menger, together with their predecessors such as [Jacques] Turgot and [Jean-Baptiste] Say) who receive particular praise; while others, whom most would regard as greater names, such as Smith and Ricardo, Marshall and [Arthur Cecil] Pigou are treated somewhat grudgingly. Why does he write them down? Because they belong to the other party. (Hicks, 1981: 238)

We now turn to some other steps Heilbroner takes in the development of Schumpeter's "vision."

Heilbroner links his concept of "vision" with history. For their discussion of the history of economics, both Schumpeter and Heilbroner look at history. For Schumpeter, "the ocean of facts has innumerable different aspects which call for innumerable different modes of approach" (Machlup, 1978: 464). He would therefore allow the "historical method in business-cycle analysis" and the "mathematical method in economic theory" (ibid.: 461). For Heilbroner, "the histories of social change, of science or literature or even fashion—in short most of the innumerable histories that can be written about America—require for their full understanding a grasp of the profound economic transformation through which America has passed" (Heilbroner, 1977: 3). He described the choice of transformation thus:

> Its cast of characters features business leaders, working men and women, inventors, not the usual presidents, generals, or patriots. Its plot ignores the great epic of American Democratic developments and dwells instead on the less familiar currents of economics expansion and conflict. Technical processes,

> such as steel-making, play a role as central as those usually accorded in political processes such as lawmaking. Enormous events like the Civil War appear only in the background; whereas matters that we ordinarily hardly bother to notice, such as J. P. Morgan's purchase of the Carnegie Steel Company, suddenly loom very large. (ibid.: 2)

On the other hand, Heilbroner does not have a proper role for mathematics. He applauds the use of mathematics as an expositional tool, such as in the explanation of growth theories.

Heilbroner's concept of a "vision" is not an invariant view in society, but a "changing concept" (ibid.: 9). The US has undergone three episodic changes recently—the depression of the 1930s, the growth period of 1945 to the mid-1960s, and the modern period, characterized by the "absence of interest in the developmental tendencies of economic society" (Heilbroner, 1990: 1098, 1101, 1106). Recognizing that the periodization of history is arbitrary, Heilbroner looks for the vision from the thought of representative spokesmen of the period. The "vision" in *The Worldly Philosophers* is "a thread that would tie together its chapters more firmly than a mere chronology of remarkable men with interesting ideas" (Heilbroner, 1999: 9). Heilbroner continues to look for the "vision" from the spokesmen, or, worldly philosophers "whose outlook I shall seek to justify as representing the most significant views of the time span in question. In all 'periods' of capitalist developments few voices attain commanding presence" (ibid.: 1098). The "vision" that the spokesmen espouse is grounded in history, and is not always understood. "If current events strike us as all surprise and shock it is because we cannot see these events in a meaningful framework. If the future seems to us a kind of limbo, a repository of endless surprises, it is because we no longer see it as the expected culmination of the past, as the growing edge of the present. More than anything else, our disorientation before the future reveals a loss of our historic identity, an incapacity to grasp our historic situation" (Heilbroner, 1960: 15).

In summary, what we get from *The Worldly Philosophers* is a view of economics framed, on the one hand, by the term "worldly," and, on the other hand, by speculative theories or models of a sample of social philosophers. Among his virtuous exposition of these two concepts is an appraisal of their performance over time. He would extend and restrict this vision over time to accommodate topical problems, and show how progress or decline were unfolding.

A Representation of His Value Judgment View

Heilbroner advanced a methodology that links values. "I want economics to make a virtue of necessity, exposing for all the world to see the indispensable and fructifying value-grounds from which it begins its inquiry so that these inquiries may be fully exposed to—and not falsely shielded from—the public examination that is the true strength of science" (Heilbroner, 1973: 143).

In *The Worldly Philosophers*, the term "worldly" refers to things such as resources, consumers, producers, economic relationships, and facts. They are the materials that philosophers want to understand. For instance, methodologists want to know the relationship between facts (F) and theory (T). Many such relationships have been formulated, but we will look at only those that Heilbroner has developed. Heilbroner referred to "economic statistics" (ES) and "economic analysis" (EA) as well. He spoke of ES in the sense that a biologist or physicist uses statistics. EA denotes not pure theory, but analysis with normative or value elements (Heilbroner, Spring 1973: 141). Heilbroner also takes a broad disciplinary matrix approach to economics, which we represented above by the acronym APPSH. The acronym covers many disciplines, and a part of Heilbroner's contribution is that he has looked at some disciplines that the classical economists have ignored.

Figure 1 helps us to correlate these thoughts. One advantage of using such a diagram is that it helps us to extract "the essential features, and . . . [makes] these features explicit in order that they could serve as a basis and guide for further work in the field" (Lawvere and Rosebrugh, 2003: 232). It does not emphasize calculations, "but much about the analysis that goes into deciding what calculations need to be done, and in what order" (Lawvere and Schanuel, 1991: xiii). Heilbroner has one foot in Marxism and the other in orthodox economics, and he employs a broad method of analysis that we have summarized in the acronym APPSH. How are we "to establish a sense of order and continuity in the face of the historic realities which confront us?" (Heilbroner, 1960: 15). Just as Galileo describes the motion of an object by transferring it into horizontal and vertical motions of other objects (Lawvere and Schanuel, 1997: 3–6), we hope to learn Heilbroner's view of capitalism by transferring its motion into other objects, such as facts and theories. The objects we will use are displayed in Figure 1, which shows the essential and realistic elements of Heilbroner's methodology and help us connect with other methodological views in the literature. For instance, both Nell (1972) and Heilbroner (1973) have advanced their own brand of methodology in defense of "value" judgments in economics. A recent review placed Nell in the camp of Plato and Aristotle based on his doctrine of essentialism, and Heilbroner in the camp of Lakatos based on the vicissitudes of capitalism (Blaug, 1983: 125).

An entry point into Figure 1 is Blaug's characterization of Martin Hollis and Nell's contribution as "all facts are theory-laden and all theories are value-laden" (ibid.: 124). This explains the pathway $V \rightarrow T \rightarrow F$ in the diagram. Blaug draws the conclusion that this is a falsification of positivism, making neoclassical economics an exemplar of positivism. He then goes on to consider the alternative position that Nell and Hollis offered based on "essence" and "realism." We must be cautious to note that "reality" falls into three groups: 1) realism, where objective reality exists; 2) instrumentalism, where we read reality from a measuring instrument; and 3) relativism, where reality is what society says is real (Casti, 1989: 46–47). Heilbroner is more inclined to instrumentalism and relativism. "While positivists can have instrumentalism, realism, and relativism in their *belief*, their *method* would be rational. Hollis and Nell maintain a rationalistic, essentialist approach to economics" (Blaug, 1983: 125). Heilbroner appears to play down rationalism: "Capitalism is assuredly a social order that draws its acquisitive energies from the unconscious substratum of behavior, and it must therefore expect to evidence both the energy and *irrationality* [emphasis added] of that motivating drive" (Heilbroner, 1993: 160).

In Figure 1, a letter represents a category, an abstract set of objects, which can be thought of as a "bag of dots" (Lawvere and Rosebrugh, 2003: 1). Arrows between letters, such as $V \rightarrow T$, represent relationships and can be denoted Mor(V, T), a morphism between V and T, which can be thought of as an arrow linking internal dots in the bags. The linking, or mapping, follows the rule: "for each . . . there is exactly one . . . " (ibid.: 3).

The three dots in Figure 1 indicate a direction that will make a triangulation commute. It means that when you select two objects, you can choose any route in the diagram and obtain the same result through a process of

$$\begin{array}{ccccccc}
V & \rightarrow & T & \rightarrow EA & & \rightarrow & WP \\
\downarrow & \ddots & \updownarrow & \updownarrow & & \ddots & \downarrow \\
APPSH & \rightarrow & F & \rightarrow ES & & & SE
\end{array}$$

Figure 1 External Diagram.

composition. For instance, the first square commutes because you can get to F from V, either through T, or through APPSH, that is, V → T → F, or V → APPSH → F.

Heilbroner on Facts

To flesh out the relationships between the variables of Figure 1, start at F, and consider what economists mean by facts. Heilbroner wrote that terms such as "labor, capital, interest, even wealth—are all historical concepts fraught with sociopolitical implications" (Heilbroner, 1973: 137). The facts Heilbroner is referring to cannot be observed in the manner of scientific facts. To the extent that facts are historical, that is, they come from the category APPSH, we can say that the "primary facts are not observed but inferred" (Stebbing, 1961: 384). Modern anthropologists have shown that the term "scarcity" is not the cause of the modern fundamental problem of economics where, for a lack of resources, wants go unsatisfied. "Rather satiety appears to be the prevailing condition of material life in primitive society . . . *insatiable commodity-hunger that we discover in adult man but not in his infancy* . . . deserves singling out as a fundamental problem concept of economics, not the trivial condition of scarcity that arises once the hunger has been instilled" (Heilbroner, 1987: 112). "Words such as wealth, waste, public, private, efficiency, value—indeed, all the interesting and important terms in the economic lexicon—embody political and moral presuppositions and premises" (ibid.: 119–120).

Facts Linked to Value, Theory, Economic Analysis

Heilbroner does not follow the argument that is based on "no documents, no history" (ibid.: 384). Rather, he looks to APPSH for "behavioral" laws for guidance. "The crucial aspect in the meaning of social behavior infuses economic analysis with values in two ways" (Heilbroner, 1973: 136–137). Economists either apply "laws" that are "partial descriptions of reality," or, with strong appeal, the "maximization" principle that is now "a prescription for conduct" (ibid.). However, there is a limit to this kind of analysis. Heilbroner "fears that liberal and radical thought is being badly weakened because it overlooks aspects of human experience dictated by an inherent human nature. . . . Heilbroner would have us borrow from the conservative tradition its long-held assumption that man cannot be totally programmed and that a certain 'unexpungeable individuality' must be taken into account in all social planning" (Yankelovich, 1973: 409).

How else are F and V associated besides our observation that facts are laden with theory, and theory is laden with values? Facts are inferred from history. "We are left, then, with the need to write history from some perspective, highlighting one theme or another from our 'total' history . . . *the choice of a theme is a decisive determinant of what we will find in 'history'*" (Heilbroner and Singer, 1977: 2 [italics original]). There we find F from having chosen T. But there is only one element, H, in APPSH. We should not forget that Heilbroner subscribed to psychoanalytic theory to help us determine our values, V, and facts, F. "The central theme of Freud's work—the persistence into adulthood of infantile dependency traits and the idealization of parental surrogates—provides essential insights into phenomena of history and society that are otherwise inexplicable" (Heilbroner, 1985: 21).

Is there a pathway from APPSH to T as well, which we can represent by the slanted three-dot line? Yes. If our value system is to reflect "obedience" to secure political institutions, and "identification" to have political action, then we must accept the concepts of markets and capital accumulation. Here lies our missing link. As Nell pointed out, "'The concept of the 'market' (like that of 'capital') is a 'theory-laden term'" (Nell, 1993: 2–3). So, it is possible to go from APPSH to T as well.

Now, how do we get from T → EA, and F → ES? We may think of theories and facts as coming in bundles, or collections of bundles, like bundles of hay. Heilbroner, Smith, Ricardo, John Stuart Mill, Marx, Marshall, and Keynes were great economists because they "were explicit in their use of facts and theories as instruments of advocacy" (Heilbroner, 1973: 139). They provide their bundles of thought. Smith advocated perfect liberty; Ricardo advocated the retraction of the Corn Laws; Mill advocated a stationary state; Marshall advocated social change; Marx advocated revolution; and Keynes advocated government intervention. These bundles have fibers that can be isolated for economic or statistical analysis. EA and ES are such fibers.

On the relation: EA → ES, "laws" (e.g. maximizing behavior) in the sense of theory, affect "facts," and "facts" (labor, wealth are socioeconomic influenced) affect theory. Therefore, the relationship between F and T seems bi-directional; but that relationship is not sufficient to make EA and ES bi-directional. Heilbroner analyzed topical instances of ES, such as the incident of inflation in the 1970s that required an expectation specification in EA. The purpose of his *Journal of Economic Literature* survey was "to inquire into the successes and failures of economic thought in anticipating the march of actual events" (Heilbroner, 1990: 1097). In an earlier work, he explained how we can link Figure 1 back to a value-laden theory with the view of science in mind: "how the economic analyst, whose analysis must include normative elements, can aspire to the position of the scientist" (Heilbroner, 1973: 141). Those pieces of arguments find their home in a grand maxim that the economist should "duplicate the methods, not the models, of the natural sciences" (ibid.: 142).

A Capitalist Representation of Figure 1

If the value system is capitalism, then we start with the capitalist values for V in Figure 1. One position Heilbroner takes involves the logical part of Smith's growth process, where the growth in output follows an outward spiral hypothesis interpretation as given by Lowe, keeping in mind that Heilbroner adds an internal hitch where a saturation point can be reached. We shall describe this process in greater detail in the dynamics of capitalism section below (Lowe, 1975). "I suggest that we begin with a scenario that is already quite familiar to us. It is Adam Smith's expectation with regard to the Society of Perfect Liberty. . . . Smith envisaged that society as bringing about a general increase in well-being for every one, but he also anticipated that after a time it would accumulate '[the] full complement of riches' to which it was entitled by virtue of its resources and geographic placement. At that point accumulation would stop, and growth with it" (Heilbroner, 1993: 123).

For Heilbroner, "capitalism can be comprehensively viewed from more than one perspective" (Heilbroner, 1985: 182–183). He defended a rigid position that "economics has no relevance whatsoever to the study of the hunting and gathering tribes who account for over 99 percent of human history. . . . Economics is about capitalism" (Heilbroner, 1995: 22). He credits three meanings of Capitalism to Marx: 1) "a process in which physical capital loses its meaning as an object of use-value to gain a new meaning as a link in a chain of transaction . . . M-C-M'," where M-C-M' represents a commodity-money system where money is exchanged for commodities in the first phase, and commodities are exchanged for money in the second phase, 2) "a network of channels of exchange—established and protected by an extensive framework of law and custom," and 3) " a structure of horizontal and vertical order," where horizontal order deals with unwritten customs and conventions, and vertical order deals with hierarchy, ownership of capital, and the like (ibid.: 23–24).

Heilbroner views capitalism as "an economic order marked by the private ownership of means of production vested in a minority class called 'capitalists,' and by a market system that determines the income and distributes the output arising from its productive activity. It is a social order characterized by a 'bourgeois' culture among whose manifold aspects the drive for wealth is the most important" (Heilbroner, 1974: 63). Capitalism and markets are sometimes used interchangeably, but they have inherent differences: "capitalism is [a] much larger and more complex entity than the market system we use as its equivalent, and a market system is larger and more complex than the innumerable individual encounters between buyers and sellers that constitute its atomic structure. The market system is the principal means of binding and coordinating the whole" (Heilbroner, 1993: 96).

Capitalism has a unique logic." I shall speak of capitalism as the social order in which a certain kind of nature gives rise to an historically unique logic" (Heilbroner, 1985: 18). Heilbroner did not look for the nature and logic of capitalism in the mere business or "invisible force field" (ibid.: 18). "Just as we have seen that a description directed only at the business aspects of the capitalist world fails to capture its ordered properties, a description aimed solely at the invisible force fields within the system should fail to convey its sense of motion, its guided historical path" (ibid.: 19). An understanding of capitalism comes from "examining the idea of the nature and logic of social formations in general, not just those of capitalism" (ibid.). We create such an understanding by accepting the distinction of societies into "primitive, imperial, feudal, and capitalist" (ibid.). In studying these phases of society, he plays down the givens of geography, and plays up the givens of "psychic endowment" (ibid.: 20). "The central theme of Freud's work—the persistence into adulthood of infantile dependency traits and the idealization of parental surrogates—provides essential insight into phenomena of history and society that are otherwise inexplicable" (ibid.: 21). In other words, when we insist on viewing social behavior as "rational action," we neglect the influence of the "psychic endowment," interplay between the ego, id, and super-ego.

Institutions, organizations, belief systems, and the support of cultural activities are like receptacles in which the "primal energies" are poured. To function, capitalism needs "the formation of monetary institutions and forms of property" (Heilbroner, 1995: 25). Production and behavior-molding activities are the outcomes, and they cut across the different levels of society. In primitive societies, we find hunters and gatherers with varying degrees of skills. Imperial and feudal societies produce peasants and lords, with special roles to play. Capitalist society includes the categories of workers and capitalists.

Heilbroner proposed a 4x4 matrix classification of the historic development of the logic of capitalism (Heilbroner, 1985: 150–152). The columns represent long periods of traits of capitalism: 1760–1848, 1948–1893, 1893–1941, and 1941–current. The rows include: Structure of Accumulation, Function of Economics and Politics, Ideologies, and the Nature of Crisis Periods.

What capitalist realizations or scenarios, and future implications, are possible within that 4x4 matrix classification? If capital size is of international scale, such as in the wave of the 1941–current period, then it is possible to have state participation, of which a modern form of strategic trade policy is a realization. Here the state promotes industries or firms, such as Boeing, that are most differentiated and would potentially gain the highest monopoly profits. As countries exploit monopoly profits, more regulation of trade and more improved mixed economies are possible. Also, on the political front, we are likely to witness the manifestation of more Free Trade Areas (FTAs), and the support of Most Favored Nation (MFN) status. Economics ideologies such as efficiency, productivity, and production under humane conditions prevail. Crises such as OPEC-generated stagflation, trade imbalances, capital flight, and currency problems are possible.

A Marxian Representation of Figure 1

If the value system is Marxian then we start with the Marxian values in V. Heilbroner is not afraid to let the Marxian "M-C-M" represent such a value system. In order to justify Heilbroner's position, we pull materials freely from his books *Beyond Boom and Crash* (1978), *Marxism: For and Against* (1980), and *The Nature and Logic of Capitalism* (1985). In *Beyond Boom and Crash,* he uses the M-C-M' model "to look into the etiology of capitalist crises as a kind of chronic disease of the system and to venture whatever prognosis seems possible" (Heilbroner, 1978: 12). In *The Nature and Logic of Capitalism,* he spoke of an "overall vision of capitalism," wanting to replace the neoclassical vision with the Marxian vision. This is implied in central concepts such as "the regime of capital," which has implications for the study of capitalist societies that affect social changes through different epochs. Other implicative points include discussions about the proletariat as a complement to the central regime of capital, where the existence of a center implies the existence of a periphery.

M-C-M' is the theory (T) that drives economic analysis such as that represented in *Beyond Boom and Crash.* "In the first phase, businessmen hire labor and buy the raw or semi-finished goods. . . . This initial phase of Marx's 'circuit' of accumulation immediately identifies two potential sources of crisis. The first is the crucial role played by businessmen's expectations. . . . A second obstacle . . . money will not even begin its tortuous journey through the system if a labor force cannot be hired, or if supplies of materials or plant and equipment are not available. When workers strike, capitalistic growth comes to a total halt" (Heilbroner, 1978: 19). In the second phase of Marx's circuit, "no money is directly involved. Rather, the money that has been turned into labor power, raw materials, and other necessities of production is now further turned into the finished products that will emerge from the factory gate" (ibid.: 20). "Interruptions of labor discipline, such as absenteeism, sabotage, 'work-to-rule' slowdowns, vandalism, or indifference will damage the process by which money, embodied in labor power and materials, becomes transformed into salable outputs" (ibid.: 21). In the third stage, "capital, now embodied in a finished good, must complete its metamorphosis back into money. . . . Changes in buyers' wants or needs . . . can reduce the value of output. . . . Events over which an individual business has no control . . . can cause markets to disappear. . . . Thus the process of completing the circle of capital accumulation by selling the output of business is always attended by anxiety and uncertainty" (ibid.: 22).

Analogous to the capitalist replication above, we can now ask what Marxian realizations or scenarios, and future implications, are possible within Heilbroner's 4x4 matrix classification for the logic of capitalism. The theory of M-C-M' yields global positioning and technological development during the 1941–current period. Increasing labor cooperation is demanded, and technology becomes essential for accumulation. Technology is transferred from developed to less developed countries during crises of more inequality.

In Figure 1, the relationship between EA and ES includes the prediction that workers' shares of output will fall, and that low wages and minimum wage laws are possible. *The Worldly Philosophers* develops visions from studying economic analysis, EA, and economic statistics, when for instances worldly philosophers call for strengthening or creating a new institutional framework. Predictions are made from the side of EA, and ES allows models of EA to be re-specified, giving a two-way interrelationship between ES and EA.

Dynamic Forces of Capitalism

Heilbroner has repeatedly attributed his vision of capitalism to the interplay of forces over time, cycles, and human interactions—between the distant past, yesterday, today, and tomorrow; the future as history; boom and crash; and the interaction of the individual with his environment. Rejecting parallels with aero, electro, thermo, and field theory dynamic views in the physical sciences, Heilbroner wanted to expand the socio-economic views of the classical economists to include the other disciplines as described by APPSH. Analogous to the psychoanalytic phases of human development, he wanted to look internally into the human psyche to explain the future scenarios of the logic of capitalism.

Heilbroner made a novel contribution by extending classical economists' views of a "hitchless" process of growth of capital. He split those processes into "external hitches" and "internal hitches" to characterize the growth process initiated by Smith. The next section looks at both of these aspects.

External Hitchless Growth Process

To Smith, the growth process is built around three laws relating to population, capital, and technology. In the first law, the rate of growth of a population depends on real wage—wages adjusted for the price level. If the wage rate or wage fund is high, then population reproduces itself through increases in new births. If the wage rate is greater than the subsistence level, then wealth in the economy will increase continuously.

Accumulation, according to Smith, depends on technology. Only accumulation with technology improves profits. Technology in turn depends on the specialization and division of labor. Specialization depends on the extent of the market and foreign trade. Accumulation improves profits by creating income, which in turn causes increases in domestic consumption.

In Smith's model, certain variables are held constant, and can be classified as natural, psychological, or institutional. The only natural constant for Smith is constant returns to scale, for the idea of diminishing returns was unknown at that time. Psychological constants include the desire of people to better their conditions, and their propensity to barter. Smith made approximately eight instructional assumptions—personal freedom, contractual relations, unequal distribution, private property, division of labor, free exchange, factor mobility, and specialization. These constants are difficult to measure precisely. They can be linked with other economic variables to create a growth theory which can be seen as a continuous process, a spiral. We can choose any point to start our analysis. An illustration follows.

Consider a high level of national wealth, which is made up of capital stock, payroll, and profits. This will create opportunities for improvement in the division of labor, causing expectation of earning profits, and thus a demand for investment funds. This in turn will cause an increase in savings, i.e. demand for funds less supply of funds, which will lead to an increase in demand for labor. Here, wage rates will go up, and will cause an increase in population. This in turn will enable employment with an improved division of labor, which will create a further rise in national wealth. This process repeats itself continuously. This whole process is faithful to the way Lowe first formulated it (Lowe, 1975).

Heilbroner has amended the Smithian growth process in many directions. In one direction he considers the growth path of the developed nations; in another, the growth path of the underdeveloped economies. His concerns in the developed areas are with the hitchless process, and in the undeveloped area with "The Great Ascent," to which he devoted a book (Heilbroner, 1963). In both the developed and undeveloped processes, he was concerned with external and internal factors. In the book, he wrote "we must look at development, not from the American standpoint, from *without*, but from the standpoint of the developing countries themselves, from *within*" (ibid.: 48 [emphasis added]). And the difference is not merely a matter of geography, the boundaries that must be crossed are those of accustomed habits of thought, of unexamined assumptions, of comfortable social and political and economic limitations, all of which may be valid enough for the consideration of American problems but which "fail to illumine the vaster problems of the emerging currents of world history" (Heilbroner, 1963: 15). We know that Heilbroner accepts that the growth process is "hitchless," a term coined by Schumpeter (1954: 572, 640), because he looked for a different kind of hitch, those that are internal to the system. In that path, he was novel. As the splitting of the atom by Ernest Rutherford led to the discovery of elementary particles, Heilbroner's splitting of the hitchless process into external and internal sources has deepened research into the logic of capitalism. Capitalism took on a broader face, starting with his broader view from the APPSH lens. We therefore take a closer look at these hitches, starting from the external side.

The Harrod-Domar model, an attempt to put dynamics into the Keynesian static framework, turned out to be unstable. By the multiplier process $Q = sI$, where s is the propensity to save, and the capital output ratio is constant, $K/Q = v$, yielding $v\Delta Q = sI$, the solution of the system, $Q = ce^{(s/v)t}$, is unstable. In Heilbroner's concrete vision, deviation from a balanced growth path will lead to "recession on one side and inflation on the other" (Heilbroner, 1978: 35). Backtracking into the history of thought, we find that Thomas Malthus determined that the capitalist system will lead to misery. If a population, x, grows at an exponential rate, c, over time, t, then $dx/dt = cx$. If food supply, y, grows at a constant rate, k, over time, t, then $dy/dt = k$. Then the ratio of $y/x = (y_0 + kt)/x_0e^{ct})$ will break down as t approaches infinity, implying misery (Hirsch, 1984: 14).

Marx also pointed out hitches in the capitalist system. In Marx's model, accumulation means a re-transformation of appropriated surplus value, S, into capital. In one version of Marx's dynamic model, we may take the ratio of fixed capital, C, to variable capital, V, and hold it constant. As accumulation, i.e. investment of surplus value, proceeds, its rate will exceed the rate of the labor supply, putting pressure on the real wage rate to rise, shrinking the rate of profit, $S/(C+V) = (S/V)/(C/V + 1)$, and eventually causing accumulation to slow down. In another version of Marx's model, as C/V rises, labor will displace technological progress, causing C to rise at a faster rate than V. Constant capital will be needed to re-employ displaced workers, which again leads to a fall in profit. We should mention that Marx postulated some counteracting tendencies, such as 1) that S/V may rise if technology affects the wage-good industry; 2) that workers may not feel worse off with the fall in wage; 3) that C may fall if technology occurs in the wage-good sector; and 4) that importation of cheaper foreign wage-goods may lower the real wage without affecting the worker. We should also mention some other views of hitches. Schumpeter holds that capitalism cannot survive (Heilbroner, 1976: 10), and Ricardo holds that capitalism will approach a steady state, based mainly on the laws of diminishing returns. We turn now to Heilbroner, who says: "My own assessment draws on both Marxian and Schumpeterian insights, without following either slavishly" (ibid.). Heilbroner weighed those hitches on the "external" side of his balance, while he sat on the "internal" side. We will discuss his side, relating it to his broad vision of the APPSH approach.

Internal Hitchless Growth

Heilbroner wrote that "if the economic history of capitalism is one of boom and bust, its psychological history is one of alternating confidence and despair. . . . Economists, like doctors, should begin with case histories" (Heilbroner, 1978: 12). Presumably, as a psychoanalyst looks for the causes of neurosis in the human psyche, accumulated through the stages of human development, we should look for internal hitches as well in economic crises. For Heilbroner, the 1973–1974 OPEC crisis, which followed the longest expansion period in capitalism history (1950–1970), exemplifies a unique hitch (ibid.: 16). In *The Economic Transformation of America* (1977), he sampled 1) the period from mercantilism to the pre-industrial era, 2) the industrialization process, 3) the Great Depression, and 4) economic changes during the present period. He looked for the limits of growth and failures, giving him a somewhat pessimistic outlook, somewhat like the pessimistic Keynes that we describe below. In describing those landmark periods of capitalism, he manipulates his argument around the internal hitches of his system.

We can discern several of Heilbroner's approaches to the description of internal hitches to growth. He starts by looking for the logic of capitalism: "So I will not be so foolish as to attempt to do that which has foiled so many—namely, to predict the future of the social order in which we live. . . . I shall be considering the prospects for capitalism from which might be called a perspective of future-related understanding" (Heilbroner, 1993: 20). In a sense, the future is in the present as the present is in the past. In his *An Enquiry into The Human Prospect* (1974), he was concerned with "life on earth, now and in the relatively few generations that constitute the limit of our capacity to imagine the future . . . *whether we can imagine the future other than as a continuation of darkness, cruelty, and disorder of the past*; worse, whether we do not foresee in the human prospect a deterioration of things, even an impending catastrophe of fearful dimensions" (Heilbroner, 1974: 13 [emphasis added]). Although countries differ in custom and habits, "they can transact exchanges in the market place, negotiate around the bargaining table or engage in board-room conferences as persons who see at least one aspect of life in much the same way . . . a way of thinking about the future that we would not have if we approached the problem from the viewpoint of one country. . . . Only by becoming aware of this orientation can we hope to discover whether there is a logic at work behind the movement of things" (ibid.: 20–21).

To elucidate his dynamic theory of capitalism, Heilbroner appealed to the developmental process in psychoanalysis, namely, what Freud and others have said of human "development" and "personalities." Heilbroner developed two traits, which he called "obedience" and "identification," in the domain of politics. Political power is what he adds to the classical socio-economic model to form the trio—social, economic, and political views of economics. He said about his novel contribution that "one cannot have political power without political obedience; one cannot have strong government without a sense of international identification" (ibid.: 102). For instance, "obedience" to authority is necessary in order to secure the institutional framework of private property, to withstand environmental threats, and to conduct wars (ibid.: 105). Similarly, "the capacity for identification—and in particular national identification . . . [is] an indispensable precondition for the exercise of political action" (ibid.: 110).

How do we understand this psychoanalytic view of human nature? "We must begin by focusing our attention on . . . the extended period of helplessness of development through which all human beings must pass and in which the elements of their adult personalities are first molded" (ibid.: 103). He summarizes the Freudian developmental process, which indicates how an infant moves from omnipotence to dependence of objects, to a state where the child seeks to "control and direct its physical and psychic energies" (ibid.: 104). The dynamic view Heilbroner takes from Freud and others need not form a new category outside of the already listed trio—social, economic, and political. As Freud would have it, the preferred developmental view should be one of "lay analysis," just as economics is sometimes defined as the study of the ordinary business of life. Freud proposes that "we must study of Ego and Id from a new standpoint, the dynamic; that is, with an eye to the forces interplaying within them and between them" (Freud, 1947: 20). The Ego represents a psychical organization in man, "interpolated between his sensory stimuli and perception for his bodily needs on the one hand, and his motor activity on the other; and which mediates between them with a certain purpose" (ibid.: 15). Everything besides the Ego is called the "It," or "Id." The interplay between the Ego and the Id tells whether things are normal or not.

The information in Table 1 helps us to bring out the parallel between Heilbroner's views and human developmental views. We draw a parallel between

TABLE 1: A Topographic View of Development

Endowment of Countries	Psychological Parallel	Troubled Economies
Developed:	Signs	
1.Abundant Capital (K)	1. Father: +++	1. Father: ++++
2. Scarce Labor (L)	2. Mother: ---	2. Mother: ----
Less Developed:		
3. Abundant L	3. Mother: +	
4. Scarce or no K	4. Father: -	

Source: Adopted from Nagera, 1981: 252.

how mother and father influence a child's development with labor and capital in capitalist development. Capital is understood to also include forces that lead to capital accumulation, and labor is used broadly as well. A narrower conception of those terms is inherent in the most evolved economic model in modern economics, the neoclassical growth model. A simplification of it holds that the growth rate of K/L is judged by its deviation from the growth rate of population, $dP/dt = n$. Deviations from $K/L = n$ are adjusted forthe savings, S; Investments, I; and identity, $S = I$. To honor the evolution of the neoclassical growth model, we would retain K, and L, but with the understanding that when Heilbroner talks of problems with population growth and environmental impacts. that they can be classified into the K and L boxes.

Heilbroner's unique position is that, as K and L grow, the system will reach a saturation point. He describes two trends: "material decline awaiting at the terminus of the economic journey, [and] moral decay suffered by society in the course of its journeying" (Heilbroner, 1975: 524). He cites hitches concealed in Smith's *The Wealth of Nations*: "at the end of the long rising gradient, we are suddenly confronted with the spectacle of a nation which has attained 'that full complement of riches which the nature of its soil and climate, and its situation with respect to other countries, allow(s) it to acquire,' and we discover to our consternation that in such a nation 'the wages of labour and the profits of stock would probably be very low.' ... Thus 'hitchless' growth has somehow terminated in general poverty, a fact that suggests that there are, after all, some very important hitches concealed in the dynamics of *The Wealth of Nations*" (ibid.: 527).

Among other passages in *The Wealth of Nations* Heilbroner cites to back up his idea of a decline are 1) "competition ... would every-where be as great, and consequently, the ordinary profit as low as possible" (Smith, 1976: 111); 2) "the usual market rate of interest ... would be so low as to render it impossible for any but the very wealthiest people to live upon the interest of their money" (ibid.: 113); and 3) "we must assume that the population proceeds relentlessly until it reaches a point at which the increase in productivity stemming from the continued division of labour is finally overwhelmed by the decreasing productivity of the land and resources available to the nation" (Heilbroner, 1975: 529–520).

We must note that it has been observed that society does have a tendency towards poverty. For instance, Pierre-Joseph Proudhon in the nineteenth century discussed problems with Smith's concepts of division of labor and competition under the title "Chaos of Economic Forces: Tendency of Society Toward Poverty" (Proudhon, 2003: 46). But Heilbroner is saying something different. By linking poverty with Smith's statement, he places the hitches internal to the system.

Elements of Heilbroner's Dynamic Model

His growth model has two main assumptions: accumulation of capital, and a benevolent directorate that oversees planning. We discuss several specific concerns for growth that are implied in his methodological framework discussed above. These concerns describe a nation embarking on an economic growth path. Just as in psychology we find that the developmental paradigm for children and adults share common traits, so too we can find common applications of the concerns below to developed and under-developed economies.

Savings and Investment

In one of his seminars on Smith, Heilbroner remarked that the idea of demand and supply of savings is not as significant to the Smithian dynamic process as it is to the Keynesian model. Early formulators of the Keynesian model such as Hicks (1937), Franco Modigliani (1944), Lawrence Klein (1947), and Don Patinkin (1949) have shown that the equality of savings with investment is critical for the understanding of macroeconomic equilibrium. Heilbroner's Keynesian equilibrium model differs in the sense that he introduces the terms "designed" or "undesigned" savings and investment (Heilbroner, 1942: 827–828). We explain his model by emphasizing the planning and the dynamic perspectives that are implied in his arguments.

In an attempt to specify the savings and investment functions, Heilbroner wrote: "The designed investment function and the designed savings function may be so shaped that they never equal each other, at any international income, although this is most unlikely" (ibid.: 828). To peek into the dynamics of his system, we can denote designed savings as dS and designed investment as dI. Correspondingly, udS and udI would be undesigned savings and undesigned investment, respectively. Heilbroner describes many possibilities, some of which can be shown in the diagram below. For example, if dS < dI, as indicated by the lower arrow, then udS will occur when dI causes increases in income over consumption. Heilbroner puts it: "if designed investment outlays exceed designed savings flows, total equality is maintained at each instant by additional undesigned savings" (ibid.: 827).

Some predictions of Heilbroner's designed savings and investment model in the long run can be made. Drawing parallels with the Lotka-Volterra predator-prey model (Abraham and Shaw, 1985: 84), Figure 2 displays one outcome where the economy perpetuates itself. In Heilbroner's words, "(o)ver successive periods of time, as the excess of one 'dynamic' factor influences the size of national income, the new economic environment will change the designed components of the two flows until, at a subsequent income level (if equilibrium is established there), the designed flows will again equate" (Heilbroner, 1942: 828). As a special case for Heilbroner, we can argue that if the savings and investment functions were to take on explicit specifications, other predictions are possible. In the special case of Nicholas Kaldor's savings function, a system can lose its stability (Medio, 1992: 242–244). Other dynamic predictions are possible, but the one Heilbroner is known for portrays an "attractor" where, through his argument based on internal hitches, the economy settles at a level of poverty.

Population Dynamics and Poverty

In one version of his internal hitch process, Heilbroner related the Smithian dynamic process to mortality rates. He cast his analysis in terms of net natural change (births minus deaths), which he conducted in three periods of analysis.

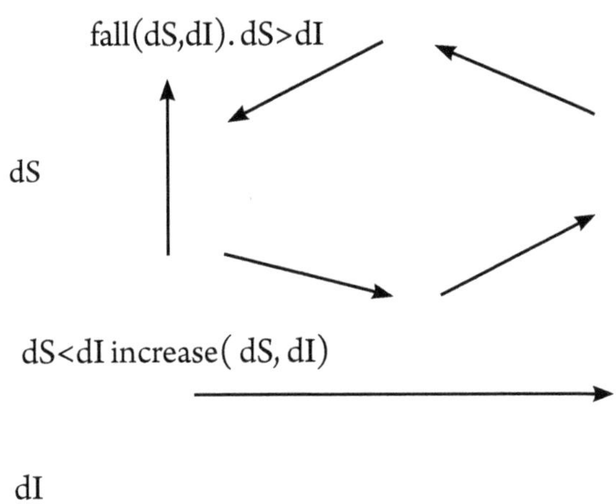

Figure 2

To analyze these three periods, we start out by setting the stage for the analysis of population dynamics. Supposing that b is the birth rate per thousand, and d is the death rate per thousand, then net natural changes is b-d. If P(t) is the population, and t is years in the future, then we write P'(t) = (b-d)P(t), or the log P(t) = (b-d) + c, where c is an integral constant. Solving for P(t), and letting the initial population base, which is also the integral constant, be P(0), yields $P(t) = P(0)e^{(b-d)t}$. In all three of his period analyses, Heilbroner concentrated only on the case where d>b, that is, net natural change is negative, b-d<0. In Period I, the labor force will increase at a steady rate. In Period II, wages will dampen the death rate and speed up population growth; and in Period III, the death rate will stabilize, leading to a higher and stable level of population growth (Heilbroner, 1973: 251).

In the case of underdeveloped countries, he would relate the internal poverty hitch to a "quicksand" nature of population growth. He attributes this phenomenon to "the incursion of Western medicine and public health into the underdeveloped area. Prior to World War II, the poorer countries were generally marked by high birth rates, but their population increase was held in check by comparable death rates. Since then, the birth rates have continued to be high, but the death rates have plunged dramatically" (Heilbroner, 1963: 57).

Environmental Dynamics

Heilbroner considered dynamic models relating to the ecological "balance" and "stationary state" of the economy. His concern is with the meaning of those terms and how they relate to each other. He defends the point of view that a stationary state requires an "unchanging population" and an "unvarying level of output per capita" (Heilbroner and Allentuck, 1972: 205). An ecological balance should be sought where "we seek to use inputs so as to minimize the chance of depleting stocks before acceptable substitutes were found" (ibid.: 207).

This argument can be cast in terms of the production economics. "Neoclassical microtheorists have consistently treated natural resources as a fixed factor and diminishing returns as an inevitable consequence of the law of factor proportion. Growth economists, on the other hand, have merged natural resources with capital, thus endowing them with manmade wealth's attribute of indefinite expansibility" (Morse, 1973: 126). With no technological progress (a = 0), it is standard neoclassical economics to write that $dk/dt = sf(k) - (n + v + a)k$, where k is capital (K) per worker (L), s is saving rate, f(k) is the production function or output (Y) per worker, n is population growth rate, v is the rate of depreciation, and a is the growth rate of knowledge. By the fixity and diminishing return assumption, k will approach a steady state value k^*, also called a balanced growth situation where all the variables will be growing at a constant rate. Heilbroner's contention is that the stationary state "would not necessarily be a society in ecological balance. This is because a society can be 'stationary' and can still be polluting the environment . . . a stationary state will still asphyxiate itself" (Heilbroner, 2001: 148). It would require an "anti-growth school . . . to mobilize the social will—how to induce us to apply *existing* technologies against the resistance of entrenched interest and ordinary people alike" (ibid.: 150). Ecological equilibrium will require "public control far beyond anything yet experienced" (ibid.: 151).

While growth theorists ignore constraints, Heilbroner is concerned that "according to existing estimates, there are not enough resources to allow industrial expansion to continue unhindered at a compound rate of seven percent a year for anything like 50 years—much less a century—with the exception of a few items such as coal and iron" (ibid.: 141). The solution to the "fundamental" problem lies in the domain of social and technological realms. He was led to this conclusion: "I have indicated some reason for optimism with regard to our technical capabilities for adaptation, I do not find it so easy to be sanguine with respect to our near-term ability to bring about the needed social and instructional changes" (ibid.: 153).

Laws and Propositions

We state several propositions that Heilbroner has made explicit in his analysis of economic development. Afterward, we state what we think is his general law that envelops all of the propositions.

Proposition I: *Economic development is not primarily an economic but a political and social process.* (Heilbroner, 1963: 16)

Proposition II: *Political and social changes required for economic development are apt to be revolutionary in nature.* (Ibid.: 17)

Proposition III: *Economic development is not a process which breeds social contentment.* (Ibid.: 18)

Proposition IV: *The Great Ascent is not assured of success.* (Ibid.: 19)

Proposition V: *The price of development is apt to be political and economic authoritarianism.* (Ibid.: 20)

A general law for these propositions is that "development is apt to be characterized by a growing gap between expectations and achievements—that is, by an increased awareness of insufficiency and a decreased tolerance for both poverty and privileges" (Heilbroner, 1962: 18). The dynamic of this law can be stated as an equation:

$$\frac{d(Development)}{d(time)} = \lambda(Expectations - Achievements) \qquad eq(1)$$

$d = derivative; \ \lambda = constant.$

In this model, climatic conditions and unavailability of resources are not the reasons for the gap between expectations and achievements, for "the deficiencies of nature can be repaired, as witness the economic progress of both Australia and Israel," and it is "not so much that resources are lacking, as that their presence is simply unknown" (Heilbroner, 1963: 33, 35). The gap in eq(1) is a result of a lack of proper social and instructional arrangements. We find in underdeveloped countries "a structure of social stratification unlike any we know from our own historic experience," and "social types and social structure do not tend to produce economic systems which are capital-creating" (ibid.: 51). But it is not "'just' a lack of capital, or 'just' a political problem, which weighs upon the poorer nations" (ibid.: 59). Rather, we embrace a combination of factors, such as we have discussed in this section, a "complex multi-causality." Ascent may depend on "a centralized directorship of effort if the Ascent is to be made at all. . . . Unfortunately, however, even the most thoroughgoing control over the social and economic energies of backward nations may yet not bring about development at a sufficient rapid pace to close the gap between expectations and accomplishments" (ibid.: 20–21).

Prediction

Heilbroner's predictions have offered varying doses of intensity, adjustments, topography, and genesis to the capitalist world. For Heilbroner, "the three organizing principles of Tradition, Command, and Market impart totally different dynamics into societies over which they hold sway" (Heilbroner, 1993: 32). They form the topography for coordinating economic activities. "If Traditional society sleepwalks through history, and Command society pursues the goals of powerful individuals or institutions, Market society is in the grip of subterranean forces that have a life of their own" (ibid.: 35).

Intensity of Economic Thought

Heilbroner has specialized in the history of economic thought. Like Keynes, he was concerned with how the thoughts of defunct economists played out in history, by their influence on human prospects. "At bottom our troubled state of mind reflects an inability to see the future in an *historic* context. . . . Unlike our forefathers who lived very much *in* history and *for* history, we ourselves appear to be adrift in an historic void. . . . The problem, then, is to establish a sense of order and continuity in the face of the historic realities which confront us" (Heilbroner, 1960: 15).

Heilbroner posits his thought in a grand design, which encompasses several disciplines. His idea of a "vision" for economists to follow is captured in this quotation: "As individuals we move into the future on the mingled accident and design of our lives. As a society we move into the future on the grand dynamic of history. It is this grandiose design which we must discover if we are to comprehend the meaning of the struggles of our time" (ibid.: 16). Our ancestors (pre-modern man) did not have "the idea of social movement, of aggregate betterment, of progress. . . . What he could not bring himself to believe was that heaven might be sought on earth, that reform might proceed from his own aspirations, that despair could give way to determination" (ibid.: 21).

Such an aggregate view of "betterment" formed an explicit psychological assumption in Smith's model of progress. It is also to be found throughout Keynes' work. In the 1930s, Keynes wrote:

> We are suffering just now from a bad attack of economic pessimism. It is common to hear people say that the epoch of enormous economic progress which characterized the nineteenth century is over; that the rapid improvement in the standard of life is now going to slow down. . . . We are suffering, not from the rheumatics of old age but from the growing-pains of over-rapid changes, from the painfulness of readjustment between one economic period and another. The increase in technical efficiency has been taking place faster than we can deal with through the problem of labour absorption; the improvement in the standard of life had been a little too quick. (Keynes, 1963: 358)

Keynes traced the success for Great Britain to the loot Sir Francis Drake took from the Spanish in 1580. Such success for Heilbroner follows from 1) a transformation from "man's subservience before nature to a mastery of it," 2) belief in "the idea of human betterment," and 3) social institutions for "spontaneous growth" (Heilbroner, 1960: 21).

Adaptability

By giving thumbs down to the marginal revolution and other deterministic views of the development of capitalism, Heilbroner argues for a different concept of equilibrium. By standing with the "worldly philosophers," he adopts a view from Freud that "the life system is governed by two trends: it moves towards zero potential but in doing so it creates new tensions" (Hartmann, 1964: 38).

Adaptability to Heilbroner is not just how a person "fits in" with society. His famous quote about history, "we cannot help living in history. We can only fail to be aware of it," is a call for adaptation (Heilbroner, 1960: 209). However, we will adapt better if we plan our affairs for the future because "planning will be the central political and economic necessity of all economic systems over the coming generations. . . . This new impetus to planning derives from the explosive character of economic processes in contemporary industrial societies" (Heilbroner, 1977: 250). This statement should be adjusted in the face of the demise of the former Soviet Union, which makes planning an "open question" conditioned on "the worst traditions of a bureaucratic autocracy, a primitive technology of communication, and the extreme pressures of the Cold War. Had capitalism been initially launched under such conditions, it too might well have failed" (Heilbroner, 1993: 152). Some policy stipulations Heilbroner makes are "to find ways of preserving the human community as a whole against its warlike proclivities," and "an awareness of the complex role that unconscious drives and fantasies play in the determination of our behavior" (Heilbroner, 1995: 117–118).

We should plan to seize on "whatever technological and organizational changes offer profitable chances for expansion," to use "public investments to provide whatever transformational impetus is lacking from the private sector," and to devise structures for "coping with inflationary pressures" (Heilbroner, 1993). Subordinated problems to be solved are the proper level of taxation;

"social contract among labor, management and government"; demand saturation, full employment, and economic crises (ibid.).

We must adapt to the possibility that our instrument may not reach its target. History, for instance, may not unleash the "forces that promise to drive society in the new direction in which we seek to move" (ibid.: 150). The driver for capital to accumulate may be deformed.

Heilbroner seems to be on the side of the Keynesian dictum that "in the long-run, we are all dead. . . . No civilization, save only the most primitive, lasts 'forever'" (Heilbroner, 1976: 101). "I suggest that this long-run termination of capitalism will occur within a century" (ibid.: 102). The future capitalism will not be supported by an "infinitely rich and vast environment." The Malthusian exponential growth model discussed above is one reason for the fall; pollution, another; tension between rich and poor nations, yet another.

Conclusions

Heilbroner was a polymath who used no math. But, as we have shown, logic and mathematical forms underscore and support his arguments. He maintained a consistent line of thought in his modern works, which trace back to his "worldly philosophers." From the worldly philosophers, he integrated the concept of the centrality and accumulation of capital into economics. Economics, he found, has vision, the underlying thread that connects his works. His works tap into a variety of disciplines—anthropology, psychology, politics, sociology, and history. He truly observed that the reaction of the individual to the environment is not limited to relationships, but moves forward and backward depending on a person's mental apparatus and instinctual developments.

In his predictions, Heilbroner saw the various disciplines as completing a mosaic form of human prospects. We can pull out a caricature of such views as: 1) the decline of business civilization; 2) the end of capitalism as we know it; 3) more cautious planning modified from lessons from the former Soviet Union; 4) psychology in the form of "obedience" and "identification" with our political system; 5) history as a signal to the future; 6) a broad vision based on all schools of thought, orthodox and heterodox; and 7) an adherence to a core of beliefs, a value system in which capital is central and capital accumulation is the goal.

We know him as a person with a strong work ethic. He did not procrastinate. Once, one of the authors handed him a term paper for his History of

Economic Thought course in the hallway of the New School. He graded it then and there.

Heilbroner was more than willing to share his knowledge with his students. In one of his seminars, he walked up from the back of the class to show a subtle curvature of a diagram. He taught his students from the textbooks of the masters, which for some was the only lifetime exposure they may have had to the "worldly philosophers." But more importantly, as he told Lall Ramrattan, he expected his students to have a feel for economics, for he believed that budding economists should have knowledge of economics buried "in the bones." Indeed, many economists interested in the "worldly" masters, have asserted that Heilbroner carries the honor of being one of the most delightful writers to read. An example is his *The Worldly Philosophers,* which Evelyn Wood Reading Dynamics made a part of their business reading for speed-readers. When told of this, Heilbroner replied to Ramrattan that it is probably because he was a "natural speed reader." Maybe it is for that reason that his reading lists are so comprehensive.

Heilbroner did not receive the Nobel Prize, perhaps because he was too broad in his approach. Or perhaps because he was too sympathetic to Marx. We see him as a man in pursuit of the truth. In that pursuit, he left no stones unturned. His legacy will be as a social scientist who integrated the diverse disciplines for the explanation, understanding, and prediction of human prospects.

References

Abraham, R. H., & Shaw, C. D. (1985). *Dynamics—The geometry of behavior, part I: Periodic behavior.* Santa Cruz, CA: Aerial Press.

Blaug, M. (1983). *The methodology of economics or how economists explain.* Cambridge: Cambridge University Press.

Casti, J. L. (1989). *Paradigms lost.* New York: William Morrow and Company.

Freud, S. (1947). *The question of lay analysis.* (N. Procter-Gregg, Trans.). London: Imago Publishing Company.

Kuttner, R. (2005, Feb.). A worldly economist. *The American Prospect Online.* Retrieved from http://www.freepatentsonline.com/article/American-Economist/140790456.html.

Hartmann, H. (1964). *Ego psychology and the problem of adaptation.* (D. Rapaport, Trans.). New York: International University Press.

Heilbroner, R. L. (1942, Dec.). Saving and investment: Dynamic aspects. *The American Economic Review*, 32, 827–828.

———. (1960). *The future as history.* New York: Harper Brothers.

———. (1963). *The great ascent: The struggle for economic development in our time.* New York: Harper Torchbooks.

———. (1970). *The economic problem* (2nd ed.). Englewood Cliffs, NJ: Prentice Hall.

———. (1973, Spring). Economics as a "value-free" science. *Social Research*, 40, 129–143.

———. (1973, Apr.-Jun.). The paradox of progress: Decline and decay in the *Wealth of Nations. Journal of the History of Ideas*, 34, 243–262. Reprinted in

———. (1974). *An inquiry into the human prospect.* New York: W. W. Norton and Company.

———. (1975). The paradox of progress: Decline and decay in the Wealth of Nations. In A. S. Skinner & T. Wilson (Eds.), *Essays on Adam Smith* (524-539). Oxford: Clarendon Press.

———. (1978). *Beyond boom and crash.* New York: W. W. Norton & Company.

———. (1985). *The nature and logic of capitalism.* New York: W. W. Norton & Company.

———. (1987, Spring). Fundamental economic concepts—Another perspective. *Journal of Economic Education*, 19(2), 111–120.

———. (1990, Sept.). Analysis and vision in the history of modern economic thought. *Journal of Economic Literature*, 28, 1097–1114.

———. (1993). *21st century capitalism.* New York: W. W. Norton & Company.

———. (1995, Jan.-Feb.). The nature of economics. *Challenge*, 38(1), 22–26.

———. (1995). *Visions of the future: The distant past, yesterday, today, and tomorrow.* New York: Oxford University Press.

———. (1999). *The worldly philosophers* (7th ed.). New York: Simon & Schuster.

———. (2000, Apr.). Happy birthday, Paul! *Monthly Review*, 51, 42–64.

———. (2001). Growth and survival. *Foreign Affairs*, 51(1), 139–153.

Heilbroner, R. L., & Allentuck, J. (1972, Aug.). Ecological "balance" and the "stationary" state. *Land Economics*, 48, 205–211.

Heilbroner, R. & Singer, A. (1977). *The economic transformation of America.* New York: Harcourt Brace Jovanovich.

Hicks, J. (1983). *Classical and moderns: Collected essays on economic theory.* Cambridge, MA: Harvard University Press.

———. (1981). *Wealth and welfare: Collected essays on economic theory.* Cambridge, MA: Harvard University Press.

———. (1937, Apr.). Mr. Keynes and the classic: A suggested interpretation. *Econometrica,* 5(2), 147–159.

Hirsch, M. (1984, Jul.). The dynamical systems approach to differential equations. *Bulletin (New Series) of the American Mathematical Society* 11, 1–64.

Hollis, M. & Nell, E. J. (1975). *Rational economic man: A philosophical critique of neo-classical economics.* Cambridge: Cambridge University Press.

Hutchison, T. W. (1970, Jun.). Economic means and social ends: Essays in political economics. *Journal of Economic Literature,* 8, 445–446.

Keynes, J. M. (1963). *Essays in persuasion.* New York: W. W. Norton & Company.

Klein, L. R. (1947). *The Keynesian revolution.* New York: Macmillan and Co.

Lawvere, F. W. & Rosebrugh, R. (2003). *Set for mathematics.* Cambridge: Cambridge University Press.

Lawvere, F. W. & Schanuel, S. H. (1997). *Conceptual mathematics.* Cambridge: Cambridge University Press.

Lowe, A. (1953). Classical theory of economic growth. *Social Research,* 21(2), 127-158.

———. (1965). *On economic knowledge.* New York: Harper and Row.

———. (1975). Adam Smith's system of equilibrium growth. In A. S. Skinner & T. Wilson (Eds.), *Essays on Adam Smith* (415-425). Oxford: Clarendon Press.

Machlup, F. (1978). *Methodology of economics and other social sciences.* New York: Academic Press.

Medio, A. (1992). *Chaotic dynamics: Theory and applications to economics.* Cambridge: Cambridge University Press.

Modigliani, F. (1944, Jan.). Liquidity preference and the theory of interest and money. *Econometrica,* 12, 45–88.

Morse, C. (1973, May). Discussion. *The American Economic Review,* 63, 126–128.

Nagera, H. (1981). *The developmental approach to childhood psychopathology.* New York: Jason Aronson.

Nell, E. J. (1993). History and vision in economics. In R. Blackwell, J. Chatha, & E. J. Nell (Eds.), *Economics as worldly philosophy* (1–11). New York: St. Martin's Press.

———. (1972). Economics: The revival of political economy. In R. Blackburn (Ed.), *Ideology in social science* (76-95). London: Fontana.

Okroi, L. J. (1988). *Galbraith, Harrington, and Heilbroner: Economics and dissent in an age of optimism.* Princeton: Princeton University Press.

Patinkin, D. (1949, Sept.). Involuntary unemployment and the Keynesian supply function. *The Economic Journal*, 59, 360–383.

Proudhon, P.-J. (2003). *General idea of the revolution in the nineteenth century.* New York: Dover Publications.

Rostow, W. W. (1986, Jun.). The nature and logic of capitalism. *The Journal of Economic History*, 46, 575–577.

Schumpeter, J. (1954). *History of economic analysis.* New York: Oxford University Press.

Smith, A. (1976). *An inquiry into the nature and causes of the wealth of nations.* R. H. Campbell, A. S. Skinner, & W. B. Todd (Eds.). Oxford: Clarendon Press.

Stebbing, S. (1961). *A modern introduction to logic.* New York: Harper TorchBooks.

Yankelovich, D. (1973, Autumn). The idea of human nature. *Social Research*, 40, 407–428.

PART XI

WELFARE ECONOMICS

Abram Bergson

Abram Bergson

The economics profession has lost a great theoretician and ambassador of Soviet economics. Born in Baltimore, Maryland, in 1914, Abram Bergson died in Cambridge, Massachusetts at the age of 89. He graduated from John Hopkins University at 19 and obtained his doctorate at Harvard University in 1940, where he became George F. Baker Professor of Economics. During his academic career, Bergson held many government positions. He served as an analyst for the Office of Strategic Services, as a member of the reparation committee in Moscow during World War II, and as a member of various military boards during that time. Bergson was a scholar of immeasurable credits and immortal renown, quite deserving of his reputation as Dean of Soviet economics.

Bergson will be remembered for establishing the theoretical foundations of modern welfare economics. His first published milestone article on welfare economics (*Quarterly Journal of Economics* 1928, reprinted in Bergson, 1982: 2-27), laid out a research program that he advanced for nearly three quarters of a century. In a sympathetic evaluation of Bergson's early contribution, Paul Samuelson noted that the concept of Social Welfare Function originated with Bergson. This idea has gained so much importance that it can be used to explain the community's social preferences (Dobb, 1968: 110-111). The welfare function allowed equilibrium to be attained at the tangency of a community indifference curve with the production possibility curve. Samuelson, a friend of Bergson, also remarked, "Bergson was the first to understand the contributions of all previous contributors, and form a synthesis. He is the first to develop explicitly the notion of an ordinal social welfare function in terms of which the various schools of thought can be interpreted with significance" (Samuelson, 1974: 219).

The abstract and general nature of Bergson's welfare function was not without controversy. Bergson actually wrote out a mathematical welfare function: $W = F(U^1, U^2, U^3, \ldots)$ and demonstrated that it is a "generalization of the Marshall-Pigou formulation; according to the latter, W being the sum of the utilities $U^1, U^2, U^3 \ldots U^n$. Also, to maximize W would satisfy the criterion of Vilfredo Pareto and Enrico Barone" (ibid.: 154). Unforeseen was an old theory of Condorcet ticking like a time bomb waiting to explode in the face of a Pareto-like efficiency frontier. This is now known as Arrow's Impossibility Theorem, which holds that unless there exists a single peak preference system or a benevolent dictator, a welfare function cannot be constructed or determined. Bergson's reaction to Arrow's Impossibility Theorem was: "it is at most only tenuously related to welfare economics. Continued affirmation otherwise can only be at the expense of confusion regarding both Arrow's real contribution and welfare economics" (Bergson, 1982: 52). Others have examined this hypothesis. What is known as the Bergson-Samuelson Social Welfare Function considers questions regarding domains of applicability in areas such as the political versus economic versus ethical in the face of Arrow's Impossibility Theorem. Further, economists such as Sen (1977) have been concerned with the information content of the social ranking of the Impossibility Theorem.

Another important stance of Bergson is in the area of planning, where he brushed against the Austrian school. Bergson picked up the controversy with Ludwig von Mises, "as to whether socialism can work at all, and how well" (Bergson, 1982: 233). Bergson proceeds on two levels with his argument. First, "Mises' contention is that without private ownership of… the means of production, the rational evaluation of these goods for the purposes of calculating costs is ruled out conceptually" (ibid.). To this view, Bergson replies that Oscar Lange and Joseph Schumpeter who favor this interpretation of von Mises, accurately observe that the works of Pareto and Barone refutes this position. Hence, if taste and techniques are given, we can calculate the values by imputation, without the help of the market.

Second, another point of von Mises, underscored by Friedrich Hayek, states that "imputation is theoretically possible; but once private ownership of the means of production has been liquidated, it cannot be accomplished in practice" (ibid.). Bergson situates Hayek and Lionel Robbins on one side of the balance, and Lange and von Mises on the other. He quotes Lange's observation that a "trial and error" method can be employed to value the means and ends. He takes followers of von Mises off the balance, and lets the scale tip in favor of Hayek and Robbins against Lange. Hayek's weight rests on his anticipation that "output, where the use of the available resources was determined by some central authority, would be lower if the price mechanism of a market operated freely" (ibid.: 235). This put the balance squarely in favor of "competitive efficiency." Bergson requires a "test on efficiency, that is, on the ends according to which the optimum allocation of resources is to be defined" (ibid.: 236). He points to Schumpeter's consumer sovereignty as a measure. This turned out to be not an idle suggestion, considering that consumer and producer surpluses are the staple measure of benefits in the Computational General Equilibrium modeling environment. Bergson also calls for a comparison of "ideals with ideals or facts with facts," implying "competitive solutions in an established socialist state where there is a unanimity on ends with monopolistic and unstable capitalism in the United States" (ibid.: 236). Such a comparison is complicated by its requirement of comparable data, such as data from the World Bank, ITC, and private sources such as Penn World Tables (PWT) and GTAP, and also CES and Cobb-Douglas a priori specifications on data, with their undermining assumptions of constant returns of scale.

The economics profession will always be grateful to Bergson for asking the hard questions, and leading welfare economists in scientific directions. As the fields he initiated continue to be vigorously researched, we cannot as yet determine which side of the debate has the analytic edge. But those that judge progress based on both structure and performance will appreciate Bergson's work for years to come.

Abram Bergson's Major Works

(1936, Oct.). Real income, expenditure proportionality, and Frisch's new methods of measuring marginal utility. *Review of Economic Studies*, IV(1), 33-52.

(1938, Feb.). A reformulation of certain aspects of welfare economics. *The Quarterly Journal of Economics*, LII(2), 310-334.

(1948). Socialist Economics. In H. S. Ellis (Ed.), *Survey of contemporary economics* (193-236). Philadelphia: Blakiston Co. & Richard D. Irwin.

(1967, Oct.). Market socialism revisited. *The Journal of Political Economy*, LXXV(5), 655-673.

(1973, Dec.). On monopoly welfare losses. *The American Economic Review*, LXII(5), 853-870.

(1944). *The structure of Soviet wages: A study in socialist economics*. Cambridge, MA: Harvard University Press.

(1961). *Real national income of Soviet Russia since 1928*. Cambridge, MA: Harvard University Press.

(1964). *The economics of Soviet planning*. New Haven, CT: Yale University Press.

(1966). *Essays in normative economics*. Cambridge, MA: Harvard University Press.

(1978). *Productivity and the social system: The USSR and the west*. Cambridge, MA: Harvard University Press.

(1987, Jun.). Comparative productivity: The USSR, eastern Europe, and the west. *American Economic Review*, 77(3), 342-357.

References

Bergson, A. (1982). *Welfare, planning, and employment: Selected essays in economic theory*. Cambridge, MA: MIT Press.

Dobb, M. (1968). *Welfare economics and the economics of socialism: Towards a commonsense critique*. London: Cambridge University Press.

Hayek, F. (1935). The present state of the debate. In F. A. Hayek (Ed.), *Collectivist economic planning* (201-243). London: Routledge.

Lange, O. (1938). On the economic theory of socialism. In B. Lippincott (Ed.), *On the economic theory of socialism* (74-91). Minneapolis: University of Minnesota Press.

Samuelson, P. A. (1974). *Foundations of economic analysis*. New York: Atheneum.

———. (1977, Feb.). Reaffirming the existence of reasonable Bergson-Samuelson social welfare functions. *Economica, New Series*, 44(173), 81-88.

Sen, A. (1977, Oct.). On weights and measures: Informational constraints of social welfare analysis. *Econometrica*, 45(7), 1539-1572.

Szenberg, M. (Ed.). (1993). *Eminent economists: Their life philosophies*. London and New York: Cambridge University Press.

von Mises, L. (1935). Economic calculation in the socialist commonwealth. In F. A. Hayek (Ed.), *Collectivist economic planning* (87-130). London: Routledge.

Index

G

H

L

M

www.ingramcontent.com/pod-product-compliance
Ingram Content Group UK Ltd.
Pitfield, Milton Keynes, MK11 3LW, UK
UKHW020058210526
471278UK00004B/94

9 781618 114662